Dazzled by Disney?

Studies in Communication and Society

Series editors: Ralph Negrine and Anders Hansen
University of Leicester

Dazzled by Disney?

The Global Disney Audiences Project

Edited by

Janet Wasko, Mark Phillips and Eileen R. Meehan

Leicester University Press
London and New York

Leicester University Press
A Continuum imprint
The Tower Building, 11 York Road, London SE1 7NX
370 Lexington Avenue, New York, NY 10017-6503

First published 2001

British Library Cataloguing-in-Publication Data

A catalogue record for this book is available from the British Library.

ISBN 0-7185-0261-2 (hardback)
   0-7185-0260-4 (paperback)

Library of Congress Cataloging-in-Publication Data

Dazzled by Disney?: the global Disney audiences project/edited by Janet Wasko, Mark Phillips, Eileen R. Meehan.
   p. cm.—(Studies in communication and society)
   Includes bibliographical references and index.
   ISBN 0-7185-0261-2 — ISBN 0-7185-0260-4 (pbk.)
   1. Walt Disney Company—Influence. I. Wasko, Janet. II. Phillips, Mark, 1954- III. Meehan, Eileen R., 1951- IV. Studies in communication and society (Leicester, England)

PN1999.W27 D39 2001
384′.8′06579494—dc21   00-067822

Typeset by BookEns Ltd, Royston, Herts
Printed and bound in Great Britain by Biddles Ltd
www.biddles.co.uk

Contents

Contents

Contributors

Coordinators

Janet Wasko (University of Oregon)
Mark Phillips (University of Oregon)
Eileen Meehan (University of Arizona)

Researchers

Australia: Virginia Nightingale (University of Western Sydney–Nepean)
Brazil: Raul Reis (California State University, Long Beach) and Roberto Elisio dos Santos and Flavio Calazans (Methodist University of São Paulo)
Canada: Malcolm Smith (University of Manitoba)
Cyprus: Mashoed Bailie (Eastern Mediterranean University)
Denmark: Kirsten Drotner (USD Odense University) and Anne Mette Stevn (University of Copenhagen)
France: Jacques Guyot (Université d'Angers)
Greece: Sophia Kaitatzi-Whitlock (Aristotle University of Thessaloniki) and George Terzis (Catholic University of Brussels, Belgium)
India: Manjunath Pendakur (University of Western Ontario, Canada) and Jyotsna Kapur (Southern Illinois University, USA)
Japan: Shunya Yoshimi (University of Tokyo)
Korea: Seung Hyun Kim and Kyung Sook Lee (Korea University)
Mexico: Silvia Molina y Vedia (National Autonomous University of Mexico)
Norway: Ingunn Hagen (University of Trondheim)
Singapore: Henry Tan (Ngee Ann University)
Slovenia: Breda Luthar (University of Ljubljana)
South Africa: Simon Burton (University of Natal)
Sweden: Gunilla Muhr (Stockholm University)
United Kingdom: David Buckingham (University of London)

United States:
  Athens, Ohio – Norma Pecora (Ohio University)
  Chicago, Illinois – Jack Banks (Hartford College, Connecticut)
  Detroit, Michigan – Jackie Byars (Wayne State University)
  Eugene, Oregon – Janet Wasko and Mark Phillips (University of
    Oregon)
  Tucson, Arizona – Eileen Meehan (University of Arizona)

Acknowledgments

The editors would like to thank everyone who participated in the Global Disney Audiences Project, especially the authors included in this volume, as well as the other researchers who administered questionnaires and interviews (see list of contributors).

Valuable research support at the University of Oregon was provided by Christine Quail, Mike Huffman, Kyoung-Ah Nam, and Shin-Joung Yeo.

For use of their photographs, thanks also to Jeremy Alden, Carlos Calderon, Mike Huffman, and Andrew Jakubowicz.

Finally, we wish to express our gratitude to Rennie's Landing for providing carrel space as well as intellectual and emotional support.

PART I

Introduction

CHAPTER 1

Is It a Small World, After All?

JANET WASKO

The image of Mickey Mouse is said to be the best-known cultural icon in the world. While it may be difficult to verify this claim, it is hard to dispute the widespread recognition of The Mouse and its maker, the Walt Disney Company. Despite their American origin, certain Disney characters and products have played important roles in the popular culture of many countries since the 1930s. In other countries, the Disney brand name more recently has become important, both culturally and economically.

As noted in Disney's Annual Report for 1998, 'The company generates revenues from more countries each year as Disney and its brands *continue to be welcomed around the world*' (emphasis added). Disney's international activities have grown over the last few years, as 1999 revenues from international sources (including U.S. exports) reached $5 billion or 20 percent of the total company revenues. The company claims that it is the world's top-ranked international distributor of motion pictures, in addition to strengths in home video, television and sports programing and consumer products. Indeed, one of the company's theme-park rides – 'It's a Small World' – both symbolizes the constant quest to expand the Disney universe and provides a popular metaphor for recent discussions of globalization trends.

The Disney company is not the only transnational media company pursuing globalization. Yet the company is a special case because of its distinctive brand name, which is associated around the world with childhood, family, fantasy, and fun. In fact, some enthusiasts (including company representatives) maintain that Disney and its characters and stories are 'universal,' and not wedded to American values and ideology.

Thus, understanding Disney's global impact and significance is not simply a matter of documenting and analyzing the continuing expansion of its products in global markets. We also need to understand more carefully the consumption or reception process and the audiences for these products. While the Disney company certainly does its own marketing research, communication researchers have paid relatively little attention to the audiences for Disney products, at either national or global level. Because the Disney company has increased its presence in international markets, as well as its seemingly 'special' brand status and appeal to children and families, an assessment of Disney's global audiences is increasingly important and long overdue.

Figure 1. Mickey Mouse truck, Washington, D.C. Photo: Jeremy Alden

The Global Disney Audiences Project

The Global Disney Audiences Project is an attempt to analyze the reception of Disney products internationally. The project included questionnaires and interviews to assess audience reactions to Disney in eighteen countries, plus individual national profiles outlining Disney's marketing activities and the specific contexts for the

Figure 2. Mikimiška shop, Piran, Slovenia. Photo: Andrew Jakubowicz

Figure 3. Mural at a small grocery in Tomaszkowo, northern Poland. Photo: Jörg Becker

reception of Disney products. Thus, the study examines both how extensively and intensively Disney products are marketed, and also how local audiences interpret these products.

This book is a report on the Global Disney Audiences Project and hopefully a contribution to understanding the implications of the expanded global distribution of cultural products. This chapter introduces the study through an overview of the issues and themes that have characterized the study of global media audiences, followed by an outline of the global expansion of the Walt Disney Company. The second chapter discusses more details about the study, as well as presenting the cross-cultural results, followed by twelve individual national profiles, which provide more depth and explanation of the different national and cultural contexts for the reception of Disney products. The final chapter presents an overview of the general findings of the study, suggesting further research that might be done on the study of Disney, global culture and cultural consumption.

Foundations for the study of global Disney audiences

The study of global media audiences for Disney products draws on a range of theoretical discussions and previous empirical studies relating to: (1) international communications; (2) global audiences; and (3) Disney and Disney audiences.

International communications

The study of international communications has been dominated by two general 'frames of thinking' – a dependency and a free-flow paradigm (see Biltereyst, 1995). This section will include a brief overview of some of the issues in the study of international communications that have informed the Global Disney project, citing representative studies which mostly draw upon a dependency paradigm, and especially those that feature analyses of the Disney company or products.

INTERNATIONAL FLOW STUDIES/GLOBALIZATION

Although the issues relating to international communications have been examined over the years, the global distribution of media products received special attention by communication researchers during the 1970s. Several studies documented the international flow of media, focusing primarily on news and television (Nordenstreng and Varis, 1974; Tunstall, 1977), as well as other media (Guback, 1974).

More recent studies have updated and deepened this analysis (see Larsen, 1990; Sepstrup, 1990; and Herman and McChesney, 1997, among many others).

As this research has shown, global distribution of media and communication products has grown dramatically during the last half of the twentieth century. In addition, there has been a consistent one-way flow of media and communication from Western countries to less developed countries. More recently, new media and information technologies have been developed within neo-liberal economic climates, leading to even further globalization of media and communication markets. Herman and McChesney (1997) describe a global convergence of media and telecommunications systems, as well as the dominance of commercial media and the weakening of public media systems. While Schiller (1991) emphasized that these developments represent a transnational form of cultural domination, Herman and McChesney argue that the U.S.A. 'provides the evolutionary model toward which the global media system is moving,' with primarily U.S.-based transnational corporations (including the Walt Disney Company) as the major players in this global system.

Whether or not it is dominated by the U.S.A., globalization has become one of the buzz words of the new century, as political and business leaders, the popular press and academics focus on the increased circulation of products and investment worldwide. A wide range of definitions of globalization have been offered, often emphasizing interconnections, networks, or flows. For instance, Tomlinson (1991: 2) argues that globalization represents a 'complex connectivity,' or 'the rapidly developing and ever-densening network of interconnections and interdependences that characterize modern social life.' In a widely cited article, Ferguson (1992) addresses the issue of differing conceptions of globalization, but also the contradictions that surround the concept. She discusses 'the existence of a global cultural economy that ignores the counter pull of localism and the rich traditions of variance,' concluding that we know more about the extent of global circulation of media products than about their political, cultural or social impact.

Studies of global media have raised a wide range of issues, but those most relevant to this study can be discussed in terms of political, economic and cultural factors, or in other words, questions that relate to global cultural production and issues that revolve around the concept of global culture and cultural identity.

GLOBAL CULTURAL PRODUCTION

It has been established that the proliferation of Western media has had an impact on the evolution and development of indigenous media or culture industries. Nationally produced media attempt to compete with global products with larger production budgets and well-developed distribution and marketing strategies. In many cases, the prevalence of global media products has inhibited local and national media production. In other instances, indigenous media companies or outlets are actually owned by transnational companies (see Guback, 1989; Sussman and Lent, 1998).

Some researchers, however, have argued that new technologies and global tendencies actually encourage the growth of indigenous media production. For instance, in their study of global music, Robinson *et al.* (1991: 4) conclude that despite 'international consumership for centrally produced and distributed popular music,' indigenization of popular music still exists and contradicts trends in globalization.

The last section of this chapter includes details on the Disney company's global businesses, which include not only global distribution of Disney products but also ownership of media and entertainment outlets in many different countries. In addition, many Disney products are produced outside of the U.S.A., which has implications for indigenous culture industries. Further discussion of these issues is included in some of the national profiles that follow, specifically for Australia, Greece, Japan, and Korea.

GLOBAL CULTURE

The international distribution of media and entertainment products has prompted concern over the homogenization of culture, or global cultural homogeneity. With the increasing proliferation of global products, some observers fear a growing global culture or mono-culture. Others argue that there is still a good deal of cultural diversity, as well as preferences for indigenous rather than global products (see, for instance, Sepstrup, 1990).

Still other researchers question whether or not globalization is actually a new development or merely a continuation of global capitalism and imperialism. For instance, Sparks (1998) considers this question as he traces the evolution of Winnie the Pooh since Disney gained the rights to the stories in 1965. He argues that Pooh has been 'Americanized' and questions whether or not Disney, in particular, is a 'global company' that produces 'global products,' and thus, whether or not globalization is really a new development.

Another concern that emerges from discussions of globalization and global culture is the issue of national and cultural identity. Researchers have traced not only the proliferation but also the influence of foreign media products on local and national cultures. While proponents of the free-flow paradigm most often argue that such products have little effect on cultural identities, dependency theorists have generally argued that the impact is significant in various ways.

CULTURAL/MEDIA IMPERIALISM

One of the key issues that involves both cultural and economic questions is cultural imperialism, a concept that emerged in communication research in the late 1960s with the intense global expansion of transnational corporations. Beltran (1976) defined cultural imperialism as 'a verifiable process of social influence by which a nation imposes on other countries its set of beliefs, values, knowledge and behavioral norms as well as its overall style of life.' Although the discussion of cultural imperialism was strongest in Latin America, Western researchers developed the concept in their work, including Schiller, Mattelart and many, many others.

The theoretical basis for cultural imperialism drew heavily on development theory. More specifically, the one-way flow of media and communications products was seen as evidence of a global imbalance, with economic, political and cultural power held firmly by Western countries.

DISSECTING THE DUCK

One of the best-known studies of cultural imperialism focuses on Disney. In *How to Read Donald Duck*, Ariel Dorfman and Armand Mattelart presented their critique of Disney comics in 1971, at a time when the democratically elected Popular Unity government was attempting to build a socialist society in Chile. Even after the new government was in place, much of Chile's television programing and 80 percent of the films shown in cinemas were from the U.S.A.; many of the newspapers and magazines were still U.S.-owned. Thus, Dorfman and Mattelart's critique was originally written to encourage the Chilean people to resist these foreign cultural products.

How to Read Donald Duck utilizes a combination of approaches, basically drawing on a Marxist critique of 'Disney ideology' that incorporates a class analysis, as well as semiotic and psychoanalytic approaches. The analysis draws upon a sample of 100 Disney comic books that were distributed in Chile in the 1970s. The authors dissect the comic books as texts, directing attention to some of the common characteristics of Disney ideology, which persuasively exemplifies the notion of cultural imperialism. One of the primary themes identified in the Disney comics is the portrayal of people of the Third World or 'the noble savage.' Specific nationalities are stereotypically represented, especially Third World countries whose people are presented as backward, primitive, savage, and/or ignorant. Typically, the Duck stories featured a quest for fortune, which is revealed and produced magically, as there is little evidence of work or production in the lands portrayed in the comics. The emphasis on consumption is evidenced by the Disney characters' constant quest for money. In his introduction to the study, David Kunzle observes:

> If important sectors of the intelligentsia in the U.S. have been lulled into silent complicity with Disney, it can only be because they share his basic values and see the broad public as enjoying the same cultural privileges; but this complicity becomes positively criminal when their common ideology is imposed upon non-capitalist, underdeveloped countries, ignoring the grotesque disparity between the Disney dream of wealth and leisure, and the *real* needs in the Third World. (Dorfman and Mattelart, 1975: 11)

While other analysts have since considered Disney's representation of foreign cultures (see Burton-Carvajal, 1994; Piedra, 1994; and Yoshimoto, 1994), Mattelart and Dorfman's study probably has had the most impact on the cultural imperialism debate.

CRITIQUES OF CULTURAL IMPERIALISM

But there also has been considerable critique of the concept of cultural imperialism, especially during the last few decades. To begin with, critics claim that the discussion itself has been more political and ideological than academic or scholarly. Indeed, 'cultural imperialism' itself has become an ideologically loaded term. Another complaint is that the term 'cultural imperialism' has been employed, when in fact it is 'media imperialism' that has been described and studied (Tomlinson, 1991; Fejes, 1981). Other scholars argue that there have been changes that negate the cultural imperialism position. Despite the increased globalization of cultural/media products, Western media no longer dominate, and indeed, even developing countries have established their own strong media and communication systems. The typical example is Brazil, although there are differing opinions about the significance of its telenovelas, which are often cited as evidence of Third World media power (Oliveira, 1988; Straubhaar, 1991).

Most important for this study is the typical critique that has bemoaned the lack of substantive empirical research on how audiences actually respond to Western media (see, for instance, Tomlinson, 1991). While a few studies have attempted to respond to this issue, it often seems that the research has been undertaken specifically to refute the cultural imperialism thesis (Robinson *et al.*, 1991, as discussed above, and Liebes and Katz, 1990, discussed below).

It seems that further research is needed to sort out the complexities of the cultural imperialist argument, as noted especially in many of the national profiles that follow, but especially Korea and Japan.

Studying (global) audiences

ACADEMIC AUDIENCE RESEARCH

The study of media audiences has been the focus of an enormous amount of academic research over the years. In a recent collection dedicated to audience research approaches, Dickinson *et al.* (1998) argue that

> All research which takes media processes as central to its analysis stems from an interest or concern with the consequences of the media for society, communities, publics, readers, listeners, viewers, consumers – audiences. The difference between approaches is, essentially, to do with the scale of analysis or the length of focus – micro or macro – chosen by the researchers in question. (p. xi)

From early efforts to study the direct effects of propaganda to more recent attempts to identify the uses and gratifications that media serve for individual audience members, the analysis of audiences has been a major stronghold of mainstream communication research, especially in the U.S.A., but also in other countries.[1] The dominant paradigm has shifted from assuming direct effects of media messages on individual audience members to more limited effects, with intervening variables influencing audience responses. Such research has typically employed quantitative methods, such as surveys, questionnaires, experiments, and closed interviews.

There also are plenty of studies of the 'effects' of Western media on cultural identity, cultural values, and the adoption of Western values (Salwen, 1991), as well as numerous studies examining cross-cultural factors related to media, mostly drawing on the traditional media-effects model and the free-flow paradigm (see Korzenny *et al.*, 1992). Although there is often a call to 'contextualize' media effects in various ways, most of these studies still do not situate the audiences within the larger framework that political economy or critical studies demand.

In addition, there is an abundance of research on children and media, which has been a major area of audience research over the years (see, for instance, Jenkins, 1998; Buckingham, 1993). In particular, there is a considerable body of research that has been directed at children and television (see, for example, Bazalgette and Buckingham, 1995). In spite of the numerous studies of children and media, little attention has been paid to audiences for Disney products, despite their ongoing significance for audiences, in general, and children, in particular.

Recent audience studies have roots in cultural studies (for example, Morley, 1980), uses and gratifications in communication research and textual analysis in literary theory (for example, Radway, 1984). The analysis of audiences has also become the major focus of reception analysis, with more qualitative research methods employed (participant observation, ethnography, etc.).[2]

Such analysis has been influenced especially by Stuart Hall's encoding/decoding model, which argues that although there are preferred textual messages encoded by producers, resistant and even emancipatory readings can be decoded by audiences (Hall *et al.*, 1981). These concepts have been pushed further by scholars such as John Fiske, who describe active audiences constructing their own liberating meanings from polysemic, open texts (Hartley and Fiske, 1978). As Liebes and Katz (1990: 19) explain, 'The new convergence on reader decodings clearly implies an active reader – selecting, negotiating, interpreting, discussing, or, in short, being involved.' While Fiske's extreme active audience model has been challenged by many critical researchers, as well as recanted to some degree by Fiske himself, there are still plenty of variations on the active audience in the audience research literature. And most often, these approaches include harsh criticism of the cultural imperialism concept, as discussed in the next sections.

DOING *DALLAS*

One of the most commonly studied examples of Western media is the night-time soap opera that became the most popular program in the world, *Dallas* (Liebes and Katz, 1990; Massing, 1986; Ang, 1985). Indeed, Liebes and Katz's study of *Dallas* is claimed to be the 'most ambitious attempt so far to examine the media imperialism argument empirically from the perspective of audience response' (Tomlinson, 1991: 48). They begin their study with a typical critique: 'Theorists of cultural imperialism assume that hegemony is prepackaged in Los Angeles, shipped out to the global village, and unwrapped in innocent minds' (Liebes and Katz, 1990: v). It is clear from their discussion that they find this assumption invalid, and continue by asking whether and how a parochial television program like *Dallas* can be universally understood, whether it is understood in the same way, and what kinds of involvement and response are evoked. The study points out that Dallas is 'not so simple-minded or so visual that anybody in the world can readily comprehend it,' but that it is 'quite complex' (*ibid.*: 3). While Liebes and Katz acknowledge the pervasiveness of American television programs, they argue that the cultural imperialism argument is valid only if it is shown that first, American messages are incorporated into programs, second, that messages are decoded by receivers in the same way they are encoded by senders, and third, that messages are accepted uncritically by viewers and allowed to 'seep into their culture.'

Furthermore, they point to three reasons why American TV programs are successful internationally: first, 'the universality, or primordiality, of some of its themes and formulae' (making the shows 'psychologically accessible');[3] second, the 'polyvalent or open potential of many of the stories and thus their value as projective mechanisms and as material for negotiation and play in the families of man;' and third, the availability of (and 'vigorous marketing of') American programs that national producers cannot provide (Liebes and Katz, 1990: 5).

The *Dallas* study compared the responses of different ethnic groups in Israel with American viewers, and concluded that viewers negotiate their reactions to the program, and become either critically or referentially involved. The study is clearly within the renewed realm of audience power, drawing on both textual and audience analysis.

Meanwhile, other studies of *Dallas* have also focused on audience responses. While Ang (1985) did not specifically focus on the issue of media imperialism, her study examines responses to watching 'imperialist' programing. She found that audiences 'negotiated' between contradictory values and the 'pleasure of the text.'[4]

Beyond the studies of *Dallas*, other researchers have considered audience use of and responses to media across cultures, mostly drawing on reception analysis, but other theoretical frameworks, as well. Only a few, however, have included Disney products as part of the research. One exception is a preliminary study by Lemish *et al.* (1998), which looked at how globalization is embedded in the lives of children and adolescents in three different countries. While television was found to be the dominant medium in children's lives, the study also discovered that Disney films were the most popular for children in the three countries under study (Denmark, France and Israel). While several themes were revealed in the mostly qualitative study, the researchers point to seemingly contradictory findings. On the one hand, the subjects adopted a global perspective on social life, but the researchers also identified the coexistence of multi-cultures, or hybrid cultures, in the lives of young people. As the researchers note, 'Our concern is to investigate how children juggle, experiment with, deconstruct and reconstruct the various global and local elements and what form of cultural identity they assume in the process' (Lemish *et al.*, 1998: 554).

Studying Disney/audiences

In addition to books produced by the company and coverage in the popular press, there is a huge literature devoted to Walt Disney, the Disney company and Disney products. The continuing proliferation and popularity of Disney recently has prompted scholars to examine this cultural phenomenon with a flood of books and articles devoted to the topic. Much of the academic work, however, focuses on biographies of Walt Disney, business histories of the Disney company, or textual readings of Disney films and theme parks (see Bryman, 1995; Wasko, 2001). However, there have been few studies of Disney audiences, either in the U.S.A. or elsewhere.

One of the few examples is Michael Real's *Mass-Mediated Culture* (1977). Real administered questionnaires to 200 individuals (primarily students) from southern California who generally had high exposure to Disneyland, as well as a wide range of other Disney products. In addition to their exposure, respondents were asked about the values represented by Disney ('vices and virtues'), as well as its perceived influence. While there was some ambiguity in assessing influence, the identification of values represented by Disney was clear and unequivocal. Respondents mentioned many of the values that have become associated with Disney, such as happiness, friendliness, honesty, innocence, industriousness, cleanliness, etc. On the other hand, most respondents agreed that Disney did not approve of sex, violence, greed, laziness, un-American activities and left politics. (More discussion of this research will be presented in Chapter 2, as the Global Disney Audiences Project was patterned after Real's study.)

The Disney universe was considered by Real as an example of mass-mediated culture, in which meaning is structured as a semiological system, 'fixing reality both by receiving and transmitting dominant patterns of perception, structures of feeling, cognitive maps and cultural norms' (Real, 1977: 84). His study confirmed two major hypotheses: 'that Disney attracts participants into mass-mediated utopian typifications and that Disney instructs through morality plays that structure personal values and ideology.' Above all, Real's research confirmed that the Disney universe is not value-free, as well as contributing to the argument that entertainment media, such as Disney, have definite effects on individuals and the social system.

Elsewhere, in a study of heroines in 1975, Kay Stone interviewed 40 women of different ages in three U.S. cities. She found that many of the women admitted that they were influenced by fairy tales, but mostly through the Grimms' translations and Disney films. However, at least some of the women were not very impressed with the passive heroines of Disney and the Grimms, and would have appreciated more active heroines, or at least more diversity, in these stories.

In another study, Jill May (1981) asked students at Purdue University about their favorite 'family' film experience and found that students preferred Disney films by four to one and animated films by three to one. May also reported that Disney was favored by both young men and women, who admitted that they wanted to expose their children to Disney's versions of classic stories and most often enjoyed watching a Disney film more than reading the story in book form.

And, finally, an attempt was made to categorize Disney audiences in the U.S.A. in Wasko (2001), in which I identified Disney fanatics, fans, consumers, cynics, resisters and antagonists. While these archetypes may not be appropriate for international audiences, some of the categories (especially resisters) have been used by the project's researchers.

Generally, then, in light of the continuing global expansion of media and communication companies, as well as the complex issues revolving around the issue of cultural imperialism, especially, there is still a pressing need to study the global reception of media products. More specifically, with its continuing global expansion and well-known brand name, Disney presents an opportunity to assess the proliferation and impact of transnational media products.

The next section briefly outlines the Disney corporation, emphasizing its international businesses and activities. Additional details about the marketing of Disney's products, as well as its influence on local media production in specific countries, will be presented in the twelve National Profiles.

The world of Disney

The Walt Disney Company was established in the late 1920s as a small U.S. entrepreneurial enterprise when Walt Disney and his brother Roy began producing Mickey Mouse cartoons. The company grew gradually, always with financial difficulties, but established itself as an independent production company in Hollywood. Never one of the major studios, the Disney brothers built a reputation for quality animation, utilizing cutting-edge technological developments such as sound and color.

The popularity of Disney's products and characters was instantaneous and unmistakable, not only in the U.S.A. but also in other countries. In the 1930s, the image of Mickey Mouse was a global phenomenon. Schickel (1968) reports that by 1937 The Mouse was distributed in one form or another in 38 countries around the world.

The company had found the merchandising that followed their films especially effective in foreign markets, and, by 1934, had opened offices in London and Paris to distribute merchandise and films. Though the films were dubbed in only three languages at the time, they were distributed in many other countries. However, Schickel notes that products based on print also became successful, as more verbal humor was added to the films:

> It was as a printed comic and as merchandising figures that The Mouse and his cohorts won many of their first audiences in out-of-the-way corners of the world (thus reversing the order of recognition that had pertained at home), and in the process increased Disney's revenue in a way that no other movie maker could so easily and consistently exploit. (Schickel, 1968: 165)

Another development was the growth of Mickey Mouse clubs, which spread the image of Mickey around the world (see deCordova, 1974).

Other stories have been passed down over the years (no doubt encouraged by Disney's public relations efforts) about the popularity of Mickey and the other characters with kings and queens, heads of state and other international political figures. Typically, these tales are accompanied with an explanation of how Disney's products/creations are 'universal,' as exemplified by the following excerpt from Schickel:

> The bold colors of the Disney cartoons, their use of animals, which have no nationality, as the major characters, their broadness and brevity, the commonality of the problems they encountered and the solutions they invented, and above all, their cheerfulness – all contributed to the success of the films in the international market. What is true of high art is also true of mass art to the extent that universality of appeal is based on success with particularities. In their uncomplicated way, the Disney craftsmen caught something of the truth of the American scene and situation at the time and, lo, found that they had touched a chord that set up responsive vibrations all over the world. (Schickel, 1968: 168)

Generally, then, the international distribution of Disney films and the merchandising efforts that accompanied them contributed to the reputation of the Disney enterprise that was magnified far beyond the relatively small company's resources.

Most of the Disney histories claim that Walt Disney was a creative and financial genius, yet they often acknowledge that the company struggled for years to achieve financial success, even while attracting critical acclaim and praise. Recently, a number of researchers have done a decent job of debunking the 'great man' approach to the Disney mythology, pointing out that Walt was no real genius. Indeed, the Disneys operated a marginal, niche company for three decades, taking advantage of technological change, but finally succeeding with the creation of Disneyland, which essentially turned the operation into a theme-park company. As one media economist argues, 'The Disney company is simply another capitalist enterprise with a history best understood within the changing conditions of twentieth-century America' (Gomery, 1994: 86).

Since 1984, ownership has shifted from the Disney family to investors who have supported management efforts to extend the corporate tentacles even more widely and more tenaciously. As with most of the major companies in Hollywood, Disney's expansion has not depended solely on motion pictures, but a wide array of business activities. Led by CEO Michael Eisner, 'Team Disney' has drawn on the Disney legacy, as it aggressively exploits the Disney name and its characters, and even boldly proclaiming that the 1990s was to be 'The Disney Decade.'

With Team Disney at the helm, Disney's corporate rhetoric changed so that the corporate name was more deliberately treated as a brand name. This practice suggests that the presence of the word 'Disney' is sufficient to produce routine, unthinking consumption, in the same way that brand loyalty supposedly means that people buy Ivory soap regardless of similar soaps offered for lower prices. While the rhetoric of branding is upbeat, it hides the interesting assumption that any Disney product is like any other Disney product, in the way that one bar of Ivory soap is identical to any other. Another shift in corporate rhetoric imported the term 'synergy' (the whole is greater than the parts) to describe Team Disney's aggressive campaigns to build Disney into both a transindustrial media conglomerate and to repackage and recycle its intellectual property to feed its various media operations. Taken together, branding, conglomerating, repackaging, and recycling proved the key to rejuvenating the sagging corporation.

Other new policies also were implemented, such as reviving the classic Disney animation, modernizing some Disney characters, rabid cost-cutting (especially on feature films), price increases at the theme parks, technological development (such as computer animation), strategic corporate partnerships, and, importantly, synergistic and global expansion. The company finally obtained one of its goals of owning its own television network, with the dramatic takeover of Capital Cities/ABC in July 1995, confirming the company's position as one of the dominant media and entertainment powerhouses in the U.S.A. and the world.

Today, the Walt Disney Company is a mammoth corporation, with revenues totaling over $25 billion, encompassing a wide array of domestic and international investments that overlap and reinforce each other. Cited as one of the 'first tier' media firms in the world, it represents perhaps the quintessential example of synergy, at least among American corporations. Obviously, the company has diversified far beyond the arena of children's or family programing and products. The aggressive marketing of a multitude of Disney products in a wide range of distribution channels all over the world has contributed to a proliferation of Disney images and characters that could hardly have been imagined in the 1930s. Disney products seem to be almost omnipresent.

Eisner has recently identified Disney's corporate strategy, as first, 'to build the greatest entertainment asset base in the world', and second, 'to simultaneously create the greatest entertainment product in the world.' However, it is also important to keep in mind that *all* of Disney's activities are guided by the same underlying philosophy, as expressed in the company's own words on their website: 'Disney's overriding objective is to create shareholder value by continuing to be the world's premier entertainment company from a creative, strategic and financial standpoint.'

It might be noted that even though international sources provided almost $5 billion of overall revenues in 1999, the company is far from satisfied. As Eisner explains:

> Our growth overseas has been strong and exciting. But we have not duplicated the level of success we have achieved in North America. As a result, Disney is in the ironic position of being one of the best-known brands on the planet, but with too little of its income being generated outside of the United States. The U.S. contains only 5 percent of the world's population, but it accounts for 80 percent of our company's revenues. If we can drive the per capita spending levels for Disney merchandise to just 80 percent of U.S. levels in only five countries – England [*sic*], Italy, Germany, France and Japan – then we would generate an additional $2 billion in annual revenue. (Walt Disney Company, 1999: 6)[5]

To assist in this effort, the company centralized its international activities in 1990, creating Walt Disney International to coordinate all overseas business. As explained in the Financial Review section of the 1999 Annual Report, 'Disney is positioning itself to capitalize on long-term international growth opportunities' (p. 13).

Many people fail to realize the actual extent of Disney's reach today; thus it may be useful to look briefly at the company's various businesses, emphasizing its international activities.

Creative content

THEATRICAL FILMS

Theatrical films still provide a strong base for the Disney company's diverse empire. In addition to consistently releasing new films, the company has been especially successful in exploiting its film library, carefully releasing already amortized products in new forms, and promoting them through its other business activities. In the mid-1980s, the company created the Touchstone label, which allowed it to produce films that would not be associated with the family-oriented, Disney brand. Hollywood Pictures was introduced in 1990, Miramax Films, a successful independent distribution company, was added in 1993, and Merchant–Ivory, an independent production company, in 1994. These moves extended the Disney film empire into markets for adult and foreign films, again providing diversification beyond the family-oriented market. For instance, successful films for the company during the last few years have included not only *Toy Story II*, *Tarzan*, and *Inspector Gadget* but also *Shakespeare in Love*, *Armageddon*, and *Enemy of the State*. Consequently, during the last few decades, Disney has regularly led the Hollywood majors in overall box-office revenues.

Buena Vista International distributes all Disney films outside North America, and claims that it is the only company to have reached $1 billion in annual box-office revenues more than five years in a row. For instance, big hits for Disney in foreign markets for 1999 were *Armageddon* ($350 million gross, with a $115 million gross in Japan alone), *A Bug's Life* (around $200 million), and *Enemy of the State* ($139 million). *Tarzan* was expected to gross $275 million by the end of its international run. Disney is also involved in distribution partnerships with other studios and co-produces selected movies in Europe and South America.

HOME ENTERTAINMENT

Buena Vista Home Entertainment distributes Disney's film labels in video and DVD formats, and has been the top video company in the U.S.A. for at least seven consecutive years; in fact, it is twice the size of its nearest rival in the sell-through business. Between 1986 and 1990, Disney's international video business expanded rapidly, with gross revenues increasing fourfold and branches in 64 markets by 1994. That same year, the company claims to hold up to 60 percent of the family video market in many European markets.

The company owns all except one of the industry's top-ten top-selling videos in the U.S.A. and all of the top-ten best-selling international titles, led for many years by *The Lion King*. In 1999, *The*

Lion King II: Simba's Pride became the top-selling made-for-video title of all time with 23 million units sold worldwide. And international expansion continues, as noted in the annual report for 1998: 'The emphasis … is on further entry into markets in Southeast Asia, Latin America and Eastern Europe.'

TELEVISION PRODUCTION

Disney's prime-time network television division has been successful in creating programing that continues to sell in syndicated markets, both in the U.S.A. and internationally. Popular programs have included *Home Improvement, The Golden Girls, Dinosaurs*, and *Ellen*, as well as a wide range of animated programing, including shows such as *Aladdin* and *The Little Mermaid*.

Walt Disney Television International (WDTV-I) coordinates Disney's international television activities, including the Disney Channels. At the beginning of 2000, there were nine Disney Channels outside the U.S.A., including France, Germany, the U.K., Spain, Italy, and the Middle East (featuring Disney programing 7 days a week, 24 hours a day to 23 countries throughout the Middle East and North Africa). New Disney Channels were being planned for Latin America, Scandinavia and several Asian countries (through the Disney Channel Asia Network).

WDTV-I claims that it is the 'leading distributor of programing worldwide, licensing some 4200 hours of programing in 1999.' This includes not only the Disney Channels but also Disney Clubs and Disney animation programs. In the 1999 Annual Report, the company boasted: 'Disney's award-winning shows continued to be among the leading programs enjoyed by kids and families around the world, out-performing the competition in their timeslots in a majority of markets, and reaching approximately 300 million viewers every week' (The Walt Disney Company, 1999: 35).

The company also has pay television agreements with other companies, such as Sogecable, Telepiu and KirchGruppe, and owns an equity stake in Latin America's leading pay television entities, HBO Ole and HBO Brasil. The Disney Weekend, a PPV service, is also available in Latin America through DirectTV's Galaxy. New investments were added in 1999, including HBO Hungary, HBO Czech Republic/Slovakia and HBO Poland.

MUSIC PRODUCTS

Disney's music properties are coordinated by the Buena Vista Music Group, and include music products from the company's motion pictures, as well as the Hollywood, Hollywood Records Latin, Lyric and Mammoth labels. Musical groups under contract with these labels during 1999 included Duran Duran, Los Lobos, Youngstown, and the Goo Goo Dolls.

THEATRICAL PRODUCTIONS

The Disney company recently ventured into the world of theater, with some success. Broadway productions of *Beauty and the Beast, The Lion King,* and *The Hunchback of Notre Dame* typically have been introduced at the company's refurbished Amsterdam Theater, followed by worldwide tours.

CONSUMER PRODUCTS

Although some histories claim that Walt Disney was not necessarily interested in merchandising, licensing activities still provided the company with much-needed revenue to continue producing relatively expensive animated films. Thus, beginning in the early 1930s, the company began to license its characters to manufacturers who produced a wide range of products that were distributed all over the world.

More recently, Team Disney has emphasized the exploitation of the classic Disney characters, as well as creating new ones, and expanding the company's merchandising activities far beyond anything the Disney brothers might have imagined. The company not only licenses its various properties to other companies but also manufactures consumer products itself. One source claimed in 1987 that 3000 companies manufactured over 14,000 Disney-licensed products. And while the company does not regularly report total revenues from merchandising activities, the annual report for 1994 noted that an estimated $14 billion in Disney products were sold around the world. More recently, the company reported that 58 percent of the licensing revenues from consumer products were from international markets. Meanwhile, Mickey Mouse is still claimed to be the most popular licensed character in the world, appearing on more than 7500 items, not including publications.

The Consumer Products division supervises an extremely wide array of products in which Disney characters are featured. Publishing includes comic books, children's books and other printed material. In 1988, over 120 different Disney magazines and comics were published in sixteen different countries, and by the end of the century, the company claimed to be the number one publisher of children's books and magazines. This activity has been especially important in some countries, where Donald Duck and Mickey Mouse comics and books have been popular for decades and have become important components of childhood memories. Even today, Disney comic books are widely read by children and adults in many countries, as detailed in the national profiles that follow on Denmark and Norway.

Music products include records, audio products and music publishing. The company's direct marketing and mail-order business features a wide range of products, but is especially strong in the infant merchandise market, with product lines such as the Disney Babies. Educational products distributed by Disney include films, videos and films strips for schools, libraries and other institutions, plus posters and teaching aids, in addition to educational toys, play equipment and classroom furniture. A new addition to the company is the Disney Software Licensing division, which distributes an increasing number of Disney computer and CD products.

The company has expanded its retailing activities considerably with the introduction of Disney Stores. By December 2000, there were 742 Disney Stores around the world providing centralized sources for Disney merchandise. But the company does not rely only on the Disney Stores to market their products. Disney has recently introduced 'product corners' in department stores and other key outlets on three continents. The company hopes to create new markets with 'Mickey & Friends,' a licensed store operation opened first in Indonesia, followed by Poland.

Further international activity is presented by Disney Online Europe, founded in 1995 to develop the company's presence in the online world. Disney Online's in-house Internet studio creates and produces the company's various websites, including `Disney.com` launched in February 1996. The company boasts that it 'quickly became one of the most popular and highly trafficked sites on the World Wide Web.' It is not surprising to hear, as well, that 'the site showcases the services and products of The Walt Disney Company, with innovative and engaging information from a variety of Disney divisions …' In January 1997, Disney Online opened a satellite office in Paris to manage the development of original content in European markets. Using the local Disney domains (disney.country domain), these websites are destined to offer European Internet users 'the same level of information about Disney products and services.' By the end of 1999, the company had reorganized its online activities around `go.com`, which now includes Disney's Internet and online businesses and *The Disney Catalog*.

One of the ways that Disney integrates its various businesses is by special 'company-wide marketing events.' For instance, during 1999, Mickey and Minnie celebrated their 70th anniversary in Japan, with a line of commemorative merchandise and department store special events. More recently, the Millennium Celebration was highlighted, with various activities planned over a fifteen-month period. In association with UNESCO, Disney and McDonald's sponsored 'a search for 2000 Millennium Dreamers – young people from around the globe who have made a positive impact on their communities.' Their reward – a trip to Walt Disney World in May 2000.

Another example of Disney's international activities that must be mentioned here is the 1995 merchandising deal that the company made to market the name, image and logos of the Royal Canadian Mounted Police – or the Canadian Mounties – internationally. It probably is not surprising that the company emphasizes the Hollywood version of the Mountie legend.

Theme parks and resorts

The Disney empire currently operates a variety of theme parks, hotels, and tourist attractions. At the turn of the century, the company owned 7 theme parks (and were planning 4 others), 27 hotels (with 36,888 rooms), and 2 cruise ships.

The original Disneyland is now called Disneyland Resort, and will be expanded to include Disney's California Adventure during 2001. The Walt Disney World Destination Resort is located on 29,000 acres in central Florida, and includes the Magic Kingdom, Epcot Center, the Disney-MGM Studios Theme Park, hotels, another entertainment complex, shopping village, conference center, campground, golf courses, water parks and other recreational facilities. The latest addition to the complex is Disney's Animal Kingdom and the Disney Cruise Lines, featuring voyages designed with stopovers at the Florida complex and Disney's own island in the Caribbean. Florida is also the site of Celebration – a 4900-acre planned community controlled by the Disney company.

Two theme parks are located outside the U.S.A., including the very successful Tokyo Disneyland and Disneyland Paris, which, after a difficult launch, is now claimed by the company to be 'the leading tourist destination in Europe.' The next site for a Disney theme park is Hong Kong, a country with a population of more than 1 billion people (as carefully noted in the company's 1999 Annual Report). Hong Kong Disneyland is scheduled to open in 2005, mostly with local funds but featuring attractions from the existing parks.

The significance of the theme parks was pointed out by Eisner, again, as he explained that immediately before and after the opening of each existing park, Disney Consumer Products revenues rose significantly. For instance, merchandise sales in Europe increased tenfold from two years before to five years after the opening of Disneyland Paris. His point? (in case anyone missed it): 'Hong Kong Disneyland could help redefine our entire company for consumers in the most populous region on the planet' (The Walt Disney Company, 1999: 7).

The company is also expanding into regional entertainment, including Disney Quest and The ESPN Zone, thus making it possible to extend the Disney 'theme park experience' without the huge investment of major theme parks.

The Disney company is constantly adding new components to this division. Future plans include another park in Europe, expanding the Disney–MGM Studios park, second theme parks in southern California and Tokyo, and extensive hotel expansion to include 16,300 additional rooms. Also, the company has recently expanded its activities in sports, adding the Anaheim Angels baseball team to their expansion hockey team, The Mighty Ducks. An international sports arena in south Florida attracts numerous sporting events which receive worldwide coverage.

Broadcasting

TELEVISION

The ABC-TV network reaches 99.9 percent of U.S. television households, while the company's ten television stations reach one-quarter of U.S. households. The company also owns interests in television production and distribution in Germany, France, Scandinavia, the U.K., and Japan.

RADIO

The ABC Radio division includes 42 radio stations; however, the various ABC Radio networks are claimed to reach 147 million listeners weekly. At the end of 1999, Radio Disney (a 24-hour children's radio service) was carried on 45 stations and reached nearly 50 percent of the U.S. market.

CABLE

In addition to the Disney Channel, Disney also holds interests in other U.S. cable channels, such as A&E, Lifetime and the History Channel. ESPN, the most widely distributed cable network in the U.S.A., is mostly owned by Disney, and was claimed to reach over 152 million households internationally in 1997. Other cable networks include ESPN2, ESPNEWS, and ESPN Classic.

Meanwhile, the company reports that 'ESPN-branded sportscasting' reaches more than 150 countries in 21 languages, making ESPN International one of the world's largest distributors of sports programing. ESPN Asia and Star Sports is a joint venture which delivers sports programing throughout most of Asia.

Disney's small world

Overall, then, Disney has successfully rebuilt and expanded, especially internationally. *Fortune* magazine claimed in 1989 that 'the company has become the archetypal American corporation for the 1990s: a creative company that can move with agility to exploit international opportunities in industries where the U.S. has a competitive advantage.' As mentioned previously, the company is still not satisfied with its international revenues. As Disney focuses on extending its global reach and deepening its market penetrations, it may shrink the economic distance between local markets and local consumers, integrating them into a small and cozy world of Disney products.

Whether the world is actually small in terms of the way that these products are received, however, is another question. Before we are able to conclude that Disney products are 'welcomed throughout the world' – thus making it a smaller world – we need to consider people's reactions to them. We turn next to a summary of the Global Disney Audiences Project, which represents, at least, one attempt to begin to understand how Mickey, Donald and their friends are received and understood around the world.

Notes

1. See McQuail (1994) for an overview of media research traditions.
2. For a discussion of reception analysis and the relationship to cultural studies, see the introduction to Hagen and Wasko (2000).
3. A more recent volume argues that the 'U.S. competitive advantage in the creation and global distribution of popular taste is due to a unique mix of cultural conditions that are conducive to the creation of "transparent" texts – narratives whose inherent polysemy encourage diverse populations to read them as though they are indigenous.' In other words, Hollywood narratives 'have meaning to so many different cultures because they allow viewers in those cultures to project their own values, archetypes, and tropes into the movie or television program in a way that texts imported from other cultures do not, thus enabling the import to function as though it were an indigenous product.' See Olson (1999).
4. For a particularly interesting critique of Ang, see Webster (1988).
5. More specifically, the company reports that the four leading European markets – France, Germany, Italy and the U.K. – generate 40 percent of the spending per capita compared to the U.S.A., while Japan, the company's top international market, generates 70 percent of the per capita spending of the U.S.A. (The Walt Disney Company, 1999: 12).

References and other sources

Ang, I. (1985) *Watching* Dallas*: Soap Opera and the Melodramatic Imagination*. London, Methuen.

Bazalgette, C. and Buckingham, D. (eds) (1995) *In Front of the Children*. London, British Film Institute.

Beltran, L. R. (1976) 'Alien premises, objects, and methods in Latin American communication research,' *Communication Research*, 3(2): 107–34.

Biltereyst, D. (1995) 'Qualitative audiences research and transnational media effects,' *European Journal of Communication*, 10(2): 245–70.

Bryman, A. (1995) *Disney and His Worlds*. New York, Routledge.

Buckingham, D. (ed.) (1993) *Reading Audiences: Young People and the Media*. Manchester, Manchester University Press.

Buckingham, D. (1996) *Moving Images: Understanding Children's Emotional Responses to Television*. Manchester, Manchester University Press.

Buckingham, D. (1998) 'Children and television: a critical overview of the research,' in R. Dickinson, R. Harindranath, and O. Linné (eds), *Approaches to Audiences: A Reader*. London, Arnold, pp. 131–44.

Burton-Carvajal, J. (1994) ' "Surprise package:" looking southward with Disney,' in E. Smoodin (ed.), *Disney Discourse: Producing the Magic Kingdom*. New York, Routledge, pp. 131–47.

DeCordova, R. (1994) 'The Mickey in Macy's window: childhood, consumerism, and Disney animation,' in E. Smoodin (ed.), *Disney Discourse: Producing the Magic Kingdom*. New York, Routledge, pp. 203–14.

Dickinson, R., Harindranath, R., and Linné, O. (eds) (1998*) Approaches to Audiences: A Reader*. London, Arnold.

Dorfman, A. and Mattelart, A. (1975) *How to Read Donald Duck: Imperialist Ideology in the Disney Comics*. New York, International General.

Fejes, F. (1981) 'Media imperialism: an assessment,' *Media, Culture and Society*, 3: 281–9.

Ferguson, M. (1992) 'The mythology about globalization,' *European Journal of Communication*, 7: 69–93.

Gomery, D. (1994) 'Disney's business history: a reinterpretation,' in E. Smoodin (ed.), *Disney Discourse: Producing the Magic Kingdom*. New York, Routledge, pp. 71–86.

Guback, T. H. (1974) 'Film as international business,' *Journal of Communications*, 21(1): 1.

Guback, T. H. (1989) 'Should a national have its own film industry?' *Directions*, 3(1).

Hagen, I. and Wasko, J. (eds) (2000) *Consuming Audiences? Production and Reception in Media Research*. Cresskill, NJ, Hampton Press.

Hall, S., Hobson, D., Lowe, A., and Willis, P. (eds) (1981) *Culture, Media, Language*. London, Comedia.

Hartley, J. and Fiske, J. (1978) *Reading Television*. London, Methuen.

Herman, E. and McChesney, R. (1997) *The Global Media: The New Missionaries of Global Capitalism*. London, Cassell.

Jenkins, H. (ed.) (1998) *The Children's Culture Reader.* New York, New York University Press.

Korzenny, F., Ting-Toomey, S., and Schiff, E. (eds) (1992) *Mass-Media Effects Across Cultures.* Newbury Park, CA, Sage.

Larsen, P. (ed.) (1990) *Import/Export: International Flow of Television Fiction,* Reports and Papers on Mass Communication, No. 104. Paris, UNESCO.

Lemish, D., Drotner, K., Liebes, T., Maigret, E., and Stald, G. (1998) 'Global culture in practice: a look at children and adolescents in Denmark, France and Israel,' *European Journal of Communication,* 13(4): 539-56.

Liebes, T. and Katz, E. (1990) *The Export of Meaning: Cross-Cultural Readings of Dallas.* New York, Oxford University Press.

Massing, H. H. (1986) 'Decoding *Dallas,' Society,* November–December, pp. 74-8.

Mattelart, A. (1979) *Multinational Corporations and the Control of Culture.* Atlantic Highlands, NJ, Humanities Press.

May, J. (1981) 'Walt Disney's interpretation of children's literature,' *Language Arts,* 58(4): 463-72.

McQuail, D. (1994) *Mass Communication Theory,* 3rd edn. London, Sage.

Morley, D. (1980) *The 'Nationwide' Audience: Structure and Decoding.* London, British Film Institute.

Nordenstreng, K. and Varis, T. (1974) *Television Traffic – A One-Way Street,* Reports and Papers on Mass Communication, No. 70. Paris, UNESCO.

Oliveira, O. S. (1988) 'Brazilian media usage as a test of dependency theory,' *Canadian Journal of Communication,* 13: 16-27.

Olson, S. R. (1999) *Hollywood Planet: Global Media and the Competitive Advantage of Narrative Transparency.* Mahwah, NJ, Lawrence Erlbaum Associates.

Piedra, J. (1994) 'Pato Donald's gender ducking,' in E. Smoodin (ed.), *Disney Discourse: Producing the Magic Kingdom.* New York, Routledge, pp. 148-68.

Radway, J. A. (1984) *Reading the Romance: Women, Patriarchy, and Popular Literature.* Chapel Hill, University of North Carolina Press.

Real, M. (1977) *Mass-Mediated Culture.* Englewood Cliffs, NJ, Prentice-Hall.

Roach, C. (1997) 'Cultural imperialism and resistance in media theory and literary theory,' *Media, Culture and Society,* 19(1): 47-66.

Robinson, D. C., Buck, E. B., and Cuthbert, M. (1991) *Music at the Margins: Popular Music and Global Cultural Diversity.* Newbury Park, CA, Sage.

Rogers, E. and Antola, L. (1985) 'Telenovela: a Latin American success story,' *Journal of Communication,* 35(4): 24-35.

Salwen, M. B. (1991) 'Cultural imperialism: a media effects approach,' *Critical Studies in Mass Communication,* 8 (March): 29-38.

Schickel, R. (1968) *The Disney Version: The Life, Times, Art and Commerce of Walt Disney.* New York, Simon & Schuster.

Schiller, H. I. (1991) 'Not yet the post-imperialist era,' *Critical Studies in Mass Communication,* 8 (March): 12-28.

Sepstrup, P. (1990) *Transnationalization of Television in Western Europe.* London, John Libbey.

Sparks, C. (1998) 'From the Hundred Aker Wood to the Magic Kingdom,' University of Westminster, Professorial Lecture Series, October 14, University of Westminster.

Stone, K. (1975) 'Things Walt Disney never told us,' *Journal of American Folklore*, 88(347) (January–March): 42–50.

Straubhaar, J. D. (1991) 'Beyond media imperialism: asymmetrical interdependence and cultural proximity,' *Critical Studies in Mass Communication*, 8 (March): 39–59.

Sussman, G. and Lent, J. A. (eds) (1998) *Global Productions: Labor in the Making of 'Information Society.'* Cresskill, NJ, Hampton Press.

Tomlinson, J. (1991) *Cultural Imperialism: A Critical Introduction.* Baltimore, The Johns Hopkins University Press.

Tunstall, J. (1977) *The Media Are American: Anglo-American Media in the World.* London, Constable.

The Walt Disney Company (1999) Annual Report to Stockholders.

Wasko, J. (2001) *Understanding Disney: The Manufacture of Fantasy.* Cambridge, Polity Press.

Webster, D. (1988) *Looka Yonder: The Imaginary American of Populist Culture.* London, Routledge.

Yoshimoto, M. (1994) 'Images of empire: Tokyo Disneyland and Japanese cultural imperialism,' in E. Smoodin (ed.), *Disney Discourse: Producing the Magic Kingdom.* New York, Routledge, pp. 181–202.

PART II

Summary of the Project

CHAPTER 2

The Global Disney Audiences Project: Disney across Cultures

MARK PHILLIPS

The Global Disney Audiences Project is, as the name suggests, an initial attempt to understand a transnational media conglomerate from the perspective of those receiving its offerings. Researchers from around the world were recruited to participate in this project and the result comprises data from eighteen countries. A total of 1252 respondents representing 53 separate nationalities voluntarily responded to questionnaires designed by the project team, and a subset of these respondents submitted to in-depth interviews designed to elicit a greater understanding of how Disney is perceived by users and non-users alike.

As one might imagine, the resultant database offers a wealth of information that could be described as daunting. However, responses also indicate a uniformity of exposure and a relative unanimity of attitude and belief that is, to say the least, surprising. An oversimplified conclusion: as far as Disney is concerned, it really is a small world after all.

Genesis of the project

As mentioned in the introduction, the initial interest in this research was engendered by a chapter in Michael Real's book *Mass-Mediated Culture* (1977) entitled 'The Disney Universe: Morality Play.' In this chapter Real reports on the results of a questionnaire returned by 192 subjects asked to respond to such questions as their reactions to Disneyland, their perceptions as to what extent they had been influenced by Disney products, and their comments on which virtues Disney approved of and which vices the company disapproved of.

Real described his respondents as 'experts' on Disney representations (Real, 1977: 49). The 192 respondents had spent a cumulative total of approximately 6500 hours in Disneyland; 45 had visited the park ten or more times, some in excess of 50 visits. The majority of respondents had been exposed to the full range of Disney offerings – films, both live action and animated, cartoons, comic books, merchandise, etc. In short, this sample was comprised of users not just tangentially aware of Disney offerings but intimately involved with Disney, consciously, actively choosing to consume Disney offerings and, one presumes, tending to agree with the premise and messages propagated by Disney representations. Indeed, of the 192 respondents only ten expressed any resistance to Disney or its offerings (*ibid.*: 70).

Of particular interest to the coordinators of the Global Disney Audiences Project were the results of the virtues and vices section of the questionnaire. Respondents showed a remarkable clarity in terms of what values Disney approved and disapproved of. Of the virtues mentioned, sixteen were repeatedly offered; of the vices, twelve received multiple mentions. Even more dramatically, on no occasion did someone designate as a vice something that the rest of the sample identified as a virtue, or vice versa. This universal understanding of Disney intentions is both extraordinary and disquieting. That any company, whether media savvy or not, could so successfully communicate a complicated and broad-based agenda without contradiction or confusion is staggering. Remember, these responses were unprompted: that is, no lists were offered as a guideline, no hints given as to appropriate limits on response. From a blank slate, if you will, these respondents not only offered general agreement on what was regarded as a virtue and a vice but also exhibited not a single instance of disagreement between the categories. Such a communication success speaks of a propaganda machine unparalleled in its concinnity. The unambiguous response is also disquieting in view of the fact that the majority of respondents denied that Disney had exerted any great degree of influence on their lives (*ibid.*: 72).

Real's intriguing research raises several interesting questions. What kind of response might one elicit from a broader-based sample, one composed of 'non-experts?' Has Disney maintained its effectiveness in terms of communicating an unambiguous ideology in the intervening 25 years? And, in this era of global media expansion, merger, conglomeration, and transnational hegemony, how do audiences outside the U.S.A. view Disney?

Figure 4. Mickey Mouse birthday party in Albany, Oregon, U.S.A. Photo: Bill Alden

The Global Disney Audiences Project is an attempt, then, to expand on Real's project both geographically and phenomenologically. In one sense it is an attempt to replicate his results; in another sense it is a totally unrelated project dealing with Disney expansion, product availability and cross-cultural attitudes toward the company.

In the next two sections of this chapter I will discuss the nuts and bolts of the project. Subsequent sections will present the results of the cross-cultural analysis and a discussion of those results.

Method

The research was conducted via a tripartite method consisting of questionnaire, interview and observation. Standardized questionnaires were administered in each of the seventeen countries outside the U.S.A. and in five distinct locations within the U.S.A. (Athens, Ohio; Chicago, Illinois; Detroit, Michigan; Eugene, Oregon; and Tucson, Arizona). The questionnaires were a combination of closed and open-ended questions designed to ascertain respondents' level of contact with, and attitudes toward, Disney at various age levels (pre-teen, teen and adult), the types and number of Disney products with which each respondent has come into contact, the values that respondents attach to Disney, and the perspective from which Disney makes its offerings (American? Western? Global?).

The questionnaire utilized in this project was the result of three separate pre-tests in which instruments of various length and difficulty were assessed in terms of quality of information gleaned and response rates. The resultant questionnaire was comprised of 49 questions and took approximately 20 to 30 minutes to complete. (See Appendix 1.)

Each respondent provided a very brief demographic sketch (age, gender, country of origin) and then reported their level of contact with Disney at various ages using a seven-point scale. Respondents were also asked to estimate the age at which they were first exposed to Disney. Subjects were next asked to express the degree to which they liked or disliked Disney at various stages of their life, again using a seven-point scale.

The next question asked respondents to list all of the Disney products, services, and presentations with which they had ever had contact. This open-ended, unprompted query was followed by a list of Disney offerings: each respondent indicated with a 'yes' or 'no' if they had personal contact with each item. This prompted list was physically separated from the aforementioned unprompted question, which appeared on a previous page. Respondents were specifically instructed to respond to questions consecutively, neither referring back to a question once completed nor referring forward to subsequent questions until all questions had been completed to that point.

The next section of the questionnaire duplicated the dichotomous structure just described, but in this instance was aimed at under-standing what respondents believed to be the values that Disney promotes or discourages, or in Real's terminology, Disney virtues and vices. The unprompted, open-ended question asked was, 'As you look back at your experience of Disney media, products, and services, what descriptions instantly come to mind? What terms express your perception of "Disney"? List as many words or phrases as you wish.' The subsequent prompted list of 'values,' on the following page (again, respondents were instructed not to refer back after completing the unprompted question) consisted of nineteen terms listed alphabeti-cally (see page 35). For each term respondents were asked to indicate whether they thought Disney promoted that concept, discouraged it, or whether they felt the item did not apply to Disney.

This list was compiled from three sources: (1) some of the terms (approximately one-third) were from Real's work, either directly specified or implied; (2) some were culled from the unprompted versions of the pre-test questionnaires; and (3) the rest reflect specific interests of the project coordinators, either to understand better how

1. Bravery	11. Optimism
2. Family	12. Patriarchy
3. Fantasy	13. Patriotism
4. Fun	14. Physical beauty
5. Good over evil	15. Racism
6. Happiness	16. Respect for difference
7. Imagination	17. Technological progress
8. Individualism	18. Thriftiness
9. Love/romance	19. Work ethic
10. Magic	

people perceive Disney or to test the effectiveness of Disney's communication efforts.[1]

The questionnaire concluded by asking respondents to indicate whether they thought Disney was uniquely 'American.' This last question has obvious cultural imperialism implications but also was designed to aid researchers in understanding the extent to which disparate cultures have embraced Disney as 'their own.'

The second leg of the research design was in-depth interviews conducted with a subset of the respondents to the questionnaires. Each questionnaire included a page asking for volunteers to participate in an interview lasting approximately 30 minutes, and provided space for prospective interviewees to list their names and phone numbers.

The interview portion of the research was much less rigid and standardized than the questionnaire section of the project. Whereas each respondent in each locale responded to the same questionnaire, the interviews were much more free-form and intentionally uncoordinated. The project leaders did provide an interview template for those researchers who wished such guidance, but by no means were these guidelines to be construed as mandatory. In fact, it was anticipated, and encouraged, that project participants would pursue lines of inquiry consistent with their own particular research interests and expertise. Thus, the interviews were conceptualized as a vehicle to allow researcher and/or respondent to follow lines of interest as suggested by responses to the questionnaire or by topics raised anew in the interview. The aim was to dig more deeply into areas of interest, and in the process enhance our understanding of Disney audiences. (See Appendix 2.)

In the event, some researchers tended to follow the templates relatively closely, while some ignored them completely; others chose to interview a number of respondents, while there were those who chose to focus on a few very in-depth interviews; some combined individual and focus-group situations (see, for example, David

Buckingham's profile of the U.K.); and some researchers declined to interview anyone at all.

It should be acknowledged that a majority of those who volunteered to be interviewed could be described as enthusiastic about Disney. Disney critics, judging from our own efforts to recruit participants, tend to prefer not to discuss Disney – period. However, even among Disney enthusiasts there was an acknowledgement of certain problems or disagreement with Disney orthodoxy (discussed in the results section below).

The last part of our tripartite research design was observation. This can be more accurately described as an individual country market survey. Each researcher was asked to compile a compendium of Disney products available in their specific location. Again, a template was provided by project coordinators to assist researchers by identifying product categories. The point of this exercise was to ascertain the extent to which Disney offerings had spread around the world and to identify any products/offerings that were idiosyncratic to a specific country or region. One by-product of this phase of the project which, in hindsight, should have been obvious was the business practice of differentially committing resources to different geographic areas (see, for example, Pecora's and Meehan's U.S. profile and Simon Burton's discussion of Disney availability in South Africa).

A couple of comments on the research method. The goal of this project was not to produce a boilerplate report on Disney, country by country. Rather, the aim was not only a broad geopolitical perspective but also individual, differentiative, diacritical examinations of Disney founded upon the perspective of audience. Thus, researchers were free to utilize questionnaire data in myriad ways, encouraged to sample outside the required frame, and given broad latitude to pursue interview and market data so as to facilitate their research interests and goals. Just as a prism refracts light to produce a color spectrum, so this approach produces a more complete picture of how audiences use and understand Disney; a more complete, diverse spectrum of knowledge.

However, in order for any cross-cultural analysis to have meaning there must be a common basis from which to analyze the subject. In this case such a commonality is the standardized questionnaire administered to a specified sample frame (undergraduate university students). The sample frame will be discussed below. The questionnaire has already been described, but the function, or purpose, of this instrument requires explication.

Questionnaire and propositions

The first section of the questionnaire seeks to identify the level of contact respondents have had with Disney at different stages of their lives (pre-teen, teen, and adult). The second section asks respondents to quantify their level of liking toward Disney at the three age levels previously specified. It has been suggested that these questions, relying as they do on memories, will necessarily be unreliable. If our intention was to accurately portray subjects' contact and affection for Disney at these previous stages in their lives, then reliability would indeed be suspect. However, we are not concerned with actual contact or feelings at the time; rather, we are interested in respondents' *current* perceptions as to how they felt and how much contact was experienced. It is our contention that it is these current perceptions that will dictate future interactions with Disney. These first two sections contribute to the following two propositions.

- P1: Respondents will report decreasing contact with Disney as they age from child to adult.
- P2: As they age respondents will report an erosion in the degree they like Disney, but such ratings will still tend to be positive.

The third section of the questionnaire is the unprompted/prompted dichotomy concerning Disney products. This section will assist in determining the level of market penetration Disney has realized in a given locality, help in identifying idiosyncratic product offerings, and give us an idea to what extent users understand their level of involvement with Disney.

- P3: It is predicted that consumers will tend to significantly under-estimate their involvement with Disney as demonstrated by an underreporting of unprompted versus prompted product usage.

The fourth section repeats the unprompted/prompted dichotomy for terms ascribed to Disney. The unprompted question serves as a barometer for the strength of a given term: that is, multiple mentions across cultures demonstrate the strength with which a given term is associated with Disney. Also, this question allows respondents to freely express their opinions about Disney, both positive and negative, unfettered by paradigmatic incursion. As will be discussed in the results section, respondents offered literally hundreds of Disney descriptors.

The prompted question allows us to focus more narrowly on themes previously identified as germane to Disney. Obviously this list could have been much more extensive. There is a fine line, however, between eliciting useful information and confusing and/or boring subjects, resulting in a concomitant lowering of response. Exit interviews after pre-test instruments utilizing more terms/values indeed indicated that the subjects reached a point of mental exhaustion.

Some exit interviews of the list ultimately used suggested that respondents suspected an agenda on the part of researchers: that we were in some way biased or predisposed to be critical of Disney. This revelation was received with some bemusement. As previously stated, the majority of terms were suggested by previous research and pre-test subjects. Furthermore, in many cases whether a term is viewed as virtue or vice is determined by context. For example, in Real's study 'individuality' was conceived of as a vice. Certainly in the context of selfishness, or failure to cooperate for the greater good, such a characterization might be warranted. But what about the rugged individualism of the American frontier (often depicted in Disney presentations)? Finally, the respondent was presented with the opportunity to indicate that Disney promoted or discouraged each term. So, even for a term like racism, which is *de facto* negative, by indicating that Disney discouraged this practice, is this not a positive outcome?

Sections three and four give rise to the following propositions:

- P4: It is predicted that the values propagated by Disney will be remarkably consistent across countries and cultures.
- P5: Consumers will view Disney as essentially benign.

The combination of P3 and P5 leads us to the conclusion that parents will tend to view Disney as appropriate for their children without fully understanding the effects the company may have had on their own development.

The last question in the questionnaire asked respondents to comment on Disney as an American company: 'Do you feel Disney is uniquely "American"? Does it promote and represent a vision of American culture that is distinct from other cultures? Please explain.'

This question engendered a significant amount of contradictory opinion. Some were concerned about cultural imperialism and the diminution of indigenous culture. Others were quite sanguine about any deleterious effects, while still others acknowledged the cultural ramifications but embraced American culture nevertheless. Perhaps most interesting were those subjects who decried against American imperialism, targeted Disney as a prime instigator and yet continued to express a strong liking for the company. These findings will be more fully explored in the results section.

The sample frame

The sampling frame was comprised of undergraduate university students. Clearly, this frame does not lend itself to any claims of statistical representativeness, nor will it be possible to generalize the results to the populace at large. However, this sample frame was specifically chosen for two considered reasons, the first pragmatic and the second pertaining to the quality of data collected.

The first reason this sample was chosen was that it was achievable. Coordinating a project of this magnitude was a complex task. Not only were we dealing with scholars from disparate backgrounds, with varied interests and research agendas, but also with myriad university and national rules and laws regarding studies involving human subjects. Individual researchers were encouraged to expand the sample frame to include other demographic groups consistent with their research interests, but in order to ensure a standardized and consistent frame from which to make inter-country comparisons, university students were targeted because of their availability and because it was determined that this group would be least likely to run afoul of any human subjects prohibitions. So the first consideration was essentially grounded in realism.

The second reason was purely research oriented. University students are uniquely situated to understand and comment on Disney, having come of age during the greatest global expansion in the company's history. They sit on the cusp of adulthood and so can discuss how they anticipate interacting with Disney as adults (for example, will they expose their children to Disney?), but at the same time are young enough to have relatively vivid memories of their own childhood interactions with Disney. This sample, then, is appropriate in that it is capable of responding to the questions posed by this research. Furthermore, it is representative in that it comprises a prime target of Disney communication efforts.

Increasingly, marketers, including Disney, target specific market niches to receive their appeals and, it is believed, be thus encouraged to use said marketer's (Disney's) products. In other words, segments of the market most likely to use a company's products are targeted by that company via advertising appeals, retail locations, product customization, etc.[2] Disney is interested in consumers who are literate, have above-average amounts of disposable income (Disney products are, by and large, not inexpensive), and have the time and inclination to pursue leisure activities. University graduates precisely fit this profile and are, therefore, a prime Disney target. Our sample frame is and will increasingly become a prime receptor of Disney appeals and likely users of Disney products; as such, these respondents are well suited to comment on Disney and its offerings.

While it is acknowledged that this sample is a non-probability sample, it certainly qualifies in the tradition of *purposive sampling*, or *expert choice* (Kalton, 1983). While the project coordinators are aware of the potential for selection bias (see, for example, Scheaffer *et al.*, 1990; Smith, 1988), there is no reason to expect that this sample, as an example of a Disney target market, will differ substantively from Disney's target market at large. And, to reiterate, no claims of general-izability or attempts to extrapolate to the populace at large will be made. This project is really more exploratory than definitive in nature; it is an initial attempt to research how audiences use and understand Disney.

Finally, it should be recognized that student samples have a long tradition in consumer/audience research.[3] It is our contention, there-fore, that the sample frame selected for this project is both relevant and appropriate.

Results

As stated earlier, 1252 students responded to the questionnaire worldwide, representing 53 separate countries.[4] The average age of respondents was 21.12 with a range of 13–52 (two respondents were under 17 years of age and fourteen were 35 or older).[5] The sample was 58.3 percent female and 41.1 percent male (0.6 percent non-response on this question).

The country reporting the youngest average age of respondents was Singapore (19.0); the country reporting the oldest average age was Sweden (24.95). Four countries reported a male–female response ratio opposite that of the world as a whole: Korea (70 percent male), India (63.6 percent male), South Africa (54.4 percent male), and Denmark (53.1 percent male). Four countries reported female–male ratios significantly higher than the world average: Slovenia (85.3 percent female), the U.K. (80.8 percent female), Australia (76.3 percent female), and Cyprus (72 percent female).

The average age at which respondents reported their first contact with Disney was 4.61 years. The country reporting the youngest average age of first contact was Norway (2.76 years), while the oldest was India (7.23 years). Nine countries (Norway – 2.76, U.S.A. – 3.24, Singapore – 3.25, Sweden – 3.61, the U.K. – 3.81, Australia – 3.91, Denmark – 4.17, Canada – 4.38, and Mexico – 4.42) had an average age of first contact under 5 years of age; while nine countries had an average age greater than 5 years (Greece – 5.21, France – 5.40, Cyprus – 5.56, Slovenia – 5.71, South Africa – 5.90, Japan – 6.45, Brazil – 6.93, Korea – 7.18, and India – 7.23).[6]

When asked to assess their level of contact with Disney at various ages, respondents indicated the following level of contact (using a seven-point scale where 1 indicates no contact and 7 indicates much contact):

Age 1–12	4.65
Age 13–17	4.03
Age 18+	3.74

These data support our first proposition which predicted a decrease in contact as respondents aged.[7] This pattern was replicated in all but four countries in our survey, as reported below:

	Australia	Canada	Japan	Korea
Age 1–12	4.53	4.54	3.62	4.28
Age 13–17	3.87	3.95	3.67	3.93
Age 18+	3.92	4.04	3.29	4.16

While these four countries do not duplicate the straight-line pattern of the rest of our sample they still demonstrate the predicted erosion from pre-teen to adult. Japan and Korea have two of the older first-contact averages, thus mitigating the distinction between the pre-teen and teenager years. Further, Korea has one of the lower levels of product exposure. This combination of both late and low exposure serves to ameliorate age category distinctions, as the level of liking by Koreans is essentially flat over time. Respondents from Australia and Canada have two of the older average ages in the sample, which may partially explain the increase in liking from teen to adult as older respondents tend to pull the average up (see note 7).

Respondents were also asked to report how much they liked Disney offerings at various age levels (again, response was measured on a seven-point scale where 1 indicated strongly liked and 7 indicated strongly disliked):

Age 1–12	2.48
Age 13–17	3.25
Age 18+	3.52

Although a slight erosion in liking occurred over time the ratings remain positive, thus supporting our second proposition. Three countries offered exceptions to this pattern:

	Brazil	Canada	France
Age 1–12	2.97	2.64	3.17
Age 13–17	4.00	3.11	4.13
Age 18+	3.93	3.10	3.17

Again, the general pattern of erosion from pre-teen to adult is evident except in the case of France, which given their reputation for resisting cultural imposition is, to say the least, quite an unexpected result.

Our third proposition predicted that respondents would tend to underestimate their exposure to Disney based on a discrepancy between the number of products they reported using in unprompted versus prompted conditions. This prediction was supported, as the unprompted average was 4.24 products per person versus a prompted average of 11.36.[8]

Highlights of respondents' consumption of specific Disney products include the following (all percentages reported to nearest whole number). Of those responding, 98 percent have viewed a Disney film; 79 percent have seen a Disney television program (not including the Disney Channel); 50 percent have seen the Disney Channel; 72 percent have rented a video and 44 percent have purchased a video; 82 percent have read a Disney book, 53 percent have read a Disney comic book and 46 percent have read a Disney magazine; 72 percent have received Disney merchandise as a gift, while 60 percent have given a Disney gift; 64 percent have been in a Disney Store; 73 percent have owned a Disney toy, 61 percent own Disney clothing; 30 percent have owned a Mickey Mouse watch and 26 percent have had Mickey Mouse ears; 54 percent of respondents have visited one of the four Disney theme parks in France, Japan or the U.S.A. – either California or Florida. (See Appendix 4 for complete results of world response to the questionnaire.)

Country by country the data offer some interesting insights. Japan reports the lowest level of film viewing (83 percent) followed, in ascending order, by Singapore (93 percent), Denmark (94 percent), Cyprus (96 percent), Korea (97 percent), Mexico and South Africa (98 percent); all other countries report that 100 percent of respondents have seen a Disney film. Japan is also in the lowest one-third in video rentals (62 percent) and is second to lowest in purchasing Disney videos at 15 percent (Korea and Slovenia report only 9 percent). Contrast this with theme-park attendance where Japan leads the world, with 97 percent of respondents having attended a Disney theme park. Ninety percent of U.S. respondents have visited one of the theme parks, after which there is a significant drop-off to 63 percent of Canadians; no other country is over 50 percent, the lowest being Cyprus with a reported attendance of 4 percent. Table 2.1 lists the countries with the highest and lowest usage for the identified product categories.

When asked to describe Disney, respondents produced literally hundreds of terms. Far and away the most frequently mentioned was 'fun,' followed in descending order by 'happiness,' 'fantasy,' 'imagination,' 'family,' and 'magic.' The results of the prompted version of this

Table 2.1 Percentage of product usage by country (highest/lowest)

	Highest		*Lowest*	
Product	*Country*	*Percentage*	*Country*	*Percentage*
Films	*	100	Japan	83
Disney Channel	Greece	100	Cyprus	8
TV	U.S.A.	94	Brazil	26
Rented video	Mexico	96	France	33
Bought video	U.K.	81	Korea	9
Video games	India	73	Denmark	9
Books	Slovenia	91	Greece	60
Records	U.K.	92	Brazil	23
Comic books	Greece	93	Japan	12
Magazines	Sweden	98	Brazil	7
Received gift	U.S.A./Singapore	87	Korea	55
Gave gift	U.K.	81	France	35
Disney Store	U.S.A.	96	Cyprus/Korea	24
Clothing	Cyprus	84	France	33
Jewelry	U.S.A.	36	Denmark/France	0
Mickey Mouse watch	Mexico	73	France	4
Mickey Mouse ears	U.S.A.	56	South Africa	1
Toys	Singapore	97	Korea	55
Theme parks	Japan	97	Cyprus	4

*11 of the 18 countries reported 100%

question offered a close approximation of the unprompted results. Table 2.2 below lists values in descending order as respondents rated the degree to which Disney promoted a given value (percentages refer to the number of respondents who said Disney promoted that value).

Interestingly, not one term failed to garner support for the idea that Disney also discouraged that value. For example, 1 percent of respondents believed that Disney discouraged 'fun,' 1.6 percent said the company discouraged 'fantasy,' while 2.2 percent opined that Disney discouraged 'happiness,' etc.

Lastly, respondents were asked to indicate whether they thought Disney was 'uniquely American.' Of those responding to this question, 49.5 percent answered yes, Disney is uniquely American, while 27.6 percent indicated that they did not believe this to be the case. (See Table 2.3.)

Table 2.2 Responses to given values, by percentage

Order	Percentage	Order	Percentage
1. Fun	95.3	11. Physical beauty	68.5
2. Fantasy	93.9	12. Technological progress	49.9
3. Happiness	88.8	13. Respect for difference	47.6
4. Good over evil	88.7	14. Patriotism	40.9
5. Magic	88.7	15. Individualism	40.5
6. Love/romance	85.1	16. Work ethic	39.2
7. Imagination	86.2	17. Patriarchy	38.8
8. Family	84.3	18. Thriftiness	24.6
9. Bravery	76.8	19. Racism	18.8
10. Optimism	76.8		

Table 2.3 Percentage responses by country to Yes/No question 'Is Disney uniquely American?'

	Yes	No		Yes	No
Australia	65.8	31.6	Korea	84.0	7.0
Brazil	51.6	32.3	Mexico	53.3	6.7
Canada	30.2	27.4	Norway	65.9	17.1
Cyprus	60.0	20.0	Singapore	76.7	23.3
Denmark	68.8	31.3	Slovenia	32.4	20.6
France	41.3	52.2	South Africa	57.8	31.1
Greece	36.7	56.7	Sweden	43.1	41.4
India	45.5	50.0	U.K.	61.5	26.9
Japan	19.8	9.5	U.S.A.	48.4	33.2

As Table 2.3 indicates there is wide variance in opinion as to whether Disney is or is not uniquely American. Opinion also greatly varies as to why Disney is uniquely American or not. The next section will discuss this range of opinion, as well as giving further consideration to the data previously presented and the introduction of information from interviews and the open-ended questions from the questionnaires.

Discussion

The data presented thus far offer the unavoidable conclusion that Disney is both universal and ubiquitous. Certainly, individual products have disproportionate distribution patterns, but the presence of Disney is unambiguous. A quick glance at Table 2.1 indicates that France offers the lowest consumption in various product categories:

for example, renting videos, giving gifts and clothing. Yet in all three of these categories one-third of French respondents had consumed the specified product. Further, 100 percent of the French respondents had viewed a Disney film, 87 percent had read a Disney book, over half had read a comic book or magazine and 63 percent had owned a Disney toy. Similarly, while only 4 percent of respondents from Cyprus had been to a Disney theme park, 96 percent had seen a film, 92 percent had owned a Disney toy, 84 percent had owned an article of clothing, 80 percent had read a Disney book and 72 percent had seen a Disney television program. Even in South Africa, where one might assume Disney's presence to be proportionally less, 98 percent of respondents had seen a Disney film and 80 percent reported owning some piece of Disney merchandise.

While Disney is often viewed from a local, and even more specifically from a child's, perspective as being indigenous (see, for example, Kirsten Drotner's profile of Denmark, 'Donald Seems So Danish'), as a company its *modus operandi* is to offer essentially standardized products, undifferentiated across country or cultural boundaries. Certainly, the company will customize certain products to specific geographic areas. Obviously, language is one area where the company modifies presentations to appeal locally, while some minor character names and references may also be altered slightly. Generally, however, the company offers standardized products, identical to the original American format, and simply recycles and repackages these offerings for local consumption. These customized packages can have the effect of making Disney offerings appear individualized. For example, respondents from Denmark, Norway and Sweden all reference Disney Christmas presentations (in addition to the afore-mentioned profile of Denmark, see Ingunn Hagen's discussion of Norway). Silvia Molina y Vedia describes how clowns dressed as Mickey Mouse or the Lion King routinely entertain families in public parks in Mexico City. Disney films are routinely dubbed using popular local actors for the voice-overs (see, for example, the profile of Greece). But none of these examples presents a product individua-lized for a local culture. The Scandinavian Christmas shows are generic (American) Disney programing wrapped in holiday packaging; the costumed characters in Mexico City are standard Disney characters; and dubbing (even using the voices of local actors) does not individualize the format, style or message of Disney films.

We can, however, recognize distinct patterns of consumption: in some cases, perhaps, because of customized product offerings; in other cases, because certain products are not offered locally. Comic-book readership is one example of cross-cultural disparity. Of the eighteen countries included in our survey only three reported less than 50 percent readership of comics: Canada (40 percent), U.S.A. (35 percent) and Japan, where just 12 percent of respondents had read a Disney comic book. Conversely, Greece (93 percent), India (91 percent) and the Scandinavian countries (Sweden – 91 percent, Norway – 90 percent, and Denmark – 88 percent) all reported exceedingly high rates of readership. Magazines showed a similar pattern, with Brazil (7 percent), Japan (13 percent), Korea (22 percent), Canada (33 percent), the U.K. (39 percent), and U.S.A. (43 percent) being the only countries to report below 50 percent readership. In contrast, the Scandinavian triumvirate (Sweden – 98 percent, Denmark – 97 percent, and Norway – 93 percent) greatly embrace this medium.

Other examples of unequal product usage are evident: for example, the Disney Channel is unavailable in several countries. But whatever media are emphasized or whatever product offerings are repackaged within a medium, Disney consistently promotes certain themes or ideas. In fact, while Disney may customize certain product offerings to a specific country or area, the values propagated by the company have been remarkably consistent across cultures.

Values

Of the nineteen terms contained in the prompted list, 'fun' and 'fantasy' came first and second in our world rankings. Only four countries failed to register these two options in their top three ranked terms (based on the percentage of respondents who agreed that Disney promoted this value): the U.K. (fantasy ranked fifth), Greece (fantasy fourth), Denmark (fantasy fourth) and France (fun fifth, and fantasy eighth). Correlating the top-ten ranked terms, the coefficient of agreement across countries is a quite impressive 95.6 percent.[9]

The terms provided by respondents in the unprompted portion of the questionnaire add insight to our understanding of Disney audiences. As previously mentioned, fun, happiness, fantasy, imagination, and family were the terms corresponding to the prompted list that were most frequently mentioned in the unprompted section of the questionnaire. Imagination and family were proportionally mentioned more often in the unprompted than the prompted section. In connection with family, a term that was frequently cited was children or childhood. This term was referred to in three distinct contexts. First, it was often suggested that Disney was designed for children. Second, there was the sense that Disney's appeal is 'universal,' attracting the child in all of us. Finally, there was a nostalgic element to this term, evoking fond memories of interactions with Disney in childhood. A 19-year-old male from the U.S.A. serves as an exemplar: 'I personally feel Disney is a reflection of what [it] is like to be a child. It doesn't matter what color or culture. People of all ages enjoy Disney because it brings out the kid in all of us.'

Color and music were often mentioned in relation to Disney. Again, childhood nostalgia was a factor here. An amalgam of sentiments might read as follows. 'Disney created a *colorful* and *magical* world, full of *cute animals* with *entertaining* stories and enjoyable *music*. It was a *safe* place where *dreams* can come true.' Or as the following list provided by a 19-year-old female British respondent more concisely states: 'Bright, colorful, harmless, fun, magic, music, dreams, fantasy, cozy, family, warm, happy, good for all ages, good quality, innocent, values.'

At the same time as Disney was seen as a warm and cozy place, many terms offered in the unprompted section explicitly criticized the company. These criticisms tended to fall into two main categories: business-related terms and content.

There seems to be a growing awareness that Disney, warm and fuzzy as it may be, is also a business. Terms such as greed, profit, merchandising, monopoly, capitalist, corporate and multinational were mentioned with great regularity. Expensive was a term also readily applied. Advertising was often mentioned, as in respondents being bombarded from all sides with Disney images (McDonald's tie-ins were specifically referred to in many countries). More content-oriented terms included cheezy, hoaky, saccharin, sterile, conserva-tive, tacky, and, in a particularly evocative descriptor from the U.K., 'yukky.'

Dealing with the latter terms first, it should not be too surprising that 18- to 22-year-olds may try and distance themselves from images and products associated with childhood. As adolescents struggle into adulthood it is natural to express disdain for those institutions and activities enjoyed as a child. Yet these expressions are belied by both respondents' ratings of their liking of Disney and other terms that they simultaneously apply to Disney. For example, the aforementioned respondent from the U.K. offered the following description of Disney films and products: 'schmaltzy, safe, clean, sweet, creative, dark, yukky, imaginative, American.' This seemingly inconsistent response to Disney is not at all unusual in our sample, particularly as it applies to Disney the business. On the one hand, respondents decry the focus on profits, the pervasiveness of Disney enterprises, the expense of participating in the Disney world, and the manipulative (another term used repeatedly by respondents) aspects of the Disney empire. On the other hand, respondents like Disney, have fond memories of earlier interactions, and testify that they will expose their own children to Disney in the future. Consider the following comment from a Japanese female, aged 21: 'Huge everlasting castle made of mass of money.' On the seven-point scale with 1 indicating strong like, this respondent rated her current liking of Disney a 3. Or consider the description of a 21-year-old U.S. male: 'exploitive, expensive, mass produced, insincere, manipulative, downright scary, only in it for the money, what would Walt think if he were alive.' This person rated his current level of liking as a 2.

This last point, 'what would Walt think,' leads us to another interesting issue with respondents: namely, that consumers seem to be able to compartmentalize Disney the business from Disney as entertainment, and to make a distinction between 'classic' Disney and current Disney. This compartmentalization is demonstrated by sentiments expressed in the quotes just cited and their concurrent liking of Disney: clearly, although the respondents do not like the business of Disney, this does not stop them from liking the products produced by the company. Further, there is a strong association with Disney animation as exemplifying what Disney *is*. When asked to comment on or discuss a Disney film, respondents invariably refer to a Disney animated feature; rarely will they offer a live-action film as an example and they never suggest a non-Disney label film (Touchstone, Hollywood, Miramax, etc.). Walt Disney is inextricably intertwined with the context and production of animation and thus the following equation tends to pertain: Walt = animation = good. Business practices are not associated with Walt but instead are ascribed to Michael Eisner and the current Disney corporate team. A 35-year-old British female puts this equation in perspective: 'Walt, I believe, could not have foreseen the extent of the industry today. To make kids smile must have been the original intention?' Or consider the following paean to Walt from Canada (female, 22 years old):

> If you watched different cartoons nowadays, it's not the same, different animation, it's not the same as Walt Disney. Like Transformers, there's so much evil. There is so much fighting. There is a good guy, but he doesn't come out and show feelings and emotions like Walt Disney movie animations; they have feelings and they portray them.

Of course, as with any group this size, there exists some cynicism regarding 'Uncle Walt' – for example, cryogenics was mentioned a couple of times,[10] and if exceptions prove the rule then in all fairness the following opinion from an Australian female, aged 18, should be entered into the evidence: 'I really don't like the old Disney films, but the more recent ones are great to watch!' But the vast majority of respondents prefer classic Disney and express a fondness for Walt's legacy. This does not mean consumers necessarily prefer *old* Disney films, but that they have nostalgic feelings for Disney animation. (One could argue that Disney's revival under Eisner is directly related to a re-emphasis on producing animated features – but that is another study altogether.) Remarkably, people are so enamored of Disney that they assume if it is animation and it is good it must be Disney.[11]

This credulity regarding Disney animation is expressed by such terms as cute, cozy, warm, clean, safe, friendly, heart-warming, carefree, enchanting, wonderful, perky, innocent, mystical, moral, etc. These feelings are seemingly hard-wired in Disney users and tend to override any misgivings about Disney enterprises when respondents are asked about the likelihood of exposing their children to Disney. Various traits are attributed to Disney, but the prevailing belief seems to be that Disney is harmless fun. As a 27-year-old female from Greece says, 'I will expose my children to Disney films and shows, because according to my experience there is no danger in them. I do not think that my children will have bad influences by watching Disney cartoons or films.' A respondent from Denmark (female, 30 years) opines that she would rather have her children view Disney features than watch 'the crap on television.' A 20-year-old female from the U.S.A. is more pragmatic: 'How can you not expose your kids to Disney? It's not realistic to think you can avoid Disney. ... I wouldn't want to rob [them] of [their] childhood.'

Kids

Disney as a rite of passage is not an uncommon notion. Another U.S. female enjoyed relating her experience of trying to watch the Disney Channel even though the signal was scrambled because her family had not subscribed to the service. And a U.S. male recalled how he was *only* allowed to watch Disney movies.

However, many respondents expressed reservations about exposing children to the business side of Disney, and resented the unending product promotions, tie-ins, and advertising. At the same time, they clung to the magic of Disney. This ambivalence is expressed by a 24-year-old French female:

> I would say that going to the movies, or buying video cassettes, that kind of thing ... I see that with my childhood, I've never been disappointed by Disney products, I found that really superb. But on the other hand, all the merchandising stuff ... it does not correspond to Disney magic world. At least, that's the image I keep from my childhood, when I was a little girl. The business breaks the myth. For me, the cassettes, I think it's very good ... However, there's too much business around it, it breaks the dream.

Despite such reservations, respondents in the great majority indicated that they would expose their children to Disney in part because they believe Disney offerings to be safe: 'if you look at the sample that's available to us, Disney is probably one of the less explicitly harmful sort of things that kids can get involved in, so ya, I just think it's cool'

(South Africa, male, 25 years). This chimera of safety was expounded upon in an impromptu conversation with a male colleague of the project coordinators in which he compared Disney to McDonald's. (I am paraphrasing the following comments.) Our colleague explained that while McDonald's cuisine may not be very nutritional, you always know what you are going to get and his children liked the food. Sometimes parents, he explained, are worn out making decisions and thinking about the ramifications for their children, and a decision to go to McDonald's is, in this context, safe. The same with Disney: his children like the colors, the music, and the cute characters. Of all the entertainment possibilities (and who could possibly research them all?) Disney (animation) remains a known quantity and as such seems a safe choice.

Finally, there is a segment that believes that any attempts to analyze Disney are foolish. Comments such as 'They are just cartoons,' and 'Disney is just about having fun,' abound: 'To me Disney is just about having a group of friends and having fun. That's something that almost everybody in the world wants' (Singapore, female, 18 years). In displaying this attitude Disney fans are emulating Walt, who proclaimed that 'We make the pictures and then let the professors tell us what they mean' (Schickel, 1985). While a majority of respondents agree that Disney is about fun, fantasy and happiness, and as such is appropriate for their children, opinion as to the perspective of Disney – U.S., Western, global – is much more divergent. This section will end with a discussion of the question, 'Is Disney uniquely American?'

Disney: uniquely 'American'?

Table 2.3 displayed a wide variance from country to country in response to this question. Overall, approximately 50 percent thought Disney was uniquely American, while 28 percent disagreed with this notion. Those advocating the former offered arguments that can be broken down into two basic categories: (1) Disney as prototypical American; and (2) Disney as cultural imperialist. Conversely, those who argue against the idea of Disney as uniquely American represent three basic arguments: (1) Not so much American as Western; (2) universal; (3) mine.

YES: DISNEY AS PROTOTYPE

First, Disney as American prototype. This argument can be broken down into two contradictory assertions: America the good and America the bad. America the good refers to the America of hope, freedom, and dreams. The 'American Dream' (not always in a positive context) was referred to by respondents in every country surveyed (one Japanese student described the concept as the 'American illusion'):

> Disney shows us the U.S. is the best country in the world. U.S. is a dream country and, you can do whatever you want in the U.S. (Cyprus, male, 19 years)

> I think Disney promote and represent a vision of American culture as cheerful, bright, hopeful and dreamful. (Japan, female, 20 years)

> I think it promotes the American culture, the American Dream. Everything is possible if you just try really hard and stand up for what you believe in. (Sweden, female, 24 years)

> American way of living – a family lives in a house, has a puppy and is happy. (Slovenia, female, 21 years)

America the bad focuses on consumerism, commodification and excess:

> 'Too much is enough' is a term used to explain American culture and I think Disney fits the description. Yes, it's uniquely 'American.' (Sweden, male, 25 years)

> The ruination of classic stories and fairy tales (and novels) for generations by simplification, cartoonification and relentless wasteful merchandising. It's American in the sense that it sugarcoats stories that would otherwise have been valuable to children and values getting *stuff* over meaning. (U.S.A., female, 20 years)

> Promotes North American culture with all the consumerism, individualism and racism that they can. (Mexico, male, 21 years)

> PR for American middle-class culture/American capitalism. (Denmark, male, 23 years)

Both of these camps, America the good or bad, seem to some extent to confound Disney and America: that is, anyone who was predisposed to like the U.S.A. can find support for this position in Disney presentations. If, on the other hand, you view the U.S.A. as in some way disagreeable, then Disney can easily be seen as promoting everything you do not like about the country. But whereas America can be tarred by Disney, Disney is not necessarily tarred by America. Again, we can see compartmentalization at work. For example, in the quote from Mexico just cited ('consumerism, individualism and racism'), the respondent rated his current feeling toward Disney as 'strongly like' (a 1 on the seven-point scale). Although it may be hard to rationalize strongly liking Disney while at the same time accusing it of promoting consumerism and racism, it is clear that those arguing that Disney represents America, good or bad, are obviously correct. In this scenario it is all about perspective.

YES: DISNEY AS CULTURAL IMPERIALIST

The second paradigm for describing Disney as uniquely American is Disney as cultural imperialist:

> Disney is a wholly American cultural phenomenon which serves to perpetuate the false consciousness of economic liberalism, gender stereotypes, patriarchy and the land of the brave and the free as a model for the rest of the planet to aspire to! (South Africa, male, 24 years)

> Uniquely 'American' (in culture and in capitalistic economic system), invasion of American culture. (Korea, male, 23 years)

Advocates of this cultural imperialist position often referred to the 'whiteness' of Disney and the Americanization of international story-lines via American accents, idiom and lifestyle situations:

> If you define American as 'vanilla white' that turns every ethnic tale the color of snow once touched, then Disney is American ... (U.S.A., African-American male, 18 years)

> Certainly Western/white culture ... (U.K., female, 25 years)

> Yes, characters have American accents. No uniquely international characters. (South Africa, male, 18 years)

> Yes, ... the whole film, everything is made on American culture, it represents American lifestyle, their way of living, etc. (India, male, 21 years)

> Yes, the characters in the movies were mostly white. The princess and prince were always American. (Korean studying in the U.S.A., female, 18 years)

There is an element of racism inherent in these comments and a minority of respondents explicitly referred to what they believe are Disney's racist tendencies. Almost 19 percent of respondents indicated, in response to the prompted list of values, that Disney promoted racism. Many respondents also expressed concern over what they perceived to be negative aspects of American lifestyle. Again, in response to the prompted list of descriptors, 39 percent believed that Disney promotes patriarchy and 69 percent asserted that Disney promotes physical beauty. Respondents concluded that this combination promoted a sexist atmosphere with dangerous consequences for female self-esteem:

Promotes an unattainable ideal that is focused on aesthetics (knowledge of sexism/racism). (U.S.A., female, 20 years)

Male oriented, male dominated, egotistical, *overpriced*, insulting to women. (U.S.A., female, 23 years)

I don't think any other culture is as obsessed with beauty and wealth as the United States is. (Korean studying in the U.S.A., female, 20 years)

In a contradictory, but intuitively attractive, insight, one respondent offered the opinion that Disney's lack of diversity makes it un-American: 'I don't feel Disney is uniquely American. That is WASP culture. America is a multiple ethnic country. But, in Disney films ethnic culture is neglected' (Japan, female, 21 years).

Respondents evidenced an awareness that Disney distorts myths and fairy tales for its own purposes ('bastardized' in the words of one respondent). As one male from Denmark (26 years) put it, Disney's rewrites of original stories make them 'too cute, too romantic.' This awareness rapidly turns to resentment when the subject matter strikes close to home:

Now, for example, *Hercules* is coming out. But I am very negative towards this particular film, because I know that they will completely distort the myth. ... But in general, when a new Disney film comes out, I am very curious to see it. (Greece, female, 24 years)

Disney was not only accused of homogenizing international myth and legend from an American perspective but also of representing the economic power of the U.S.A. and imposing the U.S. economic system on the rest of the world:

Disney is 'American' because its products reflect mainly the American way of life: e.g. the capitalist message that passes through Scrooge, the sign of the dollar, etc. (Greece, female, 22 years)

Yes ... corporate takeovers, overseas sweatshops, lawsuits, etc. are as American as apple pie. (U.S.A., male, 21 years)

Disney seems to be one of the best means of cultural standardization throughout the world. Disney takes advantage of the American hegemony over the economical market to spread the values of American society. The notion of national, regional culture doesn't exist. One unique culture may exist = Disney's culture. Disney culture introduces very average entertainment for a mass of people. Disney doesn't seek intellectual fulfillment. Its only motivation is profit-making. (France, male, 20 years)

This economic hegemony also serves to pre-empt local competition for Disney products. Much as Hollywood, in general, has worked to dominate the international film market, and thus suppress local production, Disney has tried to accroach international animation (see, for example, the profiles of Australia, Greece, and Korea). Korea presents a particularly interesting case. In their profile of the country, Seung Hyun Kim and Kyung Sook Lee place Korea's tradition of resistance to cultural incursion in historical perspective and highlight Koreans' increasing resistance to Disney in the 1990s. As Table 2.3 reveals, Korean respondents evidenced the greatest degree of unanimity in our survey, with 84 percent agreeing that Disney is uniquely American. Further, Korea ranked next to last in our survey in total number of products used per respondent, averaging 7.91 exposures per person (France ranked last at 7.74), thus demonstrating their resistance to foreign products. Yet the authors conclude that survey respondents are still more familiar with Disney than with indigenous animation productions (see the concluding chapter of this book for more discussion on this topic).

Tangentially related to arguments of cultural imperialism, but with an interesting twist, are those respondents who suggest that Disney is *not* uniquely American because American culture *is* global culture. This argument, a kind of post-imperialistic fatalism, suggests that Disney has come to represent world culture:

> Disney is the representation of American imperialism. But we misunderstand that American culture stands for world culture ... (Korea, female, 21 years)

> European stories ... Americanized ... They can pass as global only in the sense that most popular culture is Americanized. (Sweden, male, 24 years)

> Disney represents what *used* to be uniquely American, but Australian culture is very similar to American now, so it's no longer uniquely American ... (Australia, female, 26 years)

This post-apocalyptic sensibility, where it is no longer about invading another country's culture, is aptly summed up by a 19-year-old male from Singapore: '[Disney is the] only thing standing in the way of world domination by Warner Brothers.'

As previously stated, those disagreeing that 'Disney is uniquely American' tend to adopt three unifying themes. Disney is Western, universal, or 'mine.'

NO: DISNEY IS WESTERN

Those arguing that Disney is not uniquely American but rather an example of Western/industrialized culture tend to view the two as analogous. This perspective does not mitigate the cultural imperialism argument, rather it just broadens the base from which such imperialism springs:

> I believe that Disney represents both the American and European culture … (Greece, female, 21 years)

> The Disney movies do not promote American culture as such, but promote the standards of any wealthy Western culture … (Australia, female, 32 years)

> [Disney promotes] Western culture – not necessarily American. (South Africa, male, 32 years)

This Western advocacy is in many ways indistinguishable from the cultural imperialism arguments applied to the U.S.A.; it is still an industrialized culture imposing itself on underindustrialized cultures.

NO: DISNEY IS UNIVERSAL

Those arguing that Disney is universal are, unabashedly, Disney fans. They see the themes propagated by Disney as resonating for all humans:

> Disney not about being American … about the difference between good and evil, using the imagination, making people laugh, and even sharing the basic family values … (Australia, female, 26 years)

> Recognized worldwide, e.g. romance, courage, good over evil. They also often use animals as their main characters which are not necessarily American … (Australia, female, 21 years)

> The vision of Disney is one that transcends cultures. It is a message of hope, love, family, compassion, courage and respect. This is not just American. This is felt in all cultures. (U.S.A., male, 34 years)

> Disney is a dream world. It isn't 'American.' Disney is everybody's world. (Japan, female, 21 years)

> No, Disney is not American. It basically represents a free culture in which there is no place for hatred. There is love, pleasure and happiness all around you. (India, male, 22 years)

NO: DISNEY IS 'MINE'

The final category of arguments expressing the belief that Disney is not uniquely American are what I have termed 'mine.' These people have adopted many of the themes expressed in 'Disney is universal' but they have inverted the perspective to make it seem more personal. These respondents also express a childlike wonder of Disney, a naïveté that is certainly understandable, for how could a child first encountering Disney know whence it came?

> No. I never thought of Disney as American. When I was a kid I always thought of them as Norwegian. I guess Donald could have been a Norwegian duck. (Norway, male, 21 years)

> No. Growing up in Canada, Disney has always seemed Canadian to me. (Canada, male, 21 years)

And, with the last word on Disney and the U.S.A.:

> No. I believe it is universal. Values of treating others equally, having manners, loving each other, being respectful are not uniquely American. In fact I think Disney better reflects Canadian values. (Canada, female, 36 years)

Conclusion

This study offers evidence of the pervasiveness of Disney, the popularity of Disney across cultures, and the cohesiveness of the Disney 'message.' Disney products are available, in abundance, in every country surveyed. Certainly, there are distinctions in the quantity of products offered, but respondents from every country have been exposed to virtually all Disney product categories.

Disney remains very popular. Despite many objections – from thematic, business and cultural perspectives – the company's products remain desirable and respondents' overall level of liking is positive.

Disney has remained amazingly successful in communicating its core values – fun, fantasy, happiness, etc. In a sense these results replicate Real's findings, while at the same time expanding upon them to include international reception of Disney themes.

However, we have also uncovered a level of resistance and resentment of Disney not found in Real's study. Some of this may be due to the international perspective offered herein, but much of it must be attributed to a growing sophistication and awareness of Disney and its activities. In this context university students, while remaining a prime target of Disney overtures, may be particularly distinct from the populace at large. By the very nature of their studies and their surroundings they may be more cognizant of Disney business and practices. Respondents from two locations in the U.S.A. (Tucson, Arizona, and Eugene, Oregon) reported taking university classes devoted to the study of Disney and/or writing research papers with Disney as the topic. All this contributes to a level of understanding perhaps unrealized even a few years ago.

Despite this level of understanding, and despite growing concerns about Disney messages and business practices, respondents in the vast majority remain loyal to Disney. They compartmentalize different aspects of Disney and while they may disdain one part they continue to embrace other Disney offerings: 'Yes, Disney ... distinguish between the cartoon films and the theme parks ... The theme parks I think are typically American. This kind of commercial publicity stunt is very much different from the animated films' (Sweden, female, 19 years). This compartmentalization allows consumers to be critical of Disney, at times vituperative, and yet remain essentially positive in their outlook toward at least the essential Disney – animation.

As the data have shown, respondents tend to decrease their contact to Disney with age, yet remain positive in their outlook toward the company. While generally underestimating their contact with Disney, they concurrently receive and tend to agree with the core concepts promoted by the company. They have a nostalgic view of Disney and by and large consider the company to be benign: after all it's only about fun. This combination of forces tends to indicate that respondents will expose their children to Disney, thus propagating the phenomenon.

Disney has engendered a fanaticism that few other corporations enjoy. Many respondents express a fierce loyalty to Disney and report exposure to Disney that borders on the fanatic (see Introduction for a discussion of Disney 'fanatics'). One 20-year-old U.S. female reported visiting Disneyland 20 times and Disney World twice. Others report annual family vacations to one of the theme parks. At the same time, many Disney consumers refuse to consider the potential harmful effects of exposure to Disney, particularly Disney animation. This combination of loyalty and sang-froid allows Disneyophiles to be impervious to negative implications, even when offered by trusted advisers: 'it is unique ... all cultures, continents, ages and sexes. My pastor is strongly against Disney and calls Mickey Mouse an anti-Christ. I just think of Disney as fun times and happiness. It brings out the kid in me' (U.S.A., female, 20 years).

The conclusion to this book more fully discusses these and other concepts and contextualizes Disney as an American company in a global market. But first, a succession of twelve national profiles from our international project participants. These profiles are offered both from unique cultural and individual researcher perspectives. Some delve more deeply into the questionnaire data from their individual countries, while others approach Disney from a different direction altogether; all offer insight into the Disney phenomenon.

While these twelve profiles represent participation from every populated continent on the planet, it must be acknowledged that we would have preferred to increase certain areas of exposure. Africa and South America suffer from a lack of representation and we would have liked to include certain specific counties (for example, Russia and China).[12] However, taken as a whole, these twelve profiles offer a global perspective admirable in both their breadth and their unique cultural perquisite.

Notes

1. For example, Disney obviously promotes the concept 'happy' – Disneyland, 'The happiest place on earth.' Similarly such terms as 'fantasy' and 'magic' are constantly referred to in Disney's marketing, thematically in various theatrical presentations, and overtly in titles and dialog (for example, *Fantasia*). The extent to which respondents agree that Disney promotes such terms/values suggests success in terms of effectively communicating company ideals.
2. For those readers interested in segmentation and its various derivations – geo-demographic, psychographic, lifestyle, volume, etc. – see, for example, Smith (1956), Beane (1987), Weinstein (1987), Weiss (1988), Tedlow (1990), Smith and Clurman (1997), Turow (1997), Phillips (1997).
3. A randomly selected issue of an academic journal concerned with issues of consumers (and audiences) contained six articles. Of those six articles, four utilized survey or experimental techniques (the other two articles were a theoretical construct – Bettman *et al.*, 1998 – and an ethnographic study – Belk and Costa, 1998). Of those four articles, all four used student samples (Aaker and Williams, 1998; Fisher and Ackerman, 1998; Strahilevitz and Loewenstein, 1998; and Janiszewski, 1998). This example is presented not as proof of the prevalence of student samples but as evidence of the appropriateness of utilizing students as sample subjects in relevant situations.
4. For a list of the countries represented in this sample, see Appendix 5.
5. Thirty respondents were 17 years or younger. The dispersal across countries was as follows: Australia (2), Brazil (10), Canada (1), Cyprus (1), Mexico (10), South Africa (3), and Sweden (1). The two respondents under 17 years of age were from Canada and Australia, aged 13 and 15, respectively. The representation of students 35 years or older was: Australia (3), Canada (3), the U.K. (1), Norway (1), South Africa (1), Sweden (3), and the U.S.A. (1).
6. Because the U.S. sample was disproportionately large (352 of total respondents were from the U.S.A.) there was some concern that U.S. data would overwhelm the data set at large. Consequently, mirror analyses were computed, one including all respondents and one analysis conducted on the world minus the U.S.A. The differences were, with the following three

exceptions, negligible. The age at which respondents reported first contact with Disney was slightly higher in the world outside the U.S.A. (5.25 years versus a world average of 4.61 when the U.S.A. was included); the total items respondents reported having contact with from the prompted list was lower (9.81 versus 11.36); and the response to the question, 'Is Disney uniquely American?' was very slightly higher (50 percent answered yes outside the U.S.A. versus a world average of 49.5 percent when the U.S.A. was included).

7. This proposition was conceived with the assumption that those surveyed – university undergraduates – would be approximately 18 to 22 years of age and would be, for the most part, childless. In other words, contact will lessen as people age from infancy to their early twenties. One might further hypothesize that after their undergraduate years contact with Disney will experience a move back upwards, the major impetus for this renewed contact being the formation of families and the arrival of children. Indeed, while our data are too sparse to speak reliably on this point, the 34 respondents in our survey over 30 years of age (spread over ten countries) reported average contact of 3.91 as adults, slightly higher than the average for the sample as a whole. For those countries with more than three data points, only Sweden (seven respondents, average contact 3.14) reported an average below the norm. Canada (four respondents, 4.0), Australia (four respondents, 4.5), and the U.S.A. (seven respondents, 5.71) all had averages much higher than the sample as a whole. While we have no proof that these higher averages reflect the presence of children, and/or grandchildren, it seems a reasonable assumption. Comments during interviews and to open-ended questions in the questionnaire tend to substantiate this perspective.

8. Unprompted responses were lumped into categories to correspond to the prompted list presented to respondents. That is, if a respondent listed X number of products in a category, the responses were counted as 1 instead of X. For example, some respondents listed all the Disney films they had seen, others listed the various toys or clothing items they owned. These responses were counted as 1 for films, 1 for toys, and 1 for clothing to correspond to the appropriate categories included in the prompted list. If a respondent listed an item in the unprompted question that did not correspond to any category in the prompted list, it was counted as a response. Theoretically, then, it was possible for a respondent to have a greater number of unprompted responses than prompted responses even if he/she indicated that they had used every product listed in the prompted list. The most items listed by a respondent in the unprompted question was sixteen. The most items listed from the prompted list was 25.

9. This figure was calculated by totaling the number of potential choices (eighteen countries by top-ten rankings equals 180 chances to agree) and then counting the number of times individual countries' lists failed to correspond to the world rankings. As there were eight such disagreements, 172 of 180 possible top-ten choices were in agreement, or 95.6 percent concurrence. Four terms not included in the world top-ten list were

included in individual countries' lists: 'physical beauty' ranked by seven different countries, and 'thriftiness,' 'patriarchy,' and 'technological progress' ranked once each (there are a total of ten items, rather than the eight just cited, due to ties in individual country rankings).

10. At the time of Walt's death rumors were rampant that he had ordered his remains cryogenically preserved until such a time as medical science discovered a cure for his ailments. This myth persists to the present and has been remarked upon in various biographies and company histories.

11. Among those characters erroneously identified as Disney were Tom and Jerry, Wile E. Coyote, Road Runner, Bugs Bunny, Scooby Doo, and Tweety Bird. Cartoon quotes mistakenly attributed to Disney include, 'I thought I thaw a putty tat,' 'What's up Doc?' and 'That's all folks!' The feature *Anastasia* was assumed to be a Disney production. Respondents also misidentified Universal Studios and Sea World as Disney parks and one respondent described the Barbie Doll as a Disney toy.

12. In an interesting sidebar, the recent Elian Gonzales imbroglio (a Cuban child stuck in immigration limbo while various U.S. factions and the Cuban government engaged in diplomatic warfare) was from start to finish a media circus. Perhaps the greatest, or at least most often repeated, Elian adventure while in the U.S.A. was his trip to Disney World. Judging from media coverage, the greatest deprivation that a child growing up in communist Cuba (an island country a mere 90 miles from the continental U.S.A.) must suffer is the inability to visit a Disney theme park.

References and other sources

Aaker, J. and Williams, P. (1998) 'Empathy versus pride: the influence of emotional appeals across cultures,' *Journal of Consumer Research*, 25(3) (December): 241–61.

Beane, T. P. (1987) 'Market segmentation: a review,' *European Journal of Marketing*, 21(5): 20–42.

Belk, R. and Costa, J. (1998) 'The mountain man myth: a contemporary consuming fantasy,' *Journal of Consumer Research*, 25(3) (December): 218–40.

Bettman, J., Luce, M. F., and Payne, J. (1998) 'Constructive consumer choice processes,' *Journal of Consumer Research*, 25(3) (December): 187–217.

Fisher, R. and Ackerman, D. (1988) 'The effects of recognition and group need on volunteerism: a social perspective,' *Journal of Consumer Research*, 25(3) (December): 262–75.

Janiszewski, C. (1998) 'The influence of display characteristics on visual exploratory search behavior,' *Journal of Consumer Research*, 25(3) (December): 290–301.

Kalton, G. (1983) *Introduction to Survey Sampling*. Newbury Park, CA, Sage.

Phillips, M. (1997) *A Theoretical Critique of Segmentation in Consumer Markets*, Ph.D. dissertation, University of Oregon.

Real, M. (1977) *Mass-Mediated Culture*. Englewood Cliffs, NJ, Prentice-Hall.

Scheaffer, R., Mendenhall, W., and Ott, L. (1990) *Elementary Survey Sampling*. Boston, PWS-KENT Publishing.

Schickel, R. (1985) *The Disney Version: The Life, Times, Art and Commerce of Walt Disney*. New York, Simon & Schuster.

Smith, G. (1988) *Statistical Reasoning*. Needham Heights, MA, Allyn and Bacon.

Smith, W. and Clurman, A. (1997) *Rocking the Ages: The Yankelovich Report on Generational Marketing*. New York, HarperCollins.

Smith, W. (1956) 'Product differentiation and market segmentation as alternative marketing strategies,' *Journal of Marketing*, 21 (July): 3–8.

Strahilevitz, M. and Loewenstein, G. (1998) 'The effect of ownership history on the valuation of objects,' *Journal of Consumer Research*, 25(3) (December): 276–89.

Tedlow, R. (1990) *New and Improved: The Story of Mass Marketing in America*. New York, Basic Books.

Turow, J. (1997) *Breaking Up America: Advertisers and the New Media World*. Chicago, University of Chicago Press.

Weinstein, A. (1987) *Market Segmentation: Using Demographics, Psychographics and Other Segmentation Techniques to Uncover and Exploit New Markets*. Chicago, Probus.

Weiss, M. (1988) *The Clustering of America*. New York, Harper & Row.

PART III

National Profiles

CHAPTER 3

Australia: Disney and the Australian Cultural Imaginary

VIRGINIA NIGHTINGALE

The broad cultural context

> When I was young there was America, the place of Disneyland ... it
> was probably the first thing I knew about America, and it was
> probably the first thing my daughter knows ... McDonald's and
> Disneyland ... so I would say that's how I first got to know about
> America. (Mandy's interview; October 1997: 12)

Australians sometimes joke that Australia is really the 52nd state of the
U.S.A. Like Mandy's daughter, my own daughter recognized from
infancy the cultural and technological power of the U.S.A. She made
the attached drawing, Mickey as a cartoon strip, before she had turned
5 years old. My daughter and I hold very different opinions about her
creative efforts. She sees the drawings as evidence that she has never
been able to draw, while I still marvel at her ability to capture the
essence of comic-strip drawing when so young. Where she sees failure,
I see potential. Where I see success, she sees a pathetic copy. Where
she itemizes each detail of difference between her own work and that
of a Disney artist, I see similarities and her underlying insight into the
form.

A parallel debate has in the past characterized discussion of
Australian cultural production. As new waves of enthusiasm for local
production break on the rocky shores of local criticism, judgments
abound: is the new work creative or derivative? Locals, ignorant of the
work copied, imagine the copied work as original, while outsiders

Figure 5. Anna's Mickey faces

familiar with the work copied see the local version as flawed in technique or execution. More recently a consensus critical view has emerged which asserts that the creative is always derivative and vice versa. According to this view, which informs the work of Sinclair *et al.* (1996) and Cunningham and Jacka (1996), the existence of the copied work (the local version) offers hope for the future of Australian production, while its difference from the work copied holds the key to an understanding of the ways national identity is expressed through the creative process (O'Regan, 1993; Sinclair *et al.*, 1996; Cunningham and Jacka, 1996). But today, marketing strategies and merchandising licenses control engagement with entertainment products so firmly that national production has become a matter of the development of technical expertise that facilitates the participation of Australian nationals (as individuals) in global productions, or alternatively the provision of production facilities and options that attract global ventures to Australia. Local/national production is tailored increasingly to international markets.

This analysis of Disney in Australia aims to identify some of the ways the issue of a national cultural identity and its expression is assisted or hindered by the activities and the entertainment products of a major global entertainment provider like Disney. It elaborates contexts for the exploration of ideas put forward by the 38 students who completed the questionnaire for this project in 1997, focusing particularly on their written comments about Disney's 'uniqueness' or special place in their lives. It also draws on comments made by several of the students who agreed to follow-up interviews to elucidate their written comments. I have attempted to use quotations from the students' comments to provoke and challenge issues which today impact on the imagination of Australian cultural identity in the context of production for global markets.

Of the students interviewed for this project, one-third claimed that Disney is *not* 'uniquely American.' The reasons they gave for this judgement were that they believe Disney is 'universal' or 'multi-cultural,' because it provides stories from all around the world, 'not just America.' In other words, they imagine themselves as part of the same cultural formation as Disney. Some acknowledged that Disney's portrayal of other countries is 'inaccurate,' and others argued that Australian culture and American culture are the same, because both aspire to (and achieve) identical 'Western' standards of development and cultural interests. There is broad support for such a view in Australia. Many of the students who said they consider Disney *is* uniquely American cited very similar reasons to those who did not. A small number saw the values and beliefs Disney presents as 'utopian fantasies,' but the Disney ideals were not considered as 'foreign' or 'other.' Knowledge of American culture among the students was derived primarily from mass-entertainment products and news. The sense of the sameness or continuity between Australian and American culture is supported, of course, by similarities in cultural origin, which are evident in the everyday realities of life in Australia, and untroubled by first-hand experience of life in the U.S.A.

Media and the development of national identity in Australia

This questionnaire did make me realize how much Disney is involved in our life and how much money we have spent ... though not so much for our own children as they are more involved with *Thomas the Tank Engine, Bananas in Pyjamas, Play School, Budgie,* and *Star Wars.*[1] (written questionnaire: female student, 26 years, Australian)

Viewing and reading stir the desire to create, whether as imitation or improvisation (Nightingale, 1996). Yet both improvisation and imitation require an initial acceptance of the 'foreign' cultural object as an aspect of 'local' life, and recognition of a significance for the foreign object in the local context. Between my own childhood in the 1950s and my daughter's in the 1990s, and the experiences of the young mothers quoted above, millions of Australian children have no doubt embarked upon their discovery of culture by drawing Mickey Mouse or Donald Duck, without feeling any need to reflect on national identity. In the above quote, British, Australian and American products jostle for position in a seamless English-language product array, which reflects the contemporary Australian experience – as broadly based in the English language – in terms of the foundations of its story culture.

In view of the amount of American content on television in Australia, young Australians discover their national identity by solving mysteries framed by a sense of the uncanniness of local production (different accents and acting styles) and news content; or by puzzling over the significance they should attach to political comment about the Prime Minister (of Australia) compared with that about the President (of the U.S.A.). In the global idea- and media-scapes (Appadurai, 1996), Australian identity has to be discovered as 'other than' American, and the value of its difference learned:

> My culture is so saturated with American products these days that it's hard to tell [whether Disney is 'uniquely American' or not]. Call me a cynic. I call me observing the friggin' obvious. It's American … but then aren't we all? (written questionnaire: male student, 20 years, Anglo/Australian)

The dilemmas of national cultural identity in the year 2000 are very different from those that characterized my own youth. In the late 1950s, the years of my childhood, when Walt Disney was aggressively planning Disneyland as the pinnacle of his marketing power in the U.S.A., the Australian cultural imaginary was still fixated on its British heritage and tied inexorably to the British class structure. In 1953, the year of the coronation of Queen Elizabeth II, my mother fitted me out for a fancy-dress ball in a painstakingly exquisite paper replica of the coronation gown. There were two messages in the dress. I like to think that perhaps she was unconsciously willing me to reject my subordinate class status as a colonial daughter. But, alongside such ideas of resistance, the equally convincing adoration of British style, design and authority must be recognized. The predominance of British cultural iconography and imagery was at that moment still securely central to Australian national identity, and the citizenship dilemma was located in the impossibility for Anglo-Australians to disentangle Australian interests and identities from British interests and identities.

That fancy-dress ball was held in 1953, just two years before the introduction of television in Australia. Few people had heard of television, and fewer still would have predicted the transformative power the medium would exert on the sense of national identity and cultural allegiance, let alone on the hearts and minds, and shopping practices, of Australians (Nightingale, 1990). Television brought not only the *Mickey Mouse Club* (the first television program I ever saw and my first Disney memory) and the Disney presence, but in even greater volume, detailed information about American life, culture, life expectations, style and technology, packaged in televisual forms (like the summer camp serials on the *Mickey Mouse Club* and the domestic uproar of *I Love Lucy* and *The Honeymooners*) which made such

Figure 6. Virginia as Queen Elizabeth II

information available for reworking as the very fabric of Australian life. Fewer than 50 years later it is the American cultural imaginary that is 'normal' on Australian screens, that dictates the form of republic Australians would prefer, and that has all but displaced the centrality of the British monarchy from our cultural imagination.

The magnitude of the difference in development that existed between the U.S.A. and Australia in the mid-1950s is evident still in my photograph album. Somehow I managed to find two penpals in the

U.S.A. in the late 1950s, and interestingly no British penpals. The names of my American friends were lost long ago, but the presence of their photographs speaks of a reorientation then occurring in Australian cultural life. I sometimes wonder what those girls thought of their Australian penpal. The consumerism on which Disney relied for the success of Disneyland was already alive and well in the sensibilities represented in the American photographs – the newly built houses, the new cars, the immaculate dresses, the corporatized families and manicured lawns, and even in the quality of the photographs themselves. At that time, by contrast, we lived in a fibro waterfront cottage in a suburb on the outskirts of Sydney. My Box Brownie photographs featured my beloved grandmother in a home-made dress, my mother still wearing her slippers and hand-knitted sweater, and various other unplanned and unnoticed objects – an obtrusive rock, the corners of the 'Hills hoist' – all the more obvious because of the absence of such amateurish intrusions in the U.S. photographs. The 'American way' spoke eloquently from those photographs. It told of other (more professional) ways of doing and being, and fitted uncomfortably alongside the casual and makeshift Australian manner.

The changing standards of the Western world

The Disney movies do not promote American culture as such, but promote the standards of any wealthy Western culture. Disney puts you into a world where for a time something is fun, maybe a little sad, but always in the end everything works out for the best. Whether you are Australian or American, the standards of life are the same, and for a time going into a fantasy world tends to make you feel there are no barriers whether [it's] true or not. (written questionnaire: female student, 32 years, Anglo/Australian)

The imperializing thrust of U.S. culture into the Pacific in the 1950s was particularly evident in Australia in the development of new industries, especially the car industry, and in the introduction of television and its production technologies, even though the significance of television was appreciated to a lesser extent at the time. In the 1950s the first animation studios, sometimes inspired by a fascination with Disney, were established (Eyley, 1992). Such macro cultural and technological reorientations changed the nature of Australian life through their impact on the worldview of children of my generation who were writing letters to American penpals, drawing pictures of Disney cartoon characters or being taken on visits to the newly built Coca-Cola factory, where we were encouraged to marvel at the wonders of

Fordist production practices. The nation was caught up in the post-World War II fascination with U.S. culture and power, and with the potential it offered for the transformation of our own world. And, even though a taste for British product remains, we have been transformed:

> I believe Disney represents what used to be 'uniquely American.' But Australian culture is very similar to American now, so it's no longer 'uniquely American.' It's different to British culture in that the presentation of American culture is much louder and 'in your face' than what you find in English culture. (written questionnaire: female student, 26 years, Anglo/Australian, born in England)

Merchandising and improvisation

> [My Disney memories include] ... as a young child, 3 to 6 years old, I remember the *Mickey Mouse Club* showbag being bought for me at the Royal Easter Show each year; the Mickey Mouse show with the Mousketeers and the Mouseketeer song;[2] going to Disneyland when I was 4 years old (in 1977) – I still have a little book and personalized mouse hat (!); I saw *Jungle Book* when I was 7 at the Collaroy Cinema with my friend [name provided]; the Disney program [on TV] on the weekends. Most recently I have seen and have bought copies of the Disney films *Aladdin*, *The Lion King* and *Beauty and the Beast*. I read news reports of Mickey's birthday celebrations. I work in the concept section of the department store, Grace Brothers, which sells Disney T-shirts and cups, etc. (written questionnaire: female student, 20 years, Australian)

This Disney reminiscence provides an excellent example of the ways merchandising is linked to memories of not only the products themselves but also events and people of personal significance. The student starts with early childhood experiences and memories, and works forward to her current part-time sales position. The memories recounted are not of stories or characters, but of shared experiences and treasured gifts. Through mass production and merchandising, representations of foreign cultural ideas literally are translocated into domestic, work and play contexts, where they then colonize the environment. The positioning of self in relation to the ongoing flow of entertainment production appears to be the salient issue for the student, rather than any positioning by story or character identification.

A similar process is also clearly in operation in the following extended extract from Graeme's interview about the Disney questionnaire, except that he does identify a strategic use of Disney's character development. Graeme first described Disney's characterization of the 'ideal' Disney 'person', Mickey Mouse, and based on this characterization, he demonstrates how other Disney characters measure up as models for identification. Based on associations with characters, Graeme then tells how he has used Disney merchandising to challenge the seriousness of his work culture and to excuse his resistance to work regimes. In this case, however, Graeme's story emphasizes the community of Disney characters and the different possibilities they offer for identification:

> Mickey Mouse is the main role ... all the other characters have a problem ... [but] I don't see Mickey Mouse having a problem, do you? He's the only one who is good, does the right [thing], is nice to everybody ... as far as I can remember. All the others ... Goofy is just 'goofy' ... he can't do anything right! Donald Duck has got a temper problem ... which everyone thinks is really funny and can relate to ... no one can really relate to someone who's perfect.
>
> [You see] I am mixing a bit with people who are working, and also working class, more so than [most] people. It's hard when you have been [a student and] institutionalized for so long to relate to what actually happens out there ... I meet people who are on the other side of the spectrum a lot and they blow me away with their lack of ability to just let loose ... and they would not wear a Mickey Mouse watch ... now hang on a second [though] one thing is the Disney ties. Now I have one of those and I used to wear it ... You could have Pluto and you could have Donald Duck and you could have Mickey Mouse ... and sox! Don't forget sox! I used to wear the sox and the tie and the pink shirt, and no one took me seriously at work – which wasn't just the clothes I wore, but that sort of all was part of the show. Well there you go, I mean it's fun to wear the silly sox and ... what people call silly now I mean, I am sure if I was 10 years old, it would be 'what are you talking about, this is Mickey Mouse, he's not silly.' (Graeme's interview: October 1997)

Like Graeme, people everywhere disrupt and challenge the world around them in a sort of pseudo-totemic engagement with Disney merchandising which uses the playfulness of childhood and the traces of animal nature left in Disney characters to mask their resistance to oppressive domestic and work regimes. This is a much more ephemeral type of cultural production than that which results in new entertainment production. It does not linger to disrupt the cozy comfort of Disney copyright legislation. It does not challenge the integrity of the Disney image in the way even my daughter's innocent copying does. It does not offer itself as national imagery, or even as lasting imagery. In a sense the merchandise protects its user from criticism by invoking a totemic affiliation with culturally shared knowledge about the significance of Donald Duck in Disney cosmology.

The type of cultural engagement with Disney imagery that Graeme outlined depends on Disney's maintenance of a strong television presence and on planned movie distribution and exhibition to retain market share – after all, Sylvester and Tweetie, Eric Cartman and Homer Simpson are all waiting in the wings to push Disney off that tie. Ideally, the merchandise matches the mood so well that the impetus to make one's own associated images evaporates. The volume, variety and professionalism of readily available Disney merchandising are designed to pre-empt copying and divert the energy of cultural engagement into commercially exploitable re-enactments, like Graeme's tie and sox routine, or dressing up in a Disney Tigger suit to play at being Tigger. The impetus to draw your own Mickey or Donald is diminished by the ready availability of stuffed toys, dolls and other merchandise which privilege a different, and arguably less dangerous (from Disney's copyright protection perspective), type of improvisation. In this sense, the Disney presence in Australia is more controlling in its impact on Australian cultural production and Australian identity than in the pre-merchandising days.

Disney reach in Australia

The *Mickey Mouse Club* and the *Wonderful World of Disney*, the vanguard Disney productions of my youth, were long ago replaced by the *Saturday Disney* format on free-to-air TV and the Disney Channel on Pay TV. This format uses young Australian presenters to introduce the cartoons, to get excited about Disney travel packages (to Disney theme parks) and Disney merchandise of all descriptions. As in most developed countries, Disney merchandising can be found in almost every department store or shopping mall in Australia's capital cities. In addition, since the first store opened in Sydney in 1997, Disney Stores have been opening throughout the nation. The formerly widespread and relatively unfocused presence of Disney merchandising is now giving way to the concentration and controlled release of product which boutique marketing promotes. Outside this marketing strategy, comic books are still available from local paper shops[3] and specialist stores and the Disney magazine, *Disney Adventures*, is marketed to children at the supermarket, along with Little Golden Books and other Disney lines.

The relatively recent introduction of cable TV subscription services to Australia in the late 1990s launched the Disney Channel into the

Australian television environment, even though it is packaged with the second-ranking (Optus – Cable and Wireless) cable package rather than the more popular (Foxtel – Telstra, News Corp and PBL) cable package (providing Nickelodeon). The practice of coopting locals to articulate the global formats and power structures to the local population can be seen at work in all Disney engagement with Australian cultural life, particularly those where cultural production activities are required.

'I feel that one issue that wasn't mentioned [in the questionnaire] is the access to Disney theme parks. For Australians to visit one we would have to go overseas and for some people that isn't possible' (written questionnaire: female student, 18 years, Australian). The missing element in the Disney presence in Australia is a Disney theme park. Warner Bros. have established Movie World on Queensland's Gold Coast, Fox Studios have opened a studio experience in Sydney, and there is an Australia's Wonderland in Sydney which features Hanna-Barbera characters. But Disney is conspicuous by its theme-park absence. Instead, Disney operates in the newspaper travel pages, offering Australians special airfares or accommodation deals to go to Disneyland in California, Tokyo or Paris. Accounts of Disneyland or Disney World by British travel journalists are routinely reprinted in Australia from British newspapers like the *Guardian* (see, for example, Ronson, 1997) as news features rather than as paid advertising.

Disney in Australia: the production context

[Disney provides] a delightful world of brilliantly crafted characters, which entertain and educate. (written questionnaire: female student, 23 years, Anglo/Australian)

In December 1996, five Disney companies were registered with the Australian Securities Commission. They were Disney Entertainment Productions (Australia), The Disney Store (Australia), The Walt Disney Company (Australia), Walt Disney Television Animation (Australia), and The Disney Channel (Australia). Their activities include entertainment, selling merchandise, licensing the use of Disney characters to merchandisers, producing 'work made for hire' for Walt Disney Television Animation, and the production and distribution of programing. Of these companies, only Walt Disney Television Animation (Australia) is delivering product, made in Australia, back to the U.S. market.

While highly sensitive to the marketing of Disney products in Australia, none of the students who completed the questionnaire made reference to Disney's role as an entertainment producer in Australia. Their comments about Disney provided lists of either products they had been given or had bought, or described feelings they associated with Disney. Some students focused on the 'brilliance' and quality of Disney production. Others appeared to be critical of Disney simply because it is a transnational corporation. Others, who consider transnationalism and corporate capitalism to be the nature of the world as we know it, adopted a cynical tone and encouraged Disney to 'profit on!'

> Mickey Mouse emblazoned everywhere. Cheap commodified sentimentality. Outstanding animation!! Not as funny as Warner Bros. cartoons. Goofy gets a bad rap. Not as educational or 'realistic' as *The Muppets*. Great movies but overdone marketing. (written questionnaire: male student, 24 years, Latvian/Australian)

> I see the Disney Corporation, with all its merchandising and false advertising through different media genres as just another American company, obsessed on greed and wealth, that has been released on the world – like a disease. It promotes the American culture as being the only *good* culture in the world. (written questionnaire: male student, 20 years, Anglo/Australian)

> In a capitalist era I give it the thumbs up, and the battle cry: 'Profit On!' Morally I'm not so sure. Mice, dogs and ducks are better than humans and should not be substituted – more Christopher Robins required! In all, consider me overwhelmed and in awe of your power. A prayer for Walt. (written questionnaire: male student, 20 years, Anglo/Australian)

Perhaps because they were unaware of Disney's production presence in Australia, the students did not reflect on the part some Australians play in Disney's entertainment machine, or on the interdependence of Australian and transnational corporations. The Australian presence in the Disney *œuvre* is effectively unnoticeable to Australian viewers, because it is technical rather than creative in nature. It seldom has the power to include or develop local issues or themes in its output. Its activities are limited to parceling top-end Australian technical expertise for transnational consumption. It nevertheless provides some positive outcomes for Australian artists. While in the past Disney animators in Australia were employed on exclusive contracts which effectively removed them from the Australian animation production scene (Eyley, 1992), they are now employed on non-exclusive, though consequently less secure, contracts which allow them the freedom also to participate in non-Disney production. In a few cases animators who previously worked for Disney have switched to writing and illustrating children's storybooks. From a reception perspective, however, the work of Walt Disney Television Animation (Australia) is invisible, and consequently the source of little pride or specific inspiration among young Australians in spite of its scope.

Some historical perspectives

Walt Disney Television Animation (Australia) is located in Sydney and employs about 200 Australian animators. The company produces spin-off cartoon series based on Disney's major film releases and specializes in high-cost direct-to-video sell-through production. To give an indication of the scale of the Disney production financed by this company, Crayford (1999) has indicated that *Lion King II: Simba's Pride* was 'produced in Sydney over 16 months at a cost in excess of $10 million.' The creative development for such products is completed in the U.S.A., but the work is executed and finished in Australia.

Mass production in Australia of animated film began in 1972 when Hanna-Barbera established a Sydney studio. Eyley notes that 'Hanna-Barbera continued with series production, and in a relatively minor way with commercial production, until 1989 when Walt Disney Television Australia Limited virtually took over the studio' (Eyley, 1992: 6). In a feature article in the *Australian Financial Review* Peter Crayford (1999) described only two other Australian animation companies that appear to be thriving: Yoram Gross–Village Roadshow; and Burbank Animation Studios. Yoram Gross is an independent Australian animation production company which produced the charming Dot movies (for example, *Dot and the Kangaroo, Dot Goes to Hollywood, Dot and Keeto, Dot and the Whale*) in the 1970s and 1980s, and the Blinky Bill series and films in the 1990s. This company is extremely important in both Australian culture and in the film industry contexts, not least because it reflects the creative impact of European migration to Australia, post-World War II. By contrast, Burbank Animation Studios employs only five people in Australia and makes direct-to-video productions with names like *Mulan, Moses: Prince of Egypt*, and *Pocahontas*. According to Crayford (1999), its one-hour animated videos are low-cost clones that are 'made off-shore in low-cost nations such as India, China and Vietnam.'

Eyley describes how, in the past, some Australian animators of note attributed their inspiration at least in part to their early experiences of Disney animation. This was the case with Eric Porter. Eyley explains Porter's achievements in the following way:

> The Porter studios, based in Sydney and mainly a two-person operation, were kept busy through the war years by making propaganda films. Eric

Porter, an important pioneer in Australia and honored for it in 1983, was heavily influenced by Walt Disney's technique and dreamed of producing films in Australia for an international audience. (Eyley, 1992: 4)

Today, as Eyley explains it, such small-scale local studios exist mostly as service industries to Australian advertising. The importance of the skill base maintained by contract work for local advertising cannot be underestimated. It is one arena where local creativity which addresses local interests, argot and behaviors is welcomed, and it provides employment and experience for locally educated animation artists, for whom Disney is also an important source of continuing employment.

To recapitulate for a moment, the animation 'industry' in Australia, outlined by Eyley and Crayford, is composed of the following: the presence of a major global operator (Disney) which is the main employer of Australian talent in secondary production roles; an Australian-owned company which makes product for low-cost international sales (Burbank); an independent Australian animation production house (Yoram Gross) which has secured an international distribution and exhibition partnership with Village Roadshow; and small-scale animation and special-effects studios which serve the local advertising and film industries. To this list it is time to add the intervention of the Australian government via its support for the Australian Children's Television Foundation, which in 1998 released for a global audience an animation series called *Li'l Elvis Jones and the Truckstoppers*. This production attempted to redress the lack of Australian content of Australian origin in animated works by focusing on quintessentially 'Australian' representation for the international market.

According to a publicity feature on the series (Jellie, 1998), *Li'l Elvis* employed the 'Crocodile Dundee formula.' It used Australian idiom, Australian actors, references to past Australian production, and the 'wondrous colors – the deep cobalt blue of the open sky, the cadmium yellows and oranges of the earth and the pillar-box red – reflect the intensity of the Australian light' (Jellie, 1998: 8). Interestingly, Disney also used the 'Crocodile Dundee formula' for its 1990 film, *The Rescuers Down Under*. This now rather obscure Disney film was mentioned by only two of the students, but their comments about it point to problems with assumptions made in Australia and elsewhere about the meaningfulness of the so-called 'Dundee formula' for Australian audiences, and about audience concern over representation.

Virginia Nightingale

Representation: Disney's treatment of Australian content

[Disney promotes] many themes of patriotism, the American Way … every story has a happy ending, despite evil people good always triumphs. [Disney] promotes an American utopian fantasy of goodness, beauty and happiness. (written questionnaire: female student, 23 years, Malaysian/Australian)

To an extent [Disney] does promote American culture, however with the use of folk tales from around the world, it promotes universality, yet by enhancing American culture into it, i.e. American voices dubbed onto animation, commercialization and consumerism. (written questionnaire: female student, 20 years, Australian)

[Disney] is American, but universal in its themes. Usually it just uses American stories. Aladdin had an American accent. (written questionnaire: female student, 20 years, Hungarian/Australian)

These are some of the many comments the students offered concerning Disney's presentation of a vision of an idealized American culture. While most students had noticed Disney's idealization of American culture, some also commented on the ways this idealization both reflected and superimposed a Disney version of non-American cultures on the world. The students demonstrated a sense of the action of Disneyfication on national cultures, even if they appeared to say little in the context of this questionnaire about its action on their own culture. The articulation of an almost inaudible murmur of protest about Disneyfication is discernible, and a glimmer of recognition and protest that popular culture demands a capacity for self-subjugation to the tastes for mass consumption in exchange for representation is noticed:

[Popular culture] is the space of homogenization where stereotyping and the formulaic mercilessly process the material and experiences it draws into its web, where control over narratives and representations passes into the hands of established cultural bureaucracies, sometimes without a murmur. (Stuart Hall, quoted in Giroux, 1995: 46)

Two students registered statements of dissatisfaction with specific examples of Disneyfication, making direct reference to *The Rescuers Down Under* – the only Disney feature-length animated film to use Australian characters (Cody, Jake, Mara Hute the sea eagle, and a few other indigenous animals), settings (a gratuitous sweep over Sydney Harbor; the Australian outback), and issues (smuggling of endangered indigenous birds and animals; a child 'lost' in the bush). These

78

characters and themes provide an Australian setting for the international rescue mice, Bianca and Bernard, who travel from New York to the outback aboard Wilbur, their Albatross 'airliner,' to rescue a lost boy, Cody, and the wildlife he was trying to protect from poachers. The students' comments about this film amount to a mild admonition of Disney for inadequate research into Australian culture, for unacceptable representation of Australian characters, and for lacking cultural sensitivity in the portrayal of characters, contexts and issues from other cultures (in this case, Australia).

The Rescuers Down Under was released in 1990, the year after Disney's takeover of the Hanna-Barbera studios in Sydney. The film applied components of the 'Dundee formula' to the story treatment. Traces of the result of this decision are recorded in the student comments. One student remembered an 'Australian' Disney character (Jake) in the context of expressing her longing for 'something I can identify with' in Disney. The other ridiculed Disney for the choice and portrayal of Australian content in the film:

> [Disney] depicts a world as seen through American eyes. As I grew up, so much film and television was American, it became almost a 'norm.' It certainly promotes American patriotism. Whenever I see an Australian actor or reference to something Australian in American film or television, it stands out and I strain to get more, to break into American domination … I think there is a character called Jake in… [the student wrote the names of programs she guessed it might have been – *Rescue Rangers* or *Chip and Dale*]. Perhaps I crave something I can identify with rather than watching the 'other' all the time. (written questionnaire: female student, 20 years, Australian)

The character Jake was created for *The Rescuers Down Under*. Jake is a hybrid, both genetically and culturally. He is the size of a marsupial mouse (perhaps based on *Antechinus stuartii*, 120mm), but has the shape of a kangaroo rat (similar to *Aepyprymnus rufescens*, 530mm). Jake is portrayed as physically agile, courageous and competent, but as unable in the end to effect Bernard and Bianca's rescue mission because MacLeach, the evil wildlife poacher, traps him and Bianca. Jake eventually defers to Bernard and surrenders his claims for Bianca's affections. Jake's intertextual inheritance includes the physical power of Mick 'Crocodile' Dundee, compromised by the servile nature and safari-suited dress sense of Dundee's sidekick, Walter.

It is worth noting that the student quoted above remembers Disney's Australian animated character Jake, but neither Cody (the film's hero) nor the Australian landscape, Australian fauna in general, or any other aspect of the film's iconographic content. The *Crocodile Dundee* reference makes the character Jake memorable for her. The student 'forgets' the dramatic world of the film, a site where Australian-ness might be encoded. This contrasts markedly with the concern among Australian film-makers about coding the natural environment as 'distinctively Australian,' mentioned above in regard to *Li'l Elvis Jones and the Truckstoppers*. It also contrasts with the ways nationalistic sentiment plays off the representation of natural land-scapes in Australian advertising contexts. Bell and Bell (1993), for example, discuss the adoption of the Australian landscape by transnational companies to assert their Australian credentials. Disney pays similar homage, but with only tokenistic glimpses of sites of national significance. The presentation of landscape is so anodyne in this film that, apart from the few stereotypical shots of Sydney Harbor and Uluru, it is hardly recognizable as Australian at all.

The Rescuers Down Under is an exciting and entertaining film. *Sight and Sound* described it as coming on 'like an Indiana Jones movie which has been reconceived as animation, and then proceeded to push back that medium's technical boundaries' (quoted in *Halliwell's Film Guide*, 1995: 952). In spite of its technical quality, the Australian setting, the choice of character and iconography, the film's plot demonstrates a lack of sensitivity to the implications for Australians of many of the plot, character and landscape choices made. By poaching character, location and cultural themes from *Crocodile Dundee* to create distinctively 'Australian' angles for the film, Disney unfortu-nately converted the colonial triumph of *Crocodile Dundee* into a national subservience. It also created a negative overall impression of Australia for Australians through the use of a 1950s 'retro' *mise-en-scène*.

Patrick Murphy has suggested that Disney repeats a 'consistent but incoherent worldview on nature and women that is escapist and androcentric' (Murphy, 1995: 121). Murphy has noted that the Disney 'world' erases individual (animal) differences and evacuates natural character from the landscape. While this process is obvious in the way Australian animals, women and the natural environment have been treated in *The Rescuers Down Under*, a layer of national meaning, referenced by Disney's use of Australian themes and iconography, also comes into play for Australian viewers.

A student quoted earlier suggested that 'Mice, dogs and ducks are better than humans and should not be substituted – more Christopher Robins required.' The statement is a reminder that in *The Rescuers Down Under* native Australian fauna are subjected to the Disney androgenization process. All are given voices and human-like capacities for directed action, except for the symbol of the wild, the sea eagle Mara Hute.[4] None, except the eagle and the evil goanna, Joanna, act independently. As Murphy indicates, even the selection of the eagle as the symbol of the wild is a superimposition of American culture. It contributes to making the film less Australian for Australians and to the creation of the impression that the use of Australian animals is tokenistic.

Cody, the 'Christopher Robin' of *The Rescuers Down Under*, is represented as almost devoid of both character and Australian-ness. Murphy suggests that this emptying of character and agency from Disney heroes makes them difficult to identify with as figures of power. In a specific national context, it also makes them difficult to identify with as significant national characters:

> Penny and Cody do not seek to become embroiled with kidnapping jewel thieves or poachers ... Thrown into situations in which they participate in, but do not engineer, their own rescues, they conclude their adventures with only their circumstances altered; their characters remain fundamentally unchanged. Since the films do not empower their characters, they cannot possibly empower their audiences. (Murphy, 1995: 134)

For this reason Cody also fails to count as an Australian character, and so does Jake. Bernard and Bianca alone are 'empowered' by the rescue. Only their professional and personal competence has been enhanced by their experiences in the film. By contrast, Cody's mother is little more than a figure in a landscape, as are the Australian search parties scouring the bush for Cody. From an Australian perspective, a film like *The Rescuers Down Under* de-cultures a national world, and arguably perhaps, re-cultures it to fit a Disney worldview. As one student noted:

> Disney represents a fantasy of a 'globalized' America, an American culture that the world can buy but cannot have, because it is a fantasy. On the positive side, however, Disney optimism can be infectious. [But] there needs to be a greater cultural understanding on behalf of American corporations of differing cultural views – *Rescuers Down 'Under'* was laughed AT, not WITH. One cannot 'market their way into' a culture. (written questionnaire: male student, 24 years, Latvian/Australian)

Just as the Disney production misread the meaning of *Crocodile Dundee* for Australian audiences, so the student has failed to recognize that the film undoubtedly had different meanings for American audiences. From an Australian perspective, the film *Crocodile Dundee* (1986) belongs to an Australian *œuvre* that explores the nature of Australian-ness and assesses the nation's current status in world terms. It repeats from folk memory a 200-year-old question, 'How are ya, mate?' in response to which the question we never ask forms, instantly and unspoken, as if by magic: how have we Anglo, Euro, Asian and indigenous Australians, separately and together, survived the separation from our indigenous cultures, homes and loved ones? Have we overcome the legacy of the outback/wilderness experience – our exile and cultural displacement? Do we now have something of value to offer the world from our experience? Stories like *Crocodile Dundee* help Australians laugh at themselves, at our cultural isolation, and at our place in the world, but only because such stories also reassure us of our (imaginary) invincibility and comfort us with a lullaby of 'She'll be right, Mate!' before a stoical silence again descends.

Dundee stories[5] never have an unhappy ending for the local hero. They are the antithesis of Australian war stories[6] where Australian character is depicted as being created in adversity and persecution. Dundee stories begin when the wounds of war have healed, and when the Australian hero, emboldened by time and mastery of the local environment, again makes contact with the 'home' culture. But in *The Rescuers Down Under*, Jake masters neither his own local environment nor the girl. Through his inability to win Bianca as a partner, Jake demonstrates himself to be just as endangered as the sea eagle, Mara Hute. Leaving Jake in the wilderness, as Disney does in this film, causes embarrassment for Australians instead of hilarity. Jake's failure is a failure to transcend the handicaps of space, distance, and culture and a sign of national inadequacy. The only face-saving strategy is, as this student suggests, to laugh 'AT, not WITH' the film.

A similar misunderstanding is obvious in Disney's use of the lost child motif. Both in song and in film, the search for a child lost in the bush is a recurrent Australian story which exerts a powerful hold over Australian hearts and minds.[7] Potentially, the motif could work to intensify national identification, yet an unfortunate disjuncture is created in this film around the figure of Cody because of the ambiguity of his status. To the human searchers and to his mother, Cody is a lost child, but to the Rescuers he is a kidnapped child. The kidnapping, both of Cody and the native animals, occasions the iconographic use of cages and imprisonment, trapping, netting and capturing. But 'imprisonment' does not resonate with 'lostness' in Australian cultural mythology. Imprisonment shifts agency from the natural world to the human world, again demonstrating the androcentric orientation of Disney's film treatment.

Being 'lost' is a state of disorientation in the landscape.[8] In Australian films and songs 'lostness' works as evidence of the power and agency of the land to make claims on the humans who dare venture there. This understanding of the Australian land is imbued with a knowledge handed down from indigenous Australian culture of sacred sites and the dangers of unlawful trespass in its secret places. Recognition of the power of indigenous knowledge of the land over the worldview of

European Australians also reflects residual guilt over the appropriation of indigenous lands, and evokes folk memories of early isolation and vulnerability.

Kidnapping, by contrast, involves human agency and imprisonment, and invokes too easily memories of Australia's penal colony beginnings and more pertinently the assault on indigenous culture which resulted in the forced removal of Aboriginal children from their families. These are pasts the nation has expended considerable effort to forget and for which more recently the government has 'refused' to apologize, but which lend distinctiveness to Australian storytelling. Equating 'lostness' with 'kidnapped-ness,' as in *The Rescuers Down Under*, shifts the meaning system evoked away from the expropriation of indigenous lands and children, and onto thoughts of danger and vulnerability of a quite different order. It demonstrates Disney's lack of sensitivity to the range of signifieds brought into play by the application of the 'Dundee formula.' Disney's treatment of Cody's disappearance mirrors the kidnapping of Penny in *The Rescuers*, but in doing so relinquishes the opportunity to implicate more powerfully Australian experience within the film's plot.

The treatment of the other Australian characters – the endangered fauna, the evil MacLeach, the ineffectual army of searchers, Cody's vulnerable single mother – serve predominantly to demonstrate the necessity for the existence and presence in Australia of the Rescue Mice and the Mouse Aid Society, in a very thinly disguised justification for transnational interventionism. It is no doubt of some comfort to Australian viewers that the Australian 'locals' in *The Rescuers Down Under* are stereotyped less savagely than the hillbilly 'locals' in *The Rescuers*. All are, however, sacrificed, as representations, to the power of international agency over local passivity, complacency and lack of professionalism, and to the imperatives for making the film a recognizable sequel to *The Rescuers*. The treatment of Australia and Australians in *The Rescuers Down Under* is, as Murphy suggested, more a by-product of the typical Disney treatment of the environment and local characters, and of mothers and wild creatures, than a deliberate trampling on Australian sensibilities. But the unwitting transgression of 'sacralized' national conventions demonstrates a shortcoming of international entertainment where content with the potential to tug at the heartstrings is eradicated of its local meanings.

The film ends with Australia and Australians being left to enjoy a sleepy and timeless pastorale, safe from the depredations of wildlife poacher, MacLeach. The susceptibility of the environment to the rapacious plundering by evil characters like MacLeach is contrasted with the vulnerability of both Cody's mother and the sea eagle, Mara Hute, to bereavement (the loss of spouses) and to the loss of their children. Nature, women and wild endangered species are rescued for conservation in virginal isolation, secure again because of the timely intervention of the fearless international aid workers, who fly back to New York, their rescue mission successfully completed, and with Bernard's engagement ring firmly on Bianca's finger. The merciless, punishing and overwhelming 'land' of Anglo-Australian folklore is in a sense 'unrecognizable' after subjection to Disney's androgenization, which simplifies and homogenizes cultural specificity.

Conclusion

Disney is accepted worldwide and tends to stick to themes that are recognized worldwide, e.g. romance, courage, good over evil. They also often use animals as their main characters, which are not necessarily American. And more recently they represent people of other cultures, e.g. Aladdin, though not necessarily accurately. (written questionnaire: female student, 21 years, Dutch/Australian)

The comments of the students interviewed for this project indicated a broad acceptance of the stereotyping conventions of mass culture, and little negative comment about the narrowing of the range of stories recycled in the international arena. Their acceptance is based on the belief that they share 'ownership' of global international culture; that they are equal participants in its benefits. Only a few students talked openly about a desire to see more recognizably and convincingly Australian content in the mass entertainment arena.

For Australians the narrowing of story traditions is enacted both nationally and transnationally. Global media 'agents,' like Disney, promote the participation of Australian professionals in the production of entertainment products which show little evidence, in terms of textual content, of their Australian genesis. At the same time, government funding routinely recommends the tailoring of national product to international tastes in order to generate international sales and to defray local production costs. Both government and commercially operated cultural bureaucracies promote their own formulaic approaches to new Australian production for international markets. Popular imagination seems to be shifting from a focus on the development of Australian entertainment industries to a fascination with individual achievement. Australian films may attract less international critical acclaim, but while Australian actors, production and technical staff command sustained international recognition for their achievements in terms of international awards, the Australian public appears satisfied with its international identity.

Global production simultaneously sets standards of production quality and audience experience which challenge local production to match international standards and to define its distinguishing characteristics. The challenge for local production, especially in terms of the representation of national identity, is to exhibit its 'particularity' – its unity with the place of its production – while also practicing the best in technical expertise, global conventions of taste and aesthetics, and avoiding unnecessary contraction of the idea of Australian-ness to worn-out 'Dundee' formulas. As the analysis of the student comments and of *The Rescuers Down Under* demonstrates, the global corporate headquarters of a cultural bureaucracy cannot be expected to imagine an Australian production agenda.

The Australian experience of global mass culture has been characterized by an ongoing dependence on English-language programing from the U.S.A. and the U.K., and to a much lesser extent from other English-speaking countries like Canada and New Zealand. Even though, as Cunningham and Jacka (1996) and Sinclair *et al.* (1996) have pointed out, Australia exports some media products back to the Anglo-American market, this return trade is significantly less than the in-bound trade, and always has been. Sinclair *et al.* have argued that dependence on global product is not necessarily an index of prolonged dependence and underdevelopment, but should instead be understood as a precursor to the development of local production. Nevertheless, the history of the animation, film and television production industries in Australia demonstrates what a slow process such a national development might prove to be.

Notes

1. *Bananas in Pyjamas* and *Play School* are Australian products; *Thomas the Tank Engine* and *Budgie* (the helicopter) are British products; and *Star Wars* is, of course, American.
2. On a visit to the Disney archives in 1993, I discovered that Australian television channels throughout Australia had bought at least thirteen years of scheduling rights to the *Mickey Mouse Club*. Rights to broadcast the program were still being licensed, very cheaply, as late as 1981. I watched this program in 1957, and this student remembers watching it and the later version over 20 years later.
3. In Australia, newspapers are sold locally through franchises we call 'newsagencies' or 'paper shops' – stores which exist primarily to sell newspapers and magazines, but which have diversified into greeting cards, gift-wrapping paper, a small range of stationery items, lottery tickets, cigarettes, a few sweets and drinks.
4. Murphy comments on the Disney treatment of the eagle in terms of

gender and nature, and on the virtual impossibility, given the national American status of the bald eagle, of subjecting it to androgenization. The sea eagle depicted in *The Rescuers Down Under* is of the same family as the American bald eagle, though it has never been given the status in Australia that the eagle has in U.S. culture. There is greater national concern over the protection of koalas, frogs, various small mammals and freshwater crocodiles.

5. Other classic examples include *His Royal Majesty* (Efftee films); *The Adventures of Barry Mackenzie* (Columbia/Longford); *Dot Goes to Holly-wood* (Yoram Gross); even *Babe* (George Miller).

6. *Breaker Morant* and *Gallipoli*, for example.

7. For example, the song 'Little Boy Lost' was a best-seller in the 1960s; the film *Razorback* includes a similar event; children's storybooks and other treatments abound.

8. The Australian film *Picnic at Hanging Rock* (1975) strongly created this sense of the power of the landscape to swallow young lives. The 1956 film *Jedda* created a similar sense of the control of place over individual will.

References and other sources

Appadurai, A. (1996) *Modernity at Large: Cultural Dimensions of Globaliza-tion.* Minneapolis, University of Minnesota Press.

Bell, P. and Bell, R. (1993) *Implicated: The United States in Australia.* Melbourne, Oxford University Press.

Crayford, P. (1999) *Australian Financial Review,* January 23.

Cunningham, S. and Jacka, E. (1996) *Australian Television and International Mediascapes.* Cambridge, New York and Melbourne, Cambridge University Press.

Eyley, J. (1992) 'Animation in Australia: the nature of industry and its relationship to training,' paper presented at the Developing Animation Conference, Italy.

Giroux, H. A. (1995) 'Memory and pedagogy in the "Wonderful World of Disney:" beyond the politics of innocence,' in E. Bell, L. Haas, and L. Sells (eds), *From Mouse to Mermaid: The Politics of Film, Gender, and Culture.* Bloomington and Indianapolis, Indiana University Press.

Halliwell, L. (1995) *Halliwell's Film Guide.* New York, Scribner.

Jellie, D. (1998) 'Animation with attitude,' *Sydney Morning Herald,* The Guide, 2–8 March, p. 8.

Murphy, P. (1995) ' "The whole wide world was scrubbed clean:" the androcentric animation of denatured Disney,' in E. Bell, L. Haas, and L. Sells (eds), *From Mouse to Mermaid: The Politics of Film, Gender and Culture.* Bloomington and Indianapolis, Indiana University Press.

Nightingale, V. (1990) 'Women as audiences,' in M. E. Brown (ed.), *Television and Women's Culture: The Politics of the Popular.* Sydney, Currency Press.

Nightingale, V. (1996) *Studying Audiences: The Shock of the Real.* London and New York, Routledge.

O'Regan, T. (1993) *Australian Television Culture*. Sydney, Allen and Unwin.

Ronson, J. (1997) 'Disney dreaming,' *Sydney Morning Herald*, Saturday, January 11.

Sinclair, J., Jacka, E., and Cunningham, S. (eds) (1996*) New Patterns in Global Television: Peripheral Vision*. Oxford and New York, Oxford University Press.

CHAPTER 4

Brazil: Love It and Hate It: Brazilians' Ambiguous Relationship with Disney

RAUL REIS

Introduction

In 1997, an estimated 295,000 Brazilian tourists visited central Florida and most, if not all of those travelers had Disney World and its affiliated parks as their main destination. In fact, visiting Florida and Disney World has become a 'rite of passage' for middle- and upper-class Brazilian teenagers. However, youths are not the only Brazilian tourists visiting the Magic Kingdom: entire extended families, and an ever-growing number of organized tourist groups are responsible for making the 'Brazil–Florida connection' one of the busiest international commercial air routes in the world. In addition to the popularity of Disney World, Brazilians also have a history of purchasing Disney products, which are currently marketed in Brazil with some success.

Yet, despite their relatively high exposure to Disney products, when asked their opinion about the Walt Disney 'ideology,' at least some Brazilian adolescents seemed critical, skeptical, and generally negative. On the one hand, how do we explain Brazilians' fascination with Disney World, as well as other Disney products? On the other hand, how do we explain the outright critical and ultimately ambiguous views expressed by young Brazilian adults when confronted with questions that probe their relationship to the Disney 'ideology'? The answers are not easy, and they mirror the complexities inherent in a diverse and ambiguous society such as contemporary Brazil.

This chapter examines the relationship between Brazilian audiences and the multifaceted Disney entertainment conglomerate by employing multiple methodologies and sources of information. The methodologies used included questionnaires, personal interviews, observation, and informed analysis of this cultural phenomenon.[1] Besides looking at patterns of consumption of Disney services and products by Brazilian audiences, the chapter also explores the possible explanations for Brazilians' enduring/ongoing fascination with Disney.

Disney in Brazil

Disney comics had a very early start in Brazil. According to Santos (1999), they first appeared in the country in 1934 in the pages of *Suplemento Juvenil* magazine. From 1934 to the mid-1940s, Disney comics appeared in various Brazilian children's publications, but in 1946, they finally gained their own magazine, *Seleções Coloridas*.

In 1950, Editora Abril (Abril Publishing Group) bought the rights to publish Disney comics in Brazil, and launched the comic book *O Pato Donald* (Donald Duck), which included Brazilian adaptations of American and Argentinian Disney comics. However, it wasn't until 1959 that the first Brazilian team of artists and writers was assembled to produce nationally based Disney comics (Santos, 1999).

Since they first appeared in Brazil, Disney characters and comic books have become so popular that they have turned Editora Abril into one of the largest publishing groups in the country. In the 1970s, Abril's comics studio became one of the most important Disney production centers in the world, surpassing its well-established Italian counterpart (Santos, 1999).

Some authors credit the success of Disney comics in Brazil, at least partially, to the 'acculturation' of traditional characters:

> Mickey and his friends, or members of the 'Duck Family,' for example, might celebrate Carnival; or yet, a character who is originally a recluse from the Southern U.S. is transformed into a *caipira* from São Paulo's countryside, who participates in traditional June celebrations, and tells stories from the Brazilian folklore, such as the 'headless mule.' (Santos, 1999: 8, author's translation)

According to Santos, the best example of this successful acculturation is the quintessentially Brazilian 'Everyday Joe,' the character Zé Carioca, created by Walt Disney himself in 1941, and intended to strengthen the ties between Brazil and the U.S.A. during World War II. Throughout the conflict, Zé Carioca appeared with Donald Duck in several cartoons and comic books produced in the U.S.A. The

American version of the character died out after the end of the war, but it was successfully 'resuscitated' by Brazilian comic artists in the 1950s (Santos, 1999: 9).

The immense popularity of the well-established Disney comic books in Brazil (and the strong Brazilian slant that was given to Disney characters) helps to explain why it is so easy for Brazilian children and teenagers to identify Disney products with the words 'quality' and 'fun.' Besides the comic books, feature-length Disney cartoons have always done extremely well in the Brazilian movie and video markets. While most Hollywood-produced movies are released in Brazil with subtitles, Disney cartoons are promptly dubbed, and their release (as well as the accompanying merchandise) is preceded by much of the hype that also follows their release in the U.S.A.

Brazilians' fascination with Disney World Florida and all things Disney is a mass-scale phenomenon, as represented by the amount and variety of licensed products available to and bought by the Brazilian public. In 1996, consumers spent almost $500 million in Brazil on products bearing the Walt Disney logo. Distributors expected sales to increase by 40 percent in 1997, to $600 million. According to a report in *Gazeta Mercantil*, Brazil's leading financial newspaper, that volume of sales made Disney the absolute leader in the Brazilian licensing market. Disney's market share of licensed products was 25 percent in 1996, with an anticipated increase to 30 percent the following year ('Disney licensing increases,' 1997). Table 4.1 shows the range of products and the popularity among our Brazilian respondents. Each entry represents how many times the respondents mentioned having ever bought, received or used the product or service indicated.

Table 4.1 Popularity of licensed Disney products*

Product	Percentage
Clothing	83.9
Movies	100.0
Comic books	83.9
Videos – rent	71.0
Videos – purchase	22.6
Mickey Mouse watch	41.9
Jewelry	22.6
Books	80.6
Disney World	35.5
Toys	83.9
CDs/records	22.6
Household items	48.4

*By percentage of total mentions in the questionnaires

Brazilians' relationship with Disney and its products is a very ambiguous and complex one. The consumption of Disney products, especially comic books and animated feature-length cartoons, is as widespread in Brazil as in any European, Asian or other Latin American country. However, what might differentiate their relationship with The Mouse from other audiences' consumption patterns is Brazilians' fascination with Disney World and other Disney theme parks.

The infatuation with Disney products in Brazil is maintained and perpetuated by the habit of reading Disney comic books from an early age. Although 'acculturated' Disney characters such as Zé Carioca won't be found in Disney theme parks, it is the continued exposure to Disney's traditional characters, combined with the box-office success of Disney features, that helps to explain why Brazilians visit the Magic Kingdom and other Disney parks in droves. The following sections will explore this cultural phenomenon in greater detail.

Brazilian tourists in Florida

As previously stated, almost 300,000 Brazilian tourists visited central Florida and Disney World in 1997 (see Table 4.2). This represents an 8.8 percent increase from 1996, when an estimated 271,000 Brazilians visited the region. In fact, Brazil is the second largest overseas market for central Florida and Disney World, behind only the U.K., and ahead of Germany and Japan (Clark, 1998a).

Table 4.2 Overseas visitors to central Florida

Country	1996	1997	% Change
United Kingdom	899,000	949,000	+5.5
Brazil	271,000	295,000	+8.8
Germany	218,000	201,000	−7.7
Japan	130,000	113,000	−13.0

Source: Orlando Sentinel Tribune, June 1, 1998

Reputed as big spenders, Brazilian tourists are specifically targeted by central Florida businesses and Walt Disney World itself. For three years in a row, corporations such as American Express, United Airlines and the Walt Disney Company have joined forces with car rental companies, hotels and travel agencies to set up 'Temporada Mágica' (Magic Season), an early summer and mid-winter program aimed at increasing the already large number of Brazilian tourists to the area (Clark, 1997). In 1997, its second year, the program drew 9940 bookings, a 61 percent increase over 1996. With the inclusion of additional companies, the campaign was expected to draw even more business in 1998 (Clark, 1998b).

When Brazilians visit central and south Florida, they not only tour the Magic Kingdom and South Beach but also usually go on a concerted spending frenzy. Brazilian tourists spent an estimated $526 million in Florida in 1995 (Emling, 1996), which was even before 'Temporada Mágica' and other similar tourism packages had been established.

Brazilians like Florida and Disney World so much that they are not only visiting the region in unprecedented numbers but are also buying property in Orlando, Miami and other Florida vacation spots. A story in the *Ft. Lauderdale Sun-Sentinel* reported that foreign buyers were purchasing almost half of the luxury condominiums sold in Dade County, Brazilians being the fastest-growing segment among those buyers ('Foreign buyers,' 1997: 34). One Brazilian industrialist explained why he and other middle- and upper-class Brazilians were moving to or buying vacation condos in Florida: it's like Rio de Janeiro, he reasoned, with the same good weather and beautiful beaches, but without the crime and other urban problems faced in the Brazilian metropolis ('Foreign buyers,' 1997).

Visiting Disney World: a rite of passage

There is an important cultural and social component that helps to shed light on this phenomenon. Visiting Disney World and Epcot Center has become a 'rite of passage' for the great majority of middle- and upper-class Brazilian teenagers. When they turn 15, many Brazilian girls choose to visit Disney World, in lieu of the traditional, and often lavish 'festa de 15 anos' (15th birthday party) their parents would proudly throw for them. Male teenagers, who in Brazil often face peer pressure to abandon childhood habits and idols, have no qualms about showing their excitement at the prospect of a Disney World visit.

In this context, going to Disney World also has become a status symbol invested with special significance for boys and girls in the expensive Brazilian prep schools and language schools. Each additional visit may even increase the teenager's popularity among classmates and friends. Most respected are those who come to Florida on a yearly basis, and are able to shower first-time visitors with survival tips and other useful information. In this ostentatious atmosphere, where 'being cool' often equates with being able to afford overseas trips and American clothes, visiting – and liking – Disney World is never seen as childish or immature. On the contrary, not being able to 'share' the Disney experience and lingo may well prove to be 'uncool' and socially alienating.

An additional factor that helps explain the attraction to Disney parks is the vast overall influence of U.S. media on Brazilian culture. American media and popular culture (movies, TV shows, comic books, fashion) permeate every aspect of Brazilian society. It seems likely that such daily, widespread contact influences adolescents' decision to visit the U.S.A. Brazil's geographic proximity to North America and the Brazilian middle classes' relative affluence also help to explain the influx of tourists to Miami, Disney theme parks, and other U.S. destinations.

Eleven out of the 31 young adults (35.5 percent) who responded to the questionnaires used for this research project in Brazil had been to Disney World and Disney-MGM Studios. Almost all of those had also visited the Epcot Center, and three respondents in that group said they had also been to EuroDisney (see Table 4.3). The fact that our respondents were all young university students, with a middle-class background and relatively high educational level, helps to explain the high rate of overall visits to Disney theme parks. Those results also support our view of those visits as a 'rite of passage' for young, middle-class Brazilians.

Table 4.3 Visits to Disney World and other Disney parks (percentage of responses)

Disneyland, California	3.2
Disney World	35.5
Epcot Center	22.6
Disney-MGM Studios	35.5
Disneyland, Paris	9.7
Any Disney theme park	35.5
n = 31	

One of the baffling aspects of teenagers' infatuation with Disney parks is the fact that, although they have grown up with 'acculturated' Disney characters such as Zé Carioca, Brazilian tourists won't find any of those characters in the actual theme parks. It is arguable that the continued exposure to Disney comics and Disney animated features, combined with the cultural and social aspects of the trip discussed in the previous section, overrides that possible obstacle.

Mixed feelings and ambiguous relationships

In the case of Brazilian teenagers, what makes their relationship with Disney parks and products even more ambiguous and complex is the fact that a few years later, the same teenagers who visited and thoroughly enjoyed their Disney World trip, tend to look back at that and other Disney memories with less forgiving eyes. The Brazilian respondents interviewed for this project in Brazil were very familiar with Disney products, but many of them, while admitting positive feelings, memories and attitudes towards those symbols, were also very critical of the Disney 'ideology.'

Interesting emergent data refer to the word association question included in the questionnaires. When prompted to indicate which words or expressions came to their minds when they thought about Disney and its products, our respondents came up with a wide range of answers, which varied from the traditional and expected (for example, 'childhood,' 'enchantment'), to the unusual or unexpected (for example, 'useful,' 'expensive'). Table 4.4 reports some of the recurrent themes in our respondents' answers. For our Brazilian respondents, the words most frequently associated with Disney were positive ones, such as 'fantasy' (seven), 'entertainment' (six), and 'childhood' (seven).

However, 'capitalism' was the only word that came to the mind of a 17-year-old female respondent, when prompted to make a list of words she associated with Disney. When asked how much she presently likes Disney and its products, that same respondent marked 4, on a Likert scale that ranged from 1 ('I like them very much') to 7 ('I don't like them at all'). The same teenager said she had been to the three main Disney parks in Florida, and owns merchandise, such as videotapes and stuffed toys, associated with the company. Along with the previously mentioned response of 'capitalism,' the term 'consumerism' was also cited by three other respondents. However, when asked how much they like Disney products as adults, roughly one-third of the respondents (nine) marked 3, using the same Likert scale. Such an overwhelmingly positive response – which put the mean in that category at 3.93 – is at odds with many of the statements made by the respondents when answering other questions (see Table 4.5). Comparatively, when asked how much they liked Disney products as children (from 1 to 12 years old), and as teenagers (from 13 to 17 years old), the same respondents, using the same Likert scale, provided answers that swung the average pendulum from 2.97 (children) to 4.0 (teenagers).

Table 4.4 Frequency of words associated with Disney*

Words	Percentage
Childhood/children**	32.3
Fantasy	22.6
Entertainment/fun***	22.5
Cartoons	16.1
Mickey, Minnie or Donald	12.9
Consumerism	9.7
Magic	9.7
Beauty	9.7
Quality	9.7
Dreams	6.5
Joy	6.5
Expensive	6.5
Enchantment	3.2
Emotion	3.2
Control	3.2
Personal accomplishment	3.2
Sympathy	3.2

*By percentage of total mentions for question #47 in the questionnaires
**includes childhood, children and youthfulness
***includes entertainment, fun and funny

Table 4.5 Attitudes toward Disney products (percentage of responses)

	1 Like very much	2	3	4	5	6	7 Like not at all
(a) As Children (n = 31; Mean = 2.97)	22.6	22.6	19.4	12.9	19.4	0	3.2
(b) As Teenagers (n = 31; Mean = 4.0)	0	0	35.5	38.7	19.4	3.2	3.2
(c) As Adults (n = 28; Mean = 3.93)	0	14.3	32.1	21.4	17.9	7.1	7.1

Respondents could check seven different alternatives, from 1 ('I liked them very much') to 7 ('I didn't like them at all'). The questions were:
(a) 'How did you feel as a child (1 to 12 years old) about Disney products?'
(b) 'How did you feel as a teenager (13 to 17 years old) about Disney products?'
(c) 'As an adult, how do you feel about Disney products?'

When asked if they thought Disney was typically American, or if the company promoted American culture as diverse from other cultures, some respondents went out of their way to make sure we understood that they felt Disney presented the American culture as a superior culture: 'Disney promotes difference between people. Unequal superiority and fantasies which ridicule some segments of society,' said an 18-year-old male respondent. (This same respondent indicated that his current feelings about Disney represented a 3, which was a favorable response on the Likert scale described above.) 'Disney indirectly inferiorizes (abases) the Southern Hemisphere (including Latin America and Africa),' answered a 19-year-old who also said 'sympathy' and 'childhood' were the words that came to mind when asked about Disney products. 'Disney promotes a culture based on consumerism, on technology and on the masses, different in some few points, but mostly representing the cultures of first world countries,' said a 17-year-old female who has been to the Disney-MGM Studios and Epcot.

On the positive side, when answering the same question, other respondents said: 'Disney is universal;' 'they try to integrate other people in that world;' and, 'I think they want to entertain everyone.' The secret of the company's success, according to several respondents, is exactly the fact that Disney presents 'universal values,' as well as characters and stories that children all over the world love to watch.

The comments and respective Likert scale results presented in the previous paragraphs strongly support the idea that young Brazilians have a very ambiguous relationship with Disney products and ideology. The inconsistency in the responses sampled – two of the respondents with negative comments liked Disney as adults, while two of the participants who offered positive feedback recorded higher 'dislike' marks – can also be observed when we cross-reference their answers to the question: 'Is Disney uniquely American?'

Respondents who said that Disney is uniquely American tended to offer either negative (38.1 percent) or neutral (30.8 percent) written comments, while participants who said Disney was not a uniquely American phenomenon tended to write more positive (50 percent) than neutral (37.5 percent) or negative (10 percent) comments. However, those results were not reflected in the way respondents rated their own feelings about Disney – participants with the more critical comments rating higher (liking Disney more) than respondents who were less critical. Those apparently contradictory and inconsistent results also support and strengthen our view of Brazilians' relationship with Disney as very ambiguous and complex.

The interviews, conducted separately with eleven participants, provided even more insight into the Brazilians' love/hate relationship with Disney. Some respondents, for example, marveled at the quality

Figure 7. Mickey Mouse shrine, Guatemala. Photo: Mike Huffman

and high entertainment value of Disney movies and cartoons, but at the same time emphasized their reluctance to buy Disney products for themselves or their children.

The pattern of ambiguity continues when participants are asked if they would encourage parents to expose their children to Disney products. A significant majority (approximately one-third) expressed concern and even used strong cautionary language – 'I'd advise [parents] to … not buy the products to avoid raising a consumerist child' – and yet every single respondent said they would allow or encourage their own children to view Disney movies.

A young respondent who has been to Disney World and other parks told us she had had a great trip, and that she likes and admires Disney cartoons. However, when asked what advice she would give to parents about Disney products, she said she would advise them to take the children to the movies, but to avoid buying the merchandise. Buying those products at such an early age, she reasoned, 'will turn the child into a consumerist kid.'

As they mature, Brazilians tend to become less infatuated with

Disney products and the company's overall ideology. However, because of the positive nature of their early association with those products and services ('feel-good' movies, pleasant travel experiences, comic books), overall, adults still make a marginally positive assessment of Disney. The last section of this chapter will explore a cultural component of the Brazilian identity that might also help explain the attitudinal ambiguity detected in the survey.

Cultural identity as a possible explanation for Brazil's fascination with Disney

As the prevalent, stereotypical characterization has it, Brazilians personify carnival. In Brazil, carnival extends far beyond three days in February. Loud music, dancing and street partying – organized or not – seem to pop up all over the country whenever an important soccer game is played, a particularly popular political candidate has been elected, a patron saint is honored, or a relevant holiday is observed. Sometimes these spontaneous celebrations do not even need a reason to occur.

With all its rules and regulations, and its carefully orchestrated spectacle and sanitized fun, Disney World is, in Susan Willis' view, 'systematically elaborated to eliminate carnival.' Contrasting the Disney theme park and the Mardi Gras celebration in New Orleans, she further reasons that 'Disney World may well represent the culmination of the centuries' long campaign of suppression waged against carnival' (Willis, 1995: 4). But if that interpretation is accurate, how can we explain Brazilians' fascination with Disney World, the antithesis of carnival?

Several Brazilian anthropologists have proposed that the Brazilian character and identity – if such things exist – are very ambiguous, 'tricky,' and complex concepts. Roberto Da Matta (1991a), for example, has observed that the search for a definition of the Brazilian social and cultural identity should go beyond an examination of the environmental and historical conditions in which the country was built. He believes an acceptable definition of the country's social *psyche* will come from the qualitative sociological and anthropological examination of values, such as the ambiguity towards religious expression, as well as social characteristics, such as the fluid separation between public and private spaces, that are prevalent throughout the Brazilian body social.

Da Matta (1983, 1991a, 1991b) proposes that one of the central characteristics of the Brazilian 'spirit' is the middle ground, the Brazilian *jeitinho* ('way out'), sought as a solution to the conflict between a modern society based on strict, universal rules, codes and laws, and a cultural tradition built on interpersonal relationships:

> Brazil is not a dual country where one operates only with an 'out *or* in;' 'right *or* wrong;' 'man *or* woman;' 'married *or* separated;' 'God *or* Devil;' 'black *or* white' logic. ... Between the black and the white (which in the Anglo-Saxon and South African systems are mutually exclusive terms), we have an infinite and diversified set of intermediary categories in which the *mulato* represents the perfect characterization. (Da Matta, 1991b: 40-1, author's translation)[2]

Da Matta (1991a, 1991b) used the terms *sistemas relacionais* ('relational systems') and *sociedade relacional* ('relational society') to explain Brazilian society's tendency to place interpersonal relationships (kinship, friendships, and even acquaintanceships) above the impersonal character of the rules that dictate any modern society's functioning. While in countries such as the U.S.A., the U.K. and France, for example, there would be an 'enormous coherence between the judicial rules and the practices of everyday life' (Da Matta, 1991b: 97, author's translation), in Brazil personal relations give universal laws a specific *malleability* that allows them to 'bend' depending on the context in which they are applied (*ibid.*: 98).[3]

That particular ambiguity in dealing with bureaucratic, judicial and other 'formal' contexts, the already mentioned *jeitinho brasileiro* ('the Brazilian way') has spilled over into virtually every level of interpersonal interaction. In Brazil, writes Da Matta (1991a), the 'sacred' separation between public - *a rua* ('the street') - and private spaces - *a casa* ('the house') - is still very much prevalent.

A casa - a highly personal, well-protected, singular and well-defined space - would protect its members, *a família*, from the impersonality and roughness of the street. Meanwhile, *a rua* - this cruel, often dangerous, impersonal space - would constitute a public arena for earning a living, making friends and providing a perspective through which we interpret the world. More than physical spaces, *a casa* and *a rua* are Brazilian sociological categories and moral entities, 'capable of awakening emotions, reactions, laws, prayers, songs and images aesthetically framed and inspired' (Da Matta, 1991a: 17, author's translation).[4]

For Da Matta, there is, however, a 'shaded' space where those two separate worlds overlap. The resulting connection between private and public - the myriad of 'grays' in-between definite 'blacks' and 'whites'- is what best characterizes the Brazilian identity, the 'relational society' in which the impersonality of formal *loci* is touched and warmed up by the humanity of personal relations.

It is precisely in that myriad of 'grays' to which Da Matta alludes that we should go looking for answers to explain Brazilians' fascination with an ideal as *uncarnivalesque* as Disney World. Brazilians' attraction to Disney defies easy characterizations, because the 'Brazilian identity' itself is a concept that does not allow straightforward explanations.

Yes, Brazilians in general like the *unorganized* spectacle of carnival. However, the strict *organization* emphasized by Disney World – which might even be seen as an extreme representative of the rigid political and economic structure of industrial liberal democracies – might also function as a powerful magnet, attracting the Brazilian middle class exactly because it represents a break with their everyday reality of *disorganized* relational systems.

While these speculative thoughts may merit further development, additional research also would need to analyze other audience segments, as well as looking more deeply into the historical, cultural and economic influences on this Brazilian love/hate relationship with Disney.

Notes

1. Research questionnaires and interviews were administered in Brazil by Roberto Elisio dos Santos, under the supervision of Professor Flavio Calazans. The research sample consisted of 31 Brazilian university students. Due to the age, educational level, and socio-economic status of the respondents, participants were expected to be heavy consumers of media products.
2. 'O Brasil não é um país dual onde se opera somente com uma lógica do dentro *ou* fora; do certo *ou* errado; do homem *ou* mulher; do casado *ou* separado; de Deus *ou* Diabo; do preto *ou* branco. … Entre o preto e o branco (que nos sistemas anglo-saxão e sul-africano são termos exclusivos), nós temos um conjunto infinito e variado de categorias intermediárias em que o *mulato* representa uma cristalização perfeita.'
3. 'Nos Estados Unidos, na França e na Inglaterra … [há uma] enorme coerência entre a regra jurídica e as práticas da vida diária. . . [No Brasil] a possibilidade de gradação permite a interferência das relações pessoais com a lei universal.'
4. 'capazes de despertar emoções, reações, leis, orações, músicas e imagens esteticamente emolduradas e inspiradas.'

References and other sources

Clark, L. (1997) 'American Express, United team up to lure Brazilians,' *Orlando Sentinel Tribune*, December 8, p. 13.
Clark, L. (1998a) 'Visits from overseas rise 7.7%,' *Orlando Sentinel Tribune*, May 27, p. B4.
Clark, L. (1998b) 'It's temporada mágica again for Brazilians visiting Orlando,' *Orlando Sentinel Tribune*, May 11, p. 12.

Da Matta, R. (1983) *Carnavais, malandros e heróis: para uma sociologia do dilema brasileiro* ('Carnivals, rogues and heroes'). Rio de Janeiro, Zahar Editores.

Da Matta, R. (1991a) *O que faz o brasil, brasil?* ('What makes Brazil, Brazil?'). Rio de Janeiro, Rocco.

Da Matta, R. (1991b) *A casa & a rua* ('The house and the street'), 4th edn. Rio de Janeiro, Guanabara Koogan.

'Disney licensing increases' (1997) *Gazeta Mercantil Online*, June 11.

Emling, S. (1996) 'Latin tourists shop till they drop in Miami,' *Atlanta Journal and Constitution*, November 29, p. 8A.

'Foreign buyers are driving the hot south Florida condo market' (1997), *Ft. Lauderdale Sun-Sentinel*, April 12, p. 34.

'Pow wow participants are doing a victory dance,' *Orlando Sentinel Tribune*, June 1, p. 9.

Santos, R. E. (1999) 'Quadrinhos Disney: análise e evolução,' *Agaquê*, 1(3).

Willis, S. (1995) 'The problem with pleasure,' in The Project on Disney, *Inside the Mouse: Work and Play at Disney World*. Durham, NC, Duke University Press, pp. 1–11.

CHAPTER 5

Denmark: 'Donald Seems So Danish': Disney and the Formation of Cultural Identity

KIRSTEN DROTNER

> Donald Duck suits Danish mentality. He seems so Danish and not American like Mickey Mouse, who is very politically correct. Donald is so politically incorrect, that he seems Danish.

This quote from Sarah, a young Danish woman aged 20, is indicative of the reception found among a sample of 59 Danish students:[1] she speaks about a character found in a weekly comic bearing Donald Duck's name and by doing so defines her view on what it means to be Danish through an oppositional logic of what it is not. David Buckingham (1997: 2) asserts that 'Disney speaks to "the child in us all," while simultaneously constructing the meaning of "childhood."' If this is true – and I think it is – then it is evident from analyses of the Danish data that Disney constructs different meanings of childhood for different children. This is not simply because recipients differ, as one might suspect from the more facile interpretations of audience reception studies. It is also, and just as much, because markets differ – in their local histories of development, in their position in Disney's global empire and in the wider media and consumer trends of which the Disney conglomerate forms a part.

Young Sarah sums up the three main points of this chapter: first, looking at Northern Europe from a production point of view, until the late 1980s, Disney was primarily a print media phenomenon, sprinkled with intermittent feature-length cartoons released in the cinemas; there was relatively little merchandise, no Disney shops and no theme parks (EuroDisney opened outside of Paris in 1992). Second, when looking at Disney from a reception point of view, until the late 1980s, Disney was centered on reading as a weekly ritual that the majority of Danish children engaged in. Their reading was lodged within the family circle, rather than the peer group. Third, when looking at Disney from a wider cultural perspective, the reading of the weekly comic *Donald Duck* opens up processes of imagination that serve to define the readers' cultural identities: what it means to be Danish is formed through an oppositional logic of what the young readers perceive as being American (seen from the relative distance of Northern Europe, the term 'American' encompasses both the U.S.A. and Canada). This oppositional logic both reveals and seeks to overcome the complexities and contradictions of reception: the informants comfortably associate the pleasurable aspects of the comic *Donald Duck* (Anders And) with Danishness, while the more negative aspects are posited as part of 'Americanization' or 'the American way of life.'

The Danish study is indicative of the possibilities opened up by transnational comparative projects that encompass both aspects of production and reception: the existing project helps redress the existing imbalances in Disney research by focusing on processes of reception. And, in demonstrating differences of production and markets, the project also helps to redress the existing predominance of studies that take the Anglo-American markets as normative: as this project demonstrates, the Disney empire is founded on more pillars than cartoons and theme parks.

This chapter focuses on Disney production and reception in Denmark. As for production, particular emphasis is placed on Disney's print media, since in a global context this is perhaps the most underresearched and underrated element of the Disney corporation. Occasionally, to complete the production picture, trends have been included that have only materialized after the informants, on which the present project is based, have grown up. As for reception, the study is limited to young adults' memories of their childhood readings with all its methodological implications of distance in time and space. One of these implications is precisely that the informants speak from a position where they now witness dramatic transformations of the Disney landscape – transformations which add to the relevance of the more recent production information.

Kirsten Drotner

Disney print media in Denmark

Disney in Northern Europe is directed by the Walt Disney Company Nordic A/S founded in 1960. Based in Copenhagen, it administers consumer products, marketing as well as licensing to 61 license holders, 43 in merchandising and 18 in media production. Today, this company accounts for 10 percent of the total Disney sales in Europe, not including video tapes and computer games. Disney Nordic's sale of Disney products amounts to approximately 3 to 3.5 billion Danish kroner per year (c. 0.5 billion U.S.$) – again, minus video tapes and computer games. Despite its limited population of just over five million, Denmark is the best-selling Disney country in Europe (Mietle, 1997).

By far the largest license holder with Disney Nordic is the Danish-owned Egmont Group A/S, founded in 1878 by an enterprising magazine publisher, Egmont H. Petersen.[2] Today, the Egmont Group is the world's largest publisher of Disney print media, and the Nordic countries top the list of Disney magazine consumption (Christiansen, 1998). This prominent position is primarily based on their publication of the weekly comic *Donald Duck*, featuring a motley mixture of short stories and serials with Donald, his nephews Huey, Dewey and Louie, Scrooge McDuck, Gyro Geerloose and other inhabitants of Duckburg – plus an increasing number of activity pages with jokes, competitions and promotions for other Disney products. First appearing in 1949 as a monthly, through the 1950s the comic established itself as the leading weekly that was able to strike a golden mean between juvenile entertainment and adult approval at a time when Denmark, along with many other countries, was permeated – if to a lesser degree – by debates verging on hysteria over the perceived threats posed by American comics (Barker, 1989; Drotner, 1992).[3]

In terms of output, the comic had its heyday in the mid-1970s. Over the last ten years, increased competition from other media and different leisure activities has meant a decrease in weekly sales by a third. Today, *Donald Duck* sells 95,000 copies a week in Denmark, which is still a comfortable 60 percent of all comic sales in the country (*Dansk oplagskontrol*, 1997; Vilstrup, 1996).

Targeted at a readership aged between 8 and 12, it is estimated that the comic has over 700,000 readers, namely 317,000 aged between 5 and 18 (46 percent girls and 54 percent boys), and another 50 percent over 18 years old, most of them men (*Juniornøglen*, 1997/8: 52–3; Bach, 1997). In recent years, Egmont Comic Creation, publishing in 29 languages, has successfully sought to offset dwindling sales in Northern Europe by developing markets in Asia (starting with China in 1994) and a good number of countries in former Eastern Europe.[4]

The Egmont Group backs up *Donald Duck* with other Disney print media, of which the most important are monthly comic books, called *Jumbo Books* (*Jumbobøger*), brought out in 1968. They contain only short stories, many of which are Carl Barks classics, and some of which are print versions of popular Disney cinema cartoons or other blockbuster films but featuring Disney figures as protagonists. Today, the *Jumbo Books* are the top-selling book titles in Denmark – outselling by five times Barbara Cartland, for example; and unlike *Donald Duck*, these 254-page monthlies enjoy increasing sales.[5] The youngest readers are catered for by Egmont's Donald Duck Book Club, which since 1977 has brought out a total of 173 Disney titles – often print versions of feature-length cinema cartoons. The monthly news bulletin of the club also operates as a window for other Disney output, including merchandise.

Disney merchandise

As mentioned, the Walt Disney Company Nordic has overall control of Disney merchandise and its licensing in the Nordic countries. Licensing to merchandise has increased dramatically since the 1970s and 1980s, when the informants of the present study grew up. Thus, in Denmark in 1997, the following 43 merchandise license holders or distribution firms for other license holders existed (with number of holders in parentheses): apparel (5); fashion accessories (7); food (2); home furnishing (5); personal care (3); stationery (10); toys (11).[6] The following Disney merchandise products are sold in Denmark through the Walt Disney Company Nordic, thus excluding Disney products licensed in other European countries:

- *Apparel.* Socks for adults and children, underwear for children, T-shirts, sweatshirts, jogging suits, tracksuits, T-shirt dresses, skirts, caps, jumpsuits, indoor and outdoor wear, skiing garments, night-gowns for girls and dolls, pajamas.
- *Fashion accessories.* Ties, butterflies, men's wear, children's watches, bags, rucksacks, caps, scarves, mittens, aprons, bathing suits, children's hair accessories, sunglasses, belts, wallets, braces, key-rings, toilet bags, alarm clocks, wall clocks, wristwatches (adults).
- *Food.* Chocolate, ice-cream.
- *Home furnishings.* Melamine tableware, various dinner items/ dinnerware, towels, glassware, children's wooden furniture, plastic cups and plates, cutlery, lunch-boxes.
- *Personal care.* Adhesive bandages, liquid soaps, shampoo, toothbrush holders, nail-brushes, dummies, feeding bottles, rattles, nail clippers, teething rings.

- *Stationery.* Cardboard, filing articles, coloring pens and pencils, pencil boxes, erasers, ring-binders, school bags, exercise books, party goods, plastic collection folders, audio cassette cases, Christmas calendars and cards, gift tags, other Christmas items, illuminated globes, press-and-peel sticker sets, wrapping paper.
- *Toys.* Sleepover travel pillows for children, golf accessories, puzzles, games, drawing pads, balloons, sewing cards, writing paper, scraps, dress-me dolls, rucksacks, inflatable beach articles, audio products, pre-school toys, paint-by-numbers, children's costumes, stuffed or plush toys, Walkmen, clock radios, tape recorders (with radio).

There are no Disney Stores in Denmark, only in-store outlets at leading department stores. As far as can be ascertained, pirating plays an insignificant role in merchandising in Denmark, as the Walt Disney Company Nordic holds a firm grip, just as it orchestrates marketing campaigns for new cinema releases – campaigns that in recent years have included Disney trains riding round the capital region and tie-ins with McDonald's, so that families can buy joint meal and cinema tickets.

Animated cartoons on film and television

The preponderance of Disney print media in Denmark must be seen within a media culture in which reading has remained a popular, and not merely an educationally prescribed, activity with wide sections of the population, especially after the advent of television. Children and young people are the most diligent users of the public libraries, which have been effective cornerstones in disseminating not only highbrow literature but also more popular forms of print. Thus, until 1993, upwards of 80 percent of Danes under the age of 16 made regular library visits (Drotner, 1995: 15). Moreover, Danish television until the mid-1980s was a one-channel public-service system, and TV commercials on a national scale only appeared in 1988 with the introduction of a second, terrestrial TV channel. Thus, the combined effects of deregulation, increasing commodification hastened by the advent of the VCR, and transnational forms of simultaneous communication (Internet, satellite television) only came to influence the Danish media landscape from the late 1980s on – that is, after the informants for the present project have come of age. In addition, as of 1998, Denmark had no Disney Channel.

Still, what internationally counts as 'real' Disney, namely the animated cartoons, have, indeed, been part of young Danes' leisure also before that time, if not consistently. Danes living in the capital were introduced to Disney cartoons from 1932 on, when *Disney's Christmas Show* (five or six short cartoons) was televised almost every year until 1978. Since 1938, 32 feature-length cartoons have been shown in Danish cinemas (Danish Film Institute, 1998).[7] Since 1960, about a hundred Danish cinemas have closed during each decade (Bondebjerg, 1997: 204). And in the two decades from 1970 on – that is, when our informants grew up – only eight feature-length cartoons premiered in Denmark. Until very recently, then, going to the cinema to watch a Disney movie has by no means been a regular form of entertainment.

The same is true for television. In the 1960s, when Danes first took to television in a serious way, the Danish Broadcasting Corporation – still a monopoly channel – introduced the yearly *Disney's Christmas Show* on Christmas Day (and since 1992 on Christmas Eve). Every year the program offers the same shorts plus a trailer for a new cinema release, and as in Sweden it has become institutionalized as part of the Christmas festivities. Also in the 1960s, the TV channel broadcast a weekly show called *Disneyland*, and in the 1980s (1980–1, 1983, 1985–7), the channel featured a weekly show, *Så er der tegnefilm* (*Toon Time*), which included a mixture of shorts from Disney, Warner, Universal, MGM and Walter Lantz (Medieforskningen, 1998).

Today, Disney cartoons in the cinema are seen by an average of 500,000 people (10 percent of the poulation). In 1989, Buena Vista Home Entertainment brought out the first Disney video for sale in Denmark (*Alice in Wonderland*), and Danish households with children aged 3 to 10 claim an average, yearly purchase of four Disney videos that are watched 34 times on average (Bach, 1997). Since 1991, the Danish Broadcasting Corporation has followed suit with a weekly show, *Disney sjov* (Disney Fun), which included only Disney cartoons – apparently the single most expensive contract for the channel. And since 1997, another terrestrial channel, TV Danmark, owned by Disney's Capital Cities/ABC, features a similar weekly show called *Disney Venner* (Disney Friends).

From around 1990, then, the consumption of Disney cartoons changed from being an intermittent pastime to becoming an everyday phenomenon. In purely economic terms, the revenue gained from rental and increasingly from the purchase of videos has surpassed that of the cinemas.[8] In addition, the merchandising of Disney products has rocketed. This situation forms the backdrop against which our informants remember their own childhood experiences with Disney.

Figure 8. Pocahontas event held at a shopping mall in Lyngby, Denmark, before the opening of Disney's film *Pocahontas*. Photo: Carlos R. Calderon

Rituals of reception

'I have a crystal-clear image of my brothers eating cornflakes and being completely absorbed in a *Donald Duck* comic. It's a kind of childhood thing, you know.' This quote is indicative of the informants' immediate associations with Disney: the name flags memories of reading – all 59 informants have read the comic *Donald Duck* – of having a good time and sharing experiences within a family context and often between generations. In particular, the intergenerational sharing of experiences may be seen as the juvenile audience perspective on what in the literature is often referred to as Disney's nostalgia. For it is obvious that our informants' parents and even grandparents wanted their offspring

Figure 9. Pocahontas event held at a shopping mall in Lyngby, Denmark. Photo: Carlos R. Calderon

to gain a similar sense of excitement as they, themselves, remember. Thus, there is more to the desire for their children or grandchildren to read *Donald Duck* than merely securing them an approved pastime. In fact, our informants often single out their grandparents as introductory catalysts to the Disney universe:

> The very first memory I have of Walt Disney is in fact my grandmother living in Viborg [a small provincial town in Jutland], who had a big cardboard box under her bed with a whole lot of ancient *Donald Ducks* which I read to shreds when on holiday there … Looking back, it seems unbelievable, incredibly nostalgic, to see a little, old room – 7 by 5 square metres – tobacco smoke in the air, and a little, old woman sitting in the corner, rapping her stick on the floor – it is such a nice memory to keep, I think. (Bo, 30 years old)

Grandparents would often store old copies of the magazine, which many remember as holding a special attraction (characters are drawn differently and act strangely). In some cases *Donald Duck* is even seen as an intergenerational link – perhaps of particular relevance for a generation of children who have often experienced divorces in their families:

> My grandmother and grandfather had saved all these *Donald Duck* comics, which my father and my uncle had read when they were children, so the magazines were bound in big, brown bindings – they were a real hit when we came to visit my grandparents. (Anne Marie, 25 years old)

Reading *Donald Duck* at their grandparents' house (or in summer cottages) is also associated with holidays and with the pleasures of losing track of time and having no responsibilities. But in minor ways this creation of alternative time and space zones also characterizes memories of the more regular reading experiences. In fact, the pleasure of reading seems to be created in a pull between the regularity of the weekly purchase and the possible surprises it offered. Within the polarities of repetition and exception, reading was performed as a weekly ritual. Regularity is a particularly evident part of purchase, as Christina, aged 19, reveals: 'I remember my dad being with me, buying [the comics]; I think it was on Mondays, and so I got a small yoghurt and *Donald Duck*.' Most informants' parents bought the comic for them, but some also spent their own pocket money, a fact that may have added a sense of specialness to the purchase:

> Every time I got my pocket money, and I got it at the same time that *Donald Duck* came out on Monday ... I went down and bought it. I spent all my pocket money on it ... So it has played an important part, played a role, during my childhood, and in fact I bought them at the same corner shop. (Jesper, 20 years old)

The mixture of repetition and exception is also found in the context of reading:

> There was always a special atmosphere coming home, and my mother had bought some fresh bread and some juice or milk – it was all part of sitting in bed and having a good time reading. Reading the new comic for the first time, you had to have a little extra surrounding it, you see. (Christina, 19 years old)

The repeatable uniqueness of the ritual is evident in Christina's choice of words: you had to have 'a little extra' and have it every week ('always'). Many informants remember similar rituals surrounding their reading, rituals that brought about a brief suspension of scheduled leisure-time activities and helped transform, if only momentarily, familiar spaces such as the kitchen table, the couch or – as indicated in the above quote – one's own bed.

Most informants remember their introduction to Disney at the age of 4 or 5 and that interest waned around the age of 12 or 13, when other leisure activities increasingly competed for time, money and attention. If the context and process of reading during these years is formed as a weekly ritual lodged within the polarities of repetition and exception, then the function of reading seems to have been a tension between exerting individual autonomy and reinforcing a sense of family belonging. Buying the comic, perhaps even with one's own money, is remembered as a sign of individual choice:

> My dad is a journalist, you see, so he went to get the paper and all the magazines one had to have. And so I went with him, and then I surely also wanted a *Donald Duck* comic, for I was going to get something the same way. (Sigurd, 26 years old)

While juvenile autonomy is often exerted within and in relation to the peer group, buying and reading *Donald Duck* seem to have operated as signs of autonomy within the family circle and rarely in opposition to its norms. There appears to have been very little swapping and exchange of back issues between peers – perhaps because nearly all children possessed *Donald Duck*, but also perhaps because the comic was so firmly lodged symbolically within the family sphere: 'it was ours,' 'I wanted the entire collection.' The clearest example of the intricate pull between autonomy and family belonging are informants' reminiscences of how *Donald Duck* operated as an introduction to the world of reading. Little text, many pictures and a limited number of characters made the comic an obvious starting point for reading. Several informants emphasize the intimate enjoyment of mothers reading aloud, with the children believing that they can read themselves. The pictures told most of the story anyway.

The very simplicity of the narrative universe and its cardboard characters – elements that form the backbone of critical denigration (see, for example, Dorfman and Mattelart, 1975) – seem to have operated as pleasurable sources of recognition for young readers, perhaps even as signs of stability for a generation that, at least in Denmark, often experienced parental divorce and unemployment: 'It was so that you followed [the characters'] lives from week to week. Well, it was just like knowing what one's best friends had been up to, I think' (Bo, 30 years old). The narrative familiarity was spiced by textual puns, and informants often mention examples of humorous character names such as D. Ummy or S. U. R. Price. To a newly literate child, being able to detect such verbal tricks undoubtedly yielded an added pleasure.

Processes of negotiation

Only one informant was raised in a family where Disney was banned as unworthy trash – and was duly pitied by her peers for her fate. As for the norms of the Disney universe in general and the *Donald Duck* universe in particular, informants express a range of contradictions and a good many of them reflect on these inconsistencies. Clearly, the most obvious contradiction is that between their often negative evaluations as adults of Disney as a money-spinning industry and their positive descriptions of childhood pleasures. The informants often sum up their denigration of the Disney company by the term 'political correctness,' which covers what is perceived as narrow middle-class values based on individual success, a black-and-white view of the world, and an idealization of the nuclear family – all values that still reflect much critical discourse on the Disney company (for example, Bryman, 1995; Bell *et al.*, 1995; Giroux, 1997). To this list, some add gender stereotyping, while few remark on aspects of ethnicity.

Informants are well aware that their intellectual, adult evaluation conflicts with their reminiscences (and for some their continued fascination). The most prevalent tacit strategy in trying to tackle and overcome this contradiction is to equate the negative aspects not only with political correctness but also with 'Americanization' and 'the American way of life.' This leaves open a space for emotional and intellectual investment and negotiation, a space which most informants perceive not only as un-American but also as very Danish. This reflexive bifurcation, or oppositional logic, is most evident in the informants' remarks on the Disney protagonists. By far the most popular character is Donald Duck himself, who is singled out because of his unorthodox personality. He is 'politically incorrect,' 'hot-tempered,' and 'the world's most unlucky duck,' who 'behaves as wrongly as you can.' These traits are summed up by Sarah's introductory remark and by another informant, who says: 'Donald Duck I can relate to and perceive as Danish [unlike] the theme parks and the merchandise which belong to an American plastic culture.' Conversely, the least-liked figure is Mickey Mouse, who is perceived as 'Disney's nice boy,' as one 'always doing the right things – really sensible.' When Mickey is liked, it is because of the narratives involving mysteries and detection.

The informants' oppositional logic posits a binary opposition between Danish unorthodoxy and originality versus American correctness and superficiality. As noticed, in analytical terms this positioning may be understood as a means applied by the informants in an attempt to tackle the complexities of reception. Furthermore, through this process, the informants form and sustain their own cultural identities: they define what they see as being Danish through a process of contrastive validation to what they perceive as being American.

An additional, if less prevalent, strategy applied by the informants as adults involves a mode of reception that one may term 'ironic enjoyment.' This mode is used when watching cartoons, an engagement found more often with students of film and media studies than political science. Feature-length cartoons are brought out in both dubbed and original versions in Denmark, and the students insist on watching only the original versions, which they find more 'real' or 'sophisticated.' They will also parade Mickey Mouse rucksacks or T-shirts as a kitschy sign of their open attitude to popular culture. Thus, they inoculate themselves against sliding into a childish or naïve form of reception, while still being able to engage in the pleasures of the narratives and consumption.

Everyday Disney

Almost from its inception, Disney has been a household name to Danes. Since the late 1980s, however, Disney has become an everyday phenomenon in Danish children's lives, a change that has been brought about by daily or weekly TV shows, at least one yearly animated feature film, and, most importantly, the tremendous increase in the sale of videos and merchandise. It is in this context that the informants evaluate their childhood memories of Disney. And most prefer the past. They perceive the present market strategies as economic and emotional overkill, and as for the comic *Donald Duck*, some find the design 'more discount-like,' with more 'hyped' activity pages of quizzes, jokes and tests. It is regarded as bad taste to have the nephews roller-skate and use laptops. According to our informants, Disney should keep to the past, because Disney belongs to the past. As Jesper, aged 20, professes: 'They should return to the old style so that Disney can remain Disney for real. I do think this is the way to do it; it is a tradition, the institution of Disney, for me as for everybody else.'

The enjoyable ritual function of Disney reception, whether in its print or visual forms, is easily lost when Disney is ever present. In a period of ever-increasing competition in the juvenile media market, perhaps the most difficult conundrum for the Disney company to resolve over the next few years is how to keep up with the future without forfeiting their past.

'From all of us to all of you': the global and the local

The Walt Disney Company is perhaps the oldest and certainly the largest transnational media corporation for the young. Not unnaturally, economic and institutional perspectives have therefore dominated much of the more scholarly literature on Disney. Reading this literature, one could easily be led to the conclusion that the Disney corporation promotes a WASP ideology, exporting it as the all-American view of the world, and hence enhancing a cultural imperialism that tends to eliminate cultural diversity and discrimina-tion. In recent years, similar trains of thought may be found in the often heated debates around the notion of media globalization.

Within a research context, this is where the present project may serve an important function. By taking audience experiences from diverse localities as the point of analytical departure, we may refract the views both on culture and on the audiences that are often tacitly assumed or explicitly argued to exist in the literature on cultural imperialism and, indeed, on media globalization.

As regards culture, our analyses support the acknowledgement that there exists no neat dichotomy between national and international or global culture: at least parts of Disney lore are very much incorporated as aspects of the national media culture. The notion of national culture originates in a nineteenth-century conflation of peoples and places, and it is often called upon as an antidote to advancing industrialization. The term posits that it is possible to delineate a nation as a temporal and/or spatial entity and that this entity may be defined in contrast to what is not national, namely, international. Second, that it is possible to delineate culture as an essential category and a common feature of the nation's inhabitants. Third, that people take up and 'live' the national culture, i.e. that there is a fit between the official notion and the practices of a national culture.

Modern historiography has thoroughly deconstructed these pre-conditions (see, for example, Foucault, 1969; Hobsbawm and Ranger, 1992). Thus today, it is routinely acknowledged that to describe national culture is, in and of itself, a discursive intervention. Moreover, national culture is a contested and shifting process rather than an immutable entity. From this it follows that discourses of national culture are developed in relation to perceptions of other nations, other cultures. But while essentialist notions have been pried open for more processual forms of analysis, it seems important to stress the continued analytical relevance of national culture: to acknowledge the discursive nature of the concept does not necessarily imply a conceptual dissolution. Rather, such an acknowledgment may sensitize us to exchanges between national and international elements in defining a culture at a given historical moment. Furthermore, such an acknowledgement may alert us to incongruities between discourses and practices – what the Swedish ethnologist Orvar Löfgren terms Sunday and everyday culture (Löfgren, 1990: 87–89).

Of pertinence to the present project, we must distinguish between official notions of culture, which are invariably shaped by adults in power, and the understandings and interpretations made by children and young people through their everyday engagement with cultural processes and artifacts, including the media. This brings us to the second important notion, namely that of the audience. Scholars of cultural imperialism and globalization, speaking in terms of discursive dichotomies (global versus national or local), often infer distinctions of reception from differences of production: transnational or global forms of production are seen as unified forces enhancing homogeneous forms of reception, while national or local forms of production are seen as more heterogeneous in nature and hence advancing more diverse forms of reception. Inferences such as these are based on tacit assumptions, and little empirical evidence, of the audiences as duped; assumptions whose juvenile cousin is the innocent and defenseless child. As is evident from analyses of the Danish informants' memories, the Disney products have not been accepted wholeheartedly and without reservation, nor have they promoted a uniform acceptance of American values and norms. The picture is rather more muddled, the modes of reception more complex. At least in retrospect, the Disney products may have served as eye-openers to reflections about cultural identity.

A final point concerns the texts themselves. Disney products are what may be termed 'textually unmarked' by their origins: Disney comics are translated like other imported print media, and Disney cartoons are dubbed, unlike most other visual products (and many other cartoons), which in Northern Europe have subtitles, an explicit marker of 'foreignness' that even young children recognize. Translation and dubbing serve to enhance the 'naturalization' of Disney products.[9] Still, they possess visual markers, and a few informants speak about their surprise in recognizing, for example, barns and mail boxes from *Donald Duck* when first visiting the U.S.A. in adult life. For audiences outside of the U.S.A., reminders such as these may serve as a reflexive bond between mediated and non-mediated forms of culture, and in some cases as a bridge between juvenile and adult experiences.

Within a wider context of media globalization, then, comparative research carried out across nations or regions and taking the analytical perspective of the audience – and a juvenile audience, at that – serves to highlight that, even in what is perhaps the most closely guarded and

115

monitored media conglomerate in the world, so far globalization has implied differentiation based on local histories of production as much as it has implied homogenization. It has enhanced complexities of reception – and often reflection on these complexities – as much as it has ironed out cultural diversities. For future research, the central question remains: will this picture change once Disney becomes omnipresent, reaching children across the world?

Acknowledgment

The author wishes to acknowledge the financial support provided for this study by the Danish Research Council for the Humanities and the Department of Film and Media Studies, University of Copenhagen.

Notes

1. A total of 59 university students filled in the joint project questionnaire in November–December 1997 (32 men and 27 women aged 19 to 30, with an average age of 22 years and 24 years, respectively). Semi-structured, individual interviews were subsequently made with twelve of the students. All are students from the University of Copenhagen, studying either Film and Media Studies or Political Economy. Given the Danish pattern of further education, the majority of the respondents belong to the middle classes. All empirical data have been collected by cand.mag. Anne Mette Stevn, University of Copenhagen.
2. Today, the Egmont Group, comprising 110 companies in 27 countries, has five areas of production: Egmont Comic Creation (Serieforlaget), which is the largest publisher of comics in Europe; Egmont Books, which is the largest publisher of children's books in Europe, with a yearly output of over 60 million books; Egmont Magazines, which publishes 30 magazines in Scandinavia; Egmont Entertainment, encompassing videos, computer games, music and, increasingly, online services; Nordic Film and TV, established in 1992 with the purchase of the world's oldest film company, the Danish-owned Nordic Film (Nordisk Films Compagni). The turnover in 1997 was 6.8 billion Danish kroner (*c.* 1 billion U.S.$), an increase of 6.6 percent in one year (Balleby, 1998).
3. Already in 1931 Danish magazine readers were introduced to Mickey Mouse in a comic strip appearing in the family weekly *Søndags-B.T.*, while Donald Duck first made his bow four years later in *Dansk Famieblad* (Danish Family Journal) (Larsen, 1997: 177).
4. In 1996, Egmont had a 30 percent turnover growth in former Eastern Europe primarily based on successful expansion in Poland and Russia. At present, Egmont Comic Creation is one of the world's largest comic editorial offices, producing 5000 new pages per year. The basic material is

produced by approximately 50 freelance writers and artists around the world. In Copenhagen all material is collected, texts are translated into English and then distributed for re-translation into the 29 languages. Only special front pages are cleared with the Walt Disney Company in Burbank, California.

5. Other Disney print titles brought out in Denmark by the Egmont Group are as follows: *Donald Duck Extra* (*Anders And Ekstra*, 44 pages A4 format), a monthly version of *Donald Duck*, featuring more old stories and fewer non-fictional snippets (sales are dwindling); *The Steel Duck* (*Stålanden*, 96 pages B5 format), a monthly brought out since 1997 and featuring Donald Duck as superhero fighting hackers (previously published as part of the *Jumbo Books*) (stable sales with 66 percent male readers and 61 percent of the readership aged between 7 and 14) (*Juniornøglen* 1997/8: 57); *The Junior Woodchucks* (*Grønspættepatruljen*, 85 pages B5 format), a monthly featuring stories with Donald's three resilient nephews plus activity pages; *Uncle Scrooge/Adventure* (*Onkel Joakim/Eventyr*, 96 pages B5 format), alternating monthlies with dwindling sales and a content very similar to the *Jumbo Books* but with only a third of the pages for half the price; *Fun with Disney* (*Sjov med Disney*, 96 pages A4 format), published since 1986 as a reader and activity book; *The Golden Book* (*Guldbogen*, 96 pages B5 format), published every Christmas since 1994 and featuring only Barks classics; *Winnie the Pooh Magazine* (*Peter Plyds bladet*), the latest branch on the Egmont Disney tree, brought out since January 1998 and aimed at very young readers.

6. Figures of license holders include instances where a Disney commodity is produced by, for example, a Swedish license holder and distributed in Denmark, and also instances when a Danish firm distributes a Disney commodity to other Nordic countries for another license holder. Excluded are instances where a non-Nordic license holder distributes Disney products in Denmark.

As mentioned, the Egmont Group holds the most licenses from Disney Nordic, some of which are for merchandise distributed by Egmont Books such as diaries, stationery, and dress-me dolls. Egmont Books holds Disney licenses for the following categories (number of product items/titles in parentheses): activity books, including audio and picture books (252), children's games (20), children's puzzles (17), merchandise (29), music (107) (Hansen, 1998).

7. **Table 5.1** Chronology of Disney animated features in Denmark

Short title	First cinema release	Re-release	Cinema tickets sold	Video release	Video copies sold
Snow White	1938	1992		1994	190,000
Pinocchio	1941			1995	170,000
Fantasia	1941	1990		1991	10,000
Dumbo	1942			1990/7	115,000
Bambi	1943	1993		1994	115,000

Saludos Amigos	1944			
Make Mine Music	1947			
Fun and Fancy Free	1948			
Melody Time	1949			
Cinderella	1951	1991	1992	55,000
Alice	1952		1989	
Peter Pan	1954	1992	1992	55,000
Lady and the Tramp	1956	1997	1990/7	
Sleeping Beauty	1959	1995	1996	170,000
101 Dalmatians	1962	1995	1996	155,000
The Sword	1964		1993	45,000
The Jungle Book	1968	1993	1993	155,000
The Aristocats	1971	1994	1995	150,000
Robin Hood	1974		1994	110,000
Winnie the Pooh	1978		1997	85,000
The Rescuers	1978			
The Fox	1982			135,000
Mouse Detective	1987			120,000
Oliver & Co.	1989			125,000
The Little Mermaid	1990		1991	
The Rescuers Down Under	1991		1992/7	115,000
Beauty and the Beast	1992		1993	150,000
Aladdin	1993	550,000	1994	200,000
The Lion King	1994	1,000,000	1995	300,000
Pocahontas	1995	480,000	1996	180,000
The Hunchback	1996	432,000	1997	170,000
Hercules	1997	400,000 (est.)	1998	

Sources: Heinola (1998); Klarskov (1998)

In addition to the above titles, there are releases of video compilations as well as videos featuring, for example, the Little Mermaid or Aladdin in new narratives. The list also reveals that three Disney cartoons have never been released in Denmark: *The Three Caballeros* (1945), *The Adventures of Ichabod and Mister Toad* (1949) and *The Black Cauldron* (1985). This last title, however, had a video release in 1998.

8. According to Gregers Damgaard-Jensen, managing director of Buena Vista Home Entertainment, Denmark, the gains made today on a feature-length cinema cartoon represent only a tenth of the gains made from the sales of videos plus merchandise (Schelin, 1997: 1).

9. The Walt Disney Company in Burbank, California, is known to be very strict about accepting local voice castings, which in some cases call for serious negotiations with the casting directors. According to Kirsten Saabye, the director of Buena Vista Character Voices in Copenhagen, a voice 'must be similar to the American voice, but it must also work in Danish. It is important that the cinema audiences experience the movie as if it was drawn to be Danish' (Lahey, 1997: 10).

References and other sources

Bach, C. (1997) 'Rappe reklamer skal redde Anders,' *Politiken*, December 28.

Balleby, L. (1998) 'Interview with the marketing director of the Egmont Group,' *Søndagsavisen*, 14(6): 29.

Barker, M. (1989) *Comics: Ideology, Power and the Critics*. Manchester, Manchester University Press.

Bell, E., Haas, L., and Sells, L. (eds) (1995) *From Mouse to Mermaid: The Politics of Film, Gender, and Culture*. Bloomington and Indianapolis, Indiana University Press.

Bondebjerg, I. (1997) 'Fra biograf til hjemmevideo,' in I. Bondebjerg (ed.), *Dansk mediehistorie, vol. III: 1960-95*. Copenhagen, Samleren, pp. 200-43.

Bryman, A. (1995) *Disney and His Worlds*. London and New York, Routledge.

Buckingham, D. (1997) 'Dissin' Disney: critical perspectives on children's media culture,' *Media, Culture and Society*, 19(2): 285-93.

Christiansen, J. (1998) Personal interview with the marketing director of Egmont Comic Creation, January 26.

Danish Film Institute (1998) Archival information, Copenhagen.

Dansk oplagskontrol (1997) Copenhagen.

Dorfman, A. and Mattelart, A. (1975) *How to Read Donald Duck: Imperialist Ideology in the Disney Comic*. New York, International General.

Drotner, K. (1992) 'Modernity and media panics,' in K. Christian Schrøder and M. Skovmand (eds), *Media Cultures: Reappraising Transnational Media*. London, Routledge, pp. 42-62.

Drotner, K. (1995) *Mediedannelse: bro eller barriere? Om børns og unges mediebrug*. Copenhagen, Statens Information, Report to the Media Commission.

Foucault, M. (1969) *L'Archéologie du savoir*. Paris, Gallimard.

Giroux, H. A. (1997) 'Are Disney movies good for your kids?' in S. R. Steinberg and J. L. Kincheloe (eds), *Kinder-Culture: The Corporate Construction of Childhood*. Boulder, CO, Westview Press, pp. 53-67.

Hansen, O. (1998) Personal communication with managing director at Egmont Litas, Copenhagen, February.

Heinola, N. (1998) Personal communication with Danish marketing manager at Buena Vista International, February.

Hobsbawm, E. and Ranger, T. (1992) *The Invention of Tradition*. Cambridge, Cambridge University Press.

Juniornøglen (1997/98). Copenhagen, The Egmont Group.

Klarskov, J. (1998) Personal communication with Danish key account manager, Buena Vista Home Entertainment, January.

Lahey, S. (1997) 'Disney-dansk,' *Politiken*, Film Section, November 7.

Larsen, P. (1997) 'Striber og strimler,' in K. Drotner and G. Agger (eds), *Dansk mediehistorie, vol. II: 1880-1960*. Copenhagen, Samleren, pp. 167-80.

Löfgren, O. (1990) 'Medierna i nationsbygget: hur press, radio och tv gjort Sverige svenskt,' in U. Hannerz (ed.), *Medier och kulturer*. Stockholm, Carlssons, pp. 85-120.

Medieforskningen (1998) Personal information, Copenhagen, Danish Broadcasting Corporation.

Mietle, E. (1997) Personal interview with the managing director of Walt Disney Company Nordic, October 28.

Schelin, K. M. (1997) 'Kamp til stregen i Hollywood,' *Berlingske Tidende: Kultur*, 13(8).

Vilstrup, J. (1996) 'Krisehjælp til onkel Anders,' *Politiken*, July 31.

CHAPTER 6

France: Disney in the Land of Cultural Exception

JACQUES GUYOT

French people have long been acquainted with the world of Disney. In fact, Disney products appeared in France during the 1930s, along with other Hollywood film productions. Appearing on the screen before the long feature, Disney's cartoons used to be praised by movie viewers. Besides its audiovisual activities, the company also launched a series of children's magazines, which have entertained almost four generations of French people: *Le Journal de Mickey* in October 1934, *Mickey Parade* in March 1966, *Picsou Magazine* in February 1972, and *Mickey Poche* in April 1974.

Another French connection was the awarding of the Legion of Honor (one of France's top distinctions) to Walt Disney by the French consul in California in 1935 after his early success as a cartoon producer. Symbolically, his widow Lillian brought the medal back to Paris when Disneyland Europe was inaugurated in 1992.

Disney's success in audiovisual production can be explained by a number of reasons, but one seems especially important: Disney borrowed widely from the European fictional universe, thus anticipating what we could call 'world culture.' This was particularly true in France. Indeed, in 1929, the first musical short feature of the Silly Symphonies series was the clever illustration of the 'Skeleton Dance' by Camille Saint-Saëns. Other adaptations included *20,000 Leagues Under the Sea* (from the book by Jules Verne), *Cinderella* and *Sleeping Beauty* in 1959 (adapted from Charles Perrault and the brothers Grimm), *The Sword in the Stone* in 1963 (borrowing from the

Arthurian cycle, the legend of Merlin, the Enchanter), *Blackbeard's Ghost* in 1968 (inspired again by Charles Perrault, the brothers Grimm,[1] and the composer Paul Dukas), and *The Hunchback of Notre Dame* in 1996 (adapted from Victor Hugo's work).

Thus, thanks to a number of references to their own culture, French viewers are not in *terra incognita* when it comes to Disney products. But, at the same time, it is interesting that Disney has mainly recycled the imagination of other countries, like advertisers when they make television commercials. In the same way, Disney's heavy merchandising policy is often considered by the French to be unbearable and arrogant. From an ideological point of view, Disney has often been accused of conveying the 'American way of life' or of gently legitimizing American imperialism (Dorfman and Mattelart, 1975).

The Global Disney Audiences Project survey carried out in France reveals these tensions, contradictions and paradoxes.[2] But it also illustrates a general attitude towards American cultural productions, as people waiver between fascination and rejection, just as their parents and grandparents did when they discovered jazz music or American movies after World War II.

A few brief historical clues regarding the relationships between the U.S.A. and France in the field of cultural economy may help explain this attitude of suspicion. This discussion will be followed by a short inventory of Disney's audiovisual market in France, before commenting in detail on the French case study.

Audiovisual production: a cultural exception

Long before World War II, European countries had to face heavy film flows from Hollywood, and some of them adopted measures intended to protect their own film production. However, the dramatic human and economic consequences of war changed these priorities and momentarily put an end to such policies. While the negotiations about the Marshall Plan were being prepared, an agreement was signed in May 1946 between the French government representative, Léon Blum, and Secretary of State James Byrnes leading to a much more favorable situation for American movies which soon occupied nearly 70 percent of the French screens. In other words, the Americans managed to fix a quota that would have kept most of the French productions out of the cinemas.[3] In 1948, under the pressure of movie professionals backed up by a press campaign, the agreement was modified to increase the percentage of national films. The new official policy favored the French film industry and gave a second breath to the Centre National de la Cinématographie (CNC), created during the Vichy government.

Figure 10. The Disney Store in Paris, France. Photo: Carlos R. Calderon

The financial support was successful insofar as France remained one of the few countries (along with Italy and Germany) able to produce more than a hundred long features a year. More recently, in December 1993, the same attitude pushed the French to argue strongly for the exclusion of culture from the General Agreement on Tariffs and Trade (GATT). Specifically, Article 14 of the GATT explicitly defines the 'cultural exception.'

However, this effort to protect the so-called European cultural identity – a notion which is far from clear to many film directors and creators – cannot totally erase the effects of the internationalization of audiovisual markets. Thus, in 1997, American films accounted for 64 percent of the total receipts collected in European cinemas, with undoubtedly significant differences: 53.8 percent of the receipts in France versus more than 73.5 percent in the U.K. (CNC Info, 1999). When looking more closely at the French data, the situation is more worrying. In 1998, 449 new films were released: 171 with a French label, 160 from the U.S.A., 88 from Europe and 30 from other countries. However, a survey conducted over the first nine months shows that of the 28 films which were distributed in more than 300 cinemas, 20 were American and only 7 were French. A typical film is released in an average of 90 cinemas, but the figure rises to 161 in the case of American productions and drops to 61 for the French (Frodon, 1999).

The fact is that American audiovisual productions stand out in Europe, not only on movie screens but also on television and in the home video market. This is particularly true for the Disney company, which benefits both from a firmly established reputation and from a very active marketing strategy.

Disney audiovisual presence in the French market

Disney audiovisual products have a long history of distribution in France. Thus, it is not surprising that in the 1998 list of the most-viewed films in France since 1956, Walt Disney's feature-length animated films appear eleven times (see Table 6.1).

It is interesting to note that the older productions have maintained a successful and steady career. Three Disney animated features are among the top-ten films. For instance, the 1961 animated film *101 Dalmatians*, which was ranked eleventh until 1994, benefitted from the promotion of the new version, gaining more than 3 million viewers, and is now in fifth place.

Table 6.1 Overall film box-office rankings and tickets sold for Disney feature films in France

Rank	Title	First cinema release	Number of tickets in millions
3	*The Jungle Book*	1968	15,287
5	*101 Dalmatians*	1961	14,661
10	*The Aristocats*	1971	12,582
15	*The Lion King*	1994	10,123
33	*Aladdin*	1993	7314
37	*The Rescuers*	1977	7219
43	*The Hunchback of Notre Dame*	1996	6800
50	*Sleeping Beauty*	1959	6585
53	*Robin Hood*	1974	6473
66	*The Sword in the Stone*	1964	6134
92	*Pocahontas*	1995	5629

Source: CNC Info (1999)

Among the new productions, three films sold more than 1 million tickets in 1998. *The Hunchback of Notre Dame*, which was released in 1996, did quite well, with more than 1.5 million viewers; as for the live-action version of *101 Dalmatians*, it literally took off, with sales of almost 4 million tickets. More recently, *Mulan* was viewed by 4.5 million people. These films were heavily promoted in the media and through merchandising, and thus drew a large audience and appeared almost immediately on the French charts. The same was true for *The Lion King*, *Aladdin*, and *Pocahontas*, which were all produced and released within the last seven years.

As far as the video market is concerned, fifteen American movies were among the top 20 video sales in France in 1996. More importantly, the first five films released on video were produced by Disney (see Table 6.2), thus enhancing the success already enjoyed by these films in cinemas.

Table 6.2 Rankings of home video release of Disney animated films in France in 1996

Title	First cinema release	Video release
1 *101 Dalmatians*	1961	1996
2 *Pocahontas*	1995	1996
3 *Peter Pan*	1953	1996
4 *Sleeping Beauty*	1959	1996
5 *The Lion King*	1994	1995

Source: CNC Info (1998)

The 1997 data confirm that this trend is not just a passing fad: seventeen American movies are in the top 20 video sales, five of them for Disney (see Table 6.3).

Table 6.3 Rankings of home video release of Disney animated films in France in 1997

Title	First cinema release	Video release
1 *The Hunchback of Notre Dame*	1996	1997
2 *Lady and the Tramp*	1955	1997
3 *Toy Story*	1996	1997
4 *Oliver & Company*	1989	1997
5 *The Rescuers*	1977	1997

Source: CNC Info (1999)

Familiarity with Disney's fictional universe

Contrary to many surveys on political or socio-cultural issues, the respondents for the Disney questionnaire had very personal, documented and well-argued opinions, as well as extensive knowledge about Disney. This meant that all the questionnaires were thoroughly filled in, thus allowing comprehensive analysis. The 46 students who responded to the project's questionnaires unanimously showed that they were very familiar with Disney. Indeed, 100 percent of them had seen a Disney film, 87 percent had read a Disney book and 54.3 percent are regular readers of one of the company's magazines sold in France, while 50 percent had read Disney comics.

However, few of them rented videos (32.6 percent) and/or purchased them (24 percent). This phenomenon is obviously linked to the fact that this age group belongs to a generation that did not systematically own a home video recorder: ten years ago, only 30 percent of French households had a VCR. Undoubtedly, the situation is changing very quickly: in 1997, the equipment rate went up to more than 70 percent, which led to significant changes in the video market and people's audiovisual practices. Consequently, the sales of Disney video tapes took on considerable proportions: according to Buena Vista Home Entertainment, 3 million copies of *The Lion King* had been sold by the beginning of 1998 and *Pocahontas* accounted for 1,820,000 items. All of the older feature animated films are available in the Disney video catalog. As an example of their strong sales performance, *Sleeping Beauty*, one of the first Disney animated features, has sold 2,350,000 copies.

The favorite animated features among the interviewees were *The Aristocats*, *Cinderella*, *Sleeping Beauty*, and cartoons featuring Donald Duck. Most of the 46 students had recently gone to the movies to watch *The Lion King*, *The Hunchback of Notre Dame*, and *Pocahontas*. Although a basic knowledge of Disney's audiovisual world is mainly experienced through the cinema, the special television programs dedicated to cartoons, series and short excerpts from long features are also very popular. At least 60 percent of the sample watched the Disney Channel, which was broadcast on the third terrestrial channel between 1985 and 1989, or *Salut les Mickey* (1984), *Disney Parade* (1989), and *Disney Club* (1990), which were broadcast on TF1. More recently, the Disney Channel has been available on satellite and cable since March 1997, and 37 percent of the respondents watch it occasionally. Here again, France is still behind other countries in terms of network development, with only 1.6 million households (or 7 percent) linked to cable and 1.2 million (5 percent) owning a satellite dish.

The Disney products listed by the interviewees also corroborate these interests. Out of a total of 161 items they listed having contact with, 100 are directly linked to cultural productions, including 76 related to audiovisual activities (cartoons, cinema, television broadcasts, video and audio tapes, records) and 24 to books and comics. In the first category, cartoons were mentioned most frequently (58.7 percent), followed by cinema (45.6 percent). Other references were to theme parks (thirteen times), gadgets and trinkets (ten), educational items (ten), advertising (nine), and clothes (eight).

The 46 students first became acquainted with Disney materials around the age of 5, with more contact in their childhood (34.6 percent) than as teenagers (15.2 percent) or adults (10.9 percent). On the whole, they expressed a positive appreciation of Disney products, though their point of view varied considerably as they grew older: on average, 38 percent really liked Disney in their childhood, although 15.3 percent did not. This percentage shrinks drastically to 19 percent in their teens (versus 45.7 percent who disliked Disney products) and to 14 percent in their adulthood (versus 54.3 percent who held oppositional attitudes).

As we will see later, though the interviewees generally have good memories of the animated films, the Disney World is clearly identified as belonging to childhood. A 24-year-old female explained: 'It makes me think of my childhood.' Another 23-year-old woman added, 'I haven't seen [*Sleeping Beauty*] for a long time, but what I like today is the environment of the castle: everything's sleepy, the brambles, and so on. I still like the story of the princess, maybe because I'm still a little girl; it's like a child's dream.' A 20-year-old male said, 'In fact, when I was a kid, I was attracted by the cartoons, I would say any cartoon. But now, I think that Mickey is a very dull character, he's not very clever, his life is quite uninteresting.'

From leisure to business

The vast majority of interviewees had never been to a theme park abroad, and only 28.2 percent of the sample had visited Disneyland Paris since it opened in April 1992. This small number is very surprising, though the entertainment park was launched in very difficult circumstances. The intellectuals criticized it as an intolerable concession to American cultural imperialism and their campaign against what some of them called a 'cultural Chernobyl' or even the 'American nightmare,' was widely echoed by French newspapers. The convention signed between the French government and the Disney company triggered many negative reactions. It seems that Disney was granted particularly attractive loans from the state-owned Caisse des Dépôts et Consignations and a special high-speed train line and station were built to assist with transport to the park, which is situated about 20 miles from Paris. The unions mobilized against the way that people were hired and also against some of the terms of the labor contracts, among other things, Disney's grooming requirements (Lanquar, 1992). Then, questions about the economic viability of Disneyland Paris became an issue. After almost four years of substantial financial losses due to low attendance, Disney had to reduce its staff as well as its prices. In 1994, the company launched a campaign all over Europe, in an attempt to change the perception of the park. Disney was quite aware of the devastating effects of the financial problems, not just because it could ruin the whole project, but above all because it would focus people's attention 'on the park as a business organization to the detriment of the sense of fantasy the company is at pains to create' (Bryman, 1995: 80). This is consistent with Stuart Ewen's description of the political ideology of consumption: the reality of industrial labor must not appear in advertising, because it can only stain the visions of happiness projected onto the consumer's imagination (Ewen, 1977). Finally, in 1996, 11.7 million people visited Disneyland Paris, which meant profits for the first time.

The interviewees, however, clearly perceive the park as big business. One of the interviewees reported, 'What I remember above all is the commercial aspect. Everything is done to make you spend your money and they sell the same stuff everywhere.' In the same way, another explained, 'It's big business … As far as merchandising is concerned, it is incredible, all the shops they have. A good reason not to stay too long.'

Nevertheless, 71.8 percent of the sample own Disney merchandise, and 56.5 percent of them received the merchandise as a gift. Generally, the most favorite products are toys (63 percent), followed by clothes (32.6 percent), household items (26 percent) and collectibles (19.6 percent). The questionnaire shows that Disney products are readily available in shops and commonly used by the respondents.[4] However, the border between leisure and business is very thin and the systematic exploitation of the dream tends to tarnish the image of Disney, as discussed in the next section.

The perception of Disney 'imagineering' and marketing

As far as Disney media, products and services are concerned, there is a clear-cut distinction between perception of the audiovisual production and the business around it. Out of the 112 terms mentioned by the interviewees, 98 of them can be classified into five categories: (1) dream (25 words); (2) entertainment (19); (3) the world of childhood (20); (4) business and publicity (21); and (5) propaganda (13).

The words used in the first two categories are generally related to Disney's fictional world and globally reveal a very positive appreciation. The terms used included dream, fantasy, magic, imagination, funny, happy, amusing, and escapism. Respondents like Disney's animation skill as well as the narratives, as noted by a 24-year-old female student: 'Really superb, the graphics, the story, the sense of humor.' One of the male students commented that 'The cartoons are very technical, very up to date and easy to watch,' while another added, 'It is nicely drawn, the story is interesting.' All of them appreciated the structure of the narratives, based on the simple dichotomy between good and evil in which the young, good-looking and fair hero (or heroine) manages to triumph over the 'bad guys who are always punished' and the story ends happily.

The third category confirms that, for many people, Disney is primarily linked to children and thus benefits from a positive image. Words referred to in this category included childhood, souvenirs, good times, and simple morality. When asked what advice they would give a young couple with children, interviewees generally would advise them to show children the films, cartoons and videos, since they are good and creative products, full of 'fantasy and magic.' However, most of them would tell the parents to be careful, as the following examples of advice reveal:

> There are many other things to show children in order to open their minds. Keep going to Disney. [But] we must stop saying that Disney is a genius. When you compare *Hercules* to *Anastasia* by Warner Bros., Disney is way behind.

> I would tell them to look elsewhere, not to focus on Disney even if they advertise a lot. Disney is interesting in terms of dream for kids.

> We must teach children that what is shown on audiovisual media is not necessarily true … We must open their eyes if we don't want them to take what Disney says for granted.

This feeling of mistrust can be explained, on the one hand, by a rather traditional and legitimate idea of what culture should be like, namely, a plurality of experiences. On the other hand, it represents the Disney system itself, where audiovisual production and merchandising constitute the two sides of a deliberate marketing policy.

The fourth category focuses on the commercial dimension, which is considered as the least noble part of Disney's activities. As one student concluded, 'The business breaks the myth.' Business, heavy marketing policy, advertisements in the newspapers, on radio and television, bother many people. The word 'money' also is referred to quite often throughout the questionnaire: 35 percent mention it with a derogatory connotation ('easy money,' 'Disney is only interested in dough,' 'it's only a matter of making dough,' etc.). As a matter of fact, the pervasive merchandising policy exerted by Disney raises very negative reactions in a country where culture and business have been traditionally distinct fields of activity.

To illustrate this position, let's remember that in their attempts to mix culture and the economy, André Malraux and Jack Lang, who were both in charge of culture under two different governments over a 30-year interval, realized how difficult it could be for the French political system to take into account what the philosophers of the Frankfurt School called the cultural industries. In France, culture tends to remain a state business. In this sense, the 'cultural state' – to quote the title of a book from a sociologist who considers it as a modern religion (Fumaroli, 1992) – has two privileged organs in the educational system and television, but it generally extends its actions to every field related to literature, arts and even leisure. Within that context, people, whoever they vote for, tend to share this ideal conception of cultural productions as being the sole outcome of man's imagination. The responses to the questionnaire reveal this opposition between the world of creation and the logic of business. They also illustrate that the merchandisation of culture is not yet accepted by young people.

The fifth category may seem more surprising: thirteen question-naires explicitly mention words such as propaganda, manipulation, domination or influence. This represents 28.2 percent of the respondents in the sample. Here, these notions are directly linked to the idea that Disney exerts a cultural influence through its products. Indeed, their comments on the Disney vision of American culture represent very pessimistic points of view. Two other topics appear in these thirteen questionnaires – the standardization of cultural tastes and hegemony, as illustrated in two characteristic sentences from the questionnaire: 'Disney seems to contribute to cultural standardization all over the planet and takes advantage of the American economic hegemony;' and, 'Insofar as Disney is an international business company with hegemonic designs, Disney style tends towards universalism, i.e. a tasteless universalism where all the differences are erased, nothing shocking must appear, everything must be politically correct.' In this way, these responses confirm the opinion of those who point out that the anti-American attitude has not yet disappeared.

However, while 28.2 percent are hostile to Disney, another 47.8 percent think that although Disney is undoubtedly American, it is not necessarily a problem: 'Disney is American and is useful for the

American economy. It promotes typical American values like the family, but it also is universal in promoting values like love, magic and optimism.' One way or another, they believe that Disney conveys the American dream and an idealistic vision of life: many interviewees mentioned that Americans are optimistic and positive people and that Disney films echo this attitude. Thus, they clearly confirm the conclusion of the Dorfman and Mattelart (1975) study of Donald Duck, in which the authors pointed out that Disney did not just speak for the American way of life, but that it embodied the 'American dream of life.'

The reception of the 'Wonderful World of Disney'

When asked which values Disney encourages, a vast majority of the students focused on those expressing a paradisiacal vision of life and family (see Table 6.4). Magic, love and romance, good over evil, optimism and happiness, fun and family, fantasy and imagination, and bravery constitute the top-ten values that unambiguously define the 'Wonderful World of Disney.' Since Disney is dedicated to the celebration of an ever-enchanted children's universe, no wonder,

Table 6.4 Responses to the question assessing Disney values

Disney	Promotes	Discourages	Item does not apply
Love/romance	97.8	2.2	0
Magic	97.8	0	2.2
Good over evil	95.6	4.4	0
Optimism	93.4	2.2	4.4
Happiness	93.4	2.2	4.4
Family	89.1	0	10.9
Fun	89.1	4.4	6.5
Fantasy	78.2	4.4	17.4
Imagination	78.2	4.4	17.4
Bravery	76.0	4.4	19.6
Physical beauty	63.0	13.0	24.0
Respect for differences	54.3	17.4	28.3
Patriotism	47.8	13.0	39.2
Thriftiness	45.7	13.0	41.3
Technological progress	41.3	8.7	50.0
Work ethic	37.0	8.7	54.3
Patriarchy	36.9	19.6	43.5
Individualism	23.9	58.7	17.4
Racism	4.4	56.5	39.1

then, that these values appear to be widely chosen by the interviewees. It only confirms that Disney's marketing policy is well adjusted to its target.

However, this idyllic conception of life is tempered by other comments from the students. For instance, 43.4 percent of them think that Disney cartoons, films and parks reflect a caricatured and short-sighted vision of interpersonal relationships and human feelings: terms like 'childish,' 'simplistic,' 'naïve,' 'superficial,' 'idealistic,' or 'Manichean' are used several times.

On the whole, the answers show that people take Disney for what it is: a dream machine for children that can entertain the whole family. They are aware that Disney's success comes from the fact that the company anticipated what we call the globalization of culture. As an example, a 20-year-old student explained: 'As regards other cultures, Disney seems to offer a global vision of the world which goes beyond the American context.' Another student commented that 'Disney's universe can be adjusted to any culture, and I consider there is no antagonism with French culture or Japanese culture.' And yet another said, 'They haven't just created stories, but they took their inspiration in European tales and stories.' In this sense, Disney illustrates the phenomenon of cultural hybridity, which now tends to be a normal condition all over the world (Morley and Robins, 1995).

The questionnaires are interesting insofar as they provide interest-ing clues about the way people interpret Disney within their own cultural context. They also give substance to some theoretical works which have focused on encoding/decoding processes in media discourse (Hall, 1980), as well as those that analyze reception from an anthropological viewpoint (De Certeau, 1984).

By way of conclusion or the moral of the story

In the French case study, respondents often used the terms fantasy, imagination, magic and dreams. However, Disney was also repeatedly criticized because its world is too ideal, too disconnected from the problems of everyday life. Even though everyone expects a happy ending and children need to identify with a hero, Disney narratives, as well as the characters, are viewed as insipid, superficial and standardized. Many interviewees also pointed out the gap between the original tales and their audiovisual adaptations or cinematic representation ('it is too far from the original stories'). Generally, all the conflictual details are erased: for example, Frolot is the archdeacon in *The Hunchback of Notre Dame*, while he was a judge in Hugo's book. The stories and tales that inspire Disney are simplified and watered down in order to comply with 'American tastes and moral values.'

In many ways, Disney tales illustrate what Bettelheim (1976) noticed about modern tales, namely, that they were reassuring and avoided all the existential problems that give sense to life and help children grow up and mature: death, old age, etc. In other words, Disney stories prevent children from resolving, in a symbolic way, these problems and conflicts through the discovery of what Bettelheim describes as the inner turmoil of our mind.

Many people denounce Disney as an entertainment conglomerate which speculates on the exploitation of dreams and builds 'fictional towns.' But does this mean the end of the imaginary? At least, postmodernist philosophers think it looks like the simulacra of it:

> In both Disneyland and Disneyworld, it is clear that everything that can be derived from the imaginary has been caught, represented, made representable, put on display, made visual. Literally putting it on show for consumption without any metaphors is obviously a radical deterrent to the imaginary. (Baudrillard, 1993: 246)

The formula is brilliant and has the strength of an irrevocable and prophetic sentence. Undoubtedly, the power and interests of Disney are not pure fantasy and are reinforced through a new pedagogical and political interpretation of the history of other cultures (Giroux, 1995).

Despite Disney's tasteless adaptations of original works, despite this apparent loss of subjectivity and imagination, the last word is from one of the students who participated in this study: 'I think there are enough real places where you can dream, real magical places with real buildings, real characters and to my opinion, it is more interesting than just going to a Disney park.'

Notes

1. Published almost one and a half centuries apart, the *Contes du temps passé* (1697) by Charles Perrault and the *Kinder-und Hausmärchen* (1812) by Jakob and Wilhelm Grimm gather popular tales which were mostly collected in chapbooks. Many tales can be found in both books, including Cinderella, Bluebeard, Sleeping Beauty, etc.
2. The study included 46 students from the University of Rennes 2, in Brittany, France, who responded to the questionnaire. The 26 females and 20 males correspond to the sex distribution at the university. The respondents were between the ages of 18 and 24, with an average age of 20. Most of them belong to the French middle class. Five individual follow-up interviews were carried out. Frank Germaine, an MA student at

the Département des Sciences de l'Information et de la Communication, collected all the data and prepared transcripts of the interviews.

3. This event may explain the French resentment towards the Americans when the issues related to quotas were discussed within the GATT in 1993.
4. Because of time constraints, we could not prepare a market analysis of the Disney products distributed in France. However, it seems that most of the products available in France also exist in many other countries. Therefore, what would be interesting in the future is to assess the economic impact of Disney sales in France.

References and other sources

Baudrillard, J. (1993) 'Hyperreal America,' *Economy and Society*, 22(2): 243–52.

Bettelheim, B. (1976) *The Uses of Enchantment: The Meaning and Importance of Fairy Tales*. New York, Knopf.

Bryman, A. (1995) *Disney and His Worlds*. London and New York, Routledge.

CNC Info (1998) 'Bilan 1997,' Paris, CNC, No. 269.

CNC Info (1999) 'Bilan 1998,' Paris, CNC, No. 272.

De Certeau, M. (1984) *The Practice of Everyday Life*. Berkeley, University of California Press.

Dorfman, A. and Mattelart, A. (1975) *How to Read Donald Duck: Imperialist Ideology in the Disney Comic*. New York, International General.

Ewen, S. (1977) *Captains of Consciousness: Advertising and the Social Roots of the Consumer Culture*. New York, McGraw-Hill Paperbacks.

Frodon, J.-M. (1999) 'Vers le contrôle de la programmation des multiplexes,' *Le Monde*, January 30.

Fumaroli, M. (1992) *L'État culturel: essai sur une religion moderne*. Paris, Éditions de Fallois.

Giroux, H. (1995) 'Memory and pedagogy in the "Wonderful World of Disney:" beyond the politics of innocence,' in E. Bell, L. Haas, and L. Sells (eds), *From Mouse to Mermaid: the Politics of Film, Gender, and Culture*. Bloomington and Indianapolis, Indiana University Press, pp. 43–61.

Hall, S. (1980) 'Coding and encoding in the television discourse,' in S. Hall, D. Hobson, A. Lowe, and P. Willis (eds), *Culture, Media and Language*. London, Hutchinson, pp. 197–208.

Lanquar, R. (1992) *L'Empire Disney*. Paris, Presses Universitaires de France (Que sais-je?).

Morley, D. and Robins, K. (1995) *Spaces of Identity: Global Media, Electronic Landscapes and Cultural Boundaries*. London, Routledge.

CHAPTER 7

Greece: Disney's Descent on Greece: The Company Is the Message

SOPHIA KAITATZI-WHITLOCK
AND GEORGE TERZIS

Introduction: Disney in Greece

Since 1989 the Walt Disney International Company (WDIC) has developed a new and more aggressive foreign direct investment policy in Europe and adjacent regions. In line with this policy, and following a superb marketing strategy, Disney has started an extremely dynamic commercial phase in Greece, characterized by a focus on synergies and monopoly rights. Enormous profits are being made, whereas previously the company's products had predominantly consisted of printed material and films that reached only the major urban centers.

In this chapter we look at Disney's invasion of Greece from two angles. In sections I and II, Sophia Kaitatzi-Whitlock looks at the political economy of Disney and its impact on the cultural production of Greece, a small country (10 million inhabitants) with a rich cultural heritage and, until recently, with a relatively robust domestic cultural production. In this vein the sudden drop in local children's programing and magazine production and the displacement of local cultural forms are correlated with the 'total penetration' strategy of WDIC. The company's activities in Greece are mapped out in detail, particularly since the early 1990s, including the marketing strategies and tactics applied locally by the Disney subsidiary and its representatives. Moreover, these activities are placed in the wider deregulatory and conjunctural framework of the audiovisual policies of the EU.

In section III of this joint chapter, George Terzis examines the impact of Disney and the Disneyfication of culture from the reception angle, looking at local culture and social attitudes in Greece, and analyzing the responses from the project's questionnaire and in-depth interviews. In this way, the reaction of the interviewees to the domination of the Disney products is foregrounded. This combined analysis documents what we perceive as a 'Disney-mania' in Greece in the 1990s. The two strongest elements of this are: first, the defense of Disney products by Greek youth (our respondents), and second, the proliferation of Disney images on locally manufactured products in daily use.

The Disney company in Greece

Disney's arrival

The first appearance of a Disney image in Greece was in 1931 on the cover page of the children's magazine, *The World of the Child*. Four years later, in a weekly periodical called *Children's Encyclopedia*, Mickey Mouse came to rival Karagiozis, the wily, sulky, and self-derogatory anti-hero of traditional Greek shadow-theatre, and ever since then, the odds have been against Karagiozis. In 1935, Disney cartoon images also appeared on the back page of *Tam-tam*, a local cartoon magazine,[1] and in the same year, Mickey Mouse arrived in Greece in cinematic form (Malandrakis, 1998).

Towards 1950, when the upheaval caused by World War II and the civil war was not yet quite over, Mickey Mouse achieved his first autonomous appearance in print in the country of ancient myths and legends.[2] A more organized appearance in the print market began in March 1956. By 1964 those rare and still innovative, or at least 'different,' images and stories circulated in the periodical *Laughter and Happiness* (Ypsilon, 1982). Significantly, by that time, the periodical had been renamed *Mickey Mouse*, and included comics and short stories devoted only to that character. As we shall see, this exclusivity was decisive for the soaring career of this new hero in Greece. It is noteworthy that the name 'Mickey Mouse' tended to be used as a generic term for any strip cartoon.

As the prospects for these imported images looked promising, the rights were bought by Terzopoulos publishers, who have continued ever since to publish an array of Disney print products. These include a weekly and monthly periodical with an annual 'Super Mickey' edition. The stories were dispatched to Greece by the Italian mega-publisher, Montadori,[3] after prior supervision by the metropolitan Disney company, and subsequently translated and adjusted 'to the flavor of the Greek reader' for better domestic circulation (Ypsilon, 1982).

The Disney market in Greece in the 1990s

More recently, WDIC has taken the local cultural economy by storm, largely thanks to the externally imposed liberalization and privatization of the audiovisual sector in 1989, the year of the EU's Television without Frontiers policy.[4] The liberalization momentum was further boosted by the Uruguay round of the GATT negotiations and the final GATT agreement of December 15, 1993. In principle, this agreement covered all audiovisual services (Kaitatzi-Whitlock, 1996).

Thus, currently, in the Greek-speaking market (which includes Greece and the Republic of Cyprus), the complete range of Disney products can be accessed on a massive scale.[5] Notably, there are four major categories of Disney products supplied in Greece: (1) theatrical films, represented by Pro-O-ptiki, as well as video films for sale or home rental, distributed by Audiovisual Enterprises; (2) television programing broadcast by Tiletypos, owner of Mega Channel;[6] (3) magazines, books and booklets with Disney stories formatted for children, imported by Terzopoulos publishers; and (4) licensing of Disney images by the Walt Disney Company, the only company with the status of a WDIC subsidiary, which is situated in Phaliron, Athens. The others are independent companies representing WDIC interests (Himonas, 1997). Mega Channel, a private nationwide channel with some of the highest viewer ratings, has an exclusive contract and broadcasts TV programing purchased directly from the Disney subsidiary in London. Film and video distributors, Pro-O-ptiki and Audiovisual Enterprises, respectively, represent the Italian-based WDIC distribution division of Buena Vista International. A closer look at both companies is presented in the next sections.

THEATRICAL FILMS: PRO-O-PTIKI

Pro-O-ptiki represents Buena Vista International in Greece, which involves yearly contracts with cinema owners that reserve blocks of time for WDIC films, based on their anticipated success (Souganidou, 1998).[7]

In Greece, the cinema-going tradition – part of the Mediterranean outdoor lifestyle – developed in a way that led to the establishment of separate open-air cinemas for the summer season, which became part of the local romance of summer cinema-going. This meant that ordinary cinemas were not equipped with air-conditioning. So, what in the U.S.A. is a twelve-month season lasted essentially only nine months in Greece. Thus, the yearly output of the Hollywood industry had to be condensed into this shorter season, which necessarily imposed a different marketing strategy. Even box-office hits were shown for shorter periods and then were rerun during the open-air cinema season (Souganidou, 1998; Dermentzoglou, 1997).

This century-long local mode of cinema life survived the first cinema crisis of the 1980s, but is now being sacrificed to the gods of rationalized marketing.[8] To fully exploit film screenings, WDIC and other Hollywood suppliers have demanded the elimination of this 'natural' local tradition. Unable to resist, most theater owners have had to equip their establishments with air-conditioning facilities to lengthen the cinema season into the summer. This 'homogenizing' policy means that new films may now be launched in Greece even in the summer, which has the added marketing advantage of reaching schoolchildren during their summer holidays.

In the past, penetration of films in Athens and the major urban centres was high in comparison with provincial towns and rural areas. Athens remains the stronghold, with 57 to 58 percent of the total number of tickets sold in the country, followed by 13 percent in Thessaloniki, and 22 to 23 percent in the rest of the country; the remaining chunk, 7 percent of the total, is absorbed by the Cypriot market (Souganidou, 1998). Consequently, the greatest incursions and the new gains for Disney were achieved in the provinces. The weekly program, *Disney Club*, transmitted by the private operator Mega Channel, emerges as the obvious new 'Disneyfying' agent with respect to this change in the 1990s. Since Athens occupies the major chunk of the market, it sets the tone for a national marketing strategy and provides the prognosis for a film in the rest of the country. When a film is successful in Athens, it is usually successful country-wide, as well as internationally. There is no case of a global blockbuster which has failed in Athens, or vice versa. Although the policy of Pro-O-ptiki is to arrange concurrent showings in the major cities, this is not always possible, as some provincial towns have only one cinema or no cinema at all (Souganidou, 1998).

As Irene Souganidou, the Managing Director of Pro-O-ptiki, underlined, 'the cinematic market as such is presenting a marked increase over the last three years.' Since television transmits second-rate films, the cinema industry has had to reorient its supply strategy. Souganidou explained further that 'this policy by private TV channels has made us stop bringing second-rate films.' And it is this 'obligatory' selectiveness in terms of quality that accounts largely for the observed revival of the cinema industry. These changes also increased Disney's market share in Greece, both absolutely and relative to its local and international competitors. During the last few years, the market share of Disney films has been a remarkable 32 percent of ticket sales. Of the average 9 million cinema tickets sold annually, one-third is for Disney films.[9]

Tickets sales for Disney films have increased because of the overall tendency for growth in this market. Moreover, the recent introduction and successful operation of multiplex cinemas in Athens and Thessaloniki has greatly enhanced the cinema market and, of course, the possibilities for profits for Disney films (Souganidou, 1998; Himonas, 1997).[10] Consequently, despite the overall growth of the Greek audiovisual market, it is evident that Disney's own share has grown at the expense of its competitors, such as 20th Century-Fox or Sony. The disproportionate and speedy growth of Disney is thus attributable to its sharp competitiveness in marketing and promotion.

The cost of a cinema ticket in January 1999 was 1800 drachmas ($6). After taxes are deducted, this amounts to 1400 drachmas. About half of this amount, or 700 drachmas per ticket, goes out of the country as pure profit to the foreign companies or exporters, such as Disney. The commission that local distributors earn varies between 10 and 14 percent, depending on the deals that can be struck with each company. As a powerful player in the market, Disney offers a 12.5 percent commission to its Greek distributor (Souganidou, 1998).

As a vertically structured and multinationally oriented company, Disney can hardly overlook the matter of translating and subtitling. So, a special Disney division deals exclusively with the dubbing and subtitling of films and videos, contracting local artists and studios for these services (Himonas, 1997). The Disney company coordinates and supervises meticulously this post-production phase, which results in two versions of each film: one with Greek subtitles and one dubbed. Greek audiences, allegedly, prefer dubbed to subtitled copies, especially as popular actors from the domestic star system are used for dubbing. In the case of *Hercules*, for instance, nine out of ten copies of the film were dubbed (Dermentzoglou, 1997).

A film is usually booked for 5 to 6 weeks, but after that, continues to run on weekends for children in matinee shows. For the best-selling films, Pro-O-ptiki contracts 20 theaters in Athens (with 4 million inhabitants), and 10 in Thessaloniki (approximately 1.3 million inhabitants). Not surprisingly, then, over the last three years, animated features were among the ten best-selling films of the year. *The Lion King* sold 270,000 tickets and *Pocahontas* 220,000 tickets in the Athens area alone.[11]

But, however lucrative the cinema branch of the Disney company, it is far from the most profitable Disney division in Greece, as Souganidou points out:

Due partly to the costs involved in the distribution of films, including promotion and the hire of theaters, our division comes in third position in terms of revenues for the company in the Greek market. This is way behind the merchandising division and the video distribution which comes second.

So out of the four Disney divisions, by far the most profitable cash cow is that of licensing rights, which indeed provides exponential growth.

HOME VIDEO: AUDIOVISUAL ENTERPRISES

Although the copyright period for screening films in Greece normally lasts for five years, WDIC forbids the showing of its films in cinemas after the end of the first year. This constitutes a particular Disney policy. Accordingly, the company requests that its distributor destroy existing film copies after this period of time (Dermentzoglou, 1997). The objective of this remarkable practice is to be able to recycle the same product in the video format in order to generate more profits.

The Athens-based company, Audiovisual Enterprises, deals with the sale and rental of Disney videos, which attract huge revenues. Overall, Disney video sales grew by 75 percent in 1994, and in 1995 reached 120 percent, nearly doubling its previous increase. The rental of videos also grew impressively in the first quarter of 1996, increasing by 62 percent compared with the equivalent quarter of 1995 (*Disney News*, 1996: 9). *101 Dalmatians*, in fact, was reported to have sold as many video copies as cinema tickets. The company explains these successes by referring to 'the classical Disney virtues,' but acknowledged that a 'framework advertising campaign' was also applied. The latter included, among other things, contests offering various prizes such as two real Dalmatians. Thus, in terms of revenue growth rates, the video segment of Disney substantially supersedes the successes of the film division, which, of course, vindicates the Disney policy of scrapping film copies after their first year of exhibition. But this is not the end of the success story for Disney in Greece.

TELEVISION PROGRAMING: THE MEGA CHANNEL

The Disney Club is an hour-long magazino aimed primarily at children, shown on the Mega Channel on Saturdays at 8.55 a.m. and on Sundays at 9.05 a.m. The program typically consists of short trailers that refer to the events that follow the showing of a Disney feature film. It also consists of silly talk between the program presenters, Likourgos and Carolina, and guests. The presenters may also stage minor contests, which involve audience tele-participation in memory and observation tests, and quizzes. More often, participants have to remember the names of heroes or other details of the screened trailers and video clips. The idea is that the 20 guests (6 to 14 years old), as well as the viewers, have fun with the Disney characters (Whitlock, 1998).[12] *The Disney Club* has been broadcast for about five years now, always with the same presenters but with a different setting each year. For example, the first one was a big wooden boat, then a jungle, then a 'Magic Room,' followed by a setting with walls decorated with Disney heroes and images.

The fact that Mega Channel broadcasts Disney programing on a monopoly contract provides two obvious mutual advantages: competition is eliminated for the channel, and piracy – an endemic problem for MPEAA members in most foreign markets – can be controlled more easily by Disney. According to the ratings company, AGB, the program regularly receives high ratings.

LICENSING/MERCHANDISING

The products sold from the Disney base in Phaliron, Athens, are the licensing rights to print Disney images, and manufacturers compete fiercely to acquire these rights. During a three-year period ending in mid-1998, at least 4000 different products carrying Disney images appeared in Greece. Since the establishment of the Disney company in Athens, the annual rate of growth in this market has been between 40 and 50 percent (Himonas, 1997). While Disney receives a percentage of the revenues earned by the licensees, precise economic data are not regularly disclosed.

Given the guaranteed demand and profitability for these products, the question is how Disney selects its prospective licensees: 'The criteria for selection and approval of a licensee are market viability, strength, profile, good image and the attractiveness of its products' (Himonas, 1997). Thus, Disney ultimately selects its contractors according to their commercial viability. A close business relationship subsequently begins between the two parties:

> We deal directly with companies. These may be producers of books, magazines, paper goods, publishers, but also manufacturers of toys, clothing or other constructions. The company directs the licensee on how to project and apply images on their products by issuing elaborate guidelines. Subsequently, it approves their business plans. (Himonas, 1997)

Among the 4000 different products currently carrying Disney images, the most common items are toys, clothes and school products. Even though Disney films are promoted as 'family entertainment,' it is quite evident that 'the licensee merchandising predominantly targets age groups ranging from zero to 12- to 15-year-olds' (Himonas, 1997). This suggests that the industry is targeted at children and youth. Indeed, this trend is repeated in the cinema, where the largest percentage of viewers are between 15 and 25 years old (Souganidou, 1998).

Of all the Disney products in Greece – feature films, videos, television programs, printed material such as books and magazines, and licensing – the most profitable, by far, has been licensing, or the sale of rights for Disney images carried on other products. Since 1993, licensing has been growing by a huge 40 percent each year, thus becoming the greatest revenue source for Disney, at zero cost to the company, and conversely, the greatest capital flight from the Greek economy.

However, the three-year-old Disney company in Greece is merely a service company for the headquarters in Paris, which makes it difficult to gather specific economic data about the exact quantity of sales and the precise amounts of profits from merchandise made and sold in Greece.[13] Annual reports from the Paris office cover the broad region of Southeast Europe, the Middle East and Africa, and thus precise country-based data are virtually unobtainable. Evidently, this novel practice, which obstructs transparency and regulatory control of corporate practices, belongs to the spoils offered to multinationals by globalization. Yet, in spite of the growing market in licensed products, the Greek market represents only 50 to 60 percent of the sales in a comparable northern European market, such as Belgium (Himonas, 1997). In other words, despite the Disney-mania evidenced by merchandise sales since 1994, Greece is still an immature market, with a measure of what might be dubbed as 'Disney-illiteracy.'

PRINTED MATERIAL

About 35,000 Disney magazines are sold per week in Greece (Malandrakis, 1998), which represents the average of all magazines sold in the country fifteen years ago (Ypsilon, 1982). Meanwhile, 3 million copies of comic-strip booklets are sold annually, mainly by Terzopoulos publishers. Other companies that publish Disney material in Greece are Minoas, Elaphaki and Psychogios. Moreover, there are several specially designated Disney Stores in the country – usually located in the lobbies of cinemas – and thousands of ordinary kiosks selling Disney periodicals and booklets.

Seen in this light, the special attention traditionally afforded to the child within the family-centred Greek society seems to have been astutely ambushed, as the sensitivity and adoration for children will increasingly have to be filtered through Disney's commercial ingenuity. In this sense, a joyful trait of Greekness has revealed itself as an Achilles' heel and the Greek way of life has produced a perfect breeding ground for a strategic incursion of WDIC into the Greek market.

Disney's marketing strategies in Greece

But the marketing strategies of the Disney company in Greece need even further attention. As Souganidou explains:

> Synergy is a big weapon for Disney. We cooperate closely with the other divisions in the country, particularly with Mr Himonas. We coordinate our moves so as to exploit from the advent of new characters and to launch these for the activity of the licensing division. Products have to come in the right timing for the incoming film to be promoted appropriately. We may even launch a common promotion scheme about a film or the applications that new characters can take on products. It is furthermore arranged that some merchandise be sold at cinemas while promotional leaflets about films are delivered with some of the merchandising, thus we exchange among us our target groups. (Souganidou, 1998)

The full exploitation of every possible synergy – a strategy whose importance cannot be overstressed for Disney – and the control of monopoly rights, is the dual marketing strategy which emerges from WDIC operations in Greece.[14] Since Europe represents the world's most lucrative market for Hollywood products, Disney's marketing policy for Europe is crucial (Kaitatzi-Whitlock, 1996).

At least one year to six months before the screening of a film, its arrival is announced in the media, thus creating anticipation among cinema-goers. For instance, the première of *Hercules*, which was scheduled for Christmas 1997, was announced eighteen months in advance and media reporters were shown its trailers in early 1997 (Dermentzoglou, 1997). This policy suggests that long-term preparation and targeting of audiences over an extended promotional phase is paramount. During this time, small pieces of information are incessantly fed into the media, thereby keeping the company brand in the limelight. According to Souganidou, this is an indispensable strategy.

Another common marketing ploy includes the emphasis on Disney films as 'family entertainment.' This market-supplied view – however plausible prima facie – is problematic on a number of counts. One may wonder whether it is grown-ups who are being infantilized or children who are being treated as sophisticated grown-ups. Notwithstanding a critical analysis of this company slogan, its constant repetition seems to have contributed to two box-office successes in Greece in a single year. As Dermentzoglou (1997) explains 'two animation films by Disney becoming blockbusters in one year is historically unprecedented.'

The timing of Disney releases is an important strategy of the company. A Disney rerun or minor film is scheduled at the beginning of the cinema season to keep the brand alive in cinemas, as well as in the press. At Christmas, the latest films are introduced, when children are on vacation and wage-earners receive what is known as the thirteenth salary, their Christmas bonus. Products associated with the film are sold at kiosks and bookstores, further reinforcing the commercial propaganda machine. Around the same time, rumours are occasionally spread about Disney setting up a theme park in Athens.[15] So the Disney films descend on the market armed with the maximum publicity and promotion (Dermentzoglou, 1997).

Placing Greece in a European context, one can observe the even broader synergies achieved by the Disney company. Synergy with the company's theme park in Europe, Disneyland Paris, is well organized, both with the other divisions and with tour operators. Though Disneyland Paris was unprofitable at first, it has recovered due to a number of reasons, including tour tickets offered in contests and publicity sprees aimed at Disney fans in Greece, as well as the rest of Europe.[16]

Even Disney's obsession with adapting and distorting ancient myths and legends has been seen as instrumental for its marketing purposes. Why do Disney scriptwriters alter the classics? Is it to fit them into their *sui generis* genre, or to subject them to their 'happy ending at all costs' recipe? (Millar, 1997).[17] Arousing attention *per se* has recently been the goal of a number of publicity campaigns, which gives credence to the view that 'even the altering of the classical myths and tales may be a marketing ploy by Disney' (Dermentzoglou, 1997).

A variety of tactics appears imperative for the promotion of Disney films. Dermentzoglou (1997) explains the strategy used for film reviewers: 'A common commercial practice consists in the offer of gifts. This accepted form of bribery further oils the promotional machinery.' Evidently, this practice replaces honest film reviewing, as Disney films are then presented systematically in a positive and enticing light, thus blurring the boundary between advertising and criticism. According to Himonas, journalists also receive (in indirect ways) free trips and tickets to Disney venues, such as Disneyland Paris or film festivals, as well as expensive drinks. The aim is for journalists to write anything positive regarding the making of the film, the new technologies used, computer animations, the color of the scaffolding, the size of the budget, the anniversary of Disney, the peculiarities of a show, etc. If nothing else can be found to keep the Disney brand in the public eye, 'pseudo-events,' such as Disney's 75th anniversary in 1998, become useful. In this way Disney has achieved its treatment by the media as a celebrity. Along with the huge profits that these practices help to generate, an uncritical approach to entertainment is promoted.

The impact of Disneyfication on local creation

As noted previously, Disney's presence in Greece before 1989 was marked mainly by periodicals, booklets and relatively few cartoons that appeared mostly in the cinemas of the capital and a few major cities. There were no animation studios to speak of in the country until the mid-1980s, although some good quality in-house children's programs were produced by the Greek public service channels. Animation was also shown on these channels, imported from countries such as Sweden, the Netherlands, France, as well as Eastern European countries, such as Hungary, Poland and Bulgaria, where there is a strong tradition of animation production.

In 1988 the EU launched a biennial pilot project 'Measures for the Encouragement of the Development of the Industry of Audiovisual Production' (MEDIA), aimed to boost the European television-programing industry in view of future global competition. MEDIA contained a specific program called CARTOON, which addressed the animation segment of the market. CARTOON aspired to 'forward the development of animation techniques and to develop production capacity,' and therefore aimed to create a network among European animation studios by setting up organizational and financial tools to help start new projects (Kaitatzi-Whitlock, 1993, 1996). In addition, the notorious European programing quotas were supposedly aimed at boosting demand for local production in the new private channels. However, it seems obvious that MEDIA brought about too little too late, as competition was already *ante portas* long before the EC could counteract it.

Indeed, demand did rise enormously, but, alas, not for locally produced children's fiction, animated or not. Demand by TV channels for available domestic productions was nil. At best, animation studios were hired by the new channels that appeared after 1989 to produce motion picture logos or trailers (lasting only for seconds) to link diverse programs (Kostopoulou, 1998).[18]

Demand for locally produced children's fiction and TV programing was thus effectively pre-empted by unequal competition in the post-1989 era. New channels, in their struggle to survive, put out quantities of cheaply imported, ready-made products. Thus, despite the efforts of the MEDIA project to encourage local animation, channels effectively ignored local culture, quality and diversity.

Animation production, furthermore, is particularly susceptible to what is known as 'cost disease.'[19] Animation involves a large number of unique drawings, created by highly experienced artists, involving a lot of trial and error before the final product emerges (Maltin, 1980). This means production costs cannot easily be borne by a small linguistic market such as Greece.

Even if this difficult and expensive product is available in abundance in the local market, it still cannot be competitive. The average Hollywood film can be launched on the market for about 15 percent of its European equivalent purchasing value (Vasconcelos, 1994). This is largely due to economies of scale, but also to the structure of the U.S. copyright system, and the extreme rationalization of production and productivity gains of the Hollywood studios, spelling doom for film production, especially of children's programming, in other countries with minor or barely competing markets.

'We reject numerous [commercially] medium-rate films on behalf of the viewers,' stated Irene Souganidou. This statement confirms the common practice of effectively censoring quality films that may falter commercially – that is, they will not draw a mass audience. Conversely, the cinema films selected will be, commercially, in the lowest common denominator category. Exhibition in cinemas becomes prohibitive for smaller local production studios and also for less profitable artistic films. As a result of this intense competition for cinemas and because of the investments that Greek cinema owners have had to make to secure their businesses in the new era, they also have to accept only high-return films (or, blockbusters). This means locally produced films, particularly those with an anticipated middle-range popularity, come in a very poor second.

Thus, the Disney incursion, and the way it took place, has severely hampered existing cultural entrepreneurs and businesses and is likely to pre-empt future investment in the Greek film industry. Small local studios cannot possibly compete with the global Disney giant, with its high levels of R&D investment, and its vertical concentration, consolidation and its accompanying fierce strategies. Furthermore, unlike in previous decades, Disney today is omnipresent and all-pervasive. As the discussion in the following section shows, Disney has slipped easily into contemporary Greek mythology, and is now taken for granted. Unfortunately, its success also has meant the domination of the small number of distribution outlets in Greece, as well as the potential for the virtual extinction of local creativity.

The Disney audience in Greece

Introduction

In previous academic discussions, critics have suggested that Disney products exhibit a number of characteristics. These criticisms have included racism, imperialism, greed, arrogance, as well as the accusation that they are patronizing and glamorizing, distorting European cultural heritage, and promoting American 'virtues' of opportunity and individualism, effortless problem-solving, a work ethic and macho stereotypes (Schiller, 1973; Berland, 1982; Real, 1977; Trites, 1991).

In the second part of this chapter, we would like to abandon the concept of Disney products as a set of strategies of cultural imposition that ignores the way in which hegemony operates through a resignification of the knowledge and habits of people (García Canclini, 1990). As stated by Martin-Barbero (1993: 27), 'this implies reconceptualizing the interaction between the hegemonic messages and the codes perceived by each person, the different experiences that, working through fragments and shifts, remake and permanently recreate cultural heterogeneity.' To do that, a new strategy of inquiry needs to be employed, applying not only a top-down investigation but also an equally important bottom-up approach.

Thirty university students from Greece completed the project's questionnaire and five in-depth interviews were conducted. Three main criteria were used in the selection of the interviewees: different subjects of specialization (which in Greece usually implies different educational levels), different socio-economic backgrounds and different places of origin (born and lived in various regions of the country). These criteria were chosen specifically to reflect a variety of media reception.

Discussion of survey results

INITIATION

One of the striking results of the responses to the questionnaire is that all the interviewees had come into contact with Disney at an early age by watching Disney videos. A small sample of interviews with the students' parents (seven couples) revealed structural reasons for their children's early exposure to Disney products. At least one of the reasons was the clash of the parents' business life with the responsibilities of parenthood. For instance, Disney videos served as a convenient baby-sitting aid, which substituted for reading and explaining an original myth or book, taking a walk, etc.

147

RETURN TO CHILDHOOD, ESCAPISM

All of the respondents attributed their affection for Disney products to feelings of relaxation, satisfaction and nostalgia for childhood. One of the most common comments was: 'These movies make me feel like a child again.' One of the more explicit comments was: 'I like it because when you watch cartoons you become a kid again. Personally, I like experiencing again and again every feeling that I had as a child and that is why I still like cartoons. I want to feel happy, I want not to think of anything, I want to believe that everything is all right.' Another interviewee elaborated: 'It is a fact that Disney cartoons are carrying with them my whole childhood. Every time I watch them, I remember myself at that age.'

Almost all of the respondents said that Disney products transported them to a colorful dream world, with happy endings, where good guys always win and love always prevails. Indeed, the most common terms attributed to their Disney experiences were imagination, joy, laughter, jauntiness, suspense, bright colors, and happy endings. Our respondents saw these attributes as positive, and considered laughter and fun necessary for their lives.

Most of the respondents were aware of the traits attributed to Disney by critics. According to their responses, Disney creates a world where success is never a matter of hard work, but either accidental (for example, Mickey always wins because of accidental circumstances), or a matter of exploiting the right opportunity (treasure hunting being the most popular one), or being born a genius (like the Disney character of the inventor). Furthermore, it is a world where poor people/animals do not exist, people/animals do not age, and where there is no social conflict.

REPRODUCING SOCIAL STEREOTYPES

The interviewees' expectations from Disney film characters were strikingly similar. Most of them expect a fairy tale with a hero endowed with great strength and magical abilities, who stands for fairness and tries to help people/animals who are in danger, and puts the bad guys in jail. The heroine is expected to be a pretty woman with long blond hair. The responses differed slightly for male characters, as interviewees thought they varied much more than the female characters. One respondent explained: 'Goofy, for example, has almost nothing in common with Scrooge. It is not like heroines where you could say that most of them come out from the same mold.'

The Disney classical cartoon heroines represented, according to our respondents, the stereotypes of the housewife or the girl who is interested in looking nice for her boyfriend. She has some feminist views, but never applies these views to her life. She is always in the shadow of the main hero. One of the respondents said: 'They are talking about pie recipes and how their boyfriends are jealous.' Another one added: 'She also needs to be saved by the hero. She needs to be protected... Female characters in Disney simply exist, they do not have powerful roles, they do not change things. You notice them because they are the heroes' girlfriends, but their role is complementary.'

One of the interviewee's explanations of the stereotypes is quite instructive:

I think Disney products promote the mainstream stereotypes, although they do it in a very cute way. All the characters represent one stereotype. They are quite one-sided: they are either smart, or stupid, or clumsy. But in real life, people do not have only one of those characteristics. People have two or three or many more of those characteristics. But you have to follow these patterns in children's storytelling for the economy of the story and the understanding of the audience.

However, some of the other respondents were more critical:

I do not want to sound like a feminist, because I am not, but the characters Disney creates are very mainstream. They are couples who have straight relationships. Girls are interested in clothes and putting on good make-up or going to the hairdressers. Kids are always having fun, there is a rich bad guy and a poor good guy. There is a smart guy who looks like a nerd, who also does not have any other relationships or friends apart from his machines. These are the stereotypes that I do not like because they go into your mind, and you have this stereotypical-mainstream image about life, and this is so typical of American culture.

While respondents were aware of the fictitious world represented by Disney and documented by critics, they either doubted that they were adversely influenced by it or had never thought about the possibility of negative influences before. Our interviewees did not agree with the group of the critics, and in their replies to the open-ended question 'What did you or do you like/dislike about Disney?', no one immediately gave a negative answer. Indeed, some of the interviewees first explained that Disney products are good educational material and then added that even the distorted literature and myths have a lot to offer.

ATTITUDES TOWARDS DISNEY'S INDOCTRINATION

Although the interviewees were aware of the messages mentioned above, they did not consider them harmful, either for themselves or for children. In responding to the question, 'Would you expose your children or would you advise your friends to expose their children to Disney products,' the answers were 100 percent positive. For example, one of the responses was:

> I would tell them that no danger exists in exposing children to Disney products. I am myself an example, healthy I presume, of growing up, consuming them. I do not fear that my children will be badly influenced by watching Disney cartoons or films. It is just a way of growing up. I could not imagine myself not 'baptized' in this culture.

Another interviewee went one step further:

> The child has to see all of the [Disney] movies. You could talk to your child and refer to a lot of real-life situations by using examples from Disney. When you want to teach your child, for example, when you want to describe to your child what stingy means, you could say it means people who behave like Scrooge. The child would know the Disney characters and it will be easier. Or, for example the child would have a general idea about how silly a man can be when he loves a woman. You would not need to describe the situation. The child would see a Disney movie and s/he would understand. Additionally, a child could learn about nature and animals from Disney films. Like in *Lion King*. Lions are the kings of the animal kingdom. Why?, your child would ask. Well, the film proves to you why that is so. The only thing you need to do is let your child see the film.

And she concluded:

> It is necessary to expose children to Disney products. Necessary because this is the same way that I grew up and all my friends grew up. And if you meet a person who says that he was not touched by Disney films, there must be something wrong with him/her. I think that all kids like Disney. And all these stereotypes that we are talking about, I think that they are mainly reproduced and transmitted to the kids through advertisements, and other social institutions and not through Disney. I think that there is nothing harmful in Disney products.

Not only were there comparisons made with advertisements and other social institutions but also with similar products:

> Generations grew up using Disney products, products with certain values, ideals and messages that are not as violent as in the rest of the cartoons; the Japanese cartoons, for example, are extremely violent. I would say, go ahead and expose your children to Disney products. Because they are not as violent as other cartoons, like *The Transformers* or *The Rangers*, where there is one killing after another. And I would definitely take my kids to Disney theme parks, because this will be a good excuse for me to go to the parks as well.

Only one of our respondents presented a skeptical approach:

If you are a kid, you are supposed to have fun. But we should not expose children only to Disney cartoons, but also to different types of magazines, books, etc., so as to let them have every choice and to make their minds up. Different types of media content would help the children to develop the reading and decoding tools for these media and content. I am not against anything; this is what I believe as a person. So I won't forbid my child to watch anything. I do not think that any television content produces criminals, sex addicts or morons.

In conclusion, the interviewees view Disney products as part of the indoctrination necessary for the upbringing of Greek children. This could be interpreted as a necessary part of the national identity that 'consists in the ability to communicate more efficiently and over a wider range of subjects with members of one large group than with outsiders,' as argued by Deutsch (1966: 97) in a more functionalist communicative approach to the issue of national identity.

RESPONSES TO DISNEY'S SUCCESS

When respondents were asked 'To what do you attribute the success of Disney?' they were eager to point out the quality of the products. Only one mentioned expert marketing, and even in this case, he did not imply manipulation of tastes or control of the market: 'Very good marketing. Products that make you relax. Good products with good promotion. You are going away from your problems, and at the same time you are entertained. They are all time classics, because they have quality.' While one respondent explained, 'Because Disney products express in a right way what is right or wrong,' the following response was more typical:

Because Disney stories are mainly fairy tales and they can attract all ages … they bring out our emotions. You will either laugh or cry. There is no chance that you are going to leave the theater with bad feelings. And especially when you are tense. I mean, I see a Disney film and I am relieved, I am emptied from all the troubles and emotions that made me tense.

So, the success of the Disney products is attributed to the hard work of the producer and the escapism provided, which is considered as a necessary ingredient in everyday life.

THE PROMOTION OF A NORTH AMERICAN LIFESTYLE

It was clear from most of the interviews that respondents under-estimate their exposure to Disney. However, they do not always associate Disney products with the U.S.A. or a North American lifestyle. As one interviewee noted:

I think Disney could represent Europe or Australia in the same way. In my opinion, Disney tries to put in different heroes/heroines, with behaviors and mentalities of all the people in the world ... I think Disney is universal. It never crossed my mind that Disney could be something American. Furthermore, compared with all the other U.S.-made media products representing the American culture that we are bombarded with, Disney is very small. Some Disney films might present some habits of the American everyday life, but this is logical.

But there is also the absence of a comparative framework for these respondents. When asked whether Disney promotes a North American lifestyle, respondents were also asked about the differences between the world as represented by Disney and Greek reality. However, Greek students usually know little about Buddhist ideologies or black African cultures, for instance, so they view the white Christian Western lifestyle, and as a result, Disney, as universal products. Notably, even the more sceptical approaches restrained from accusing Disney products directly:

Well, they promote consumerism, but this is not due to Disney alone. We live already in a consumerist-capitalist society. There is a supermarket in every other corner in my city where daily I buy useless things; Disney should not be blamed for that.

There are two important things to note here: first, that the worldview of the interviewees is occupied mainly by Western values that are considered as the global norm, when actually these characteristics are concentrated mainly in the northern hemisphere; and second, that capitalism is considered an inescapable reality.

IDENTIFYING WITH DISNEY CHARACTERS

Although the interviews started with the question 'Many people tell us that their favorite character was Mickey Mouse ...,' none of the respondents preferred him as a character. This is in contrast to the amount of literature which is devoted to the success of this character. One interviewee explained, 'I am quite indifferent towards this character; and I am also very curious why there is so much promotion and publicity for the character of Mickey and not for the others.' Actually, only one interviewee liked him as a character, while a few liked Mickey as a design, thereby concurring with the claim about the attraction of the character's roundness (Brockway, 1989: 31–2).

One of the female interviewees stated that she enjoys Donald Duck more than any other character, precisely because he resembles her character: 'Clearly, I enjoy his self-destructiveness, as well as his temper. I also enjoy his underdog position, which I share with him due to my low grades at school and to my place in a patriarchal family.' Also, the fact that Donald always gets his punishment did not seem to influence our respondents in the direction suggested by the literature, namely, the promulgation of the values of society (Berland, 1982: 96). An example of a common response was: 'My favorite character was Donald because he was cute, he had a very funny voice and I liked the fact that he was clumsy.'

None of our respondents perceived the punishment of Donald as intimidating. As one of them explained,

> I am not a horse which is fed with a sugar ball when it jumps well, and a whip when I don't. I always perceived that the punishment that Donald got was worth the trouble, since the pleasure of being lazy or expressing my temper was and still is much more appealing to me, and can compensate for most of the punishments.

This view reflected the opinion of three other interviewees, who said the same thing in different words: 'At the end of the day, I could not blame Disney stories for reproducing social morality, especially when I think about the conservative morals of the fairy tales that my grandmother used to tell me.' It is noteworthy, once again, that our respondents presented comparisons with other social institutions.

DISTORTION OF TRADITIONAL MYTHS

We also found evidence that the audience gets upset with the distortion of myths, literature, or historical events that they are familiar with, but not those introduced to them for the first time. In particular, none of the respondents said that they would go to see the Disney version of *Hercules*, because it would be 'a boring distortion of the Greek mythology.' However, they did not mind, and even appreciated, the 'distortion' of French, Danish, and English literature (*The Hunchback of Notre Dame*, *The Little Mermaid*, and *101 Dalmatians*) or Arabic mythology (*Aladdin*). As one respondent commented:

> Now, *Hercules* is coming out. But I am very negative towards this particular film, because I know that they completely distort the myth. From what I read in the newspapers and the magazines, it is a complete distortion of the Greek mythology and this bothers me. I like the fact that they are using a Greek myth and they make it known all over the world, but I would like them to give to the world the real story. If they want to do it differently, they should call it differently. They should call it Megacles instead of Hercules.

On the other hand another respondent had this to say:

The Little Mermaid was modernized, more modernized than I expected, but I wasn't annoyed at all. I knew the story, so I actually enjoyed the better designs of the cartoons, the colors, the music; it was like watching an old American musical in cartoon form.

In conclusion, our interviewees considered the distortion of the national myths of 'others' as acceptable in the process of globalization, but at the same time they were annoyed when their national myths, around which their national identity is partially constructed, are distorted.

Conclusions: Disney-mania in Greece

Audience survey conclusions

The 'Disney-mania' which swept Greece in the 1990s may be accounted for in part by the recent and speedy urbanization of the country. The parents of young children are today the first generation of Disney-literate groups. Total Disneyfication is only prevented by the degree of Disney-illiteracy that obtains still in the more rural areas of the country, for Disney culture is typically urban. It would seem that the lack of genuine children's symbolic goods production created by WDIC's domination will have grave social and cultural repercussions, such as a discrepancy in identity and self-conception between generations.

The respondents in the Greek study represented a generation that has grown up with Disney products, and most of them felt obliged to defend Disney, which they identified with their childhood memories. In fact, they were generally reserved towards what they found to be rather an offensive questionnaire, only identifying problems with Disney content when presented with more elaborate questions. Even then, they were extremely defensive, comparing them readily with other products or factors: 'Japanese cartoons are more violent,' 'our society is consumerist-capitalistic anyway,' and 'consumerism is promoted firstly and foremost by advertising and other institutions and not by cartoons.'

Indeed, asking the interviewees about the possible negative influences of Disney goods, and the effects these might have, was like asking them to deny their own childhood or to betray themselves. It is also possible to argue that the abundance of Disney products that makes them so mainstream, along with the scarcity of alternatives, means that the respondents cannot deny their consumption and the gratification provided by them, which may be similar to a denial of the mainstream religion of the country.

Furthermore, many of those interviewed view the stereotypes projected by Disney products as natural or as inherent in the social system. They refuse to see them as an outcome of Disney content or as commercial propaganda. They even have difficulty acknowledging that such stereotypes might be reinforced by Disney stories. It is interesting that none of the respondents remembered anything in Disney about treasure hunting, nor did they identify greed or individualism in Disney products, as observed by Disney critics, such as Dorfman and Mattelart (1979). More specifically, only 7 percent of answers attributed individualism to Disney products, and only 3 percent found Disney content projecting any racism. By contrast, values such as fun, good winning over evil, imagination, happiness, fantasy and love/romance were identified in the Disney world by 90 to 100 percent of the sample.

Generally, then, the Greek participants in the study seemed unwilling to critique Disney and its products, with the majority of the respondents agreeing with the following response: 'Why does everything have to be political? There are times to deal with politics and times to relax.'

Political economy conclusions

Two main factors facilitated the advanced Disney incursion into the Greek market in the 1990s. First, Greece, as a member of the EU, had to accommodate community liberalization and deregulation policies. Policies such as the 1989 Television Without Frontiers Directive, moreover, reshuffled the media and cultural goods industry in a way that predominantly benefitted Europe's competitors, namely, the Hollywood majors. The channel proliferation created by this legislation led to a demand for cheaply imported programing.[20] Second, Disney had all the advantages of a global corporation able to benefit from economies of scale. In other words, it could recoup its production costs in the home market and thus undercut any local competitors. It had also the prestige of the English language, the world's lingua franca. Above all, Disney's enormous experience in this field, and the formidable marketing strategies it deployed, made for certain success.

It is hard to determine exactly how much money the Disney company generates from the Greek market, as precise revenue figures cannot be obtained. Indeed, there is a confusing lack of transparency, because the WDIC subsidiary in Athens essentially operates from abroad, although from within the 'frontierless European audiovisual market.' Thus, dependent subsidiaries or representing agencies can avoid providing turnover or profit data, representing the breaking down of the conception and operation of a national economy. Nevertheless, due to its linguistic specificity, the Greek market is still treated by the company as a national market, particularly with respect to marketing and promotional campaigns.

Trends suggest that Disney will continue to oust locally produced cultural goods, marginalizing local artists and story writers and eventually eliminating them from their home market. Furthermore, it seems likely that the Disney company will further increase its market share over international and Hollywood competitors, despite overall growth in the entertainment market.

The effects of this development can be seen in the declining popularity of traditional local cultural modes, as well as in newly developing forms of leisure activities, especially among the youth. The way Greek people have occupied their leisure time is being rapidly transformed, as Disney moves into the previously fallow periods of the evenings, summer, and the Christmas and Easter holidays. As we have seen, WDIC is one of the main forces behind the twelve-month cinema-screening season, creating an intensification of cultural consumption unprecedented in this part of the world.

In addition, the company's 'industrialized' stories, however monolithic and banal for some, are made irresistible to increasingly dynamic audiences by a systems approach to promotion and marketing. The company's policy of branding dictates the deployment of incessant promotions to keep the brand constantly in the public eye, with the licensing of Disney images playing a particularly important role. In other words, the company is the message!

Notes

1. Published by Petros Pikros and Themos Andreopoulos.
2. Pechlivanidis publishers.
3. The Italian school of Disney – Romano Sarpa, Giorgio Cavagiano, Guindo Scala, etc. – largely created the early Disney mystique in our part of the world (Malandrakis, 1998).
4. The Greek state's TV monopoly was found to be unacceptable by the European Court of Justice in 1989. Private, advertising-financed channels were then set up, following the liberalizing tenets of the Treaty of Rome.
5. The linguistic criterion is adopted here for the definition of the Greek market. The Disney satellite channels received in Greece which are not subtitled or dubbed for Greek audiences are therefore disregarded. The Greek diaspora accounts for a small section of the Greek-language market.
6. Audiovisual Enterprises belongs to the Vardinogiannis group (dealing also in shipping, oil, publishing and audiovisual interests), which also owns a 20 percent share in Teletypos, owner of Mega Channel.

7. Pro-O-ptiki is the exclusive representative of two major Hollywood production companies, Walt Disney Company and Sony, as well as various independent producers. Buena Vista International includes three different labels: (1) Walt Disney Pictures (children's and family films plus cartoons), (2) Touchstone Pictures, and (3) Hollywood Pictures (Souganidou, 1998).

8. Souganidou points to the success of cinema in overcoming two consecutive crises, the one caused by video rentals in the 1980s and the other arising from the proliferation of TV channels in the 1990s.

9. These figures do not cover the entire cinema ticket sales in the country but the companies represented by Pro-O-ptiki: Disney, Sony and some independents. Pro-O-ptiki is the biggest and most robust Greek film distributor.

10. Village Warner, the joint venture of Warner road centre and Village multiplex cinemas, is the most recent 'cinematic' event in Greece (Souganidou). Spentzos films is a distributor who deals with independents.

11. Pro-O-ptiki will not give precise economic data, on the grounds that it is not just the agent of Disney but the representative of a number of production companies.

12. These descriptions come from a written account prepared by Ekavi-Louise Whitlock (12 years old).

13. These service offices operate on the so-called 'cost plus' basis under which invoicing of all licensing activities takes place in France, and specific country offices have no legal obligation to publish annual reports of their transactions.

14. Globally, the Disney company has two different marketing divisions with two directors. One is devoted to the production and marketing of its films in the U.S.A., while the other heads its overseas marketing (Souganidou, 1998).

15. According to Jack (1997), there are company plans, which have been approved by shareholders, to introduce a second theme park in Europe.

16. The company announced a sharp increase of 7.5 percent in net income for 1997, along with a rise in the number of visitors, from 11.7 million in 1996 to 12.6 million through September 1997. Approximately 34 percent of the visitors had been to the park at least once previously. In addition, hotel occupancy rose from 72.2 percent to 78 percent, and per capita spending rose from 248 francs to 251 francs, while total revenues rose 10.2 percent to 5.5 billion francs (Jack, 1997).

17. Belying reactions by members of the French cultural elite, ticket sales for Disney's happily ending *The Hunchback of Notre Dame* were huge. A recent opinion poll found that more French citizens consider EuroDisney, rather than the Eiffel Tower, as the symbol for Paris.

18. Natalia Kostopoulou, cartoonist and lecturer in animation, was interviewed by the author in March 1998. Despite receiving distinguished awards, she was about to quit this trade.

19. Also known as Baumoll's disease, this means that production costs will keep increasing, irrespective of productivity gains, due to the uniqueness and creativity of a 'talented labour-intensive' industry (Baumoll and Baumoll, 1997).

20. The transmission of children's TV programing has increased by 15 to 20 percent worldwide over the last ten years and will increase further due to the second wave of digitized specialized channels.

References and other sources

Baumoll, H. and Baumoll, W. J. (1997) 'The mass media and the cost disease,' in W. S. Hendon, D. V. Shaw, and N. K Grant (eds), *Economics of Cultural Industries*. Akron, OH, The Association of Cultural Economics.

Berland, D. (1982) 'Disney and Freud: Walt meets the id,' *Journal of Popular Culture*, 15(4), pp. 93-104.

Brockway, R. W. (1989) 'The masks of Mickey Mouse: symbol of a generation,' *Journal of Popular Culture*, 22 (Spring): 25-34.

Carlanter, *Le Monde Diplomatique*, Greek edn.

Davis, S. G. (1996) 'The theme park: global industry and cultural form,' *Media, Culture and Society*, 18(3): 399-422.

Deutsch, K. W. (1966) *Nationalism and Social Communication: An Inquiry into the Foundations of Nationality*. Cambridge and London, MIT Press.

Disney News (1996) company newsletter published by the Disney company/ Greece.

Dorfman, A. and Mattelart, A. (1979/1982) *How to Read Donald Duck: Imperialist Ideology in the Disney Comics*, Greek edn. Athens, Ypsilon.

García Canclini, N. (1990) *Hybrid Cultures* (in Spanish, *Culturas hibrida*). Mexico City, Grijalvo.

Jack, A. (1997) 'EuroDisney's fortunes turn as numbers of visitors rise,' *Financial Times*, November 14, p. 13.

Kaitatzi-Whitlock, S. (1993) 'European broadcasting: policy-making and implementation,' MA dissertation, City University, London.

Kaitatzi-Whitlock, S. (1996) 'European audiovisual policy-making: an elusive target,' Doctoral thesis, University of Westminster, London.

Malandrakis, A. (1998) 'Mickey, the politician,' *Kyriakatiki Eleftherotypia* (Athens weekly), March 22.

Maltin, L. (1980) *Of Mice and Magic: A History of the American Animated Cartoons*. New York, McGraw-Hill.

Martin-Barbero, J. (1993) 'Latin America: cultures in communication media,' *Journal of Communication*, 43(2).

Millar, P. (1997) 'Walt Disney Co.: lock up your legends,' *The European*, August 28/September 3.

Miller, A. C. (1997) 'New Disney game: lobbying,' *Los Angeles Times* Service, September 3, 1991.

Real, M. (1977) *Mass-Mediated Culture*. Englewood Cliffs, NJ, Prentice-Hall.

Schiller, H. (1973) *The Mind Managers*. Boston, Beacon Press.

Sidiropoulou, O. (1998) 'Crowds for *Anastasia*,' *Exoussia*, April 1, 1998, p. 22.

Trites, R. (1991) 'Disney's sub/version of Andersen's *Little Mermaid*,' *Journal of Popular Film and Television*, 18(4) (Winter): 149-51.

Tunstall, J. (1977) *The Media Are American*. New York, Columbia University Press.

Vasconcelos, A.-P. *et al.* (1994) *Report by the Think-Tank on the Audiovisual Policy in the European Union.* Luxemburg, OOPEC.

White, R. (1988) *Media, Politics and Democracy in the Developing World,* Center for the Study of Communication and Culture. London, Longman.

Ypsilon (1982) 'Introduction to the Greek edition,' in A. Dorfman and A. Mattelart, *How to Read Donald Duck: Imperialist Ideology in the Disney Comics.* Athens, Ypsilon.

The following interviews were conducted by Sophia Kaitatzi-Whitlock:

Dermentzoglou, Alexis, film critic, Elliniki Tileorassi 3 (ET 3), September 10, 1997, Thessaloniki.

Himonas, Michalis, Managing Director, The Disney Company, November 1997, Athens.

Kostopoulou, Natalia, cartoonist and lecturer in animation, March 15, 1998, Thessaloniki.

Souganidou, Irene, Managing Director, Pro-O-ptiki (film distributors), April 13, 1998, Athens.

Whitlock, Ekavi-Louise, January 10, 1998, Thessaloniki.

CHAPTER 8

Japan: America in Japan/Japan in Disneyfication: The Disney Image and the Transformation of 'America' in Contemporary Japan

SHUNYA YOSHIMI

How to read Donald Duck in contemporary Japan

Several years ago, I asked my undergraduate students from several universities in the Tokyo area to read and comment upon Ariel Dorfman and Armand Mattelart's book, *How to Read Donald Duck* (1975). I was astonished when I read the reports. Many of the students expressed a negative reaction to their analysis of Disney comics. One student wrote:

> Up to now, the name Disney has been associated with Tokyo Disneyland, animation, and Mickey Mouse, but this *How to Read Donald Duck* constantly surprised me. When you say Disney, you think of peace and things that give children something to dream about. But, I felt this impression fall with a great crash.

However, this was a rather mild reaction. Another student commented: 'I grew up surrounded by Disney characters, and I like Disneyland. My first impression after reading the book was anger, because I felt as though the authors were thinking in such a pessimistic way, and I wanted to doubt their personalities.' Still another student wrote: 'Honestly speaking, it is something I do not even want to imagine. I even felt betrayed.' All of the students were shocked by the severe criticism of Disney in the book and admitted that they wanted to completely deny such criticism.

Among the students, there were some who went a step further and criticized the authors' analytic point of view. For example, one student commented:

I love Tokyo Disneyland. One step into Tokyo Disneyland and I feel as if I've entered into a fantasy world – as though I'm lost in a distant, foreign country. When I do not visit Tokyo Disneyland for over a half a year or so, there are moments when I get the sudden urge to go. Then, I get nostalgic about the times when I've been there.

This student admits that she is fascinated by Tokyo Disneyland, but resists the position offered by Dorfman and Mattelart:

Why do they have to go digging into things bad, being so critical? I was extremely angry and felt the images of Disneyland in me were being destroyed ... It is no fun when our Donald Duck is analyzed this way. I have my own image of Donald Duck, [who is] bad more than anything. The characters do not exist for the purpose of being subjected to cultural debate.

The student also comments on the point noted by Dorfman and Mattelart regarding the lack of personality and sexual dimensions of the Disney characters: 'If I met the characters at Tokyo Disneyland and they had human elements, I would definitely be disappointed. Mickey is all the more adorable to me because he doesn't speak and he's cute, and that is the essence of it all.' In the end, she concludes, 'I don't even want to listen to such argument that tries somehow to discover ideology in the text. It's like being woken from a dream.'

Many students expressed the same kind of criticism. One stated that 'the authors are thinking too deeply.' He contends such criticism of the world of Disney is unique to these authors. Therefore, since 'everyone thinks the Disney characters are cute and likes Disneyland, it is strange to read into it so deeply and to be so critical about it.' Similarly, another student responded to Dorfman and Mattelart's criticisms of Disney:

Does any child or adult who reads Disney's books think that way? I think hardly anyone does. Disney has given children and adults many dreams and I think it will continue just as it is. In the end, what sort of significance is there to destroying dreams by analyzing and re-analyzing Disney in this way and by asserting such criticisms as 'the content also has such and such meaning.'

She concluded by saying: 'Disney's comic strips were not written for the purpose of criticism. So, if you don't like them, then don't read them.' Yet another student wrote: 'When I read the book, I felt completely dissatisfied. All I could think was that it was the bias of scholars [that produced such a critical attitude].'

For the author of this chapter, *How to Read Donald Duck* is a pioneering study that succeeded in analyzing critically the structure of Disney as a cultural text. Dorfman and Mattelart are not content with a simple structural analysis; rather, they adopt a critical position in relation to cultural imperialism while keeping the realities of the Latin American political economy in the background. The book reveals the fundamental characteristics of Disney comics by concretely analyzing several aspects of the story. For example, Dorfman and Mattelart delve into the significance of such issues as the absence of fathers for the main characters, the exclusion of 'sex' from the world of children, and how this world is controlled by an outside, arbitrary power. They also look at the relationship between children and the inhabitants of foreign lands, where the children bring with them the technologies of the civilized world. The children are continually portrayed as adults (= empire) and the local inhabitants as children (= colony).

In his discussion of cultural imperialism, John Tomlinson (1997) critiques Dorfman and Mattelart's analysis as limited because they cannot provide convincing evidence that shows how the ideology they find in the Disney comic has influenced the average Chilean reader of the comic. And, furthermore, Tomlinson criticizes them for stopping at only reading the comic politically as an 'imperialist text.' Indeed, Dorfman and Mattelart use a combination of Marxist and psycho-analytic methodologies to interpret the texts. Consequently, there is no guarantee that Latin American children in the 1970s were reading the Disney comics in a way that justifies such an analysis. Nevertheless, they raise an important question: how can the world of Disney permeate the cultures of peripheral developing countries and become so immensely popular?

The rejection of *How to Read Donald Duck* by contemporary Japanese young people, however, is completely different than the critiques leveled by proponents of cultural studies. It is surprising that they rejected this book so strongly, since they were born long after this classic Disney critique was first published. Their stubborn affection for Disney differs from the affection Latin American children might have shown toward Disney comics in the 1970s. It is also dissimilar to Dutch women's interest in *Dallas*, which Ien Ang (1985) has carefully analyzed. Most of my students not only feel that their favorite cultural object is being criticized but also that their self-identities are being fundamentally questioned or denied. To that extent, they can see no distance between themselves and the world of Disney. I would like to illustrate this with an example that symbolically expresses this lack of distance. At the parade which is held nearly every day at Tokyo Disneyland, one often sees spectators, welcomed by the advancing 'Mickey' and 'Donald,' lining up dolls of the characters along the

Figure 11. Japanese people waiting for a Mickey parade at Disneyland in Tokyo

parade route. It becomes a spectacle in which the audience tries to affirm that they themselves are also characters in the world of Disney. For these people, even more than as an exterior object of desire, Donald Duck and Mickey Mouse are characters who exist internally, inside each consumer.

In this chapter, I will clarify the relationship between contemporary Japanese people and the world of Disney by looking at the historical process of cultural Americanization in Japan. The strong influence of cultural Americanism on Japanese mass culture is definitely not a recent development. Indeed, the process began over 70 years ago, as well as after World War II, when the social and cultural consciousness in Japan formed an increasingly deep and layered relationship with 'things American.' At some point during this process, the world of Disney was introduced and gradually became accepted as the core of what people in Japan perceive as Americanism. In order to evaluate the seemingly distance-less relationship between Japanese youth and the world of Disney today, it is necessary to review the historical context of cultural Americanization and its transformation, in addition to the role that Disney culture has played in such changes. Therefore, this chapter will present an overview of Americanization in Japan

Figure 12. Japanese postcard. Photo: Valentin-Hoa-qui

between the two world wars, and then discuss Americanization after World War II in the context of the full-scale importation of Disney movies and Disney products. Finally, I will discuss the changes in the structure of cultural Americanization during the 1970s.

'America' in Japan before World War II

Cultural Americanization did not begin in Japan under American military and economic pressure following World War II, but had started in earnest long before, in the late 1920s, when Hollywood films, consumer goods, and American lifestyle began to captivate middle-class inhabitants of large urban environments, such as Tokyo and Osaka. This is the reason why Takanobu Murobuse wrote in 1929, in his book *America*:

Where could you find Japan not Americanized? How could Japan exist without America? And, where could we escape from Americanization? I dare to even declare that America has become the world, Japan is nothing but America today. (Murobuse, 1929: 4)

He continued by observing that the U.S.A. had exported its civilization not only to Latin America, Japan, China, and India but also to England, Germany, France, communist Russia, and the eternal city, Rome. The world was entering into the age of America, when the U.S.A. would dominate not only the dollar (the economy) but also world civilization based on the dollar (Murobuse, 1929). Looking at it now, Murobuse's argument is a very crude statement of cultural imperialism, filled with many illogical jumps and exaggerations. Yet, it is important to note that such arguments about Americanization were already being discussed extensively in the 1920s.

From the end of the 1920s to the 1930s, Japanese monthly magazines often featured fictional articles on 'America,' and writers took up relevant subjects. For example, Itaru Nii wrote in 1929 that the world had reached the age in which the colors, smells, and sounds of various nations were rapidly melting together. It was the 'cocktail age' and Americanism poured over this new world. According to his observation, the young were intent on jazz, and willingly imitated the hairstyles, make-up, and fashion of Hollywood movies, which began to flow into Japan in large numbers at this time. Working in an American-style building, watching a baseball game, or going for a drive on Sunday afternoon, and dancing or going to the movies at night; all of these became fashionable in major urban areas during this time. Nii noted the correspondence between the vogue of Americanism in lifestyle and 'Russianism' in social thought. In Japan, 'a man who adheres to Russian ideology often prefers American tastes, and a "modern boy" who keeps the American way of life also knows well about socialism.' In Japan, these two tendencies were not contra-dictory, but concurrent (Nii, 1929: 62–3).

Souichi Oya (1929/1981) seized on another aspect of contemporary Americanism, which had spread among large cities such as Osaka, claiming, 'Osaka is Japan's America.' He wrote that Japanese moder-nization from the late nineteenth century on had been led by the governmental elite in Tokyo, and it had persistently followed the model of European nations such as England, France, and Germany. As a result, Tokyo became an urban center full of Western imitations. During this period, 'America was seen as a colony of Anglo-Saxon origin, and Russia as a developing country stretching out over Asia.' But such cultural geopolitics drastically changed after World War I. Out of this upheaval, two types of new cultural center come to the front:

Russian and American. In particular, 'America, with its enormous capital and the propaganda ability of Hollywood films, is sweeping over Europe, its cultural motherland which was exhausted during the war, and also over Asian countries, even over the whole world.' Oya compared this cultural condition of Europe with that of Tokyo after the Great Kanto earthquake of 1923. Oya further argued that, as the culture of Tokyo had been able to develop through imitating European countries, this copy would likely fall into decay when the original lost the force of previous days. Instead of Tokyo, it was Osaka that came to the fore, and it was popular American culture that became prosperous in Osaka (Oya, 1929/1981: 153–4).

Of course, Osaka's pre-eminence in modern life was short-lived. After the 1930s, Ginza in Tokyo became the center where Americanism would fully flourish in prewar and postwar Japan. During the Meiji period, Ginza was a clear imitation of a typical Western-style main street in Victorian London, and was similar to avenues in the British colonies (Fujimori, 1982). After that, French fashion strongly influenced the taste of the elite and the bourgeoisie who gathered in Ginza, and French-style cafés began to emerge. But after the 1930s, both British and French styles were suddenly overtaken by American consumer culture. Kousei Ando, in his book *Ginza Saiken* (*Detail Watch of Ginza*, 1931), wrote:

> It is Americanism that dominates Ginza today. If you look at pedestrians on the sidewalks, you find at once that their styles and behavior are completely imitated from American movies ... The majority of restaurants in Ginza do not serve French dinner with wine, but American lunch with beer. You can hear American jazz in every café ... Instead of French taste, Ginza is filled with the Americanism of large capital, speed, and the movies. Today, most Japanese want to understand the world only through America. (Ando, 1931: 29)

It is this Ginza of Americanism which became the prominent center of Japanese consumer culture from the 1930s to the 1960s. By the 1960s, more than 500 shopping streets all around Japan were named after 'Ginza' to emphasize their 'modern' image (Hattori, 1976).

It is important to note that the flourishing Americanism in large Japanese cities after the late 1920s did not merely import American culture, but remade it in Japan. Although 'America' was so often said to have swept over Japanese popular culture, the latter was not reduced to dependency on American mass-cultural products, but strove instead to naturalize and reinvent them. So, already in 1943, in the midst of the war against the U.S.A., Ikutaro Shimizu pointed out that the prevailing Americanism in contemporary Japan was not the same thing as the original Americanism in the U.S.A. According to his sociological view, when fragments of American culture were imported to Japan, it was impossible to keep their original functions, because the functions of culture were always dependent on context. In particular, he stressed, elements of leisure and consumption disproportionately proliferated in Japan, while Americanism originally meant the basic philosophy which was threaded through all aspects of American life and culture. In Japan, all modern leisure and consumption patterns after the late Taisho era tended to be called 'Americanism.' Another difference is that, in Japan, Americanism was strongly related to private, domestic life, while the original was an expression of American public consciousness (Shimizu, 1943).

In a sense, this private character of the Americanism in Japan derived from the structural change of Americanism itself in the 1920s in the U.S.A. As described in many sociological studies, including Robert and Helen Lynd's *Middletown* (1929) and Frederic Allen's *Only Yesterday* (1931), mass consumption had swept over American life in the 1920s. Through this process, the Americanism in the U.S.A. came to be more and more related to the private life of mass consumption. The advertising industry expanded and commodities such as the automobile, radio and household electronic appliances became the symbolic elements of Americanism. The relationship between the consumer life in the U.S.A. and the Americanism in Japan can be exemplified by the Seikatsu Kaizen ('Life Improvement') movement. The advocate of this movement, Koukichi Morimoto, studied consumer economics at Johns Hopkins University and his concept of 'cultural life' was strongly influenced by the image of private life within the American middle class. He established the Association for the Cultural Way of Life in Tokyo to proliferate the rational knowledge of life among housewives by using correspondence education, which was popular in the U.S.A. at that time. Although Morimoto's movement did not succeed at the time, similar ideas of 'cultural life' widely prevailed and continued to have an influence on the image of 'modern life.'

'Disney' as a symbol of Americanism

From the late 1940s, the process of widespread, overwhelming Americanization began to spread throughout Japan. In other words, the 'America' that infiltrated the everyday consciousness of Japanese urban dwellers before World War II expanded to all of Japan. For instance, the small Japanese–English pocket guide, *Nichibei eikaiwa techo*, was published just a month after the end of the war and sold 3 million copies in two months. After the NHK radio program *America*

Tayori (News from America) began in 1948, in which listeners heard the latest information from Washington, it soon became a very popular program (Ishikawa, 1981). Also in 1950, Asahi Shinbun held the enormously successful American Exposition in Nishinomiya, an Osaka suburb. The exposition displayed many American symbols such as 'the White House,' 'Lincoln,' 'the Statue of Liberty,' 'the New York Skyscraper,' 'Niagara Falls,' 'the Western Frontier,' and 'Television.' These examples show that a kind of popular desire for 'America' existed shortly after the end of the war. The military and economic force of the American Occupation Forces was not the only, or even the main, reason for such a desire. Rather, there was a continuity of Americanism in Japan from the prewar to the postwar period.

Based on this continuity, the Japanese public had already begun to associate images of Disney's films and Disneyland with 'America' as the symbol of 'richness' and 'newness.' For example, as early as 1948, Japanese film critic, Tahei Imamura focused on Disney movies as well as the two faces of changing Americanism in the context of his discussion of animated feature films. Imamura insisted there was nothing that better expressed the perspective of Americanism under the advanced stages of capitalism than animated films, which were at the height of their popularity at this time. At the core of this Americanism was the unqualified praise of machine technology. For Imamura, American animation was 'a modern myth celebrating the machine in place of the gods.' Furthermore, its imaginative power was 'constructed from machine tools, spindles, wheels, pistons, springs, motors – all of which are produced by large capitalist industry.' Modern Americans personified the power of the machine just as ancient Greeks had personified the power of nature. In other words, it is a myth praising the modern gods Rockefeller, Ford, and Western Electric. Imamura asserts that, just as in Popeye cartoons, the locus of imaginative power in Disney movies is the dynamism and speed of the machine. For example, a buffalo chasing Mickey Mouse is transformed into a streamlined locomotive increasing its speed, or a pelican into a heavy bomber, or an elephant into a cannonball. A running rabbit stops with the sound of screeching brakes, and as a beaver uses its tail as a screw, we hear the sound of a motor boat: 'Pastoral nature, which is the most distant from technology, becomes mechanized. Thus, all of nature is seen through this perspective of Americanism as it exists under the advanced stages of capitalism' (Imamura, 1948: 150–1).

On the other hand, Imamura argued that the stories express a kind of 'humanism.' All of the main characters are weak animals – a mouse, a duck, a dog, a piglet and a sheep – who are always rescued from some adversity. According to Imamura, this kind of 'humanism' is always expressed together with mechanical rationalism in the early Disney films. For example, when the piglet presses the button of a machine to punish the wolf, this machine grabs the wolf by the neck, chokes him, hits him on the head, breaks his back, tars and feathers him, shoves him into a cannon, and finally shoots the bad wolf to the moon. The piglet's military strategy is embodied in the carefully programed conveyor-belt system. In Disney movies after the Great Depression, however, the relationship between 'humanism' and 'technologism' changes from optimism to a slightly more distorted connection. In addition to this transformation, the leading character changes from Mickey Mouse to Donald Duck, and we see him more often being trifled with by machines, than operating them himself. Imamura sees this transformation as a criticism of machine civilization, similar to that offered in Charlie Chaplin's *Modern Times* (1936).

It is symbolic that Japan's leading film critics began to take up the theme of Disney movies in their writings from the late 1940s. In fact, it was around 1948 that American animated films began to be shown again after their suspension during the war. The first full-length foreign animated film to be shown in Japan after the war was *Gulliver's Travels* by the Fleischer brothers, which opened in April 1948. It was the screening of a print that was imported before the war but had been kept in storage for the duration of the war. At about the same time, short Popeye cartoons, also by the Fleischer brothers, began to run in the theaters. Two years later, in the autumn of 1950, however, Disney's monumental animated classic, *Snow White*, opened in Japan, thirteen years after it had first been seen in the U.S.A. in 1937. The popularity of this movie attracted a wider audience beyond the typical animation fans in Japan. Subsequent Disney movies shown in Japan in the early 1950s included: *Bambi*, spring 1951 (U.S. opening, 1941); *Song of the South*, autumn 1951 (U.S. opening, 1946); *Pinocchio*, spring 1952 (U.S. opening, 1940); *Cinderella*, spring 1953 (U.S. opening, 1950); *Alice in Wonderland*, summer 1953 (U.S. opening, 1950); and *Dumbo*, spring 1954 (U.S. opening 1941). Japanese movie-goers, who lived in poverty immediately after the war, were completely overwhelmed by these films. Along with these feature-length films, Disney's short animated cartoons were shown in theaters. As many as 211 Disney cartoons, including Mickey Mouse, Donald Duck, and Pluto cartoons, as well as the Silly Symphony series, were imported from the U.S.A. and shown in the Daiei theater chain.

The following excerpt from Tezuka Osamu's memoirs shows how Japanese animation fans experienced Disney films:

> Whenever a feature-length Disney film came to town, I rushed to see it. Once, I heard about a showing in Kyushu and I even took a plane in order to see it. I think I saw *Snow White* over 50 times and *Bambi* over 80 times. In the case of *Bambi*, I bought bread in the morning, went to the

theater and stayed there all day. After the last showing, I stayed in a cheap inn which was infested with fleas and ticks just so I could rush back to the theater the first thing in the morning. I acted just like the groupies of popular singers today. Finally, during the show, I turned my back to the screen and watched the audience laugh and cry – enjoying it as if it were my own. (Tezuka Productions, 1998: 86)

Indeed, Tezuka was a unique fan. He absorbed the world of Disney almost as the nucleus of his identity, and from there, proceeded to shape the framework of postwar Japanese animation. However, all of Disney's films, even the ones made before and during the war, were shown within just a few years during the 1950s. Because of this compressed time-frame, the cultural influence of Disney on children and their parents was overwhelming. Indeed, *Kinema junpo* (*Cinema Quarterly*), Japan's leading film journal, ran a special issue on Disney films in 1955. Though it was a typical special issue focusing on the history of Disney movies and Disney's production organization, we can begin to understand just how deeply Japanese movie-goers were absorbed in Disney films.

During this period, the world of Disney imagery permeated the living rooms of Japanese homes via the television set. In 1958, Nippon Television started broadcasting the biweekly TV program *Disneyland*. Originally produced by Disney for the ABC network in the U.S.A., it had a considerable impact on Japanese viewers, strengthening their image of the U.S.A. At the beginning of the program, Walt Disney himself would appear and address the audience, followed by Disney cartoons and documentary films edited for television. Masako Notoji points out that

> when children saw this program on a black-and-white television in a tiny Japanese living room, it was bright, sparkling, and wonderful. Interestingly enough, this program was coupled with the live broadcast of professional wrestling. One week it was the dazzling world of Disney and overwhelmingly rich America, and the following week, at the same time on the same channel, the kids watched Rikidozan (a very popular Japanese wrestler at the time) beating monstrous American wrestlers. For these Japanese children, it was inferiority and superiority alternating each week. (Notoji, 1990: 3–4)

In addition to this television program, Riidaazu Daijesuto Sha began publishing a magazine for children called *Dizunii no kuni* (*The Kingdom of Disney*) in 1960, which was succeeded by Kodansha's *Dizunii rando* (*Disneyland*) in 1964. During the 1960s, Disney films such as *Peter Pan*, *Lady and the Tramp*, *Sleeping Beauty*, *101 Dalmatians*, and *Mary Poppins* opened one after another. Before the

1970s, Mickey Mouse was the most popular character, in terms of character merchandise, among children.

Furthermore, in a related development, Japanese real-estate and railway investors began to think about inviting Disney to join with them in building another Disneyland in the suburbs of Tokyo. The Oriental Land Company, which would become the parent company of Tokyo Disneyland, was established in 1960. The following year, the president of Keisei Electric Railways, Tokyo Disneyland's major investor, visited Walt Disney Productions in the U.S.A. Thus, the preparations for inviting Disneyland to Tokyo were gradually put into place throughout the 1960s, until 1972, when surveyors from the Oriental Land Company visited Walt Disney Productions. As I will discuss later, from the perspective of the consumer, the success of Tokyo Disneyland in the 1980s was made possible due to a change in cultural values that occurred at the end of the 1970s. From the producer's perspective, however, Tokyo Disneyland's success was rooted in the popularity of Disney from the 1950s and 1960s. So the image of Disney as a symbol of American 'wealth' and 'innovation' overwhelmed most Japanese people throughout the 1950s and 1960s, encouraging a sense of envy and desire for the American lifestyle.

Such Americanism, which deeply permeated the everyday thinking of most people in the postwar period, was not limited to these images of wealth and innovation. In addition, 'America' in postwar Japan was also a symbol of 'emancipation' and 'resistance' for urban youth. In particular, the youth subcultures of jazz, rock and roll, and comics soon spread from American military bases to urban entertainment districts, a trend that reflected Dick Hebdige's discussion of Americanism in postwar England (Hebdige, 1988). Then postwar music culture, from jazz in the late 1940s to the rock-a-billy boom in the late 1950s, was strongly influenced by American radio programs. In the middle of the 1950s, the 'Sun generation' emerged, strongly influenced by Shintaro Ishihara's best-selling novel, *The Season of the Sun* (Mabuchi, 1989). From the end of the 1950s to the early 1960s, the emerging 'Roppongi generation' and 'Harajuku generation' hung out in Roppongi and Harajuku, where, near the American military facilities, the cultural influences of the American army remained. So the youth culture formed a layered structure of oppositional values, with 'America' as its symbol.

Transformation of 'America' in 1970s Japan

On the one hand, the Japanese yearned for 'America' as a symbol of wealth and innovation, and they integrated it into their everyday lives.

On the other hand, Japanese youth accepted American popular culture as a symbol of emancipation and resistance. In any case, the 'America' of that period was 'America' as symbol. In contrast, from the 1970s, 'America' in Japan went through a certain structural transformation, from 'America' as symbol to 'America' as system. As the success of McDonald's in Japan and the birth of Tokyo Disneyland demonstrate, cultural Americanization continued to expand from the 1970s. Yet, 'America' stopped being a symbol of wealth and innovation and of emancipation and resistance. During the 1970s, 'America' in Japan was diluted of its symbolic character and came to operate at the deepest level of everyday life.

One of the fundamental reasons for this change was, of course, the rapid economic growth from 1955 to 1973. During this period, Japanese people eagerly purchased a wide range of electronic goods and other commodities for their home, and began to enjoy their own economic affluence. Thus, by the middle of the 1970s, Japanese consumers began to feel that they were no longer poorer than their American counterparts. The once strong sentiment of envy, which had dominated Japanese everyday consciousness, gradually decreased. It should be noted here that in the mid-1970s, the new generation which had been born during the period of postwar rapid economic growth were now teenagers. As the consciousness and behavior of this generation were very different from the previous generation, they were often called the *shin jinrui* ('new humankind') by the mass media. In particular, this new generation began to enjoy consuming style and culture as completely commodified artifacts. 'America' had become not so much a symbol by which people were fascinated, but an artifact which people could repeatedly consume (Kato, 1985).

It was around this time (1983) that Tokyo Disneyland (TDL) opened in a Tokyo suburb. Throughout the 1980s, TDL came to symbolize the transformation of Japanese cities during the 'bubble economy.' But the success of Tokyo Disneyland in the 1980s was not simply an extension of 'America' as a symbol in postwar Japan. Rather, this success clearly shows the structural transformation from the 1970s mentioned above. The fact that TDL can draw such large numbers of people (about 15 million people every year) is based largely on the power of a system which offers up for consumption various self-images within a commercial landscape, not one based on a direct reference to 'America.' In other words, if it can be said that TDL is a kind of 'America' in Japan, this 'America' is a system of consumption, which constructs self-identity as consumable, or as something to be colonized. The rest of the chapter focuses on the cultural politics of TDL and reconsiders the process of Americanization in contemporary Japan.

On the one hand, it is immediately noticeable upon entering TDL that one is contained in a completely self-sufficient area. The space is designed to block views, and one is barely able to see the outside world. In TDL, there is nothing that reminds visitors of Urayasu, where TDL is located, or even suburban Tokyo. The reality produced in the park maintains its consistency, since contradictory elements from the outside are almost completely shut out (Myerhoff, 1983). This attempt is tactical, and employs other methods as well. For instance, Marin points out that the parking lot and the ticket counter function as filters to 'neutralize cars and money, and transform them into "utopian" something else' (Marin, 1973: 337–8). Visitors not only part with their vehicles and money at the entrance but also are not allowed to bring food and alcohol into the park. This policy, and the constant cleaning up, keep TDL in a sterilized state. Furthermore, one's view is not only blocked from what is outside the park but also from what is outside the particular 'land.'

In order to illustrate this well-designed strategy, it is important to understand that TDL is not a descendant of the nineteenth-century amusement parks. It is based on a completely different concept and the imagination of Walt Disney, who never stopped cultivating different media to express his world. From comic books to animation films, short black-and-white silent movies to longer talkies in color, from two-dimensional movies to three-dimensional Disneyland, these changes were all a continuation of Disney's imagination (Thomas, 1983). As a result, the essence of Disneyland is much closer to cinema than to amusement parks.

For example, when examining the lack of overview in TDL, it is important to take into account that Disneyland was fundamentally based on the concepts of film-making. The space does not offer an overview because it is designed with cinematic effects in mind; specifically, visitors become two-dimensional movie characters as they go through different attractions in the park, and this transformation is a necessity if they are to enjoy the space. A female college student says,

> I've been to TDL four times, but always with different friends or relatives, because there must be new surprises with each visit. You cannot say 'Oh, I know this attraction,' even if you have experienced it. You must say 'Gee!' or 'Oh, that's so cute!' and pretend that it's your first time.

And when one becomes a movie character on the Disney screen, it is difficult to step out from the depthless space of different 'first time' images.

On the other hand, people enjoy meeting the Other in the frontiers of Disneyland. In TDL, all of the 'lands' that constitute the major attractions have the same semantic structure. So, for example,

Fantasyland provides a representative example of how visitors meet the Other in these frontiers. Fantasyland is semantically the heart of Disneyland, and the location from where the Disney fantasy spreads so widely. It is also the place where movies, television, picture books, and comics come together and capture the imagination at the physical level. Most importantly, however, Fantasyland is also another 'frontier' – specificially, the frontier of fantasy and fairy tales. The Others in this frontier are fairies, dwarfs, small animals, insects, and other imaginary creatures, such as witches, pirates, and creatures that live at the bottom of the sea.

It is often pointed out that fantasy is the very foundation of Disney's imagination, and that his commercial success owes much to folk tales. This, however, is by no means blind adaptation. Disney did considerable work on the stories before taking them into his own world, and this structural change is what we must consider here. The best example is *Snow White and the Seven Dwarfs* (1937), Disney's first full-length animation film, which also received an Academy Award. The original story collected by the Grimm brothers is that of death and rebirth, a common theme in folk tales. Snow White's stepmother exiles the princess to the woods, where dwarfs save her from death. In one version, the princess is taken to the home of cannibal dwarfs, which shows that these dwarfs are aliens from a strange world, and the princess is in, what Victor Turner called, a 'liminal' situation. When she learns that the princess is alive, the stepmother tries to kill her with different tricks. In each attempt, the princess dies, but is always brought back to life by the dwarfs. Death and rebirth in a liminal situation is the basic pattern when stories are based on a rite of passage. In the end, the princess escapes death by the poisoned apple and returns to the kingdom. The original story ends quite dramatically as the stepmother is tormented to death, forced to dance wearing red-hot iron shoes.

The original oppositions in the story between the kingdom and the woods, and between the queen and the dwarfs, are completely destroyed in Disney's version. There is no hint of violence in his fantasy. Disney deleted the part where the queen dances herself to death in the iron shoes and her tricks are cut down from three to one. More importantly, the strange dwarfs of the woods become adorable characters. They are given names like 'real people' and all hints of their strangeness are removed. When Disney was working on this film, he was concerned with these 'aliens' more than anything else and wanted to turn them into lovable characters. In the end, he succeeded in eradicating the original structure, and reduced the contrast between the kingdom and the woods to mere background. He also changed the focus to center on the princess, the friendly dwarfs, other cute little creatures of the woods, and the prince who saved Snow White. Disney's *Snow White* is not at all a folk tale of death and rebirth, but the fantasy of a young girl surrounded by cute, adorable pets and dreaming of a prince.

Disney similarly transformed other folk tales. Typically, instead of opposing the external and the internal, unknown nature is colonized as part of the familiar kingdom. The performers of this 'external' world are adorable, tamed little creatures. Through this process Disney killed the sense of time that generates folk tales. In Disney's fantasy world, the 'external' is already a part of the internalized world, where everybody is domesticated into a cute being. And, this same structure functions in other lands as well. The strange 'exteriority' that was colonized in Fantasyland is the 'Wild West' of Westernland, the 'tropics' of Adventureland, and the 'strange planet' of Tomorrowland. Thus, all Others in this 'kingdom of dreams and magic' are tamed, and there is no room for an 'external' world to exist. In Disneyland we experience only the continuous reproduction of the 'happy present.' Visitors tour different sets, but never through different experiences, because what seems varied on the surface is structurally the same.

'Disneyfication' in contemporary Japanese society

The resemblance of contemporary Japanese society to Disneyland can be seen in two ways. First, everyday reality in Japan after the 1970s has become an extension of the 'screen' created by the media, in the same way that Disneyland is a three-dimensional Disney film. Indeed, downtown areas, shopping centers, tourist sites, and even living quarters are losing their depth and width, increasingly resembling a flat TV screen. One example of this spatial change is the Seibu Group's space planning around Shibuya, Tokyo. After the late 1970s, Shibuya became one of the most fashionable meeting places in Tokyo, and young people preferred to gather there more than in Shinjuku, where the radical cultural movements had once assembled in the 1960s. This change was initiated by the redevelopment of the Kouen Douri (Park Street) district in Shibuya, managed by the Seibu Group, one of the largest retail companies in Japan. In 1973, Seibu built a new commercial building called Parco in the middle of Kouen Douri, on the way from Shibuya to Harajuku, another fashionable gathering place for young people after the 1970s. Thus, Seibu created a new image of Shibuya around Kouen Douri and presented this area as the open theater of cultural consumption where every consumer took a role through consumable self-images.

Like Disneyland, Seibu's space planning packaged an area as an enclosed space, and employed three main strategies. First, to give exotic names to locations in order to set them up as 'stages.' Accordingly, the scenery became exotic and ever-changing, as if someone had cut out photographs of foreign cities and pasted them on. Also, the new exotic names helped to cut off outside areas, and transform the streets into a space with its own reality. Second, the area was made into a sequence of separate individual spaces, in contrast to the traditional department store, which typically has an overview. Each boxed space has its own particular genre, connected by intricate maze-like paths. Third, this new commercial space produced a 'segmented sensation,' because unlike older downtown areas that contained a variety of different elements, each of these spaces was constructed according to its own 'theme' and 'taste' (Yoshimi, 1987).

What the Seibu Group did in Shibuya was to take a designated area out of the surrounding region, and to transform it into a theater through the accumulation of sequences. This kind of planning was an obvious sign of a new trend in the production of space, which Disneyland carried out in a more deliberated way. The transformation of downtown into a shopping mall in the 1970s was, in a way, analogous to the shift from amusement parks to Disneyland in the 1980s. One writer wrote in 1983,

> Disneyland begins with Main Street, buildings that take after the belle époque period of the early 20th century. Somehow it's all familiar … and a moment later I realize that the place is just like Spanish Street in Shibuya or Pension Street in Kiyosato, that have Swiss, German, Spanish, etc., everything but Japanese settings. Partially and on a smaller scale, Disneyland's structure had already existed from the 1970s in Japan. (Sansijin, 1983: 330)

The transformation of space planning paralleled the transformation of the discursive structure. Indeed, the discursive system of Disneyland in the 1980s had also been preceded in the previous decade. As Disneyland tamed strangers from the external world and made them into adorable creatures, contemporary Japanese society also produced a discourse to colonize strangers. For example, the word *kawaii*, originally used to express affectionate feeling towards small animals and children who are too weak to support themselves, started to exert an influence on young people in the mid–1970s. Young girls would employ *kawaii* handwriting, collect *kawaii* goods, and make friends with *kawaii* characters in a *kawaii* room, thus become *kawaii* girls themselves in a world of fantasy. In other words, *kawaii* is a credential for inclusion in this imagined community of fantasy. All that is *kawaii* is taken in, and all that is not *kawaii* is denied entrance. By looking at the world through this *kawaii* discourse, it is possible to shut out problematic reality from perception. The system of *kawaii* that started to influence young people in the 1970s seems quite innocent on surface, but it is in fact surprisingly cruel.

The spread of this *kawaii* system conforms to numerous other phenomena. Today, the objects of *kawaii* culture also exist as room decorations for children's playrooms, gift shops, and building façades in suburban shopping. If, as in my analysis of *Snow White*, the colonization of the external world could be called 'Disneyfication,' a system of broad colonization exists in contemporary Japan that could be called 'cutification.' Ken Ohira, a psychiatrist, provides a wide range of examples to show that there is a tendency among contemporary Japanese people to avoid confrontation by recognizing both themselves and others as a set of goods. People turn themselves and others into goods or pets by 'sterilizing the uncertain and the dark sides' from their everyday consciousness (Ohira, 1990: 217–18). Needless to say, this was the same system used in Disneyland to tame strangers from the 'external' world and change them into *kawaii* beings. Contemporary Japanese young people 'sterilize' the external within themselves and take on the roles of *kawaii* kids in never-neverland just as Disney transformed the strange dwarfs in the medieval woods into cute, lovable characters.

Conclusions

So far, I have discussed the spatial-discursive structure of TDL and its correspondence with the transformation of the Japanese cultural landscape after the 1970s. What can we conclude from these discussions in terms of the structural change of 'America' in contemporary Japan? As noted in the opening section, TDL has usually been referred to as 'America in Japan.' Its origins and successes are seen as the culmination of postwar 'Americanization.' Even criticisms of TDL (for example, 'in trying to sell American images, the park would become too American to be smoothly managed by the Japanese' ['Disneyland,' 1983]) seemed to accept as self-evident that TDL was an imported artifact from the U.S.A. According to this view, the cultural meanings of TDL were endorsed by the meanings of the original Disneyland in Anaheim, and thus TDL might be seen as the new symbol of 'America,' which represented wealth and innovation in Japan from the 1920s.

Mary Yoko Brannen (1992) has presented an effective critique of this position. Instead of regarding TDL as a derivative of American civilization, or a mere copy of the original Disneyland in Anaheim, she emphasizes the process of re-contextualization of Disneyland in the

Japanese cultural context. She maintains that this re-contextualization was a specifically Japanese construction of cultural consumption. For example, Main Street U.S.A. in Anaheim is the World Bazaar in Tokyo. She says of Tokyo's World Bazaar:

> the storefronts are full-size, as opposed to the three-quarter scale of the original ones, and the façades face Main Street directly, rather than being set at an angle, resulting in a less intimate welcome ... plus the covered walkways and glass roof over the entire World Bazaar give Tokyo's Main Street the feel of a large suburban shopping mall.

Brannen insists that this commercial character of TDL can be explained by Japanese gift-giving customs. According to Brannen, visitors can buy many mementos at the World Bazaar, a function of TDL that is based on the strong cultural needs of Japanese visitors.

If this re-contextualization can be called a strategy of 'making the exotic familiar,' there is another kind of re-contextualization which may be called 'making the exotic exotic.' Against the Western idea of cultural imperialism which operates to a certain degree, Brannen emphasizes that a different type of cultural imperialism is at work in TDL: 'This Japanese form of cultural imperialism operates by continually reinforcing the distinction between Japan and the Other, by keeping the exotic exotic.' For example, the treatment of *gaijin* ('foreigner,' usually Western and white) employees at TDL is complex. There are two categories of *gaijin* employees: cast members who dress up as Peter Pan, Snow White, or Cinderella, and authentic crafts people, such as Swiss clockmakers, glassblowers, and silversmiths:

> These gaijin employees function as 'authentic artifacts' with whom Japanese guests can have their pictures taken to legitimate the experience of foreign vacation. To maintain their distinction as exotic, gaijin employees are asked to speak only in English and not to wear name tags, presumably so that guests do not relate to them as individuals. Rather than function as facilitators of the Disneyland experience, gaijin employees are put on display. (Brannen, 1992: 230)

Although Brannen's analysis of TDL as an artifact re-contextualized in Japanese culture is more useful than the cultural imperialists' view in which TDL is a symbol of American cultural dominance all around the global village, I must take issue with her view of the Japanese cultural context itself. In her analysis, it seems that there is a kind of stable continuity in Japanese culture and identity. She explains the commercial character of the World Bazaar by the gift-giving needs of the Japanese, and she keeps the space of the 'exotic' limited to foreign people. In this process of re-contextualization, Japanese culture, the context, seems to remain the same as it has always been. In contrast, I have argued that the very 'context' in which Japanese society re-contextualized American artifacts had structurally changed in the 1970s. The younger generations of Japenese born after the 1960s, who constitute the majority of TDL visitors, no longer have the same background and identity as the preceding generation. So, if the similarity between TDL and the shopping mall can be explained by the gift-giving needs of the Japanese, this 'gift-giving' might be very different from the traditional one.

Regarding this contextual change, Marilyn Ivy's (1995) analysis of the advertising campaign of 'Exotic Japan' produced by Japan National Railway from 1984 is also persuasive. Ivy compared this campaign with the preceding 1970s campaign of 'Discover Japan,' and concludes that the Japanese have clearly exoticized themselves. According to Ivy, the important point is that 'Exotic Japan' was written in *katakana*, the Japanese script used to transcribe foreign languages, as if 'Japan' itself had been interjected as the foreign, as something that entered from the outside. As foreign people usually are not expected to be able to read *katakana*, this 'Japan' represents the foreign for the Japanese. Thus, at the level of the script, 'Exotic Japan' established Japan as elsewhere, as Other. Yet the message of this advertising was 'an almost comically stereotypical description of Japan as seen by westerners' (Ivy, 1995: 50-1). Although the basic structure of the exoticism, and of Orient-alism more broadly, remains and penetrates throughout society, Japanese people stand on both sides as 'Westerner' and as the Other. In other words, all of Japan becomes exoticized for the Japanese themselves: here the native becomes the foreign.

It is also important to consider the increase of TDL's visitors from Asian countries and the diffusion of the cultural artifacts remade in Japan after the late 1980s. In the late 1980s, TDL saw a considerable increase in visitors from other Asian countries. According to the Oriental Land Corporation, foreign visitors amounted to 6 percent of all visitors, almost all from East and Southeast Asia. This phenomenon triggers some questions: is this Disneyland experience for Asian visitors the same as the experience of American Disneyland for Japanese? Is the postwar relationship between 'Japan' and 'America' being reproduced in a different phase? For example, Shinobu Yoshioka (1989) gives an interesting description of how 'Japan' functions as a symbol of wealth and innovation in today's Thailand. Japanese pop stars frequently appear in Thai magazines for the young, and famous Japanese brands are copied by the Thai fashion industry. At the same time, a Thai magazine editor says, 'You know how they say *kakkoii* ['stylish'] and *kawaii* in Japan? We have come to use the same expressions here in Thailand.' It seems that a kind of fictionalization or self-exoticization process has also already begun in Thailand. In this process of self-exoticization, both the U.S.A. and Japan have become detached from existing nations; they become the focusing/vanishing points of perspectives in the world reconstructed on a hyper-real level as a universe of commercial goods. Unlike colonization forced by cultural imperialism, the hyper-realization of the external/internal relationship which Disneyland so cleverly actualized is embedded in commercial artifacts, spaces, and performative relationships, and spreads in Japan as well as to other Asian countries. There is the possibility that a Disneyfying (cutifying) society may eventually transcend national boundaries. We must follow these transformations from various aspects, with the constant reminder that these changes constitute the spatial-discursive system of contemporary global capitalism.

References and other sources

Allen, F. L. (1931) *Only Yesterday: An Informal History of the 1920s*. New York, Harper & Brothers.
Ando, K. (1931/1977) *Ginza saiken*. Chuoukouronsha.
Ang, I. (1985) *Watching Dallas: Soap Opera and the Melodramatic Imagination*. London, Methuen.
Brannen, M. Y. (1992) '"Bwana Mickey:" constructing cultural consumption at Tokyo Disneyland,' in J. J. Tobin (ed.), *Re-Made in Japan*. New Haven, CT, Yale University Press.
'Disneyland: arubaito daiboshu no amai sasoi no ura no daishougai,' *Shukan Shinchou*, April 14, p. 48.
Dorfman, A. and Mattelart, A. (1975) *How to Read Donald Duck: Imperialist Ideology in the Disney Comics*. New York, International General.
Fjellman, S. M. (1992) *Vinyl Leaves: Walt Disney World and America*. Boulder, CO, Westview Press.
Fujimori, T. (1982) *Meiji no Tokyo keikaku*. Iwanami Shoten.
Hanes, J. E. (1996) 'Taishu bunka/kai bunka/minshu bunka,' in S. Yoshimi (ed.), *Toshi no kukan toshi no shintai*. Keisou Shobou, pp. 91–136.
Hattori, K. (1976) 'Ginza, soshite ginzanization,' *Toshi Mondai*, 67(5): 63–80.
Hebdige, D. (1988) *Hiding in the Light*. London, Routledge.
Imamura, T. (1948) *Manga Eiga-Ron*, Shin-Zen-Bi Sha.
Ishikawa, H. (1981) *Yokubou no sengoshi*. Taihei Shuppansha.
Ito, S. (1986) *Jiorama-ron*. Libro Port.
Ivy, M. (1995) *Discourses of the Vanishing*. Chicago, University of Chicago Press.
Kashiwagi, H. (1990) *Shouzou no nakano kenryoku*. Heibonsha.
Kasson, J. F. (1978) *Amusing the Millions: Coney Island at the Turn of the Century*. New York, Hill and Wang.
Kato, N. (1985) *America no kage*. Kawade Shobou Shinsha.
Lynd, R. S. and Lynd, H. M. (1929) *Middletown: A Study in Contemporary Culture*. New York, Harcourt, Brace and Co.

Mabuchi, K. (1989) *'Zoku' tachi no sengoshi*. Sanseido.

Marin, L. (1973) *Utopiques: jeux d'espaces*. Paris, Éditions de Minuit.

Matsushita, K. (1959) 'Taishu tennousei-ron,' *Chuoukouron*, 74(4): 30–47.

Miyoshi, M. and Harootunian, H. D. (1988) 'Postmodernism in Japan,' *South Atlantic Quarterly*, 87(3): 388–444.

Myerhoff, B. (1983) 'Disneyland no junchi sare shokuminchika sareta souzouryoku,' in Y. Masao and V. Turner (eds), *Misemono no jinruigaku*. Sanseido.

Murobuse, T. (1929) *America: sono Keizai to Bunmei*. Senshinsha.

Nii, I. (1929) 'Americanism to Russianism no kouryu,' *Chuoukouron*, 4(6): 59–66.

Notoji, M. (1990) *Disneyland toiu seichi*. Iwanami Shoten.

Ohira, K. (1990) *Yutakasa no seishinbyouri*. Iwanami Shoten.

Otsuka, E. (1991) *Tasogaredoki ni mitsuketamono*. Ota Shuppan.

Oya, S. (1929/1981) 'Osaka wa nihon no beikoku da,' and 'Osaka bunka no nihon Seifuku,' in *Oya souichi zenshu*, vol. 2. Souyousha, pp. 146–58.

Sansijin (1983) 'Disneyland-kou,' *Usio*, August, p. 330.

Sayers, F. C. (1965) 'Walt Disney accused,' *The Horn Book Magazine*, November/December, pp. 602–11.

Schickel, R. (1985) *The Disney Version: The Life, Times, Art and Commerce of Walt Disney*. New York, Simon & Schuster.

Shimizu, I. (1943) 'Teki toshiteno Americanism,' *Chuoukouron*, 58(4): 81–8.

Takayama, H. (1985) *Me no nakano gekijou*. Seidosha.

Tezuka Productions (1998) *Tezuka Osamu Zenshi*. Akita Shoten.

Thomas, B. (1983) *Walt Disney: An American Original*. New York, Simon & Schuster.

Tomlinson, J. (1977) *Cultural Imperialism: A Critical Introduction*. Baltimore, The Johns Hopkins University Press.

Tsurumi, S. (1956) 'Nihon chishikijin no America-zou,' *Chuoukouron*, 71(7): 170–8.

Yamane, K. (1986) *Hentai shoujo moji no kenkyu*. Kodansha.

Yoshimi, S. (1987) *Toshi no Dramaturgy*. Kobundo.

Yoshimi, S. (1989) 'Yuenchi no utopia', *Sekai*, 528: 293–306.

Yoshimi, S. (1992a) *Hakurankai no seijigaku*. Chuoukouronsha.

Yoshimi, S. (1992b) 'Simulacres no rakuen,' in K. Taki and R. Uchida (eds), *Zero no shujigaku*, Libro Port, pp. 79–136.

Yoshimoto, M. (1989) 'The postmodern and mass images in Japan,' *Public Culture*, Spring: 8–25.

Yoshioka, S. (1989) *Nhonjin gokko*. Bungei Shunju.

CHAPTER 9

Korea: Disney in Korean Mass Culture

SEUNG HYUN KIM AND KYUNG SOOK LEE

Introduction

Since the early 1990s, cultural globalization has become a salient factor in Korea. After the 1988 Seoul Olympic Games, the Korean government opened up the film market, as well as other cultural industries, and since then, the products of transnational companies (TNCs) have inundated urban and rural areas. Consequently, the cultural experiences and lives of Koreans have been greatly influenced by distant forces.

As major agents of global capitalism, TNCs try to enlarge their markets through open-door strategies and global organizations. Global capitalism both promotes and is conditioned by cultural homogeneity and cultural heterogeneity (Robertson, 1992). Although we cannot ignore the centrality of global capitalism, the process of globalization is also propelled locally.

One of the major aspects of globalization, global consciousness, is promoted by mass media and public policies in Korea. While globalization was presented as a catchphrase of the former Kim Young Sam government in South Korea, North Korea has been consistently criticized for closing out the rest of the world after the end of the Cold War. In contrast, the public discourse in South Korea proclaimed globalization as a good and useful survival strategy in a rapidly changing world.

Since the introduction of Korea's globalization policy, various changes have taken place in people's everyday lives, such as the high demand for well-spoken English and the use of the Internet. Many people feel that they need to change in order to fit into the ever-changing world. However, we need to be careful when responding to the process of global change. For example, one can easily find voices in the public discourse which emphasize the benefits of information technologies, and consider global consumer culture as an increase in consumer diversity and sovereignty. On the other hand, supporters of the notion of cultural imperialism argue that national culture should be protected from the TNCs. Interestingly, when publicly responding to the invasion of foreign cultures, policy-makers and the cultural industries take both of these views.

While it is not clear that globalization as a national objective can help enhance the quality of people's lives, it is also uncertain that the concept of cultural imperialism is still effective in explaining contemporary cultural developments. It is necessary at this point to reconsider the effectiveness of the cultural imperialism argument, which has been a major perspective in analyzing cultural flows in international communication since the late 1960s. However, the rapidly changing social and cultural climate of the 1990s is different from the 1970s, and thus cultural imperialism should be challenged from various positions within the study of international communications and cultural studies, including the active audience theory (Roach, 1997). Thompson (1995) argues that the cultural imperialism thesis is simply too rigid and one-dimensional to explain a global situation which is in considerable flux. But what is an effective framework to explain these cultural changes? The research into cultural imperialism was focused on how many cultural products of TNCs from the centers were distributed and how they influenced the cultural industries and mass cultures in the peripheries. To overcome the simplicity of this argument, it is now necessary to consider these cultural encounters in particular contexts.

As an example of a revised approach, this chapter describes, historically, the reception of the products of the Walt Disney Company during the process of cultural globalization in Korea. The discussion focuses on the ways that foreign culture works and has been represented in the local context, especially considering the historical context of the reception of Disney products. The chapter also briefly discusses the responses of audience members who have grown up experiencing Disney products.

The Walt Disney Company is an appropriate case study because it is a leading transnational media company with global impact. Futhermore, Disney products are encountered and used in Koreans' everyday lives and are the most popular cultural products in South Korea. Indeed, the leading Disney characters, Mickey and Minnie, have been popular in Korea for a long time. The genre of animation has been socially recognized and established as a cultural mode of entertainment due to Disney's popularity in Korea. Above all, Disney products are closely related to the national and cultural identity of the U.S.A., which has been deeply involved in the modernization of Korea.

Before considering the Disney company's activities in Korea, however, the historical context and concept of globalization need more careful attention.

The historical context and interpretation of globalization

Globalization can be defined as 'a social process in which the constraints of geography on social and cultural arrangements recede and in which people become increasingly aware that they are receding' (Waters, 1995: 3). While the concept of globalization seems to justify the spread of Western culture and capitalism, it also implies that, because of the growing systematic and reciprocal interconnectedness of different locales, various groups and minorities from around the world can communicate their situations and opinions to the whole world (Thompson, 1995). The positive aspect of globalization is that it demands the world to reflect seriously on the universal, modern Western-centered history, as well as particular critical discourses opposed to it (Robertson, 1992). Tomlinson (1997a) suggests that the iconoclasm of globalization forces us to rethink critical traditions as well as dominant academic traditions, especially cultural imperialism as a critical discourse of cultural globalization.

Cultural imperialism emerged as an antithesis to the modernization theory in the late 1960s (Roach, 1997). The concept has been used mainly in developing areas of the world to analyze the economic, media, and cultural imbalance between the Third World and developed countries, and has provided the fundamental framework for the analysis of global cultural phenomena over a long period.

Although it emerged as the antithesis of the modernization theory, cultural imperialism is based on the same assumption that history develops in one direction and progresses in a linear form, in which the underdeveloped countries model themselves after developed Western countries. It assumes that information and cultural products flow in one direction on the basis of binary oppositional relationships such as advanced/unadvanced, developed/underdeveloped, center/periphery, etc. However, cultural imperialism does not consider the complex dynamics between and within these relationships, and tends to ignore the difference and inequality among diverse groups and minority cultures (Appadurai, 1990).

Cultural imperialism also assumes that culture is organic, self-contained, and fixed within boundaries. Thus it proposes that self-contained traditional culture can be destroyed with the imposition of another self-contained dominant culture (Tomlinson, 1991). Here, the local becomes a pure culture and the global is the destroyer of the local culture (Ang, 1996). Such a view is very attractive, because many countries are concerned about the cultural homogenization of American consumer culture. Also, when considering the inequality and poverty of large populations around the world, we cannot ignore the cultural imperialism perspective. Tomlinson (1997a) suggests three reasons to assimilate cultural globalization to the cultural imperialism concept: the ubiquity of Western cultural goods, the long history of Western imperialism, and the centrality of capitalism as a cultural influence. But he suggests that contemporary cultural aspects be framed rather differently, because we might ignore the various dynamics and ambiguity which are generated from the global–local cultural encounters if we insist only on the framework of cultural imperialism. The framework also is unlikely to recognize the cultural meanings which are articulated in the particular context of global–local interaction.

Tomlinson (1997a) properly suggests that we should look beyond the self-evidence of global cultural goods, approach global culture as a dialectic, and recognize globalization as a complex decentralizing process. It is difficult to analyze the complex and rapidly changing cultural aspects in the existing binary oppositional framework of the cultural imperialism thesis. Robertson (1992) claims that the social sciences in the past have considered the objective versus subjective, and the individual versus structural determinism, and should avoid perspectives based on these binary oppositions. Robertson's critique may be applied to the concept of cultural imperialism, which needs to consider cultural, interpretative, and subjective aspects in cultural globalization, as well as structural aspects.

Culture does not change in a moment, but interacts with other elements, transforming itself slowly. Global cultural changes, especially, cannot exist independently from the long history of imperialism and colonialism around the world. Cultural change and cultural identity are deeply related to history and people's memory of history in different regions and locales. If we want to approach the cultural globalization phenomena as a dialectic, we should recognize cultural change within the historical context of modern imperialism and colonialism in the Third World. We will also have to consider the particular cultural changes in context with the long process of globalization, beyond the distribution of the cultural products between center and periphery.

How can we examine the complexity and ambiguities of cultural encounters in the particular context? Here, it is necessary to extend the context to the global world, to interpret cultural globalization specifically in historical terms. In this chapter, we will depend on the interpretation of representations of cultural products in the local context based on historical materials, data, and interviews with people in the Korean cultural industry. The representation of cultural products has an important role in the articulation of cultures, because the cultural intermediaries – for example, advertisements, advertising events, criticism, news stories, etc. – primarily provide and inscribe their images onto consumers. Thus, we will examine the historical context, representation of products, and responses of audience members in order to describe the reception of Disney products in Korea since 1990.

The historical context and reception of Disney products before 1990

Due to the geopolitical position of Korea, Koreans have often experienced invasions – large and small – from neighboring countries during their 5000 years of history. Consequently, the Korean people are very sensitive to outside forces. Unfortunately, this unique situation has been used by power groups to control and restrain any opposition from the grassroots. The numerous invasions endured during this long history have been memorized and engraved into what is called Korea's pure cultural identity. Koreans undoubtedly feel similar to each other, because they believe that they have preserved their long history and pure blood against the world. Thus, during the relatively recent process of modernization in their history, their feelings towards anything foreign have been related to these experiences.

The first intense experience with Western culture and modernization in Korea began in the last quarter of the nineteenth century when several powerful states – Japan, China, Russia, the U.S.A., Britain, and France – competed in conquering Korea, occupying East Asia, and moving into the Asian continent and the Pacific region. Here, modernization means 'the process of change that puts a primary value on scientific, technological, social, economic, political and cultural innovations in order to achieve progressively higher levels of productivity, wealth, income, consumption, democratic participation and cultural pluralism' (Tehranian and Tehranian, 1997: 121). At the time, the Chosun Dynasty of Korea had two oppositional foreign policies related to modernization which divided the power elites: 'the closed-door policy' and 'the open-door policy.' These political differences between elites who were ill-prepared for modernization brought chaos, which eventually led to Korea becoming dependent on foreign forces.

As a result, the modernization of Korea was demanded from the outside world, with Japanese and American modes becoming dominant. While the main elements of Japanese modernization were science, technology, and nationalism, in the U.S.A. it was a combination of science, technology, and individualism (Song, 1997a). The U.S. influence was especially essential to the modernization of Korea as a diversionary force against Japanese colonization. For that reason, Korean people considered the U.S.A. as a supporter of modernization and liberator from Japanese colonization (Yoo, 1997). Furthermore, after experiencing Korean independence from Japan and the Korean War in 1950, the U.S.A. has apparently become a friendly nation and represents a utopia to many Korean people.

As du Gay *et al.* (1997) proposed, cultural identity is constructed and transformed according to similarity and difference; it needs to be distinguished from others. During the process of Korean modernization, the U.S.A. and Japan have been positioned as the superior others. In other words, Koreans differentiated their culture from Western and Japanese culture. Modern military and educational systems in Korea were established during the Japanese colonization between 1910 and 1945. But after independence from Japan, Korea's modern institutions – including the mass media – were established and operated by the U.S.A. The Korean people's expectations towards the U.S.A. as a supporter of independence and modernization were transformed into trust of American-style modern institutions, technological applications, and scientific thought (Yoo, 1992).

Under Japanese domination from the 1920s, the modern mass media – including film, records, and radio, etc. – were introduced and represented the dominant trends in Korean mass culture. The cultural mode of film was popularized in the cities, where other facilities of mass culture existed. The major consumers of mass culture were the middle class, and Western cultural products were introduced as end-products (Yoo, 1992). At that time, books and magazines were the only sources of mass media for children.

Disney's Mickey Mouse was introduced to Koreans in 1935 through the 'Dolbo and Mickey' comic strip in the *Chosun Ilbo* (daily newspaper), which imitated the original Mickey (Son, 1996). It is reported that Disney's animated films were seen by the U.S. Army after the Korean War in 1950, and several directors who were interested in animation viewed these films (Kim, 1977).

However, the Korean people were unable to view animated films until *Peter Pan* was introduced in 1957. Film importers advertised the film with messages such as 'Welcome families with children' and 'Let's go to the island of dreams with the eternal boy, Peter Pan.' *Cinderella* was screened during the summer vacation of 1962, together with an advertisement emphasizing that it was produced by 'A great master, Walt Disney.' *Pinocchio* appeared in 1963, accompanied by a film magazine account which praised the film as 'The masterpiece of the perfectionist, Walt Disney' (Lee, 1963). As soon as Korean children showed enthusiasm for Disney films, other animated films were imported. While Max Fleischer's *Gulliver's Travels* was advertised as better than *Snow White* or *Peter Pan*, the name of the producer was not disclosed (*The Dong-a Ilbo*, 1961). UPA's *1001 Arabian Nights* was advertised as 'an animation film produced by Stephen Bosustow who produced *Snow White*' (*The Dong-a Ilbo*, 1962). Because Walt Disney was recognized in Korea, advertising focused on his fame and the fantasy in his films in an effort to attract a wide audience, from young children to older adults.

According to film critics, Disney animated films were evaluated as 'something which was produced by the producer with excellent technique and brilliant ideas as well as large capital in the developed country' (*International Films*, 1962; Lee, 1963). Critics also thought that the films were useful for children and families, especially because there was no other mass medium for children except comic strips, a similar but primitive genre that had become popular among children during the Japanese colonization period. At first, the comic strip was categorized as high culture, but the elitist caricatures were soon regulated by the Japanese colonial government. Thereafter, the content of comic strips and books was changed for children and adults seeking purely entertainment. After independence from Japanese colonization, the import of Japanese cultural products was prohibited by law. But Japanese comic books still were copied illegally and remained available to Koreans, who had no appropriate entertainment during this period. Most illegal comic books contained obscene and inferior content, and were lent and read in dark and seedy rooms. Although this was the only type of entertainment for children and teenagers, it eventually developed a bad reputation. Thus, the comic-book genre came to be perceived as the lowest type of mass culture in Korea (Son, 1996). In addition, Japanese cultural products have been considered inferior by Koreans with memories of colonization.

Although some Korean people have used the Japanese language and some products since the colonial period, the government banned all Japanese cultural products, and users of Japanese goods were criticized as turncoats. In this historical context, while the Korean people perceived the illegal comic books from Japan as uneducational and harmful for children (Son, 1996), they believed that the animated films of Disney had a scientific and educational quality. In Anderson's terms (1983), the images of these cultural products were associated with the imagined cultural and national identities of the two countries in Korea. Furthermore, a public recommendation by the Minister of Education – which was cited in a newspaper advertisement – made people believe that Disney products were good and educational (Whang, 1990). As a result, Disney films came to represent American fantasy and the success of modern science which could help the modernization of Korea.

When the television broadcasting system was introduced and established during the 1960s, animation became a part of regular programing and children could watch animation at home. The first Disney series was *Disneyland*, which was aired weekly on TBC-TV from 1967. Japanese animation also was aired on television, although Japanese films were prohibited from being shown in theaters. Because the country neither had the facilities nor the capacity to produce a variety of programs, broadcasting companies screened imported animation for children during the early evenings. Thus, animation on television, including Japanese films, developed as a genre for children.

Today, children have become accustomed to watching Disney animation on television, especially Disney cartoons on KBS Channel-2, which merged with TBC-TV in 1980. But there are also many animated films imported from Japan, even though people express concern about the negative influence they have on children. On the other hand, there are also claims that the doors should be open to Japanese culture, creating more opportunities for good-quality cultural products in this era of globalization.

To summarize, then, Disney animated films were the first cultural products for children which were available in sociable, public places after the Korean War. The audience perceived them as educational materials and the mass art of an advanced country. Compared with Japanese animated films, people believed that Disney products reflected scientific development and the fantasy of American moder- nization. In contrast with Japanese films, Disney animated films were not affected by any legal restrictions from the Korean government and attracted no criticism from the audience or mass media before 1990. Since then foreign film distributors, as well as other cultural products, have moved intensively into the Korean market, as discussed in the next section of this chapter.

Cultural change after 1990

After trade negotiations between Korea and the U.S.A., resulting in amended film regulations in 1986 and copyright laws in 1987, the Korean film market was forced to open its doors to TNCs. Previously, the Korean film market had been sustained by profits gained from the import of foreign films, which were then reinvested in domestic film production. Under these circumstances, foreign distributors threatened Korean film markets, which in turn lacked autonomy and competitiveness as commodities. The market share of foreign films in Korea is typically quite high, representing an average of 79 percent of total box-office revenues, or about $2.5 billion annually (The Ministry of Culture, 1997). When the market was opened up in 1988, foreign distribution companies rushed in – UIP-CIC and 20th Century-Fox Korea were established in 1988, followed by Warner Bros. in 1989, Columbia Tristar in 1990, Walt Disney Company (Korea) in 1992, and Polygram in 1995. Consequently, the Korean film, home video, and merchandising markets have become battlefields for foreign distributors.

From 1992 through to the end of 1996, Walt Disney Korea released a total of 46 films in Korea, attracting over 8.3 million customers. More than 50 percent (or about $41.6 million) of the profits have been sent back to Disney headquarters in the U.S.A. (The Ministry of Culture, 1997). In 1996 alone, Walt Disney Korea sent 57.2 percent, or about $8.1 million, of their total profits back to the parent company (see Table 9.1). Some of the Disney films that have opened successfully in first-run theaters include *The Lion King, Aladdin, Pocahontas, The Jungle Book, Toy Story, The Hunchback of Notre Dame, 101 Dalmatians*, and *Hercules*.

Table 9.1 Distributors' profits in Korean film market, 1996

Distributor	No. of films	Audience size	Revenues[a] (in U.S.$)	Exported profits [b] (in U.S.$)
UIP-CIC	17	5,816,514	19,333,476	10,201,244
20th Century-Fox Korea	11	3,158,785	13,213,186	6,606,593
Warner Bros.	7	1,091,100	7,862,764	4,717,659
Columbia Tristar	7	1,564,064	6,159,435	3,079,718
Walt Disney Korea	11	3,155,565	18,815,375	8,158,989
Totals	53	14,786,028	65,384,236	32,764,201

Source: Parliamentary inspection by the Ministry of Culture (1997)
a profits from Korean market
b profits exported to U.S. parent company

Although the Korean animation industry has sufficient production competence, the financial system is weak and thus dependence on imported animation is common. When exporting animated products, the companies usually follow the OEM (Original Equipment Manufacturing) method, which resulted in about $92 million in 1996. However, the industry has suffered due to the lack of the complete animated works for export (The Ministry of Culture, 1997). Apparently, Korean manufacturers are not willing to produce animated films because of the high costs and a small domestic market. The companies lack worldwide distribution networks, as well as competence in pre- and post-production; thus subcontracted production is regarded as more stable. Furthermore, as noted above, the profits earned from imported animated films and related products are not reinvested in Korean animation production, as more than 50 percent is sent back to the parent companies.

More specifically, domestic animation and some related industries have been weakened and restructured because of Walt Disney Korea. After the success of Disney's films, several large Korean companies (Samsung, Cheilchedang, Sangyong, etc.) invested in the production of animated films, but were unsuccessful and eventually gave up. Following concerns about Disney's cultural and industrial influence, a group of anti-commercialist animators and cartoonists planned to produce local animation films which would reflect the Korean spirit and feelings. The so-called 'anti-Disney camps,' together with CIC, Fox, and other domestic animation companies, focused their resistance on Disney in 1997. They actively began to offer animated films and challenged Disney's monopoly of the Korean market. But, these local animated films were not supported by the audience because of their poor quality and unfamiliarity. Thus, Disney has been able to maintain its powerful influence on the Korean animation industry, as well as its cultural influence in Korea.

Disney's strategy of market performance and reordering also has been prominent in the video industry, which began in Korea in 1982. In the early stages, small-size videotape manufacturers operated illegally without meeting the facility standards due to economic difficulties. Thus, by 1988, illegal video distribution represented 60 percent of the market. As the Korean video industry reached its maturity, the rate of VCR ownership in Korea grew to 80 percent. Although there was rapid growth, the quality was poor and the video market was mainly dominated by small-size manufacturers in the rental business. However, after the major American distributors – including Disney – entered the Korean video market, they were able quickly to dominate the Korean companies. Buena Vista Home Entertainment (Korea) was established as Disney's second overseas division after

Japan, and directly distributes videotapes, CDs, etc. in Korea. By the end of 1997, the company had released a total of 249 videos, including 110 animated films (The Korean Council for Performing Arts Promotion Database).

In response to the aggressive market invasion of foreign film companies such as Disney, the market-oriented domestic companies have been concentrating on distributing imported products rather than producing their own content. Animated films for children are sold directly to consumers, while imports for adults are largely centered on video rental stores. Buena Vista Home Entertainment (Korea) has seriously influenced this market with advanced marketing strategies and capital. For instance, the company constructed various distribution networks, forming and leading sell-through markets (direct sale to consumers). At the same time, small-size Korean film and video distributors and producers either disappeared or were merged with larger companies. By extending the existing video rental store system to the sell-through system, they caused over-competition among rental houses and the collapse of small-size producers.

The revenues for Buena Vista Home Entertainment (Korea) between 1994 and 1996 reached over $57.8 million, of which about $26.3 million was profit (Table 9.2).

Table 9.2 Annual revenues and profits for Buena Vista Home Entertainment (Korea), 1994–6

Year	No. of video titles sold	Annual revenues (in U.S.$)	Annual profits (in U.S.$)
1994	33	13,227,500	4,782,500
1995	40	18,758,750	8,628,750
1996	41	25,892,500	12,888,750

Source: Statistics of Cultural Industries, Ministry of Culture (1997)

More specifically, Disney expanded the sell-through of videotapes by diversifying distribution networks. For example, they explored new distribution outlets, such as supermarkets and department stores, with the help of Cheilchedang, a local company which recently expanded its business to include the distribution of audiovisual products. In one year, Disney distributed 50 different video titles, including films and direct-to-videos. The volume of sales (150,000 tapes) was considered successful, in light of Korea's weak economy (*The Electronic Times,* 1997: 10, 31).

To sell the Disney products, Cheilchedang introduced various promotional techniques, including the installation of large monitors in supermarkets and the distribution of promotional pamphlets with Disney characters. Both package and telephone sales were used for the first time, as well as the sale of videotapes in rental houses. Disney had an additional advantage with consumer-direct-corners for their products set up at video rental stores.

Disney also prompted disputes because of the low 35 percent margins given to local sales agencies. The local agencies receive only 5 to 10 percent of the total revenues, because they must pay 20 to 25 percent of the margin to department or retail stores. Furthermore, the agencies cannot take any distribution margin from outlet stores, which sell the products at a 20 percent discount (*The Electronic Times*, 1997: 8, 13). Also, Disney required a minimum guarantee (minimum sales limit) from the local agencies. Burdened by the high cost of maintaining large storage space, the local sales agencies eventually dumped their products illegally onto middlemen.

Other examples indicate that Buena Vista Home Entertainment (Korea) fully realizes the local context of its marketing strategies. When the previous government tried to fulfill their globalization policy, one of the requirements was learning English, and thus the number of private English education centers and educational materials have increased. With a local multi-content developer, Disney's Korean subsidiary began producing and distributing English videotapes and multimedia English software with Disney animation. Special video-tapes, CDs and audiotapes for learning English utilized characters from Disney films, such as Aladdin, Winnie the Pooh, etc. (*The Electronic Times*, 1997: 10, 17). In addition, scenes from the Disney classics and television series were used in a series of special collections: for example 'Mickey Specials,' 'Donald Specials,' etc.

Disney also arranged for tie-in promotions with Kellogg's and McDonald's, a result of the long-term cooperation that existed between these companies in the U.S.A. Since the end of 1996, Walt Disney Korea has accepted the PR strategy from Disney headquarters, with various promotional activities at McDonald's: customers receive paper bags decorated with pictures of Disney characters, while various promo-tional materials, such as posters, pamphlets and mobiles, are displayed at McDonald's outlets. These American fast-food restaurants are located in every corner of the city, while young consumers now easily find the tie-in promotions around college campuses and shopping centers.

Walt Disney (Korea) also has benefitted from indirect advertising by holding various special events. In efforts to combat criticism of Disney's commercialism and its negative influence in Korea, the company has tried to enhance its image with children through special events and free programs, including children's painting and writing contests, and, of course, previews of each new animated film. The company also has held a number of humanitarian events, such as raising funds with UNICEF for North Korean children, which was coordinated with the preview of *The Hunchback of Notre Dame*; and for children suffering from cancer, which was linked with the preview of *Sleeping Beauty*. These events were promoted in Disney's advertisements, as well as drawing the media's attention, thus producing indirect advertising.

While Walt Disney Korea plans these various local marketing strategies, the company also draws on the traditional popularity of Disney. For instance, new films are typically advertised as 'the masterpiece of Walt Disney; superior to *Snow White* and *The Little Mermaid*. Experience the pleasure and excitement.' In other words, the popular trust of the Korean audience is used to sell Disney products. Even other film companies compare their products with Disney films in their advertisements. The words most frequently used in the Disney ads are 'Walt Disney,' 'Mickey,' and 'Minnie.' As we discuss below, this aspect is similar to the response of audience members, who associate Disney with Mickey and Minnie over all other characters. According to interviews with the PR coordinator of Buena Vista Korea, 'In Korea, the other characters are not as popular as Mickey and Minnie. Although other Disney animation films became big hits, the characters were never popularized in Korea as much as in other countries.' These points suggest that the representations of cultural products by intermediaries may influence their recognition or image.

It is important to recognize that there have been mixed feelings about Disney in Korea since 1990. On the one hand, the company's aggressive invasion of the Korean market was criticized because of both negative cultural and industrial influences. But despite these anti-Disney feelings, which stem from the reduction of domestic companies' market share and assumed negative cultural influences, Disney products are still popular, and the animated films are considered to be educational, as well as good entertainment for children and families.

Furthermore, these polarized evaluations of Disney are tied to Koreans' historical national feelings about the U.S.A. The animosity towards American commercial culture – symbolized by Disney, Coca-Cola, and McDonald's – was stirred up because of both the aggressive marketing invasions of the 1990s and the anti-Americanism prevalent since the Kwangju struggle for democracy in 1980.[1] Even though children, who are the main audience, have enjoyed Disney products for a long time, the evaluation of Disney has changed in Korea. Thus, it is necessary and appropriate to analyze the current feelings and experiences of audience members by discussing the reception of Disney culture in Korea.

Historical context and audience response

Recent mass-media analysis, especially on cultural imperialism and cultural studies, has placed more emphasis on audience reception than on media texts and production. Therefore, this chapter briefly analyzes some of the responses of the Korean audience to Disney products and interprets the results in a historical context.

The respondents sampled in this analysis were college students in Korea who have generally experienced Disney products since they were very young. The study was designed to investigate what kind of experiences the students had with Disney and how these experiences mixed with their current feelings and impressions. The sample included 114 students from Korea University in Seoul, who were asked about the experiences, impressions, and values they associate with Disney. The first stage involved structured questionnaires to elicit general responses, followed by in-depth interviews with ten college students in June 1997 to gather more specific data.

Generally speaking, the respondents' first experience of Disney occurred when they were about 7 years old. As they grew older, their liking for Disney products diminished. In everyday life, they experienced Disney through various products: animated films in theaters (97.3 percent), on television (83.2 percent), through video-tapes and discs (71.7 percent), records and CDs (70.8 percent), and comic books (52.2 percent). However, their possession of Disney materials was lower than their experience rate. The possession rate was only 56.1 percent, while the experience rate through rentals of Disney products was 70.2 percent. According to the in-depth interviews, they found it easy to watch Disney animation on television without any special effort.

The respondents also were asked about their immediate image of Disney: 'As you look back on all your experiences of Disney, what kind of image instantly comes to your mind?' The responses were as follows: 'animation' (36.8 percent), 'Mickey Mouse' (13.5 percent), 'cuteness' (12.3 percent), 'capitalism' (8.6 percent), 'children' (6.8 percent), 'fantasy' (6.1 percent), and 'dream and hope' (5.5 percent). In Korea, it seems that the audience generally thinks of Disney as the symbol of animation. Furthermore, in the in-depth interviews, the respondents usually associated Disney with Mickey and Minnie.

To the next question, 'Do you like Disney products and why?,' the respondents answered that they did not have a chance to choose any other cartoons or other similar entertainment. They could not help but choose Disney because they have been told that Japanese animation was morally debased, and Korean animation was uninteresting and inferior. In fact, in the in-depth interviews, audience members criticized Japanese animation and comic books, and even thought that they had a bad influence on children. The respondents claimed that Disney was better than Japanese animation in many respects, and they had more positive feelings towards Disney.

It may not be surprising to find these ambivalent feelings towards the U.S.A. represented in the responses. Because the audience has been taught the ideology of anti-communism, the U.S.A. naturally is presented as a friendly nation that defends liberal and democratic nations from the threat of communists. The historical context of anti-communism has encouraged people to form positive feelings towards American products, even in animation. However, anti-Americanism has been prevalent on college campuses nationwide since the Kwangju uprising in 1980, and thus most college students have experienced anti-Americanism.

While the students evaluated Disney products as helpful for education and wanted to recommend them for children, they still showed resistance towards American commercial culture. Many of them explained that American culture was reflected in the cultural products of Disney and made their tastes more Americanized in their everyday lives. In this context, the respondents' dual feelings about Disney can be summarized as pleasure and commercialism, familiarity and antagonism. This is represented in the in-depth interview of a female student, who said:

> The United States has been a fantasy land to me. My younger sister likes American-made products very much. Before I entered university, I also liked them. Now, I realize that I have been mindlessly yearning for the United States. I know that I have been unconsciously Americanized. But children like the products of the United States and they are inclined to adopt American lifestyles. Perhaps the reason is that the American products are better than ours. It is also easy to encounter American culture through television advertising and the other mass media.

Respondents also identified Disney as American culture rather than global culture, with 92 respondents agreeing that 'Disney is typical American culture.' While many of the respondents felt a moral duty to consume Korean animation and products, they have become accustomed to the styles and tastes of Disney, and explained that 'It is not easy to find pleasure and familiarity from Korean animation.'

In general, the data have shown that people's feelings towards Disney are intermingled with the imagined cultural identity of the U.S.A., and that the impact of Disney on Korean mass culture is reflected in the tastes, values and familiarity of the audience.

Summary

Studying cultural changes on an international level, mass-media researchers have focused on how many cultural products from the center are distributed to the peripheries, and how these products influence the structure of cultural industries and mass culture in periphery countries. The most popular framework used to explain the cultural dependency that exists between the Western world and the Third World is 'cultural imperialism.' However, contemporary global changes and the global awareness of these factors have prompted researchers to explore new ways of thinking and to consider a new framework to explain the current cultural flows in the social world. To overcome the polarized views of cultural imperialism, it is necessary to consider the particular context of cultural encounters during the process of globalization and to interpret the deeper meanings beyond the mere facts of cultural distribution.

As a major agent of cultural globalization and a leading TNC, the Walt Disney Company has introduced popular cultural forms into Korea. We have seen how the U.S.A. and Japan have been deeply involved in modern Korean history. During the process of modernization in Korea, Disney's animated films represented American fantasy and provided educational materials for children. Disney animated films also mobilized children and other family members as an audience during the development of mass media in Korea. Compared to the illegally imported Japanese cultural products, Disney products have been warmly received by the Korean audience.

Nevertheless, after opening the door to foreign distributors or TNCs at the beginning of the 1990s, the Korean mass media and cultural policy-makers expressed their concerns specifically about Disney's influence on Korean mass culture and cultural industries. At the same time, they proposed that the Korean animation industry should develop by learning Disney's animation techniques and innovative ideas.

In the meantime, Walt Disney Korea introduced various marketing techniques and reshaped the map of the cultural industry with their strong capital and marketing know-how. Thus, Walt Disney Korea changed the local market and distribution networks, especially changing an inferior cultural production industry into a distribution-centered industry.

However, the Korean audience, which previously felt positive about Disney, became ambivalent after 1990 as Disney products inundated the Korean market. Walt Disney Korea continued to attract consumers with various products, advertisements and special events. Audience members had more opportunities to consume Disney products, which became more familiar than domestic cultural products. In addition, audience members who had experienced anti-American movements since 1980 also began to resist Disney products. Since 1990, the increasing critiques of American commercial culture and the relative inferiority of domestic cultural products have influenced attitudes about Disney. Therefore, we can say that these ambivalent feelings about Disney historically originated from the globalization process in the early 1990s.

The survey respondents reported that they were more familiar with Disney products than with Korean animation and characters. While they consciously want to like Korean cultural products more than Disney products, they say that they cannot resist the familiarity and pleasure of Disney. It might be said that they suffer from guilty consciences from consuming Disney products. On the other hand, they still evaluated Disney products as educational and helpful, even recommending and choosing them as presents for children.

As a result, it can be argued that the ambivalent feelings towards, as well as the trust of, Disney products is associated with the historical context of modernization in Korea. Furthermore, Koreans' feelings about Disney are intermingled with their feelings about the U.S.A. Additionally, the products of Disney and Disney itself are considered symbols of American culture and are associated with the cultural identity of the U.S.A. in Korea.

Note

1. The Kwangju incident occurred after the death of long-time dictator Park, when Koreans had a chance to democratize Korean society, but ex-president Chun Doo-hwan, with the help of the U.S.A., led a successful bloody coup. After the struggle, anti-American movements actively developed around the college campuses, along with many student boycotts against American products.

References and other sources

Anderson, B. (1983) *Imagined Communities: Reflections on the Origin and Spread of Nationalism*. London, Verso.

Ang, I. (1985) *Watching* Dallas: *Soap Opera and the Melodramatic Imagination*. London, Methuen.

Ang, I. (1990) 'Culture and communication: towards an ethnographic critique of media consumption in the transnational media system,' *European Journal of Communication*, 5(2–3): 239–60.

Ang, I. (1991) *Desperately Seeking the Audience*. London, Routledge.

Ang, I. (1996) 'In the realm of uncertainty: the global village and capitalist postmodernity,' in I. Ang (ed.), *Living Room Wars: Rethinking Media Audiences for a Postmodern World*. London, Routledge, pp. 162–80.

Appadurai, A. (1990) 'Disjuncture and difference in the global cultural economy,' in M. Featherstone (ed.), *Global Culture: Nationalism, Globalization and Modernity*. London, Sage, pp. 295–310.

Beltran, L. R. and Fox, E. (1979) 'Latin America and United States: flaws in the free flow of information,' in K. Nordenstreng and H. I. Schiller (eds), *National Sovereignty and International Communication*. Norwood, NJ, Ablex, pp. 33–64.

Biltereyst, D. (1991) 'Resisting American hegemony: a comparative analysis of the reception of domestic and U.S. fiction,' *European Journal of Communication*, 6(4): 469–97.

Boyd-Barrett, J. O. (1982) 'Cultural dependency and the mass media,' in M. Gurevitch, T. Bennett, T. Curran, and J. Woolacott (eds), *Culture, Society and the Media*. London, Methuen, pp. 174–95.

Joo, C. Y. (1997) *The Interpretative Positions of the Audience and the Invitations of Television Drama*, Doctoral thesis, University of Glasgow.

Dorfman, A. and Mattelart, A. (1971) *How to Read Donald Duck: Imperialist Ideology in the Disney Comics*. New York, International General.

Du Gay, P., Hall, S., Janes, L., Mackay, H., and Negus, K. (1997) *Doing Cultural Studies: The Story of the Sony Walkman*. London, Sage/The Open University.

Featherstone, M. (1990) 'Global culture: an introduction,' in M. Featherstone (ed.), *Global Culture*. London, Sage, pp. 1–4.

Featherstone, M. (1993) 'Global and local cultures,' in J. Bird, B. Curtis, T. Putnam, G. Robertson, and L. Tichenor (eds), *Mapping the Futures: Local Cultures, Global Change*. London and New York, Routledge, pp. 169–87.

Fejes, F. (1981) 'Media imperialism: an assessment,' *Media, Culture and Society*, (3)3: 281–9.

Fejes, F. (1984) 'Critical communication research and media effects: the problem of the disappearing audience,' *Media, Culture and Society*, 6(3): 219–32.

Ferguson, M. (1992) 'The mythology about globalization,' *European Journal of Communication*, 7(1): 69–93.

Friedman, J. (1994) *Cultural Identity and Global Process*. Thousand Oaks, CA, London and New Delhi, Sage.

Giddens, A. (1990) *The Consequence of Modernity*. Cambridge, Polity Press.

Giddens, A. (1991) *Modernity and Self-Identity*. Cambridge, Polity Press.

Golding, P. and Harris, P. (1997) *Beyond Cultural Imperialism*. London, Sage.

Grossberg, L. (1996) 'Identity and cultural studies: is that all there is?' in S. Hall and P. du Gay (eds), *Questions of Cultural Identity*. London, Sage, pp. 87–107.

Grossberg, L. (1997a) 'The cultural studies' crossroad blues,' unpublished paper presented at the Cultural Studies Workshop, Seoul, Korea.

Grossberg, L. (1997b) 'Globalization, media and agency,' unpublished paper presented at the Cultural Studies Workshop, Seoul, Korea.

Hall, S. (1996) 'Who needs "identity"?' in S. Hall and P. du Gay (eds), *Questions of Cultural Identity*. London, Sage, pp. 1–17.

Hamelink, C. J. (1994) *Trends in World Communication*. Penang, Malaysia, Southbound.

Han, C. W. (1997) *A Study of Comics, Cartoons and the Animation Industry in Korea*. Seoul, The Farm Comics.

Han, C. W. (1998) *The Economics of Animation*. Seoul, Communication Books.

Hannerz, U. (1997) 'Notes on the global ecumene,' in A. Sreberny-Mohammadi, D. Winseck, J. McKenna, and O. Boyd-Barrett (eds), *Media in Global Context*. London, Arnold, pp. 11–18.

International Films (1962) 'The original writer of Cinderella,' *The International Films*, March. Seoul, The International Films News Sa, p. 71.

Jensen, K. B. (1987) 'Qualitative audience research: toward an interpretive approach to reception,' *Critical Studies in Mass Communication*, 4(1): 21–36.

Kim, H. G. (1997) 'The cultural globalization: the theory and reality,' *Nova Humanitas*, 1: 276–97. Seoul, Hangil Sa.

Kim, S. H. (1996) 'Mass media and the global culture,' in S. W. Lim and H. C. Choi (eds), *The Korean Society and Journalism*. Seoul, Nanam, pp. 605–33.

Kim, Y. W. (1977) 'A consideration on Korean animation: a comparative study of Korean animation and foreign animation,' MA thesis, Graduate School of Communications, Ewha Women's University.

Klugman, K. (1995) *Inside the Mouse*. Durham, NC, Duke University Press.

Lee, H. W. (1983) 'Fantasia: the harmony of arts and the child's heart,' *The Films*, October. Seoul, The Films Sa, pp. 84–5.

Lee, Y. J. (1963) 'Review of *Pinocchio*,' *The Film World*, March. Seoul, The Film World Sa, p. 122.

Liebes, T. and Katz, E. (1986) 'Patterns of involvement in television fiction: a comparative analysis,' *European Journal of Communication*, 1: 151–71.

Liebes, T. and Katz, E. (1990) *The Export of Meaning: Cross-Cultural Readings of Dallas*. New York, Oxford University Press.

Mattelart, A., Delcourt, X., and Mattelart, M. (1984) *International Image Markets*. London, Comedia.

Martin-Barbero, J. (1993) *Communication, Culture and Hegemony*. London, Sage.

Ministry of Culture (1997) *Statistics for the Cultural Industries*.

Mohammadi, A. (1997) *International Communication and Globalisation: A Critical Introduction*. London, Sage.

Moores, S. (1993) *Interpreting Audiences*. London, Sage.

Morley, D. (1994) 'Active audience theory: pendulums and pitfalls,' in M. R. Levy and M. Gurevitch (eds), *Defining Media Studies: Reflections on the Future of the Field*. Oxford, Oxford University Press, pp. 255–61.

Morley, D. (1996) 'EurAm, modernity, reason and alterity or, postmodernism, the highest stage of cultural imperialism?' in D. Morley and K. S. Chen (eds), *Stuart Hall*. London, Routledge.

Negus, K. (1997) 'The production of culture,' in P. du Gay (ed.), *Production of Culture/Cultures of Production*. London, Sage/The Open University.

Ritzer, G. (1996) *The McDonaldization of Society*. Thousand Oaks, CA, Pine Forge Press.

Roach, C. (1997) 'Cultural imperialism and resistance in media theory and literary theory,' *Media, Culture and Society*, 19(1): 47–66.

Robertson, R. (1992) *Globalization: Social Theory and Global Culture*. London, Sage.

Schiller, H. I. (1976) *Communication and Cultural Domination*. New York, M. E. Sharpe.

Schiller, H. I. (1989) *Culture, Inc.: The Corporate Takeover of Public Expression*. New York, Oxford University Press.

Seaman, W. R. (1992) 'Active audience theory: pointless populism,' *Media, Culture and Society*, 14(2): 301–11.

Silji, A. (1988) *East of Dallas: The European Challenge to American Television*. London, British Film Institute.

Smoodin, E. (1994) *Disney Discourse: Producing the Magic Kingdom*. New York, Routledge.

Son, S. I. (1996) *The History of Cartoons in Korea*. Seoul, Press V.

Song, D. Y. (1997a) 'What does modernity mean for us?' *Contemporary Thought*. Seoul, Mineum Sa., pp. 100–16.

Song, L. H. (1997b) *Animation School*. Seoul, Seoul Moonwha Sa.

Tehranian, M. and Tehranian, K. K. (1997) 'Taming modernity: towards a new paradigm,' in A. Mohammadi (ed.), *International Communication and Globalisation*. London, Sage.

Thompson, J. B. (1995) *The Media and Modernity*. Cambridge, Polity Press.

Thompson, K. (1997) *Media and Cultural Regulation*. London, Sage/The Open University.

Tomlinson, J. (1991) *Cultural Imperialism: A Critical Introduction*. Baltimore, The Johns Hopkins University Press.

Tomlinson, J. (1997a) 'Globalisation, culture and cultural imperialism,' in A. Mohammadi (ed.), *International Communication and Globalisation: A Critical Introduction*. London, Sage.

Tomlinson, J. (1997b) 'Internationalism, globalisation and cultural imperialism,' in K. Thompson (ed.), *Media and Cultural Regulation*. London, Sage/The Open University.

Wallerstein, I. (1991) *Geopolitics and Geoculture*. Cambridge, Cambridge University Press.

Waters, M. (1995) *Globalization*. London and New York, Routledge.

Whang, G. B. (1989) *A Study on the Structural Characteristics of the Videogram Industry in Korea*, MA thesis, Graduate School of Communications, Seoul National University.

Whang, S. G. (1990) *A History of Animation*. Seoul, Baeksoo Sa.

Yoo, S. Y. (1992) *A Study on the Process of Modern Construction of Popular Culture in Korea*. Doctoral thesis, Graduate School of Communications, Korea University.

Yoo, S. Y. (1997) 'Cultural identity of the yellow colony: an Americanized modernity,' *Media and Society*, 18: 81–122.

Plus various articles from the daily newspapers, *The Dong-a Ilbo* and *The Electronic Times*.

CHAPTER 10

Mexico: Disney in Mexico: Observations on Integrating Global Culture Objects into Everyday Life

SILVIA MOLINA Y VEDIA

Besides its formal presence in specialized stores and advertisements, Disney images are informally present in daily life and local culture in Mexico. Donald and Mickey comics, among others, have been on sale at magazine stands for over 50 years. Figures of Snow White and the Seven Dwarfs, Pluto, Goofy and Pinocchio adorn the walls of daycare centers and kindergartens. At children's parties, glasses, plastic utensils, disposable plates, games, decoration – that is, almost all the paraphernalia that defines the childlike condition of a children's party – bear images from some of the best-known or most fashionable Disney cartoons. It is possible to find Mexican piñatas shaped like Donald, Peter Pan or Hercules and, sometimes, fireworks in the popular festivals also represent favorite Disney characters. Every so often, a clown dressed as Mickey Mouse or the Lion King appears to pep up the families that have gathered in Chapultepec and other public parks in Mexico City. The presence of Disney products and services is normal in these situations, and, in fact, it would be strange not to find them. Indeed, this illustrates how Disney has appropriated the urban landscape in this city, contributing to the colorful disorder that characterizes it.

The 'informal economy' is also involved in the production, distribution and marketing of Disney products and services. In Mexico City, Disney products sold in shopping malls and specialized businesses are easily confused with those sold at street-side stands, offered by street-corner vendors or pirated merchandise on sale in the infamous Tepito market.[1]

This chapter explores the levels of exposure to Disney products and services, especially among a specific group in Mexico City, as well as the meaning attributed to these products and the fantasies they evoke. The object is to demonstrate how people have made Disney products and services 'theirs' and how this contributes to the 'soft' integration of Mexicans into the global culture.[2]

The extended presence of Disney products in Mexico City feeds social fantasies, thus maximizing the products and services' power of attraction. At the same time as social fantasy absorbs the products to tell its own stories, it also promotes their acceptance. This is their entry into the market. Such access, however, isn't simple. It supposes that society elaborates fantasies based on the fantasies sold by the products, connecting the latter in some way with its own self-representation.

This study attempts to delve deeper into the way in which this connection is made between the Disney fantasy world and Mexican people, or, at least, a specific group of Mexican people. The study is based on a survey and interviews with mostly young adults with some college education from Mexico City's urban middle class. The interpretation of the data included comparative observations and contextualizing references culled from previous studies on typical Mexican traits, the population of Mexico City and the impact of globalization.

Two sets of issues (or hypotheses) have been examined in this study. The first relates to the appeal of Disney products in Mexico. It is suggested that Disney products and services have the following main characteristics: (a) stimulation of collective dreams and fantasies by the local Mexican culture; (b) a simple linkage with sets of socially promoted values; and (c) a tendency toward general, unquestioning acceptance of global culture.

The second set of issues relates to the acceptance of global culture promoted by Disney products and services, and is characterized by: (a) unquestioned operation in local Mexican culture, since the image promoted is interpreted at the social and personal levels as an exemplary manner of stimulating fantasy and happiness in children; and (b) openness toward new products and services of the global culture, presented from its 'friendly' side.

The theoretical framework for the study has been drawn from German sociologist Niklas Luhmann's theory of 'self-referent' and 'autopoeitic' societies. The theory of self-referential systems maintains that systems can differentiate only by self-reference, which is to say, only insofar as systems refer to themselves (be this to elements of the same system, to operations of the same system, or to the unity of the same system) in constituting their elements and their elemental operations. Following Humberto Maturana, Luhmann uses the concept of 'autopoiesis' to characterize the recursive operations of self-referential systems. According to Maturana, such systems constitute 'networks of productions of components that recursively, through their interactions, generate and realize the network that produces them and constitute, in the space in which they exist, the boundaries of the network' (Luhmann, 1995: xx and 9). In other words, 'self-referent' refers to any system that contrasts all observation with its own criteria of selection and evaluation, while 'autopoeitic' refers to any system that evolves from the complexity produced by the system itself.

In addition, the concept of social fantasy has been used to understand Disney's role in Mexican culture. Social fantasy is the set of imaginary representations that produce a social system. It may be neatly differentiated from self-representation and representations of 'others' that a system may make, because it selects objects and creates 'histories' that do not correspond to reality, whereas self-representations and representations of 'others' are elaborated and precisely based on reality, although they later distort that reality.

The next section presents the results of the survey, followed by a discussion of the in-depth interviews, in order to explore the specific manner in which social self-representation and fantasies built around Disney products and services are related.

The survey and the subjects

As noted previously, respondents to the questionnaire were all Mexican college students and all belonged to the urban middle class. Although the study sample was relatively small (45 questionnaires), the interviews provided further confirmation or clarification of the results. Of those surveyed, 66.7 percent were women and 33.3 percent men, a ratio that coincides with the distribution of men and women as reported in the 1990 national population census data (51.99 percent women and 48.01 percent men).[3]

Over 66.7 percent of the respondents were aged between 17 and 19 years old (the rest were below 30). This age group (17–19), in turn, represents 3 percent of the total population in Mexico City, according to the 1990 census.

Disney contact and stages of life

As expected, given the type of products and services offered by Disney, all respondents were introduced to Disney in childhood, the majority before 5 years of age (60.5 percent). Between the ages of 5 and 10, 32.6 percent of the population under study entered into contact with Disney, and the remaining (6.98 percent) between 10 and 15 years old.

The survey results confirm the impressive popularity of Disney products in Mexico City's urban culture, surpassed only by the presence of another firm (Coca-Cola, also of U.S. origin). It might even be possible to argue that nearly all Mexico City inhabitants are familiar with Disney products and have experienced direct contact with them. (This observation also is confirmed by further data from the survey, which is discussed below.)

According to the majority of those surveyed, it is during childhood when Mexicans are not only introduced to Disney products but also have greatest contact with them. This contact diminishes during adolescence and is even further reduced in adulthood. Nevertheless, with respect to the type of contact they established during childhood, adolescence and adulthood, the population under study seems to have a false image, which was confirmed in the in-depth interviews. In reality, the information interviewees revealed about Disney services and products shows that, in daily practice, there is far greater familiarity than they admit. This familiarity is proven in the enormous quantity of Disney products they are able to identify, many of which are recent, which implies that they are not the product of childhood experiences.

The existence of this false or distorted image supports Riding's (1985: 13) observation that Mexicans 'suffer when trying to explain themselves' and are confronted by their own contradictions. These may be revealed either when on many occasions 'logic doesn't work' for them (*ibid.*: 17), or from the fact that at other times, 'empty promises and outright lies have no intrinsic value' (*ibid.*: 22).

Disney in popular Mexican taste

With respect to the taste or distaste for Disney products and services, around 69 percent said that they liked viewing, owning and enjoying the products, although more than 13 percent expressed various shades of dislike, and the rest (approximately 18 percent) oscillated between both positions.[4]

In adolescence, as stated above, the respondents maintain that contact with Disney products and services is reduced, although enjoyment prevails (around 38 percent enjoy them, while 33 percent do not, and 29 percent are undecided). Nevertheless, the number of people who express extreme enjoyment alters dramatically, falling from around 31 percent during childhood to just 9 percent in adolescence.

The explanation offered in the interviews for this evolution in tastes is rooted in the marked interest in adolescence to differentiate oneself from childhood and its characteristic values and objects, as well as a certain sense of shame in admitting that some childhood values and objects are still maintained. This leads to rejection or hushing up.

The like–dislike relationship is modified radically in adulthood, when – according to those surveyed – distaste prevails over liking by 40.5 percent to 33.3 percent (the rest expressed an ambivalent posture).

Although in most interviews, which complement the surveys, this change is attributed to a reorientation of taste due to the distinct perspective of adult life, there are elements which leave room for doubt. In any event, this relationship does not always hold true, for two reasons: first, those surveyed acknowledge more positive than negative values in Disney products and services; and second, the respondents are perfectly up to date on new products, which allows us to suppose that they have also entered into voluntary contact with the products, and it is difficult for someone to choose voluntarily something he or she dislikes. The problem of liking or disliking Disney products will be dealt with in greater detail when we specifically analyze the interviews in a later section.

Remembering Disney

It is also interesting that those surveyed remembered fewer products than they are aware of and possess. The number of Disney products they remember is far less than those they acknowledge having given, received or bought as gifts, and those they have consumed through the mass media.

Those surveyed remembered products and services only to the extent they were mentioned in the questionnaire. This was confirmed when, several days later, a number of the respondents asked if they could fill out the survey again because they had recalled more items. While this was not allowed, it is still considered an important fact in itself and showed that the survey stimulated reflection in the population under study.[5]

Disney products as gifts and exchange

As far as products received as gifts, almost 69 percent have received some Disney product; more than 55 percent have at some time given such a product as a gift; and nearly 58 percent have bought Disney products (the discrepancy is due to the fact that, on occasions, when those surveyed gave Disney products, they chose the gift while their parents paid for it; thus, it is not incorrect to say they have given more than they have bought). Finally, around 44 percent have been in a Disney Store at some time.

Everyone surveyed had given or received some Disney product. Among such products, those that were given or received most frequently as gifts are, in decreasing order of importance: toys, clothing, Mickey Mouse watches, collectable items, artwork, jewelry, Mickey Mouse earrings and domestic utensils. Collectable objects also acted as exchange objects and stimuli for the fantasy re-creation of Disney stories, as adapted by the children and adolescents in their games.

In contrast with the frequent presence of Disney products and objects in daily life, only 4.4 percent of the population studied have belonged to a Disney Club. This should come as no surprise, since organized sociability is not characteristic of Mexicans (see Paz, 1968; Ramos, 1934; and Riding, 1985).

The most popular Disney products

As for Disney products distributed through the mass media, 97.8 percent of those surveyed have seen movies and videos, 88.9 percent have owned books, and 80 percent have read comics or seen television series. Nevertheless, only a small percentage has accessed the Disney web page on the Internet (6.7 percent). This is not necessarily due to lack of interest, but because access to the Internet in Mexico is not as extensive as in other countries.

In any event, movies and videos are the media that prevail in making Disney products available; but products such as video games, magazines, publications, albums, tapes, CDs, etc. have been accessible to 45 percent of those surveyed. This gives us an idea of the wide availability of these products, and is confirmed by the fact that all of those surveyed have had frequent access to at least two of these media.

Memories and pleasant associations with Disney

In spite of the fact that the adults surveyed expressed a certain distaste for Disney products, the words, descriptions, images and phrases that come to mind instantly when thinking about Disney are, in general, pleasurable. The majority (59.5 percent) have positive memories that translate into images of entertainment and fun, fantasy and imagination, happiness, childhood and innocence, colors, fondness, etc.

In contrast, some negative perceptions – alone or mixed with positive associations – were also detected, including disillusionment, sadness, disappointment, manipulation and racism. Similarly, it is necessary to point out that a considerable percentage of those surveyed (around 33.3 percent) did not respond to the question on the words, descriptions, images and phrases that came to mind when evoking Disney, and 4.4 percent stated they did not associate Disney with anything in particular.

The values that characterize Disney

Regarding the values that Disney products and services promote or discourage, magic and fun were unanimously cited. These were followed by (with small discrepancies): fantasy, triumph of good over evil, imagination, happiness, optimism and physical beauty. Similarly, in spite of certain discrepancies, the prevalent opinion was that the products promote the family and courage.

Opinions were further divided on the issue of the work ethic and technological progress, although the idea that these values are promoted prevailed by a small margin. Values such as thrift and patriotism were seen by the majority as not attributable to Disney products and services, closely followed by those who considered that Disney does promote those values. In the case of a work ethic, technological progress, thrift and patriotism, and in spite of the fact that they were mentioned in order of importance, the ratios here showed fewer contrasts than in the rest of the categories. In the same vein, no great differences were apparent in the responses to the question of whether Disney promoted, discouraged or was indifferent to individualism, patriarchy and racism. In these cases, opinions were divided and it was impossible to define any of these three categories as prevalent.

This lack of definition in the responses may be due to the fact that the type of patriotism promoted by Disney does not equate precisely with Mexican patriotism, which would be the frame of reference used by many of those surveyed to contextualize the item. As for individualism, this is a value undergoing change: it is accepted by younger social sectors but rejected by the older sections. At the same time, the rejection of this value is usually more verbal than actual, which indicates that the value itself is conflictive and must be interpreted with caution.

Regarding racism, Mexican society in general does not consider itself to be racist, since it is itself the product of racial mixing and because, from a smaller perspective, for certain sectors, being racist means rejecting people of color or Jews but not marginalized indigenous sectors in the country. Thus, the category of racism is not frequently used in Mexico, nor are allusions about the race to which one belongs. This does not mean that racism is non-existent, but rather that it is not defined as a problem in the social imaginary.

In spite of these latter observations, when analyzing all of the responses, Disney is generally associated with spreading positive values, which – as already stated – seems to contradict the distaste the company produces in adults.

Contradictory ideas about Disney

Two possible interpretations may be derived from the analysis of the contradiction between manifestations of distaste for Disney and the simultaneous acknowledgement of mainly positive values. On the one hand, the questionnaire listed a high proportion of positive values and a minimum of negative values. This may explain the positive tone of the responses. In other words, the questionnaire was initially flawed in orienting the answers toward mainly positive values regarding Disney products and services.

On the other hand, it is also possible that the responses of those surveyed contained real contradictions, at least from an exclusively logical point of view. This is not surprising in Mexican culture, where logical consistency is not considered important but more pragmatic, as previously noted. This is revealed in classic Mexican expressions such as 'Yes, yes, but no' or 'neither yes nor no, but on the contrary.' In fact, a good part of the misinterpretations and conflicts that arise when a member of another culture desires to understand or communicate something to Mexicans lies in the particular code and semantic system produced by their culture, which feeds on traditions, bad habits and the survival of ancestral values, and is oriented (or obliged to orient itself) toward the Western way of life and – more recently – the First World.[6]

Disney's promotion of American culture

There was disagreement when it came to the question of whether Disney promotes or discourages a vision of U.S. culture.[7] Twenty-four percent failed to respond. This may be due to the direct nature of the question, which contrasts with the fact that such forwardness is not viewed well, and at times is considered dangerous, in Mexican culture. Those who did respond to the question (the remaining 76 percent) generally avoided negative or direct responses. Only one of the respondents openly stated that Disney discourages U.S. culture.

Among those wh.o answered the question, most were aware that the U.S. culture is promoted but made no further comments, or gave a nuanced response, such as: 'Yes, implicitly,' 'Disney only promotes the best of the United States,' 'It only promotes aspects of the American lifestyle,' 'It promotes an American culture that doesn't exist, because the culture is governed by values that contradict those found in Disney.'

To a lesser degree, some answers deviated from the original question, another signal that this type of direct question, in which Mexicans might feel obliged to expose a position they would rather not exhibit, results in the formulation of unexpected responses. For instance: 'It only promotes a very capitalist vision,' 'On occasions, it promotes racism,' 'Disney is interested in promoting itself as universal culture, although perhaps not properly American,' 'It alters stories impressively,' etc. Similarly, it is possible to find comments such as the following: 'It discourages other cultures, such as the Mexican, that dream of being a faithful copy of the American.'

Although rejection of Disney or U.S. culture is evident in some comments, only one response – far removed from the original question – was categorical: 'Alienating. It promotes plastic fun.'

In any event, almost all responses contained some degree of rejection or distance from Disney and/or U.S. culture. This can be attributed to Mexicans' particular nationalism, since any talk of the promotion of U.S. culture immediately precipitates efforts to reaffirm their identity and demarcate themselves from the neighboring country, declaring the existence of limits with this 'close environment.' In cases where American culture is not treated as explicitly as in this survey, a distinct proclivity to accept, almost without criticism, all that comes from the U.S.A. may be detected. In general, mention of the U.S.A. is irritating for Mexicans, because it arouses nationalist positions and old resentments.[8]

First set of issues: the appeal of Disney in Mexico

The social perspective that emerges from the survey results allows us to address the first set of issues concerning social fantasy and Disney products and services. Regardless of whether one's personal position is approval or rejection, the associations of Disney with childhood, family and happiness reflect values deeply rooted in Mexican culture, in which children are the most valuable, family support and protection are necessary to survive, and the greatest pleasures are parties, laughter, song and other manifestations of contentedness. The sets of values that Disney promotes are simple and have a positive complement in Mexican culture: the same values – for example, courage – are shared and any difference between the meaning the concept may have at the local and global levels is not significant for those surveyed.

In addition, the acceptance of global culture is implicit, because the coincidence of values that Disney products and services promote fits easily in the local culture; rather than an imposition from outside, they appear as a prolongation or continuation, as something that naturally adheres to local culture. The perception of global culture thus remains partially veiled by its soft interaction with local culture.

Towards the interviews

At the end of each questionnaire, the respondents were invited to participate in interviews to talk at length about the subject. It is important to note that the majority of people who refused to be interviewed were those who rejected Disney products and services. Those who accept and like Disney products, in contrast, generously offered their time and, in several cases, proposed more interviews to talk about a topic that, undoubtedly, produces enjoyment and pleasure. In fact, the intensity of the affection for Disney was somewhat surprising. Around 40 percent of those interviewed expected at least the possibility of continuing the contact established in the interview or offered the interviewer some small gift (candy, pens, buttons) with Disney characters stamped on them.

The next sections, then, consider information gathered from the interviews and explore the relationship between Disney and personal fantasy, as well as issues relating to global culture.

Disney in personal fantasy

Personal fantasies refer to those forged by individuals. They are part of individual thought, although in contrast to other thoughts, they do not aspire to truth or convert themselves into deeds, but rather are recognized as fiction and play, as a pure exercise of imagination and desires. On the other hand, personal fantasies are independent from social fantasy. Although in the case of Disney products and services, it would seem that there are certain continuities, this appearance is false, for the fantasies are merely elaborated based on the same objects.

Everyone may take a character and identify with it, choose which stories to get involved in (from which new stories will be woven), approach diverse objects in accepting or not socially patterned selections of preference, and decide based on his/her own criteria (to accept or reject) – that is, self-referentially – what to do and how to use or re-elaborate these fantasies.[9] The interviews analyzed below reflect how such self-referential operations work.

Identity and identification

Frequently, the interviewees alluded to the form in which they or some family member or friend fantasized about the characters and their stories. For instance, brown-skinned girls with beautiful black eyes dreamed about being blonde and blue-eyed, like some of the Disney heroines. Among the men interviewed, the ideal of the ever-young Peter Pan remained alive. The examples cited are hardly casual: in all cases, they imply denial or rejection of a real condition and an orientation towards a model of beauty or a condition – eternal youth – that is out of reach. Styles of living and consumption, such as tinted hair and youthful clothing, are related to the need to adjust one's personal condition to the idealized model upon which the identification operates.

The interviewees referred to extreme cases as well, such as elderly persons who, living alone, fill their houses with the images of their favorite character and join collectors' clubs for that character. In these cases, Disney products seem to dull the pains of aging and give them the opportunity to relive their childhood and the imaginary universe created by Disney. Similarly, they find in the dolls and clubs virtual company that disguises their loneliness.

First personal contact with Disney

In all cases, the majority of the interviewees acknowledged that their first contact with Disney products and services was through their families and was maintained for many years. Therefore, it is hardly strange that longing for the family when ties are weakened or have disappeared leads many Disney sympathizers toward ritual consumption of its products.

The intensity of the family link in Mexican culture is strong, even when the country is experiencing a transition toward smaller families. The Sunday meal with the family is a ritual, as well as birthday and anniversary celebrations. And, it is precisely at birthday parties where Disney products and services are most intensely present, as the well-known Disney images adorn the party hall or reunion site, decorations, piñatas, entertainment, gifts, and utensils (glasses, spoons, forks, napkins, place mats, trays, etc.).

In addition, families watch videos and movies together. Frequently, it is the parents who introduce their children to the consumption of Disney objects and contribute to orienting children in their first fantasies, repeating and telling stories from movies and books.

Imagining the world

From a very young age, children's fantasies are based on characters and stories and, at times, they ask themselves if people in other parts of the world think alike. Situating themselves in the space of imagination, Disney products and services induce many to speculate on the way in which they are perceived in other parts of the world. Around 80 percent of interviewees have imagined at some time what it would be like to hear Mickey Mouse speak in English or Japanese, or 'how they would view him in Africa.'

The idea that Disney is distributed throughout the world, far from surprising the interviewees, rather confirms that they have already thought out this idea for themselves, representing it with images, interpretations, anecdotes and memories. In this way, it may be said that from the point of view of personal fantasies, Disney is not only part of 'received' global culture but also 're-created' culture. Moreover, it leads us directly to imagine and reflect on some aspects of globalization: for example, sharing with others the same hobbies, using the same objects, being part of the world market, having similar access to fantasy, being spectators of the same events, or having common experiences.

Configuration of a global culture

From the point of view of configuring a global culture, the internationalization of Disney products is projected both at the level of internationalization of the products and services and at the level of messages. But both are retaken and reinterpreted by the local culture. Far from depriving globalization of its generalizing quality, this is what allows the culture to be assumed as proper. In other words, certain forms of appropriation of the global culture and, in this case, of Disney products and services, on the part of individuals, is undertaken in the context of links with pre-existing forms considered 'acceptable' by the local culture. Thus, for example, in the case of Disney, the colors, music and songs are utilized for a festive, fun and happy atmosphere at parties, in much the same way as existed in Mexico before the arrival of Disney. The romanticism of some stories is also compatible with Mexican culture, in the same way that the multitude of collectable dolls are used by children to illustrate their own fantasy stories.

Personal appropriation and fantasy

Some of the interviews demonstrated the various ways in which original versions of Disney objects and services are transformed into personal experiences. One of these experiences illustrates this transformation process:

> My mother always told me that she had read in a magazine that Walt Disney was inspired to create Mickey Mouse by a little mouse that

peeped out in the studio when he stayed there to have lunch. And once, she stayed working until late in her office. There was no longer anybody there and she still had to work. She took out her snack and while she was eating, the mouse appeared. Only that she had a terrible fear of mice and when she saw it, she shouted and left running, leaving her work for the following day. She commented on what had happened the night before to her co-workers and asked them to help her look for the mouse and take it out of her office. But the help proved unnecessary: the rat [mouse?] was dead in the same place where my mother had seen it when she shouted and ran out. It died of fear when my mother shouted.

The interview concludes: 'My mother got sad because she noticed that Walt Disney had seen a little mouse and became inspired to create Mickey, whereas she felt that she had killed Mickey Mouse.'

Beyond the anecdotal value of this tale, the important thing here is to understand how through the story there exists a process in which information about the way a Disney character was created is introduced into the life experience of a person (the mother), who in turn identifies with Disney, projecting the information perceived into her own experience and integrating it with the original. Thus, there is a continuation and tight linking of the experience or initial information spread socially through a magazine with her own experience.

With perhaps less dramatic arguments, the interviewees narrated diverse anecdotes that show how, among those who most enjoy Disney products and services, they frequently produce this type of personal projection, which on occasion – as in the 'death of Mickey Mouse' – are transformed into family anecdotes.

Social fantasy and personal fantasy

The dimension of personal projections is relatively distinct from the way in which social projections are configured. Nevertheless, in the social dimension – as affirmed in the preceding example – there is also a special form of appropriating Disney products and services that complements their global character with the peculiar local form (Mexican) of integrating them into daily life for consumption.

In this way, it is possible to agree with – in spite of the divergent theoretical framework – observations such as those of Lie (1997), who argues that globalization not only concerns the creation of large-scale systems but also social transformation at the local level. To this we would have to add that globalization also has a personal impact, enriching individuals with stimuli for imagination and thought. Similarly, personal appropriation redefines globalness, particularizing and diversifying it.

Information gleaned from the interviews indicates that globalization provokes transformations in personal systems. One of the ways in which individuals must change is observed in children: they tend to update their information about stories and main characters for use in their own games and in conversation with other children, as well as to manifest socially their own level of importance (in relation to other children) by showing others that they have more or newer toys, items of clothing or knowledge. At the family level (generally the parents), change is also produced because, in their eagerness to entertain their children with Disney, they often adapt their budgets to go to shows, buy video games or visit Disneyland, Disney World or Epcot Center. They may also modify their home decor, not only in the children's rooms but also in other spaces; or become familiar with the stories and comics so that they can talk with their children and read them bedtime stories.

Weak global identity

The low participation rate in Disney Clubs, as well as hits on the web page revealed by the survey, coincides with a weak definition of identity between people who enjoy Disney services and products. In reality, the idea that 'everyone loves Disney' virtually implicates the Disney public, while at the same time there is no contact other than common enjoyment and the occasional, informal contact that might exist when looking at store displays, renting a video or going to the movies. This coincides with previous observations on globalization and the feeling of weak global belonging (see Tomlinson, 1996).

In fact, this weak sense of belonging to a global community is contrasted with the intense interpenetration with Disney stories and characters. Children's theme parties based on *The Little Mermaid* or Mickey Mouse, as well as small children (3 to 5 years old) who see *Aladdin*, *The Lion King* or *Hercules* several times a week for months on end, prove the intense identification with stories and characters. Much less common than the personal relationship with these products is the group relationship with them, concretized in, for example, some video games and activities spontaneously organized by the children themselves.

'I don't want to be interviewed. I don't like Disney.'

Finally, we were able to obtain information from those who refused to be interviewed and stated that they had little connection and interest in Disney products and services. By asking those who declined to be interviewed the reason for their refusal, we were able to obtain information relevant to the study.

Individuals who did not want to be interviewed refused for two reasons: first, because – according to them – they do not have contact with Disney products and services; and, second, because the reference to Disney irritates them for ideological reasons. Yet, some observations that were made related to both of these responses, which reinforced the previous observation that Mexicans are inconsistent in their judgements, have difficulty explaining themselves, or simply lie.

In the first instance, despite denying frequent contact or interest in Disney products and services, it was noted that the youngest subjects (17 to 21 years old) often wore socks, T-shirts, patches or Disney characters on their backpacks. When asked how it was possible to deny contact and, at the same time, habitually use such objects, all responded with an initial moment of confusion. Some were surprised and said they hadn't noticed. Others said that it didn't really have anything to do with Disney, but was merely fashionable or simply 'looked nice.' A few others were at a loss what to say and walked away annoyed, while some laughed and avoided further comment.

In the second place, among those who held that reference to Disney irritated them, the most frequent comment centered on Disney as an instrument of U.S. ideological penetration aimed at undermining Mexican identity and culture. They cited a fear of losing identity based upon the notion that their own culture could be affected or have less chance of prevailing over American culture.[10] Less frequent was the argument – typical of leftist discourses of the 1960s – that 'Disney is an instrument of Yankee imperialism.' In some cases, the nationalist and leftist perspectives coincided with the rejection of Disney products and services.

Appreciation of Disney

The fact that some refused to be interviewed because they 'disliked' Disney should not distort the fact that the great majority of Mexican people accept and enjoy the company's products. These individuals acknowledge that, although Disney has transformed the urban land-scape to a great degree in billboards, children's centers, parks, walls, posters on passenger buses and other public transport, etc., this presence has not been seen as conflictive, but pleasant. This prevalent form of appreciation has a lot to do with the fact that Disney services and products are, fundamentally, aimed at children. It is important to point out that a good deal of the appreciation and interest in these products is related to the high regard for childhood that exists in Mexican culture, yet it is also true that Mexico does not have its own cultural production to compete with that offered by Disney.

More observations on personal fantasy and social fantasy

It is also interesting that the instances of fantasies developed with elements taken from Disney products and services are less frequent than the use and relationship that each individual maintains with those products. In some cases – above all, among adults – there is a real disparity between closeness to the products and consciousness of their proximity that may inhibit personal fantasy.

Nevertheless, in those cases where interest or enjoyment of Disney products and services is strong, fantasies become interwoven with life stories: romantic interpretations of childhood where a movie, a heroine, the seven dwarfs, enchanted forests with small, talking animals, etc. are remembered; games shared with other children that re-create adventures they have seen in the movies; or the pleasant evocation of protecting, affectionate parents who opened access to these fantasies by giving stuffed animals as presents, decorating birthday parties, taking them to Disney movies or buying Mickey and Donald Duck comics. There also are negative fantasies, when children were unable to go to Disneyland because there was not enough money, or they did not receive the Disney products they so badly desired.

Personal fantasies, therefore, focus on subjectivity. In contrast, social fantasies stimulated by Disney are situated (a) at the level of collective expectations oriented toward and emanating from the shows, (b) in the stimulation of a social imaginary that feeds upon magic, colors, stories and characters, and (c) in the ability to evade reality and inhabit a virtual world where the impossible becomes possible and transcends quotidian conflicts.

The second set of issues: global culture

The various observations presented up to this point and the data that back them up allow us to address the second set of issues related to global culture. This is due – above all – to the general acceptance of Disney products and services in Mexico. It should be remembered that nearly everyone is familiar with the products and the vast majority have enjoyed them since childhood, as well as the fact that although adults declare they dislike Disney, they frequently wear Disney clothing, or when considering special programs for small children in the family, they generally resort to its products.

The very familiarity that at times makes Disney's daily presence in Mexican society 'invisible' erases a good part of its transnational origin. Also, giving Disney characters Spanish names (Goofy is 'Tribilín,' Daisy is 'Margarita,' Minnie is 'Mimí,' etc.), and the use of famous actors' and singers' voices in dubbed movies shown in Latin America, makes forgetting the foreign origin easy at the moment of consumption.

In spite of the fact that people throughout the world are very familiar with Disney products and services and can fantasize about them, they do not manifest the same rejection as other types of communication, services and products of foreign origin.[11] In the interviews, we found that people justify their acceptance of Disney because the products form part of their own experiences and memories. This distinguishes the company radically from other objects, services and communications of foreign origin and worldwide coverage.

Thus, Disney presents aspects of globalization that are socially and personally accepted. The common sentiment among the interviewees was, as expressed by one respondent, 'if all that came about from globalization were like Disney products, there would be no problem at all in accepting it.' And, more specifically, they gave a variety of reasons: 'Because it's good for children'; 'Because it's fun for them [children]'; 'Because it's colorful'; 'Because it always looks for the good side of human nature'; 'Because I like it,' and 'Because it's not very violent.'

Despite the confirmation of this set of assumptions or hypotheses from the opinions and points of view expressed by those interviewed, the result is hardly definitive. Just as the question of whether Disney transmits American cultural values provoked a strong reaction in people, if the interview had asked a question about possible connections between Disney and American culture, or implied that Disney somehow affected Mexican identity or being, the answers would have been quite different. In fact, the interviewers stimulated interviewees to talk about the subject and intervened only to prevent subjects from getting off the topic and to extract the greatest quantity of information possible.

Conclusions

Disney promotes, probably without meaning to, a soft insertion of the Mexican urban population into global culture. Through its products and services, Disney generates universally recognized names, values, and images that extend into the social dimension toward the heart of the family, and in the personal dimension, toward dreams and fantasies.

Through Disney, rather than erupting locally, globalness penetrates the local, becoming part of it, reconstituting and remaking it through daily use, ubiquitous presence, and the certainty that it is totally dispensable. Therefore, it may be present in the close environment not only without creating conflict but also giving pleasure.

To the extent that Disney (as well as McDonald's, Coca-Cola, Kentucky Fried Chicken, Pepsi Cola, Ford, Mercedes-Benz, Sanyo, Toshiba, and IBM) penetrates everyday life and settles there through their products or services, an aspect of globalization is projected that differs from the perspective of conflict with local agencies that some authors have suggested (for example, Lie, 1997). This is the soft, friendly side of globalization, whose penetration is so intense and persistent that it resounds in all local ambits and generates specific forms of appropriation (generally, particular forms of consumption, but also tastes and values).

The daily interpenetration between the global and the local provokes, via ecological resonance in both systems, a series of evolutionary transformations that tends to strengthen structural linkage and continue the process with increasing intensification. In fact, the two are producing semantic offers appropriate for this linkage, founded on their cultural horizon and the self-referentiality with which the codes operate. These offerings have to do with, for example, the opportunities for consumption and the use of time (above all, free time), but have distinct meanings in the global system and in each local system.

In this way, if we take up the Disney case in Mexico City, as well as many other locations, the objects of Disney are appropriate, recommendable, and appreciated as gifts for children, and this is part of society's own culturally backed perspective; on the other hand, Disney's offerings follow patterns of global promotion through which the company manages to envelop people in the 'Magical World of Disney.' The acquisition of products does not imply that buyers really feel the magic of Disney, but that the slogan of Disney has achieved its purpose: it resonates positively in the local sphere, which responds by accepting its products. This perspective neither sustains the thesis that history is moving towards the homogenization of culture nor ensures that diversity will be truly 'diverse.' In fact, as Lie (1997: 148) states, 'Diversity exists not only *between* cultures, but also *within* cultures.'

Seen in this light of 'soft' interpenetration, the phenomenon of globalization and the system it implies offer an extraordinary opportunity for the evolution of local systems that, in turn, redefine globalness in projecting images that extend from the enemy that appears as an invincible hydra to fantasies that lead to Never-Never Land. In Mexico City, at least, Disney represents a chance to escape the routine and to dream, in spite of unemployment, public insecurity and pollution. Disney does not offer an alternative to urban or individual problems, just the momentary possibility of forgetting them and simply enjoying the fantasy.

George Gerbner (1997: 17) has maintained that 'it is more probable that the synergy of media linked in networks and the consolidation of the electronic market reduce than increase the diversity of the total orchestration of cultural resources.' However, it might be argued that Disney products and services in each process of interpenetration are no more than pretexts, facts, resources. Each system, upon observing the products, denatures them, redefines and appropriates them, making them something different than the conceptions of the original promoters. Thus, through this process of appropriation of objects and reconfiguration of images, diversity proliferates in spite of all attempts to homogenize culture.

Notes

1. Pirating includes the illegal reproduction of trademark or copyright products. The Tepito market is a Saturday market in a downtown Mexico city neighborhood of the same name, where a large number of businesses sell imported contraband merchandise.
2. 'Soft' implies any form of integration that oscillates between absence of conflict concerning change and a preference for change.
3. Data on the general population is from the National Institute on Statistics, Geography and Informatics (INI), Mexico.
4. This seems to be due principally to the fact that in the movies and videos, the evil characters and their actions, or the tragedies that befell the good characters, provoked an anguish that was barely compensated for by the characters they identified with, happy circumstances, and the visual and musical effects that accompany the good characters.
5. The possibility of a new study on the same subject, applying focus-group techniques, for example, could be a way of extending and clarifying the information presented here.
6. On the dualism in the Mexican perspective on culture, see Bonfil Batalla (1991), and García Canclini (1990), Chapter II.
7. The responses to this question presented difficulties that should be treated quantitatively, since the same response may include various contradictory considerations, which implies that each question is answered in more than one way.
8. It should be remembered here that Mexico lost a great part of its national territory following the U.S. invasion of the country.
9. According to the theory of self-referent and autopoeitic systems, society provides selections of culturally patterned meanings which the same society or its members may elect, according to their own self-referent perspectives.

10. It must be remembered that animosity against the U.S.A. is nurtured from primary school in Mexico. As noted previously, this is due to the U.S. invasion and the loss of national territory, in addition to the more or less normal rivalries that usually exist between bordering countries, and is acccentuated by the fact that the U.S.A. is the most powerful country in the world, whereas Mexico is a developing nation.

11. In general, Mexicans reject all foreign products that are decoded as a form of invasion, lack of respect, threat to autonomy, dumping or antagonism.

References and other sources

Bonfil Batalla, G. (1991) *México profundo*. Conaculta, Mexico.

Braman, S. and Sreberny-Mohammadi, A. (1996) *Globalization, Communication and Transnational Civil Society*. Cresskill, NJ, IAMCR-Hampton Press.

García Canclini, N. (1990) *Culturas híbridas*. Mexico City, Conaculta-Grijalbo.

Gerbner, G. (1997) 'Marketing mayhem globally,' in J. Servaes and R. Lie (eds), *Media and Politics in Transition: Cultural Identity in the Age of Globalization*. Leuven-Amersfoort, ACCO, pp. 7–9.

Lie, R. (1997) 'What's new about cultural globalization? Linking the global from within the local,' in J. Servaes and R. Lie (eds), *Media and Politics in Transition: Cultural Identity in the Age of Globalization*. Leuven-Amersfoort, ACCO, pp. 141–55.

Luhmann, N. (1989) *Ecological Communication*. Chicago: University of Chicago Press.

Luhmann, N. (1995) *Social Systems*. Palo Alto, CA, Stanford University Press.

Luhmann, N. (1997) *Organización y decisión. Autopoiesis, acción y entendimiento comunicativo*. Barcelona, Anthropos y Universidad Iberoamericana.

Luhmann, N. and De Georgi, R. (1992) *Teoría de la sociedad*. Mexico City, Universidad Iberoamericana, Universidad de Guadalajara, Instituto Tecnológico de Occidente.

Paz, O. (1968) *El laberinto de la soledad*. Mexico City, Fondo de la Cultura Económica.

Ramos, S. (1934) *El perfil del hombre y la culture en México*. Mexico City, Cultura.

Riding, A. (1985) *Vecinos distantes, un retrato de los mexicanos*, 29th edn. Mexico City, Joaquín Mortiz-Planeta.

Servaes, J. and Lie, R. (eds) (1997) *Media and Politics in Transition: Cultural Identity in the Age of Globalization*. Leuven-Amersfoort, ACCO.

Steyn, J. (ed.) (1997) *Other than Identity: The Subject, Politics and Art*. Manchester, Manchester University Press.

Tomlinson, J. (1996) 'Global experience as a consequence of modernity,' in S. Braman and A. Sreberny-Mohammadi (eds), *Globalization, Communication and Transnational Civil Society*. Cresskill, NJ, IAMCR-Hampton Press.

CHAPTER 11

Norway: Norwegian Memories of the Disney Universe [1]

INGUNN HAGEN

Christmas and Donald Duck are strong associations that Norwegians make with Disney, which has come to play a significant role in everyday life in Norway. This chapter provides a profile of that role, giving particular attention to the characteristic ways Norwegians consume these products, both materially and psycho-socially.

The two most salient findings in the data are the predominant position of *Donald Duck* comics as the most popular Disney product in Norway, and the strong association between Disney and the Christmas season in this country. This consumption of the weekly *Donald Duck* comic magazine and also the Christmas cartoon rituals were the two features emphasized by students when asked to describe their childhood Disney memories.

The chapter begins with a discussion of the experiences that were expressed in students' memory descriptions, followed by an elaboration of the memories of the enjoyable weekly habit of reading the *Donald Duck* comic magazine. Second, the chapter will also discuss how Disney animated cartoons stand out in students' memories as a significant part of celebrating Christmas in Norway. The next section explores the feelings that were associated with the Disney memories. While most of the students' childhood memories of Disney were linked to pleasure and desire, attention will also be directed to the more critical comments made by the respondents in hindsight.

In order to discuss the stronghold of the *Donald Duck* comic magazine in Norwegian culture, the present distribution and readership of the popular magazine will be presented, based on statistical information. Initially, the *Donald Duck* comic magazine achieved such a breakthrough in distribution when it was introduced in the late 1940s that Norwegian childhood in the 1950s was described as 'growing up in Duckburgh' (see Dahl *et al.*, 1996). Some of the historical fluctuations of the *Donald Duck* comic magazine in Norway also will be presented in this section.

Another major aim of the chapter is to describe the extent of young people's contact with Disney products, and also their perceptions of these products. For this purpose, the experiences of students – based on their answers to our survey study – will be discussed. Both the memory descriptions and interviews were conducted with young people, who represent today's and tomorrow's parents. How adults and parents feel about Disney is important for whether Disney products will be introduced to and thus consumed by new generations. These young informants were children in the 1970s and 1980s, at a time when the Disney market situation was very different. But their views in hindsight are also shaped by the Disney products available today.

Thus, the present market situation of Disney products in Norway must be analyzed, as well. In this country, like elsewhere, the availability of Disney products has changed radically in the 1990s. While numerous Disney products have been available and quite popular in Norway for decades, the recent abundance of Disney products is significant and provides the background for the memories and perceptions of young adults. The present Disney market situation, together with the intensification of the promotion of Disney merchandise, also provides the context for the group interviews with children.

The section exploring children's use of and feelings about Disney products, based on these interviews, constitutes the last part of the chapter, and demonstrates that today's children in Norway experience a Disney-saturated childhood. There is a strong degree of intertextuality, in the sense that Disney stories are available in several media. While Disney stories and products clearly were sources of enjoyment to children, the abundance of products also seemed to result in some 'overkill.'

Five sources of data were utilized to develop this chapter: (1) descriptions given by psychology students of their significant childhood memories with Disney;[2] (2) actuarial data about the sale and consumption of Disney products in Norway; (3) questionnaires eliciting information from media students about their contact with and perception of Disney products;[3] (4) a limited market investigation concerning the availability of Disney products in a Norwegian city;[4]

and (5) group interviews with young children regarding their use of and feelings about Disney products.[5] The unique, qualitative picture of our findings will become increasingly clear as the data from all these sources are revealed.

Disney memories I: climax of the week

The childhood memories of a group of psychology students offer a vivid picture of the significance of Disney products in Norway. Although memories are rich sources of data, they reconstruct past experiences in a selective and romanticizing way. There is a tendency to make the past more idyllic and better than it was, or vice versa, but always in the light of present experiences (see Höijer, 1998).

According to the research design, students were asked to report one or more childhood memories about their experiences with Disney products.[6] The data included descriptions of several kinds of Disney materials, including books, movies, merchandise, and the Disneyland theme park. However, two prevalent clusters of data reveal what are the most salient findings: these students emphasized their experiences with the *Donald Duck & Co.* comic magazine and the animated Disney programs shown at Christmas time.

Buying *Donald Duck* became a weekly ritual that lasted for years in the lives of many Norwegian children. A number of students had nostalgic memories of the comics, which they considered 'exciting' and 'funny.' For Norwegian children, getting *Donald* (as the comics are called in Norway) was the high point of the week, as one 25-year-old male explained: '[It was] a great climax to buy *Donald* every Tuesday.' The comics were published once a week – on Tuesdays – which for some years has been the day when new colored magazines were issued in Norway. Another 25-year-old female student stated that she took 'great pleasure in buying *Donald* comics once a week.' This consumption habit was something she continued during her years in elementary school. However, the joy of reading Donald was not limited to childhood. The same female student admitted that she still likes to read old editions of the comic.

Naturally, it heightened the enjoyment for the youngsters to purchase the comic as soon as possible. One 27-year-old female student's statement was typical: 'What I do remember about Disney, is that it was *very* important to get a hold of the *Donald* magazine as soon as it arrived in the store when I was little [a child].' However, the same student emphasizes that in her childhood the *Donald* magazine was not accompanied by many additional products. Now she feels that there are 'enormously much more Disney things.' This is an example of how respondents' sweet Disney childhood memories have become tarnished by today's perceptions of merchandise overload.

Another salient finding is that the psychology students also remembered who introduced them to the *Donald Duck* comic magazine and with whom it was read. A 24-year-old male recalled how he was introduced to the magazine by his grandmother while visiting her when he was 4 or 5 years old. Her introduction led to the establishment of regular and, eventually, weekly consumption. The Disney study in Denmark also highlights the role of grandparents as introductory catalysts to Disney products, and the fact that it is often the grandparents and parents who want children to have the same childhood experiences that they themselves enjoyed (see Drotner's chapter in this volume).

Typically, *Donald Duck* was first enjoyed in a family setting. A 30-year-old female recalled how she and her brother used to read *Donald* comics and pocket books, but not on a regular basis. Another 24-year-old male student recalled how, when he was around 7 years old, an elderly man who visited them borrowed his *Donald* comics and that they talked about what a nice magazine it was. He wrote that he wondered back then 'how could an old man read *Donald*?'

The university students also describe rather concrete and vivid memories related to their *Donald Duck* purchases. In the words of a 25-year-old female: 'Once a week for many years in my childhood, I got money from my parents so I could run down to a store [on] our street to buy the weekly *Donald* magazine.' The same female student reflected on her own experience and memories: 'The magazine was read in a hurry, and I do not think the stories or drawings really stayed with me as a memory. It is more the joy over the *Donald* magazine itself and perhaps the illustrations [on] the front page that I remember the most.' In any case, it is obvious that these young people still remember the joys and amusement they associated with reading the *Donald Duck* magazine.

In describing the pleasures of reading *Donald*, some students mentioned specific stories. One example is a 24-year-old male, who recalled a story involving Uncle Scrooge and Donald diving for Scrooge's money that had been lost in the ocean, where they encountered mermaids etc. – a fairy tale, indeed. The same man claimed that he learned much from the *Donald* comics, such as foreign words and general knowledge. He emphasized that this was especially the case with the Carl Barks serials.[7]

The main pleasure in getting the *Donald* magazine was obviously to read the stories and look at the drawings. However, it is important to recall the comments of the female student who indicated that it was the event of purchasing the comic, and the pleasure of viewing the illustrated cover, that she remembered most. There were also ways to prolong the joy of reading and rereading the comics. Several students mentioned that they used to collect the magazines in special cover boxes. The same female student quoted above said: 'After some time I got the *Donald* cover boxes where I could collect the magazines according to year and number; something I put a lot of work into.' She continued: 'Now these cover boxes are nicely arranged in the bookshelves at my parents' house, and it happens that I enjoy the stories still.'

In addition to the cover boxes, people often kept *Donald Duck* in big cardboard boxes, thus providing the possibility that the magazines might be enjoyed later by siblings, grandchildren, great-grandchildren and others. Some students described how they borrowed *Donald Duck*, rather than having to buy the magazine. One male student explained that through friends and family, he always had access to plenty of Disney comics, especially *Donald*. Thus, children often have access to old issues of *Donald Duck* inherited from other members of their family.

As indicated above, memories of reading *Donald Duck* were often rather specific. According to Höijer (1998), what stands out in memory is often based on experiences that were perceived as a significant contrast to the flow of everyday life. This also could be related to the ritual aspect of comic magazine consumption: it happened regularly and it was elevated to a nearly ceremonial level (Hagen, 1992). Höijer and Findahl (1984) theoretically account for the connection between memories (as with *Donald Duck*) and social relations: for example, who introduced and shared in the initial joy of the comic. This is a typical feature of memory, that human actors, but also places, became quite central. Thus, it bears repeating that home is the place where *Donald* was typically consumed.

To summarize, then, we have found that buying and reading the *Donald Duck* comic magazine was a weekly childhood habit that left memory traces. But as will be illustrated in the next section, Disney products were also linked to annual occasions.

Disney memories II: the Christmas icon?

The second dominant feature in the students' memory descriptions is the strong association between Disney and Christmas in Norway. In the words of one 25-year-old female student: 'I primarily associate Disney with animated cartoons. For me, Disney is connected to Christmas celebration because then the *Disney Cavalcade* was shown'. This quote indicates that Disney animated programs are, or at least have been, an important Christmas icon in Norway. This is due, at least in part, to the broadcast monopoly that existed in Norway during the 1960s and 1970s, and to the *de facto* monopoly that existed during the 1980s.

The Norwegian Public Service Broadcasting Corporation (NRK) maintained a monopoly on television in Norway between 1960 and 1981,[8] during which time, popular culture products like Disney animated programs were a rare event.[9] However, from 1979 to 1989, NRK showed the *Disney Christmas Cavalcade* continually.[10] Christmas was virtually the only time during the year that Disney cartoons were available on television in Norway. The monopoly implied that most Norwegians were stuck with the often paternalistic NRK. This situation continued for much of the 1980s, even though the monopoly was formally broken. Deregulation meant that NRK increasingly faced competition from cable and satellite channels. Still, it was only in the 1990s that multiple channels became a reality for the majority of the population in Norway.

The 1980s correspond with the time when most of these psychology students were children. In the material on students' childhood memories, half of the respondents mention that their Disney memories related to Christmas. Also in the survey, which will be discussed below, a number of interviewees explicitly mentioned their exposure to the Disney Christmas show. A 22-year-old female psychology student stated that 'Disney memories are obviously also related to Christmas.' She explained why:

> It is not Christmas in our home if my brother and I cannot watch the animated cartoons that are broadcast in the morning. Now we have watched them for so many years that we know the lines almost by heart. We have favorite scenes that we look forward to – which are as funny every time.

Even though this respondent and her brother know the lines by heart, the joy lies in the repetitious nature of what has been established as a Christmas ritual; it is just not Christmas without it! Just as in the case of *Donald Duck* comics, a key part of the memory is the presence of the person with whom the show was enjoyed.

NRK broadcasts its Disney show once a year and it often shows many of the same stories.[11] Thus, the experiences of watching Disney animated programs during Christmas has become repetitive and ritualistic. It is the experience of seeing a discrete event, or a once-and-only-once occurrence. The broadcast has become a unique tradition, as emphasized by a 25-year-old female respondent:

> One strong Disney memory I derive from the Disney animated cartoons that are shown every Christmas. These are films that have been replayed

several times, so I know them 'by heart.' There is much excitement and expectation attached to these films, and I suppose it has become a tradition to watch them every Christmas.

Clearly, watching the Disney Christmas show, with its oft-repeated, familiar films, was a ritual surrounded by high expectations. Knowing stories by heart – and still enjoying them – is a way of taking pleasure often associated with children. However, this seems to be a more general phenomenon related to the construction of Christmas, as we shall see below.[12]

Some of the students interviewed said that they missed the Disney animated cartoons when they were not broadcast. One example is a 23-year-old female student who said that it was a 'sad Christmas' when NRK did not schedule the *Disney Christmas Cavalcade*, explaining that she recalls this absence because there was something special about the Disney cartoons. In her words: 'They were more joyful and colorful and represented something [other] than the "ordinary" (NRK) children's television.' Indeed, Disney cartoons might have been experienced as adventurous and imaginative, in contrast to the more pedagogical tradition of children's programs made available by NRK during the monopoly years.[13] A 30-year-old female student said that she still watches the Disney animated programs on the morning of Christmas Eve, but not *The Disney Hour* (which was broadcast weekly during the 1990s). The latter would be 'fake,' she suggested, implying that this is not part of the Norwegian (Christmas) 'tradition.'

Due to the repetitious nature of these Disney Christmas shows, several students also remembered specific Disney cartoon stories. Two female students mentioned that *Lady and the Tramp* was among their favorites because the story was so romantic.[14] *Lady and the Tramp* is also part of NRK's present Disney Christmas show (*From All of Us to All of You*). *The Jungle Book* was another Christmas cartoon story mentioned by a 24-year-old male student, who suggested that the animated Christmas programs – like other Disney films – were 'swallowed raw.' The same student claimed that he still likes the old films, and equates animation with Disney.

The fact that Disney animated cartoons were mainly available on Norwegian television during Christmas for a decade contributed to establishing Disney cartoons as Christmas icons. For many, the annual Disney show became an important part of the Christmas tradition, almost like Santa Claus and the Christmas tree. To watch the show became an annual ritual embroidered with nostalgic feelings. In the multi-channel environment of the late 1990s, NRK again started to broadcast the Disney Christmas show,[15] in an attempt, along with other media, to construct the showing as a Christmas tradition.[16] For instance, despite its absence during most of the 1990s, the show was explicitly announced as a 'Christmas tradition' in 1998's TV program magazine:[17] 'the day [Christmas Eve] will not be the same without *Donald Duck and His Friends.*'

In other Nordic countries, Disney's animated programs have developed a more established position. In Denmark, for example, the Danish Broadcasting Corporation (Danmarks Radio) introduced the yearly Disney Christmas show on Christmas Day in the 1960s. In 1992, this public service broadcasting institution moved their Disney program to Christmas Eve (see Chapter 5). In Sweden, the association of Disney animated cartoons with Christmas seems even stronger. Under the heading 'Constructing the Perfect Christmas,' the Swedish ethnologist Löfgren writes:

> Since the 1960s the most popular television program of the year is an hour of Walt Disney cartoons shown in the afternoon on Christmas Eve. Attempts to change the content or the timing of this event have always met storms of protest. Most Swedes have structured their celebrations around this media event – to miss the Disney show and the sing-along with the Swedish voice-over to Jiminy Cricket's 'When You Wish Upon a Star' – is to miss a sacred (and very Swedish) Christmas tradition. (Löfgren, 1996: 107)

The Disney program has been broadcast in Sweden for 30 years, and is the most popular program in the country, with over 4 million viewers. As one journalist explains, 'everybody' has to watch it.[18] In the words of one of Löfgren's informants, who dislikes her children's lack of religious Christmas rituals: 'Without Donald Duck's Christmas, it wouldn't be Christmas' (*ibid.*: 110). While less established in Norway, the *Disney Christmas Cavalcade* clearly became a significant part of Christmas festivities for children in the 1980s.

In the memory descriptions of these students at least, Disney animated cartoons were associated with Christmas. Norwegian media continue to construct Disney animated cartoons as something that is a part of Norwegian Christmas celebrations. Mostly, the students' Disney memories, like those of the *Christmas Cavalcade* and *Donald*, were sources of positive feelings. But as we shall see below, Disney memories also contained more mixed feelings.

Disney memories III: pleasure, desire, disappointment and critique

In the elaboration of the psychology students' memories of Disney products, several products, such as *Donald* pocket books and other books, biscuits, costumes, figures, and Disneyland, were repeatedly mentioned. These items were often referred to as something the students took pleasure in or desired, just as they did when reading *Donald* or watching Disney's Christmas show. For example, one male student said that he remembers very well when he got his first Disney hardback book, something that was described as a pleasurable experience. The book was called *I, Goofy*, and the student described it as 'fantastically big for a small boy.' The book consisted of Goofy stories and comic strips from many years, but the student wrote that he found the oldest stories – which included 'Spooky Ghost' – the most exciting and exotic. In hindsight, he felt that the older series contained more psychological depth – in his opinion, 'Goofy was more human then.'

An example of desire is seen in the comments of a 30-year-old female student about some of Disney's illustrated books. She described them as 'the great Disney books that "all" the other children had.' She had wanted to acquire them, but never succeeded. The books referred to are four hardback, illustrated fairy-tale collections, the Norwegian version of the Disney family book series, *Disneyland – From the Wonderful World of Walt Disney* (the volumes had titles like *Fantasyland*; in Norwegian: *Eventyrland*). These four volumes were often found in Norwegian homes.[19]

However, the memories of pleasure and desire were not universal. In the data, there are reports of disappointment with some Disney products, and especially criticism towards the later development of Disney products. One example is the two female students who briefly mentioned that they had been to Disneyland. One wrote that she did not regard it as a special or significant memory: 'Too commercial,' was her explanation. The other student said that she had been to Disneyland when she was about 10 years old. 'I had really looked forward to it,' she said. However, she explained that afterwards she had felt a bit disappointed. These two students were not very impressed by what they perceived as the commercial atmosphere of Disneyland.

Some of the students also had critical comments regarding the current commercial practices of the Disney corporation. One woman said she did not recall so many products (merchandise) when she was a child. She wrote: 'Now I feel there are enormous amounts of Disney-things.' She continued by describing an episode in a store selling bed linen, where she had noticed that many of the products were decorated with Disney motifs. Also shopping in the store was a 3-year-old girl who wanted her mother to buy bed-sheets with a Disney theme. Instead of giving in, the mother listed all the Disney items the girl already owned. This made an impression on the female student, who called the episode (ironically), 'Sleeping with Disney.' Similarly, in the student accounts reported by Wasko (1996), many noted the increasing commercialization of the Disney company, or commented that practices seemed less intensively commercial when they were children.

Feelings of disillusionment also were expressed by a male student who recalled how Disney cartoons made him laugh when he was around 5 years old, but how as an adult (after 18), he had changed his views: 'I became more and more aware of Disney as a "money machine." By this I mean all the effects (toys, clothes, etc.) that accompany the new films, which I perceive as invitations to a "consumption party." ' Furthermore, he felt that the merchandise and promotion of consumption are unhealthy tendencies in society, something that he thinks has an impact on his attitudes toward new Disney films. This seems to reflect the 'backlash' that Wasko (1996) describes in relation to Disney's intense marketing and merchandising efforts.

There also were indirect critical comments, like those of a female student who had watched a video of *Bambi* with her $3\frac{1}{2}$-year-old nephew, including the scene where Bambi's mother is shot. Even though it was unclear whether the nephew had understood the film, he continued to ask about Bambi's mum for weeks. The student felt bad about the way her nephew reacted, and said she regretted allowing him to watch the film. The implication seems to be that even 'innocent Disney' can be scary for children, if they are too young for the message.

It also is interesting that one of the male students mentioned non-Disney characters when asked about Disney. He recalled his joy on getting a Superman costume and his trauma about a Kermit soap that had melted. He explained that he subsequently tried to avoid 'Disney heroes in soap.' Here the characters and effects from other comics and films (Superman and Kermit) were confused with Disney products (although *The Muppets*, including Kermit, was recently acquired by the Disney company – see Buckingham, 1997). In other words, the producers of popular entertainment are probably not always that clear to children, or even to adults.

The disappointment and disillusionment that were reported by some students did not, however, overshadow the pleasurable moments Disney products had brought to many of them. Still, the increased commercialization and aggressive marketing of Disney created second thoughts for some of the students.

Donald Duck & Co. – a popular breadwinner

The design for this study included gathering information about Disney products in Norway. As it turns out, the actuarial data not only is consistent with but also actually highlights the psychology students' memories.

Worldwide, Norway is second only to Finland in terms of the percentage of the population who read the weekly *Donald Duck* comic magazine (Gisle, 1998). In Norway, the primary symbol of Disney is this weekly comic, which is still widely consumed by Norwegian children. Since the comic was first introduced in December 1948, it has been enormously popular.[20] In fact, the *Donald Duck* magazine is the most popular comic in Norway, a country in which the consumption of comics generally is very high.[21] At present, the circulation of *Donald Duck & Co.* is around 170,000 – quite a number in a country with a population of only 4 million people. More than two-thirds of Norwegians (or 69 percent) will read *Donald Duck* if they read comics.[22] In fact, *Donald Duck* is the most read comic, regardless of age and geographical location (Vaage, 1998).

The total readership, however, exceeds the number of copies sold. It is estimated that *Donald Duck* has about 1.1 million readers, of which 750,000 are supposed to be over 15 years old.[23] However, the main target group of *Donald Duck* is the 8- to 12-year-olds.

Donald Duck is not only the most popular comic but it also holds a prominent position among magazines generally in Norway. Indeed, *Donald Duck* is second largest in circulation among magazines sold in stores. If subscription magazines are included, it is ranked fourth.[24] In addition, this widespread circulation has not changed much since the 1970s.[25] From 1948 to 1979, the comic experienced a steady increase in circulation, but since then, circulation has fluctuated. The highest two years were 1979 and 1986, when the circulation was 250,000.[26] In recent years, the number has been lower, for example, 167,000 in 1996, and 177,000 in 1997. However, the number of published issues alone does not fully indicate the magazine's position. Initially, and for many years, *Donald Duck* had very few competitors. In today's market, however, the comic magazine faces competition from other Disney media products, as well as from other companies. More recently, the market has not been expanding, since the number of children in Norway has been decreasing.

Nevertheless, *Donald Duck* is the Disney product that has been and still is the most widely distributed and integrated into Norwegian culture. Indeed, *Donald* is not only good business but is also the main breadwinner for Egmont Serieforlaget, the company with the license to publish *Donald* and many other Disney comics in Norway.[27]

The situation is similar in other Nordic countries. According to Drotner, the Nordic countries top the list of Disney's magazine or comic consumption, and *Donald Duck* is prominent in this picture. While the Danish-owned Egmont Group A/S is the world's largest publisher of Disney print media, the circulation of *Donald Duck* is much smaller in Denmark than in Norway. *Donald Duck* sells 95,000 copies in Denmark, where the population is about 5 million. The circulation of comics in Denmark also has decreased by a third in terms of weekly sales during the last decade. In terms of output, Drotner characterizes the mid-1970s as the heyday of the printed comics in Denmark.

Although Norwegian consumption of *Donald* has decreased, especially compared to the peak years of 1979 and 1986, consumption still remains relatively high. Thus, one might wonder why the consumption of *Donald Duck* continues to be relatively high in Norway, when its readership has been declining in other countries where the Disney comics have had a similar status (as in Denmark)? A number of explanations might be offered. One reason is that a relatively literate population, as in Norway, tends to spend more time on printed media – like newspapers, colored magazines and books – compared to other countries, even after the introduction of television (Vaage, 1998).[28] Besides literacy, the Norwegian climate encourages indoor activities, such as reading, for large parts of the year. People who read – and thus have a high level of cultural capital, to use Bourdieu's (1984) concept – often try to encourage such skills in their children. In particular, the high consumption of colored magazines published weekly easily creates situations where parents (often mothers) buy a magazine for themselves (or the family) and *Donald* for the children. Another aspect is the Norwegian population's high level of economic capital. A good (oil) economy, low unemployment, and a rather equal distribution of wealth has allowed the general population to continue regularly to buy print media for themselves and for their children.

As demonstrated in this section, the *Donald Duck* comic magazine has been and still is a very popular Disney product in Norway. But as we shall see below, Norwegian children have also been exposed to numerous other Disney products for decades.

Being a part of the Dreamworld? [29]

The second source of data for this study, the structured questionnaires, may sharpen the understanding of the extent of young peoples' contact with and perceptions of Disney products.[30] The average age of the 41 media students who responded to the survey was 23, their ages ranging from 19 to 41 years old.[31] Only seven students were older than 25, which means that these interviewees had their childhood exposure to Disney products in the 1970s and 1980s. However, their perceptions also might be influenced by the Disney products available as they grew up in the 1990s.

It was clear from the survey that the students had extensive contact with Disney products, especially as children. Most of the interviewees (92 percent) said they had some or much exposure to Disney materials as children. In fact, no one said they did not have contact with Disney material in their childhood. Even though, as expected, contact with Disney materials declined with age, half of the respondents answered that they continued to have contact with Disney materials as teenagers and as adults. Contact with Disney products also started at a very young age, with the average first contact at 3 years old. All of the respondents had contact with Disney products before they were 7 years old.

How did these Norwegian students feel about Disney? Almost half of those surveyed (46 percent) responded that they strongly liked Disney products as a child, while half liked them more moderately. Only one person declared a strong dislike for Disney products, regardless of age. The general picture is that these students kept their positive attitude towards Disney as they grew up. However, as they grew older, they felt disappointment and developed critical attitudes, in much the same manner as we saw in the psychology students' memory descriptions.

The survey indicated that the students had been in contact with a number of Disney products, the most common being magazines, pocket books, cartoons and films. Some respondents also mentioned products like figures, toys, watches, jewelry, clothes, thermoses, lunch-boxes, shampoos, socks, theme parks, and specific films. Disney characters like Donald Duck, Goofy and Mickey Mouse also were mentioned.

A great majority of our survey sample (90 percent) also had owned Disney merchandise and received or given such products as a gift. Toys and clothing were among the most common products. Even though there is a Mickey Mouse Detective Club in Norway, only two of those interviewed had Mickey Mouse products like ears or a watch. This could indicate something about Norwegians' relationship to Disney products: namely, that Disney is associated with Donald Duck more than with Mickey Mouse. The hot-headed, underdog figure of Donald is more familiar and more appreciated – due mainly, perhaps, to the popularity of the *Donald Duck* comics – than Mickey, who, in most parts of the world, is the symbol of the Disney empire. The same is the case in

Denmark (as Drotner reports in Chapter 5), where Donald is perceived as Danish and politically incorrect, in contrast to the more politically correct Mickey Mouse. Related to this, it might be interesting to note that when analyzing Disney characters using psychoanalytical concepts, Berland (1982) characterized Donald Duck as a representation of the id, while Mickey Mouse is regarded as an ego-ideal.

According to the survey, some Disney products have not been widely available in Norway. Few respondents had watched the Disney Channel, played video games, or been in contact with Disney educational products. Only four of those surveyed had visited the Disney home page on the Internet. This obviously relates to the market situation and to what has been available, especially when these students were children. The Disney Channel, for example, has not been available on cable television in Norway.[32] However, access to the Internet is growing rapidly.

One interesting aspect of the survey is that more respondents had been to a Disney theme park in the U.S.A. than in Europe. Three had visited Disneyland, California, while six had been to Disney World in Florida, and five had been to the Epcot Center and MGM Studios. In contrast, only three interviewees had been to EuroDisney. This can be explained by the fact that EuroDisney did not open until 1992, while these students were children in the 1970s and 1980s. Moreover, perhaps Disney theme parks are also a more obvious destination when visiting Florida than when visiting France, because Disney is considered an American phenomenon.

The questionnaire also requested a description of the respondents' instant perceptions of Disney. The most common words used to describe their experiences were entertainment, humor, fun, happiness, excitement, friendliness, fantasy, and colors. The students suggested that Disney provides uncontroversial, innocent entertainment that makes one happy. However, many also found Disney to be commercial and moralizing, and that the products promote American values. Still, most respondents associated Disney with positive memories, with childhood, Christmas, gifts, holidays, family, and celebration. When describing the typical Disney story, many mentioned the classic battle between good and evil, and also that the stories always have happy endings. Some also mentioned Disney characters such as Donald Duck, Mickey Mouse and Goofy, etc. It was also common to associate Disney with comic magazines and films.

However, students also had mixed feelings about Disney products. They associated them with both high quality and high technology, as well as with negative words like garbage and plastic. In particular, the media products – movies, cartoons, and magazines – were associated with quality. Other products (merchandise) like figures, clothes, watches, etc. were seen as commercial, mass-produced, and of low quality. Many of the respondents had critical comments about Disney, explaining that it gives children and others a distorted impression of life and reality. Others cited Disney's effective marketing, and how the company uses children to put pressure on parents to purchase their products. They perceived the Disney company as representing the typical American values of commercialism, materialism, and mass production. The products also are judged to be expensive.

In the following discussion, a continuous emphasis is placed on the way the Disney world mirrors the values of the American Dream. A prime example of this is the viewpoint expressed in the data about Disney theme parks. It bears repeating that these critical remarks must be seen as adult reflections of childhood and later experiences, and may not represent views in childhood.

When asked about a list of values that Disney could be said to promote or discourage, the majority of interviewees replied that the company promotes fun, magic, good over evil, family, imagination, happiness, love/romance, optimism, and bravery. Half of the interviewees also suggested that Disney promoted technological progress, patriarchy, and patriotism. One interesting result was that almost half of the interviewees (48 percent) stated that racism did not apply to Disney. This view contrasts with the arguments of several researchers (for example, Claudine, 1996; Miller and Rode, 1995; Smoodin, 1993) that Disney does promote racism through its use of racial and ethnic stereotypes and caricatures. This denial of racism could be interpreted as related to the fact that discourses of race are often suppressed in Norway, which traditionally has been a rather homogenous society.

More than two-thirds of the survey respondents felt that Disney is American and promotes 'the American Dream.' Disney was seen to promote entertainment, individualism, consumer culture, materialism, mass production, industrialization, bravery, and business – all values associated with American culture and society. Many respondents tried to nuance their statements by arguing that these values could be regarded more and more as Western or universal. Those who did not think of Disney as American (seven of the 41 interviewed) argued that the Disney characters and products could be seen as a reflection of Western culture, with its emphasis on happiness, family, individualism, and capitalism. Some interviewees stated that they had felt Disney characters were Norwegian when they were children, since the characters had Norwegian names and the text was in Norwegian. Even though most respondents viewed Disney as American, these reflections again represent their adult view. Some emphasized that they did not think of Disney as American when they were children, but gradually became aware of this.

The general impression from the questionnaire was that these students had not associated Disney with American culture when they were children. The Disney characters and values were perceived as more universal, and Disney products were seen as a way to live out the dream of a happy, unproblematic life. Most respondents had subsequently developed a critical attitude, but they still associated Disney products with positive words like fun, imagination, entertainment, happiness, magic, etc. This positive view was combined with a critical attitude towards the values that Disney represents, and which are thought of as American: commercialism, materialism, mass production, and consumption. This may reflect an ambiguous or ambivalent relationship to Disney: while they love the entertainment, the fantastic characters, the imagination, the fun – the innocent dreamworld of Disney – and most of them continue to take part in 'the wonderful world of Disney,' they also condemn the business of Disney.[33]

To summarize, again, Norwegian students had extensive exposure to a number of Disney products, which they mainly associated with something positive. But many of the students had developed more mixed feelings towards Disney products as they were growing up. Still, Disney media products were mostly appreciated, while the overload of Disney merchandise was regarded unfavorably.

Disney everywhere: availability of Disney products

In an attempt to study Disney thoroughly, a limited market analysis of the availability of Disney products in Norway was conducted. As has already been indicated, a number of Disney products have been available and popular in Norway for several decades. But during the 1990s Disney merchandise and media products have become more available and their promotion has intensified. This market situation provides the backdrop against which young people evaluate their Disney childhood memories. The following market analysis is especially important for understanding the experiences children have with Disney products today.

Visits to a few local stores in one Norwegian city, Trondheim, provides a concrete picture of the extensive and intensive way ordinary Norwegians are exposed to Disney paraphernalia in their daily lives.[34] For example, 47 different Disney products were found in a large department store (OBS!), which sells food, clothes, houseware, videos, music, electronic equipment, toilet articles, etc. Items that were particularly prevalent were various articles of clothing, especially socks. In Bruun Libris, one of the largest bookstores in Trondheim (which also sells toys), 27 different kinds of Disney products were identified, most of them in the children's department. The most salient products were the Disney Home Videos, books and animated cartoons, and a shelf reserved for Winnie the Pooh merchandise (called 'Ole Brumm Torget' or 'Winnie the Pooh Marketplace'). However, one does not have to go to a large store to find Disney products, as smaller kiosks also have a variety of products on sale. In one of the local outlets of the national (news-stand) kiosk system ('Narvesen'), thirteen different kinds of Disney products were observed, including mostly magazines, comic books, story and activity books, read-along books (book and audiotapes) and some videos, but also a few toys, some candy, and Disney bubble bath. All in all, videos, comics and books are the most prominent products available in Norwegian stores. In many places, Winnie the Pooh products, recently absorbed into the Disney empire, are prevailing over the classic Disney characters like Donald Duck and Mickey Mouse.

In order to provide a more detailed picture, the following section details the prevalent and popular products from the market analysis.[35] It has been difficult to get a complete picture, since the distribution system for Disney is quite complex. For example, the company sells its licenses to different distributors in various European countries and a number of Disney products are imported to Norway in this way. Still, the market analysis provides an overview of the general picture.

Clothes for adults and teens: The most readily available articles of clothing with Disney motifs are socks, nightgowns, pajamas, and underwear. These are widely sold in Norway, although other articles, while available, are somewhat harder to find.

Products for toddlers, babies, infants: There is a wide array of clothing (like T-shirts, pants, shirts, pajamas, underpants) available for this group, along with many other products – such as toys, stuffed soft animals, plastic cups, bottles, plates, mobiles, lamps, etc. Bedroom furniture is not currently available in the Norwegian market, but soon will be.

Housewares: Numerous products are available, such as coffee cups, plates, bed linens, clocks, and towels.

Toys, games, children's furniture: Most items are available in Norwegian shops (except the aforementioned children's furniture), including soft toys, stuffed animals, dolls, action figures, games, etc. The availability of action figures seems to fluctuate, depending on the launching of blockbuster Disney films. In the summer of 1998, when this market analysis was performed, the shops contained many leftover materials from *Pocahontas* and *Hercules*. Stuffed Winnie the Pooh animals and figures also were quite prevalent.

Personal adornment: Even though a number of products – like jewelry and Mickey Mouse and Winnie the Pooh watches – are found in Norway, you may have to search quite hard. Key chains, badges, etc. are easier to find.

Decorative products: There are many items in this category, most of them decorations for children's rooms. Examples include figurines, posters, framed artwork, pillows, and framed Winnie the Pooh Classics.

Recreational equipment: Few items in this category seemed to be available in Norway, except for bicycle helmets.

Food products: Nestlé sells food products with Disney motifs on the packages. Also, egg packs were decorated with Disney motifs. Other items included ice-cream and candy. However, when a new Disney film production is launched in Norway, McDonald's often sells Disney figurines along with children's meals. A new blockbuster film may even generate a special menu (like the Hero-burger that appeared in connection with the launching of *Hercules*).

Personal hygiene products: Many products – such as soap, shampoo, perfume or cologne, bandages, hairbrushes, combs, toothbrushes, cups/glasses, and bubble bath – can be found, but mostly these are products for children.

Paper and stationery goods: A number of products are available in this category, such as pencils, pencil boxes, pens, other school supplies, stationery, cards, postcards, wrapping paper, and party goods like paper plates, cups, table covers, party favors, napkins, hats, straws, stamps, and desk butlers.

Carry-alls: These items included book bags, backpacks, and purses.

Media products for purchase and rental: Disney media products can be found practically everywhere in Norway. They include magazines, picture books, story books, comic magazines, books that compile Disney strips, activity books, home videos, records, audiotapes, CDs, trading cards, CD-ROM books, and games for use on the computer.

As noted previously, the comic magazine, *Donald Duck*, is particularly dominant in the market. In the 1990s, an average of 170,000 to 175,000 copies have been sold every week. *Donald Duck* is also supplemented by a number of other more irregularly published comic books and magazines.[36] Many other Disney publications also are displayed prominently in bookstores, video and toy stores, along with numerous Disney Classics videos, storybooks and 'read-alongs.'

Computer material, on the other hand, varies in availability and popularity. The *Donald Duck* comics have their own homepage (www.donald.no) provided by Egmont Serieforlaget, which is mainly a promotion site for the *Donald Duck* magazine. Here, one can order a subscription to the comic magazine, but also the *Donald Duck* 'anniversary book series.'[37] In addition, there is much information about Duckburgh and facts related to Donald and other figures, along with jokes, competitions, etc. In 1998, this page had an average of 5000 to 6000 hits daily.[38]

Subscriptions to Disney pages are also increasing in popularity. The Norwegian company Tele2 reports that 80,000 people subscribe to the Disney game page on the Internet (the Norwegian version of Disney Blast).[39] The Disney home page also is available, which includes detailed information about Disney media products, as well as heavily promoting Disney merchandise.

CD-ROM products do not seem to have caught on in Norway. Indeed, one computer software and video shop (RAM&ROM) indicated that they were trying to get rid of Disney's CD-ROM products because they were not selling.

Media outlets: There are three main outlets related to Disney audiovisual products. First, of course, Disney movies are shown in theaters. In Norway, the big Disney films are often launched right before Christmas, with recent examples including *Tarzan* in 1999, *Mulan* in 1998, and *Hercules* in 1997.[40] In addition, other Disney films are shown regularly. For instance, the movie theaters in Trondheim showed six different Disney animated films during 1997.[41] Some historical information may also illuminate today's situation: although Disney animated cartoons have been shown in Norwegian cinemas since before World War II (for example, *Snow White and the Seven Dwarfs*, in 1937), many of the classics produced during the early 1940s only came to Norway after 1945 (see Dahl *et al.*, 1996). These films provided the foundation for the popularity of Disney figures in Norway.[42]

Second, Disney programs are broadcast on Norwegian television. For instance, NRK broadcasts Disney shows like *The Disney Hour* (1997–8, and again in 1999).[43] *The Disney Hour* was first broadcast by the commercial Norwegian channel TV2 (1996–7).[44] NRK also broadcasts the annual Disney Christmas show, discussed earlier. In addition, TVNorge (a commercial channel available on cable) broadcasts shows for adults like *Life Works* and *Dangerous Minds*.[45]

Third, Disney videos can be either purchased or rented, although more often, Disney films tend to be sold rather than rented.[46] Disney films are now available in many grocery stores, book and video stores, etc. Animated videos seem to dominate the market.

The greatest difference between the 1990s and the earlier years is the availability of Disney merchandise. Disney spin-off products are promoted everywhere, even in the traditional comics. Especially after a new Disney film, toy stores, bookstores, supermarkets and airports are filled with follow-up merchandise.[47] This is just one indication that more Disney products are available for children today.

Generally, then, we can conclude that Disney has a high profile in Norway, both through various media products and in the increasing abundance of merchandise. The interesting question is what role these products play in the lives of today's Norwegian children.

A Disney-saturated childhood?
Group interviews with children

In the following section, the focus is on how today's children experience Disney products.[48] It is important to examine how children receive Disney products, as they are the main targets for many of them (Buckingham, 1997). Since Disney has become an inescapable part of growing up (Jackson, 1996), it is also vital to study how Disney products are used, as the following interview extract with a 9-year-old girl illustrates:

Q: Do you read anything?
A: Yes, I most often read *Donald* magazines. The most joyful [thing] I do is reading *Donald.*...Then I read some books. Donald books. Donald is the funniest I know of. ... I can't sit and eat without having a *Donald* magazine. So I sit morning, dinner and evening with a *Donald* magazine.[49]

This quote illustrates how Disney products may be integrated into everyday life, as the girl combines reading the still-popular *Donald Duck* comics with her daily eating habits.

One area of particular interest is the kinds of associations children of the 1990s have with Disney. When asked what they thought about when hearing the word Disney, most of the interviewees immediately said Donald or Donald Duck. In addition, a number of other comics or cartoon figures were mentioned: Mickey Mouse, Huey, Dewey, and Louie, Uncle Scrooge and the B-gang, Goofy, Daisy, Simba, Cinderella, Snow White, Pocahontas, and the Lion King. One girl also immediately showed the interviewer the ring she was wearing, which was decorated with a motif from *101 Dalmatians*.

Disney's *Donald Duck* magazine was the most popular Disney product among the children in our group interviews. Half of the interviewed children corresponded with the target group for the comic magazine (8 to 12 years old). The other half were younger (6 to 8 years old). Still, all of the children had access to and read the *Donald Duck* comic. Reading, however, is a relative term. For some of the first-graders, this meant looking at the pictures or 'singing the letters together,' as a 6½-year-old girl explained.

Several of the youngest children explained that they had access to boxes and drawers full of *Donald* magazines at home. Many of the older children subscribed to *Donald Duck*, while others bought it every week or more occasionally. Some of the children were, or had been, collecting *Donald Duck* and stored them in special boxes. Old *Donald* magazines also were a thrill, as expressed by an 8½-year-old boy: 'When I go and visit someone who has old *Donald* magazines, I just throw myself over the reading material.' One of the boys, aged 9½, said he was beginning to lose interest in the magazine. Although he still liked it, he no longer found it so important. The other boy in his group, however, said that the *Donald* magazine was one of the few things he read.

The interviewed children also were familiar with other Disney comics, such as Mickey Mouse, Uncle Scrooge, and Huey, Dewey and Louie. Some children mentioned magazines about Simba, Winnie the Pooh, and Ariel. Other (non-Disney) comics like Asterix, Tom and Jerry, Superman, The Phantom, Batman, and Spiderman also were mentioned. In addition, these children had a number of pocket books, especially *Donald* pockets. Some children preferred the pocket books to magazines, because they included more reading material.

What about Disney animated programs on television? A number of these children mentioned that they have watched *The Disney Hour*, and several of them found it exciting.[50] The fourth-graders also were well aware of its broadcast time. However, the program was not a priority for everyone. A 7-year-old who said she likes *The Disney Hour* explained: 'It is not so often I get to watch it.' Asked why, she replied: 'Often I do not watch it, because I have other things to do.... For example, if I do other things, then I forget *The Disney Hour*.' The girl apparently prefers social company over the program. 'I also tend to forget it [*The Disney Hour*],' her 7½-year-old male classmate added. Apparently, Disney cartoons seem less important when they are available all the time. Still, the children mentioned both *The Disney Hour* and other Disney cartoons as sources of pleasure.

What about the children's association of Disney cartoons and Christmas? Even though some of the children responded that they do watch Disney cartoons during Christmas, this did not appear to be an immediate association for them. The fourth-graders, who said they watch Disney cartoons during Christmas, responded to a question about whether they connect Disney films with Christmas in the following manner: 'Yes, because then there are many such films with snow and such' (boy, 9 years). Another interviewee said: 'And then when Donald has his Santa Claus cap on, then everybody is in front of the tree and looks at the presents' (8½-year-old girl). The children seemed to think the question was about Christmas motifs in Disney films, which suggests that they lack the association between Disney and Christmas, that was so prevalent in the memory descriptions of the psychology students.

These children seemed well acquainted with Disney films that have been playing at the cinemas. Examples mentioned include *101 Dalmatians*, *Lady and the Tramp*, *Flubber*, *Bambi*, *Hercules*, *The Lion King*, *The Hunchback of Notre Dame*, and *Aladdin*. The children made an interesting distinction throughout the interviews between cartoons and what they call 'proper films,' which are films other than animated cartoons. When it comes to cartoons, this category was often equated with Disney. One 8½-year-old girl explained: 'Almost all animated cartoons, it is almost Disney all of them. Because Walt Disney has made all films and he became very old. And he was very clever to invent them.' These children were also aware that while their own peers watched animated cartoons, older children prefer so-called 'proper films.'

Disney animated videos seemed very prevalent among the children interviewed. The Disney videos they mentioned owning included *Lady and the Tramp*, *The Lion King*, *101 Dalmatians*, and *Aladdin*, films about Donald, Pluto, Goofy, Uncle Scrooge, Winnie the Pooh, *Cinderella*, *Snow White*, and a *Duck Tales* film. *The Lion King* seemed to be the most popular video, and one 7-year-old boy tried to explain why: 'It is the world's very best Disney film I know of.'

Disney videos seemed to be in abundance in some families. One 7½-year-old girl revealed that she had a shelf full of Disney films, while another girl (7 years old) said: 'I have two boxes full of videos, and one of the boxes I can hardly close.' These were mostly Disney films, she said. With children's ability to exaggerate, two boys claimed: 'I have many thousand videos' (6½ years), to which his 6-year-old classmate responded: 'I have many millions.' In general, then, owning Disney films seemed to be quite common. Some children also mentioned that their families rented Disney films.

Disney books also were popular among the children interviewed, and included *The Jungle Book*, *The Lion King*, *Hercules*, *The Hunchback of Notre Dame*, *Pocahontas*, *Cinderella*, and *Aladdin*, along with books about Winnie the Pooh, Donald, Goofy, and Ariel. A few of the interviewees mentioned that they had been members of the Donald Duck Book Club. One 7½-year-old girl explained: 'First my mum signed me up for the Donald Duck Book Club, but then I quit because mum did not want to spend more money at it.' The book club may easily become expensive, since it is not only a source of Disney books but also of spin-off products.

How aware were these children about Disney as a brand name? Even the first-graders seemed to recognize Disney films. When asked:

'How do you know whether it is a Disney film or not?' they responded: 'It says if it is a Disney film' (boy, $6\frac{1}{2}$ years old). 'You do hear if it is a Disney film. It cannot be named Donald if it is a proper film' (girl, $6\frac{1}{2}$ years old). One 7-year-old girl explained: 'It says Disney on them, it usually says on films and magazines, so we can see the difference.' Still, the large quantity of Disney films available makes brand consciousness more difficult. In the words of one 9-year-old boy: 'There are so many Disney films, so you hardly know what is Disney or not.'

The children interviewed were also well acquainted with Disney merchandise, and some of them wore Disney socks at the interview. A $6\frac{1}{2}$-year-old girl had *Lady and the Tramp* socks, while a $9\frac{1}{2}$-year-old boy wore a pair decorated with motifs from *101 Dalmatians*. While socks indeed seemed to be a very common product, some children apparently possessed an abundance of Disney products. One $7\frac{1}{2}$-year-old said he had a drawer full of Lion King, Goofy, and Mickey merchandise and other such items. Other products mentioned included cups, glasses, straws with figures like Aladdin, Donald, and Simba, plates with the Lion King and Winnie the Pooh, Winnie the Pooh figures, Lion King pictures, jigsaw puzzles of Donald, Mickey and the Lion King, T-shirts, shorts and many other items. Some of the children claimed that they just received the Disney products, but one 9-year-old boy admitted that, at least at an earlier age, he asked for new Disney things, like figures or videos, when they were available: 'Otherwise, I would continue nagging,' he said.

What concept did these children have of the Disney products' original nationality? Only the youngest children (the first-graders) thought that Disney was Norwegian, as one $6\frac{1}{2}$-year-old girl explained: 'They have to be Norwegian in order for us to understand them.' Many of the other children had experienced Disney products from other countries, such as Sweden, Denmark, Germany, France and Italy. One $8\frac{1}{2}$-year-old boy even knew the name of several Disney figures in Portuguese. In an attempt to explain Disney's nationality, one 7-year-old boy suggested: 'Disney may be Norwegian, Swedish and German in different countries.' One girl in the second grade argued that Disney is 'actually English.' Still, several of the children seemed uncertain about the nationality of Disney; they felt that these products were Norwegian, even if they knew they were sold elsewhere, too. One $8\frac{1}{2}$-year-old girl had desires related to this: 'I wish it [Disney] was Norwegian, because then you could go to Disneyland … and you could get to buy lots of films and other things. There could be more stores where you could buy such different things.'

As indicated above, Disneyland was a particular object of desire for some of the children. A few of them had been to EuroDisney, and several of the others wished to go there. One $8\frac{1}{2}$-year-old girl who had been to EuroDisney described her experiences in the following manner:

> We slept in a hotel ... a big house. We could go out behind it, and there was the entrance to EuroDisney ... There were different kinds of merry-go-rounds and a ghost house. It was a bit spooky ... I thought so when I was younger.

The girl went on to describe the gloomy darkness inside the ghost house, the voices they heard, and the grinning witch they met. 'When I got out I almost cried,' she said. One $9\frac{1}{2}$-year-old boy had been to Disneyland Paris the previous summer. He said that they had bought T-shirts and other things, and that he thought it was fun. He explained: 'It was nice. You could do lots of different things. There were such merry-go-rounds and ... lots of things.' When hearing about this, his classmates immediately expressed a desire to go to Disneyland. Some children said that their families had made plans to visit Disneyland in the future.

Consumption of Disney products seems integrated into the family setting. These children appeared well aware of the feelings their parents, sisters and brothers had towards Disney. For example, several of the children said that their fathers had collected *Donald Duck* magazines. One 7-year-old girl, whose stepfather supposedly did not appreciate Disney, said: 'but my mum, she just *loves* Disney, because she has been to Disneyland.' Conversely, another girl ($8\frac{1}{2}$ years old) explained the background to her mother's negative feelings: 'My mum does not like to buy the *Donald* comics so often, because there is just one thing [a figure] in the *Donald* comics, and then I and my sister and brother are three, so there is [an] argument about who is supposed to get that figure.' One $9\frac{1}{2}$-year-old boy, whose father is divorced said: 'And then my dad has a new girlfriend who is collecting Disney classics,' while another $7\frac{1}{2}$-year-old boy explained: 'I have two smaller brothers. They like Disney. If mum says "Do you want to watch Disney," they shout with joy.' One $6\frac{1}{2}$-year-old girl said that her older siblings 'like proper films better,' and referred to the fact that her older sister had recently bought *Titanic*.

It was apparent from these group interviews that Disney products were an integrated part of the everyday lives and culture of these children. A number of the children also mentioned that they occasionally play-act Disney figures and stories. For example, one $6\frac{1}{2}$-year-old girl said she had played Sleeping Beauty in kindergarten. Other children mentioned that they had played the Lion King, Donald Duck, Huey, Dewey, and Louie, and Ariel. An $8\frac{1}{2}$-year-old boy explained: 'Sometimes I play that I am Goofy, and then I make mistakes and such things.' Three of the girls said that they enjoyed running around pretending to be the Lion King. Another 8½-year-old girl reported playing Cinderella and Sleeping Beauty, although the latter was considered boring.

These excerpts from the group interviews suggest that children's everyday lives are saturated with Disney products. This familiarity with the company's products also was illustrated by the fact that when one child introduced episodes from any Disney media product, the other children would fill in the story. An example is provided by the 8½-year-old boy's description of his movie experience with *Flubber*: 'It was fun to watch when *Flubber* was made. Then he lifted him up and asked: "Do you have a cold?" And then he sneezed. The little slimy creature.' This description was followed by an elaboration of the Flubber story from a girl in the same interview group. Such continuation of stories was widespread in the interview material and strongly suggests that the children knew the Disney stories very well. Generally, the interviewed children seemed to have an in-depth knowledge of Disney's fictional universe. Through their intense discussions of Disney stories, they also demonstrated how much they enjoyed certain scenarios.

Another noticeable feature in these interview discourses was the degree of what Buckingham (1998) – quoting Marsha Kinder – calls 'trans-media intertextuality,' in which a story in one medium can easily be associated with the same story in another medium, or with merchandise. For example, when *The Lion King* was discussed, someone else was reminded that they had a book about the film, then another one might say they had *Lion King* 'sing-a-longs,' or even *Lion King* socks, etc. The impression was that some of the children gradually got tired of the stories and figures in this way. To quote one 6-year-old girl: 'I do not like Disney so much.' Another girl (7 years) and one 8½-year-old boy felt that Disney was 'so-so,' while two girls (8½ and 9) described how they became tired of certain Disney books, in this case *Aladdin* and *The Jungle Book*. This seems to indicate that with Disney stories available in so many forms, the company runs the risk of tiring out these young consumers.

As this section has demonstrated, Norwegian children today are overly familiar with Disney's figures and fictional universe. Also among these children, the *Donald Duck* comic magazine seems to have maintained its leading position, despite the many other products available. However, Disney's transmedia intertextuality seemed to 'wear out' certain stories, and thus made them less attractive for some children.

Conclusion

What is the significance of Disney products in Norway? Through the memory descriptions of young people, we can see that the dominant Disney product – the *Donald Duck* comic magazine – is surrounded by positive, nostalgic feelings about a childhood pleasure that some still enjoy.[51] According to the classic work, *How to Read Donald Duck* (Dorfman and Mattelart, 1984 [1975]), Disney comics present themselves as innocent, non-political children's fantasies, when, in fact, the comics actually promote American capitalist and imperialist ideology. In Norway, especially, the *Donald Duck* magazine has remained popular for over half a century. Even among adults, the magazine is associated with innocence.

This chapter has presented a discussion of how Disney's animated cartoons have become associated with Christmas, due mostly to the lack of such entertainment during the rest of the year. In Norway, as in Denmark and especially Sweden, Disney's Christmas show became a ritual, and a sacred part of Christmas traditions. However, the significance of the Christmas memories related to Disney seems almost out of proportion. Indeed, the media themselves take an active part in the construction of Disney as a Christmas ritual and tradition.

However, young people also were exposed to a number of other Disney products that were sources of pleasure as well as disappointment. Exposure to Disney products had been part of the experience of all the interviewees, starting from a very young age. Most of the informants reported having positive feelings about Disney as children. Many of them also remained positive, but to a lesser extent as they grew older. Especially when considering the business practices of Disney in later years, some of the young people were critical of Disney's increasing contribution to the commercialization of children's culture. Such descriptions of Disney as a money machine were, however, reflections made by adults in hindsight. The exaggerated promotion of merchandise and increased consumerism were Disney practices disapproved of by young people.

The young people's relationship to Disney could be characterized as ambivalent or ambiguous, like so many of our everyday practices (cf. Hagen, 1992, 1994). The interviewees had positive perceptions of Disney characters and products, which they associated with fun, imagination, entertainment, happiness, and magic. They had maintained much of their childhood love for the fantastic characters and fictional dreamworld of Disney. However, as they became adults, they had gradually come to associate Disney with other values: namely, commercialism, materialism, mass production, and consumption.

These contradictory feelings seem to be rooted in the distinction between media products and merchandise. The media products like comics, books, and animated cartoons were associated with high quality. The merchandise (such as figures, clothes, watches, etc.), on the contrary, was seen as commercial, mass-produced, and of low quality. Such ambivalent feelings among youngsters ought to be thought-provoking for the Disney company, at a time when there is ever-increasing promotion of more Disney merchandise than any-body's heart might desire. If this continues, Disney may well face the backlash that Wasko (1996) discusses in relation to intensified merchandising. After all, it is young people, like the ones interviewed for this study, who will introduce and maintain habits of Disney consumption for future generations.

Compared to the memories and experiences of people who were children in the 1970s and 1980s, the present situation is characterized by an abundance of Disney products. Of course, the more critical comments by young people are reflections of the merchandising of the 1990s. In the Norwegian stores visited by researchers for this project, Disney merchandise was found in virtually every thinkable category, including clothing, houseware, toys, games, jewelry, decoration, food, hygiene, paper goods, and carry-alls. This means that Disney merchandise is entering all spheres of family life, and especially childhood.

The market analysis also illustrated that in the 1990s, media products are in abundance. The *Donald Duck* comics now experience competition from numerous magazines, pocket books, books, tapes, and videos. Disney animated cartoons – once limited to Christmas – are now available the whole year around on television, in the movie theaters, and through videos. What happens when it is like Christmas all year? Do Disney's animated cartoons lose part of their unique charm? Time will tell. But the Internet seems to be increasing in popularity, with new potential for people to be informed about the Disney universe, Disney media products, and, last but not least, new merchandise.

As Buckingham suggests, this proliferation of new media technologies and forms of distribution implies that children are increasingly being targeted and constructed as consumers or potential markets. He characterizes Disney's practices as a classic example of the horizontal integration of previously distinct media sectors:

> Right from the early days of the Mickey Mouse clubs, merchandising and subsequent theme parks have been a key dimension of the enterprise – and in fact, it is these aspects which have guaranteed its continuing profitability. However, this horizontal integration is now moving to a different scale. Once you have seen the latest movie, you can catch the

spin-off episodes on the Disney Channel, meet the characters at the theme park, visit the Disney store at your local mall and stock up [on] the video, the posters, the T-shirts, and other merchandise; and if you are being digital, you can check out the CD-ROM, visit the website and so on. (Buckingham, 1998: 47)

Even though a few of the products mentioned – like the Disney Channel, theme parks, and Disney Stores – are not available to most Norwegians, Buckingham perfectly characterizes a process that is taking place in Norway. The consequence of this new media environment is the transmedia intertextuality mentioned earlier.

What will happen to children when the company has reached such a level of horizontal integration that a Disney-saturated environment is created? As this study indicates, children today are still fascinated by the Disney characters and stories provided by different media outlets. Although the *Donald Duck* comics still appear to be the number one source of enjoyment for young children, Disney animated programs were also highly appreciated, on television, at the movies, and on video. The children interviewed did not associate Disney with Christmas, as the university students did. Numerous Disney books also were consumed by children. However, the abundance of media products, and the fact that the same stories and figures were available in numerous media also meant that some children got tired of them.

While these Norwegian children often owned an abundance of Disney merchandise, enthusiasm for these products in no way compared to the positive feelings many children seemed to have towards Disney's media products. An interesting question is what Disney experiences will remain with these children as significant childhood memories? And what will their adult images and perceptions of Disney be? And, for the present, the question posed by Giroux (1995) remains: to what extent will Disney – through their promotion of 'innocence' – be able to mask their aggressive marketing techniques and transform children into active consumers?

Acknowledgments

I would like to thank Richard Alapack for the constructive comments he made on earlier drafts of this chapter. I am also indebted to my research assistants Leif Johnny Johannessen and Mitja Samoilow for the valuable groundwork they did in the Norwegian Global Disney Audiences Project. I am grateful to the (here nameless) students and children who provided insight into how Disney products may be received and remembered. Finally, thanks to Amedeo Giorgi and Dan

Y. Jacobsen, who provided useful comments and inspiration at different stages of the project.

Notes

1. The title of this article makes reference to Real's (1977) discussion of the 'Disney Universe,' a term also used by the Disney company itself. According to Real, the concept also 'brings to mind the universality of Disney's worldwide spread' (*ibid*.: 81).
2. This first data set consists of fourteen Disney memories, in which a group of students were asked to recall some of their childhood experiences with Disney products. The students' memory descriptions were written by the students themselves in February 1998.
3. This second data set consists of 41 questionnaires utilizing media students as respondents. The questionnaire was developed for the Global Disney Audiences Project, and was administered in September 1997.
4. The market analysis was based on the checklist developed by the Global Disney Audiences Project, and was mainly performed by Mitja Samoilow.
5. Sixteen children were interviewed by the author and research assistant Mitja Samoilow. The children were from first, second, third and fourth grade (aged 6 to $9\frac{1}{2}$) and were interviewed in groups according to grade level. Each group included four children – two girls and two boys. Each interview was conducted by the two researchers: while one directed the conversation, the other kept track of who said what.
6. The fourteen students were in their mid-twenties (ages ranged from 22 to 30 years). Hence, they were children in the 1970s and 1980s. Nine of the students were female, while five of them were male. Their descriptions of childhood experiences with Disney products are quite short, between a half and one page, but nevertheless proved very informative.
7. In Norway, there is a strong fan culture for *Donald Duck & Co.*, calling themselves Donaldists. These fans – often young men – take special interest in *Donald Duck* classics, especially those drawn by Carl Barks. Such fans are often collectors of the old magazines, and many are very knowledgeable about the Disney universe, both the development of the company and the fictional world. One of the fans, a comics creator himself, claims that Norwegians have a religious relationship with Donald: 'Donald Duck is already a religion in Norway today. A love for the old Barks stories is being inherited from generation to generation in such a way that they continue to buy a magazine where the quality has sunk to a miserable level' (Christopher Nielsen, cited in Riesto, 1998: 46). Nielsen has himself published an underground magazine parodying the Disney figures.
8. Thus, NRK had a monopoly on broadcasting television in Norway for two decades. Still, even though Norwegian television was deregulated in 1981, it was not until the 1990s that cable access became widespread. Norway got its second national terrestrial channel in 1992, with the establishment

of the commercial TV2, which, despite being commercial, also had public service obligations as part of its license conditions.

9. The program magazines (*Programbladet*) from the 1960s and 1970s (NRK did not keep proper archives for this time period) revealed that *Christmas in Disneyland* was broadcast on December 26, 1964, and *Disneyland* on December 26, 1965. In 1979, Disney's *From All of Us to All of You* (or *Donald Duck og vennene hans*) was broadcast twice: on January 1, 1979 and December 24, 1979. In 1980, the same show was broadcast on December 26, 1980.

10. *The Disney Cavalcade, From All of Us to All of You*, was first shown on Christmas Eve 1979 and after that, every Christmas for the next decade, including 1989. Then it reappeared in 1997 and 1998. (Source: Åke Källqvist, Chief Editor in NRK's Drama Purchase. Fax dated January 22, 1999.)

11. However, there are sometimes small variations. For example, two new stories appeared during Christmas 1998: one from *Mulan*, the box-office hit of the year, and the other from *Lion King II*.

12. This seems to relate to the role of television in contributing to the national calendar (for a discussion, see Scannell, 1988). Another program that has become part of the Christmas tradition in Norway is the comical performance show, *The Butler*. The same episode has been broadcast by NRK on the evening of December 23 for 20 continuous years. Even though people know every line, watching it is part of getting in the mood for Christmas. *The Butler* also is broadcast in other countries, such as Sweden, and appears on seven German channels on New Year's Eve.

13. For an analysis of NRK's approach and strategies towards children, both in terms of program policies and programs in the 1960s and 1970s, see Bakøy (1999).

14. The story of *Lady and the Tramp* was also mentioned as a strong memory from the movies.

15. The 1998 NRK broadcast of *From All of Us to All of You* (or *Donald and His Friends*) was broadcast at 2 o'clock on Christmas Eve, which is the main Christmas celebration day in Norway. The show had 32 percent rating among 3- to 11-year-olds and 13 percent rating among those over 12. In 1997, the same show had ratings of 23 percent for 3- to 11-year-olds, while 12 percent was the average ratings for those over 12 years old. (Ratings provided by Karin Hake in NRK's Research Department.)

16. The project on Disney consumption in Norway resulted in two interviews with this author: by one of NRK's national radio channels (NRK P2's *Verdt å vite*, December 20, 1998) and by the regional paper in Trondheim (*Adresseavisen*, December 24, 1998). Both of the journalists wanted to focus on Disney's animated cartoons as a Norwegian Christmas tradition.

17. This is the literal translation of the show's title in Norwegian (*Adresseavisens TV-Magasinet* December 18–24, 1998, p. 5).

18. These claims are made by Åke Källqvist in an interview in Berntsen (1998).

19. These books were quite visible on shelves in Norwegian homes in the 1970s, as they came in bright colors like red, blue, orange, etc. The

American publication appeared in 1965, and the Norwegian publication followed immediately. According to Birgitte Frostad of Egmont Hjemmet A/S, the books were incredibly popular, and soon sold out (phone conversation, February 1, 1999).

20. *Donald Duck* was initially published monthly. Originally, the character had been introduced in Norway in 1935 as a strip figure in a colored magazine. According to the Donald Internet page in Norway (http://www.donald.no), the character was then called Teodor And (*and* is the Norwegian word for duck). However, the publication of the *Donald Duck & Co.* comic magazine is generally considered the official introduction of Donald Duck in Norway. At least, the 50th anniversary of Donald was commemorated in 1998, after a celebration in 1984 marking 50 years since Donald's first appearance in the film *The Wise Little Hen* (1934).

21. According to Gisle (1998), Norway ranks second only to Japan in terms of comics sale per capita (http://www.donald.no/bibliotek/no_bib_walt.html).

22. On average, 9 percent of the Norwegian population read comics daily in 1997 (see Vaage, 1998). This number could be an underestimate since the population used by Vaage from the Norwegian Bureau of Statistics is between 9 and 79 years old, thus ignoring children under 9, who are prime targets for *Donald Duck & Co.* It might also be noted that most comics are published weekly or monthly, and *Donald Duck* is one of the few comics for children that is published weekly.

23. These numbers were provided by Ellen Marie Turter, Marketing Director for Egmont Serieforlaget (the Norwegian branch of the Danish-based Egmont company) in a telephone interview, January 8, 1999. The total number of readers for *Donald Duck* was estimated in a readership survey by MMI (Markets og Mediainstituttet). Egmont Serieforlaget has a license to produce *Donald Duck* in Norway, along with many other magazines. Other branches of the Egmont company produce Disney books, magazines, tapes and other merchandise.

24. The figures were provided by Ellen Marie Turter.

25. For example, in the first half of 1972, the circulation was on average 176,750 (Gisle, 1973), although the population was smaller at that time.

26. These figures were provided by Ellen Marie Turter. While Turter was willing to discuss circulation numbers, she would not disclose information regarding the company's income or profit related to the sale of *Donald Duck*.

27. According to journalist Christian B. Ramm (1998), Egmont Serieforlaget – the main publisher of comic magazines in Norway – had a total revenue in 1997 of 273 million kroner ($39 million). This was an increase of 30 percent (58 million kroner or $8.3 million) from 1996. The net income of the company increased from 46.6 million kroner ($6.7 million) in 1996 to 56 million kroner ($8 million) in 1997. These results for Egmont Serieforlaget were attributed partly to the increased marketing and sale of the *Donald Duck* comic magazine.

28. In fact, Norway is among the highest in the world in terms of the number of newspapers consumed daily per capita. Thus, it could be labeled a press

nation, as opposed to many other countries where television is much more important to the general population (NOU, 1992; Høst, 1998).

29. Research assistant Leif Johnny Johannessen conducted much of the analysis of the 41 survey interviews, thus providing the background material for this part of the chapter. He also developed an annotated bibliography related to the Disney project in Norway.

30. It should be noted that this is a small (in terms of survey research) and not a representative sample. As for the characteristics of the sample, student populations are often overrepresented by people with a middle-class background. Another factor is that these are students of the social sciences and humanities. Moreover, the fact that they study media might have resulted in increased reflections about their own media habits.

31. Over two-thirds (68 percent) of our sample were female students. This could relate both to the fact that more women took the 'media audiences' course from which these interviewees were recruited, or it could mean that the female students were more willing to answer than their male counterparts (female students often tend to be more 'dutiful'). Moreover, the majority of these students were Norwegian, reflecting the fact that Norway is still a rather homogeneous country. Only two of the interviewees had other backgrounds: one was Norwegian-Australian, and one Finnish-Norwegian.

32. According to the cable company Telenor Avidi, only families with satellite dishes can receive the Disney Channel.

33. Ambivalence refers here to mixed or contradictory feelings, not the classic psychoanalytic meaning of the term implying a love/hate relationship (Hagen, 1992). Merleau-Ponty describes ambiguity as a more adult phenomenon than ambivalence: 'It consists in admitting that the same being who is good and generous can also be annoying and imperfect' (Merleau-Ponty, 1964: 103). Following Merleau-Ponty, then, these students' relationship to Disney would be called ambiguous.

34. Trondheim is the third largest city in Norway, with about 170,000 inhabitants. It is a university city located in the middle of Norway.

35. These lists are based on visits to stores by the author and research assistant Mitja Samoilow. Another source was telephone conversations with Tormod Eek of the Walt Disney Company, Norway.

36. Examples of such comic magazines in Norway are *Uncle Scrooge*, *Dumbo* and *Winnie the Pooh*.

37. A series of fifteen books was launched in connection with Donald's 50th anniversary (see http://www.donald.no/bibliotek/no_anbefal.html) and have been published annually since then. All the books contain so-called classic Donald Duck stories written by Carl Barks, with introductions by various Donald experts (or Donaldists). One can also order other books, like the complete issues from the years 1948 to 1954.

38. According to Ellen Marie Turter.

39. This information is provided in the newspaper article 'Ingen jul uten Donald' ('No Christmas without Donald') written by Trude Blåsmo (1998), which for the main part is an interview with the author of this article.

40. Other Disney films shown in Norway were, for example, *The Hunchback of Notre Dame* (1996), and *Pocahontas* (1995). Like elsewhere, *The Lion King* was one of the biggest hits.

41. These films included *101 Dalmations, The Lion King, The Hunchback of Notre Dame, The Aristocats* and *Lady and the Tramp*. Ticket sales for these films amounted to 3,579,280 NOK, or about $511,325, according to Harald Schølberg, Trondheim Movies Office (fax sent on July 16, 1998).

42. Examples include *Pinocchio* (1940), *Fantasia* (1940), *Dumbo* (1941) and *Bambi* (1942). Later, in the 1950s, *Cinderella* (1950) and *Lady and the Tramp* (1955) were quite popular films.

43. *The Disney Hour* was broadcast by NRK on Monday afternoons for one and a half years (January 6, 1997 to June 15, 1998). Ratings during this period were on average 6 percent (aged 3 to 11) and 2 percent (for those over 12 years of age). The reruns on Sunday mornings were much more popular among children – and perhaps rather appreciated by sleeping parents. The average ratings for 3- to 11-year-olds were 19 percent, while it was 2 percent for those over 12 years of age (these ratings were provided by Karin Hake, NRK's Research Department). On Sunday, January 17, 1999 the ratings were: 3 to 11 years – 17 percent; 12 years and more – 2 percent. (Source: Åke Källqvist, Chief Editor of NRK's Drama Purchase, fax sent on January 22, 1999.)

44. According to Frode Ormberg in the Program Archives of TV2 (telephone conversation, January 12, 1999). *The Disney Hour* on TV2 had the following ratings in 1997: 6 percent for ages 3 to 11, and 0.7 percent for those over 12 years. In 1996 the ratings were 8.61 percent for 3 to 11 years and 1.2 percent for 12 years or older. (These ratings are based on MMI's TV-meter data, and provided by Anette With of TV2's Program Department, fax sent on February 2, 1999).

45. *Life Works* had ratings of 1.5 percent among those who can receive this channel (about 45,000 viewers over 12 years old). (These ratings are Norwegian TV-meter data, provided by MMI.) The audience ratings for *Dangerous Minds* was 1.2 percent of those with access to the channel (about 36,000 viewers). (These figures were provided by Kjersti Kongstorp, Research Director at TVNorge AS, fax sent on July 13, 1998).

46. According to Stine Temte, Marketing Director at Buena Vista Home Entertainment (owned by Walt Disney, Norway), action films for teenagers dominate the video rental market, while families with children often buy Disney films. Examples of the most popular animated videos bought in 1998 include *Hercules* (74,763 copies sold), *Beauty and the Beast Christmas* (52,820), and *The Little Mermaid* (52,184). By comparison, the most popular feature film was *Titanic* (247,220). (These figures were provided by Stine Temte, fax sent on February 1, 1999.)

47. In Norway, there are no specialized Disney Stores.

48. This section is based on the previously mentioned group interviews – four groups making up a total of sixteen children, with ages ranging from 6 to 9½ years of age. The children were recruited from a school in Trondheim and the interviews were conducted in October 1998.

49. The girl was interviewed by Agnieszka B. Jarvoll, one of my graduate students, who wrote her thesis about families' relationship to television and other media.
50. As indicated earlier, *The Disney Hour* was broadcast by TV2 during 1996/7 and later by NRK.
51. A 13-year-old Norwegian boy told the author that most Disney products were regarded as too childish for his age. 'It is not something you brag about having used, at least,' he said. An exception was the *Donald Duck* magazine, which he felt could still be read for many years.

References and other sources

Adresseavisens TV-Magasinet, December 18–24, 1998.

Bakøy, E. (1999) 'Med fjernsynet i barnets tjeneste. NRK-fjernsynets program-virksomhet for barn på 60- og 70-tallet' ('With television in the service of the child. NRK TV programing for children in the 1960s and 70s'). Ph.D. dissertation, Trondheim, Norwegian University of Science and Technology (NUST).

Berland, D. I. (1982) 'Disney and Freud: Walt meets the id,' *Journal of Popular Culture*, 15(4): 93–104.

Berntsen, J. E. (1998) 'Donald og vennene korter ventetiden' ('Donald and his friends shorten the period of waiting'), *Adresseavisens TV-Magasinet*, December 18–24.

Blåsmo, T. (1998) 'Ingen jul uten Donald' ('No Christmas without Donald'), *Adresseavisens TV-Magasinet* (Trondheim, Norway), December 24.

Bourdieu, P. (1984) *Distinction: A Social Critique of the Judgement of Taste*. Cambridge, MA, Harvard University Press.

Buckingham, D. (1997) 'Dissin' Disney: critical perspectives on children's media culture,' *Media, Culture and Society*, 19(2): 285–93.

Buckingham, D. (1998) 'Reconstructing the child audience,' in M. Haldar and I. Frønes (eds), *Digital Barndom* ('Digital Childhood'). Oslo, Ad Notam Gyldendal A/S, pp. 34–51.

Claudine, M. (1996) 'Re-reading Disney, not quite Snow White,' *Discourse*, 17(1): 5–14.

Dahl, H. F., Gripsrud, J., Iversen, G., Skretting, K., and Sørenssen, B. (eds) (1996) *Kinoens mørke. Fjernsynets lys. Levende bilder i Norge gjennom 100 år* ('The Darkness of the Cinema. The Light of Television. Living Images in Norway through 100 Years'). Oslo, Gyldendal Norsk forlag.

Dorfman, A. and Mattelart, A. (1984) *How to Read Donald Duck: Imperialist Ideology in the Disney Comics*. London, International General (1st edn., 1975).

Giroux, H. A. (1995) 'When you wish upon a star, it makes a difference who you are: children's culture and the wonderful world of Disney,' *International Journal of Educational Reform*, 4(1): 79–83.

Gisle, J. (1973) *Donaldismen: en muntert-vitenskaplig studie over Donald Duck og hansverden* ('Donaldism: A Merry Scientific Study of Donald Duck and His World'). Oslo, Fakkel.

Gisle, J. (1998) 'Om Walt Disney' ('About Walt Disney')
(http://www.donald.no/bibliotek/no_bib_walt.html).

Hagen, I. (1992) *News Viewing Ideals and Everyday Practices: The Ambivalences of Watching Dagsrevyen*, Doctoral dissertation, Department of Mass Communication, University of Bergen.

Hagen, I. (1994) 'The ambivalences of TV news viewing: between ideals and everyday practices,' *European Journal of Communication*, 9(2): 193–220.

Höijer, B. (1998) *Det hörde vi allihop! Etermedierna och publiken under 1900-talet* ('That We Heard All of Us! Electronic Media and the Audience during the Nineteenth Century'). Värnamo, Fälth & Hässler.

Höijer, B. and Findahl, O. (1984) *Nyheter, förståelse och minne* ('News, Comprehension and Memory'). Lund, Studentlitteratur.

Høst, S. (1998) *Daglig mediebruk* ('Daily Media Use'). Oslo, Pax forlag.

Jackson, K. M. (1996) 'Walt Disney: its persuasive products and cultural contexts,' *Journal of Popular Film and Television*, 24: 50–2.

Löfgren, O. (1996) 'The great Christmas quarrel: on the moral economy of family ritual,' in J. Frykman and O. Löfgren (eds), *Force of Habit. Exploring Everyday Culture*. Lund, Lund University Press, pp. 103–19.

Merleau-Ponty, M. (1964) 'The child's relations with others,' in J. M. Edie (ed.), *The Primacy of Perception*. Evanston, L, Northwestern University Press, pp. 96–155.

Miller, S. and Rode, G. (1995) 'The movie you see, the movie you don't: how Disney do's that old time derision,' in E. Bell, L. Haas, and L. Sells (eds), *From Mouse to Mermaid: The Politics of Film, Gender and Culture*. Bloomington and Indianapolis, Indiana University Press.

NOU (1992) *Mål og midler i pressepolitikken* ('Goals and Means in Press Policy'). Oslo, Statens forvaltningstjeneste.

Ramm, C. (1998) 'Gode tall for *Donald & Co.*' ('Good numbers for *Donald & Co.*'), *Finansavisen*, July 21.

Real, M. (1977) *Mass-Mediated Culture*. Englewood Cliffs, NJ, Prentice-Hall.

Riesto, M. (1998) 'Norsk tegneserie tirrer Disney' ('Norwegian comics teasing Disney'), *Adresseavisens TV-Magasinet*, January 29.

Scannell, P. (1988) 'Radio times: the temporal arrangement of broadcasting in the modern world,' in P. Drummond and R. Paterson (eds), *Television and its Audience: International Research Perspectives*. London, British Film Institute.

Smoodin, E. (1993) *Animating Culture: Hollywood Cartoons from the Sound Era*. New Brunswick, NJ, Rutgers University Press.

Vaage, O. F. (1998) *Norsk mediebarometer 1997*. Oslo, Kongsvinger, Statistics Norway.

Wasko, J. (1996) 'Understanding the Disney universe,' in J. Curran and M. Gurevitch (eds), *Mass Media and Society* 2nd edn. London, Arnold, pp. 348–69.

CHAPTER 12

South Africa: Disney in South Africa: Towards a Common Culture in a Fragmented Society?

SIMON BURTON

Introduction

The transition to democracy in South Africa has understandably generated a lot of debate about the cultural contours of the new society, and foregrounded the role of cultural resource providers (particularly the media) in both the maintenance of apartheid and the construction of what has come to be affectionately known as the 'Rainbow nation.'

Considering the position of the U.S.A. in the years of cultural isolation, and its pre-eminence in any consideration of the implications of 'globalization,' thinking about the Disney phenomenon and its impact on South Africans raises a number of questions. Is there global cultural penetration in South Africa? Are there discernible patterns of cultural appropriation across the diversity of groups in South Africa?[1] And, is South Africa being 'Americanized'?

The intellectual aspects of these debates have tended to be negative, exemplified by Ted Leggett's caustic comment: 'The most virulent of the media colonists are the Americans, the masters of the form. Eager for the "sophistication" and "success" that American culture represents, some South African youth are ready to embrace the marauding hordes' (Leggett, 1997: 98). The reality on the streets of South Africa's urban centers is one of stylish hairdos, sneakers, baseball caps and baggy jeans, worn to the accompaniment of *kwaito* (indigenous hip-hop) and Kentucky Fried Chicken. This process of Americanization, of the youth in particular, has its roots in television, and to a lesser extent in the cinema, and is beginning to kick back into sports (for example, the growing popularity of basketball). However, the Disney product range (as an identifiable source of cultural 'goodies') remains one which is largely perceived as a childhood phenomenon. Of course, the interesting exercise of tracing the predispositions constructed in childhood into young adulthood would require a much deeper analysis than is possible in this chapter. But this study at least begins to examine these issues by looking at the presence and reception of Disney products in South Africa, as well as considering the South African case within a global context.

Disney, the entertainment provider

The Disney presence in South Africa would seem to be relatively slight, with no theme parks or Disney Stores, no dedicated Disney Channel, and no high-profile magazines, comics or educational products. Nevertheless, the students surveyed had a high level of awareness of many of these products. The Disney icons, Mickey and company, are in evidence, but one is more likely to encounter clothing, toys and collectibles associated with one or more of the recent films, such as *The Lion King*, or, more recently, *Tarzan*. It is probably true to say that the current Disney presence is derived from these recent films and the accompanying merchandising sector of the Disney enterprise.

According to the company, Disney has had a presence in South Africa for over 25 years. Prior to 1997, products (excluding film and videos) were made available through a local company responsible for licensing to manufacturers. Normally, this would mean paying for the rights to use a Disney character/s (Donald Duck, Mickey and Lion King derivatives being the most popular) with strict quality control (approval of artwork, privileging certain chain stores over others), for which a fee was paid and then a percentage of sales taken. One company official reported that in 1997, the annual revenues from Disney products (mostly toys and textiles) in South Africa was about 300 million rand (or $66 million) ('Disney sets South Africa subsid,' 1997).

Since 1997 a wholly owned subsidiary, Disney Enterprises Southern Africa, has been responsible for marketing Disney merchandise, not only in South Africa but also in the rest of the continent. As company officials explain:

> Southern Africa is one of the exciting new markets in the world. We are
> confident Disney Enterprises Southern Africa will help open up new

avenues for Disney involvement in the region. South Africa will provide the platform for the group to move into the rest of Africa, where it has had very little exposure to date.... The whole idea is to use South Africa as a base to go into the rest of Africa. We don't know Africa. We don't know what the potential is. We have a lot to learn, and we are here to do that. (Pearson, 1997)

The aim of company officials is to 'be on the lookout for unique cultural and marketing ideas that could be taken from South Africa into new markets;' however, 'heavy capital investment' in South African partnerships was not expected.

A central platform for the promotion of Disney merchandise also has been created through a collaboration between the South African Broadcasting Corporation and the Consumer Products division within Disney in the form of sponsorship of the afternoon cartoon slots on TV1, the most popular channel among Africans. This initiative is specifically aimed at 5- to 6-year-olds, with a view to 'acclimatizing' them to Disney. This mirrors a series of collaborations between local companies and the various elements of the Disney corporate structure. For example, Nu Metro has the rights to video, Ster Kinekor has the rights for certain films, M-Net (a pay-TV station) has contracts with Buena Vista International to re-flight films from the Touchstone, Hollywood and Miramax stables, and so on.

Each of these entertainment arenas (film, video and merchandise) will act collaboratively when the occasion warrants it. For example, the recently released *Tarzan* movie saw a sophisticated marketing drive involving Ster Kinekor, Shell petrol garages and Disney enterprises. This is probably no different from other countries, and simply points to the interlocking and piggy-backing which characterizes the entertainment industries.

The movie industry in South Africa is dominated by two companies, Ster Kinekor (about 68 percent of market share) and Nu Metro. Speaking informally to the managing directors of these organizations revealed that the movie industry in South Africa is on a flat line at present, where expansion is only contemplated after 'deep' research, and then only into environs which offer a 'total entertainment experience' – shopping center multiplexes. With the average age range of 16 to 23 years (and falling) constituting 75 percent of the movie-going populace, issues of peer pressure, 'out-of-home entertainment experiences,' disposable income, largely intact apartheid metro planning and transport all feed into a stagnant cinematic milieu for the majority of South Africans. Ster Kinekor has made a brief foray into opening up the cinematic option for people living in what are still loosely called 'townships' or peripheral residential areas, mostly constructed or appropriated as a response to the old Group Areas legislation, which, although long gone, divides the country into segments dominated by one or other race group. This adventure, through a wholly owned subsidiary, Moribo (a company set up as a Black economic empowerment project, which, like many other such initiatives, has targeted the media/entertainment sectors of the economy), sought in 1996/7 to broaden access for township residents, but without much success, notwithstanding the attempt to transform cinemas into community centers (for meetings, etc.). Another failed attempt to draw Africans to the cinema was the disastrous effort to indigenize *The Lion King* by having it translated into the Zulu language, which resulted in the withdrawal of the prints and heavy losses.

The captains of these cultural resource providers contend that it is the emerging African middle class which is at the forefront of those wanting the 'out-of-home experience,' and the current 10 to 15 percent of movie audiences at large multiplexes (largely situated in White areas) is made up of the trickle of African, Colored and Indian residents of these gradually more integrated neighborhoods, and 'visitors' from further afield. While the video rental market continues to grow apace, it is not clear how this growth is spread, nor its contribution to a rounded sense of the Disney project, with all that this means for widespread identification with Disney products of all kinds, and the construction of a meaningful 'place' for Disney in popular consciousness.

The All Media Products Survey (1999) highlights the difference between Black and White (the division is theirs, not the author's) in terms of cinema attendance: a meagre 10.2 percent of the former having watched a film in the last year, compared with 58.7 percent of the latter group, while only 1.2 percent of the Black age group 16 to 24 years went to the movies in the previous seven days, compared with 24.8 percent of Whites. It is common knowledge that radio is a far more accessible medium than television for Africans in general, although claims of a 77 percent daily viewership among the growing African middle class have been made (Independent Newspapers, 1999), a figure that is close to that for the White group as a whole. This emerging African middle class, or 'patriotic bourgeoisie,' as it is sometimes referred to, is extremely small, and we currently find ourselves embroiled in a debate about the role of this new social force.

Thus, we find that even though Disney's presence in South Africa may be far less than in many other countries, there are enough Disney products for the brand to be recognized. What Disney means to some South Africans is the focus of the next section.

Studying the Disney audience in South Africa

During the latter half of 1997, 30 questionnaires were administered to students at each of the universities of Natal (Pietermaritzburg campus), Rand Afrikaans (RAU) and Cape Town, totaling 90 in all. These universities were chosen in order to generate a reasonable spread of opinions, with the University of Natal servicing a large Indian community, the University of Cape Town a large Colored community, and RAU attracting the large Afrikaans-speaking White community. All three have significant numbers of African students.

Due to the difficulties of establishing category proportions at these universities and limited time available to fieldworkers, it was decided to use a form of convenience sampling which resulted in sub-populations of Africans (26 percent), Indians (9 percent), Coloreds (10 percent) and Whites (56 percent). These group proportions do not mirror the demographics at South African universities (as a whole), where Black students do outnumber White students. Furthermore, none of the universities visited fall into the category of the ethnic- (read 'race') based campuses created in the apartheid era (except perhaps for RAU), with both the universities of Cape Town and Natal holding long pedigrees in the struggle to open tertiary education to all. Slightly more males (54 percent) than females (46 percent) were interviewed, which does reflect the gender breakdown fairly accurately. Students were all interviewed outside the main library on each campus. In addition, a short pilot was undertaken to test for language, and it was decided to explain some terms (for example, thriftiness).

It is worth remembering that the students interviewed are unlikely to have been part of the death throws of apartheid, and that many Black students may already have tasted some form of integration through the 'Model C' schooling system (previously all-White primary and secondary schools whose de-racialization in the early 1990s created a platform for the de-racialization of the education system as a whole).

More qualitative data was gathered in the form of nine in-depth interviews, which provided some additional background on the meaningfulness of Disney in a South African context, but reproduced to a large extent the kinds of categories already established in the questionnaires.

Different Disney experiences

Unsurprisingly, it is Black South Africans who come to experience Disney much later than other groups in South Africa, with a reported average age of 10.3 years at first contact, as compared with 4.6 years for White, 4.25 for Colored and 3.2 for Indian students. Furthermore, the proportion of African students who indicate 'little contact' with Disney remains relatively stable through childhood, teen years and adulthood (just over 60 percent). White students, on the other hand, display a much more intuitively normal process of diminishing contact with Disney as they get older (from 50 percent who cite lots of contact in childhood decreasing to 18 percent in adulthood). In the case of Indians and Coloreds, the small sample sizes militate against any firm conclusions, but there does seem to be a tendency for both groups to have early contact which tails off as they grow older.

In terms of liking/disliking Disney, I have taken the liberty of drawing conclusions on the basis of dividing the original seven-point scale into one with two poles, liking and disliking (dispensing with the important nuances, because of the small number of questionnaires). African students, while not displaying the same degree of 'liking,' sustain this liking for much longer. Starting with 61 percent in childhood through 61 percent in teen years, it falls to 54 percent in adulthood. Indian students are not far behind this pattern, starting off at 75 percent, sustaining this through the teen years, and falling to 50 percent in adulthood. Colored students demonstrate a much sharper decline, with 78 percent liking Disney in childhood, 67 percent in teen years, falling to 33 percent in adulthood. White students show the sharpest decline between childhood (72 percent) and teen years (54 percent), leveling off to 44 percent in adulthood.

From a gender perspective, it is clear that women have the most contact with Disney, and they remain ahead of men even as contact diminishes with age. A similar configuration can be found when looking at students' reports of how much (and when) they like Disney. Women (as children, teens and adults) consistently find Disney more likeable (78 percent in childhood, 68 percent in their teens and 54 percent in adulthood) than men, who are about 15 percent behind at each stage.

The most accessed Disney products are Disney films (98 percent), across all race groups, closely followed by video rental, books and comics (78 percent), and TV shows (70 percent). For African students, access to film (91 percent) is followed by comic books (74 percent), books (65 percent), TV shows and magazines (56 percent), and video rental (44 percent). White students, on the other hand, have all accessed films, and high proportions have accessed video rental (86 percent), books (80 percent), comics (76 percent) and TV shows (74 percent). There are significant differences between groups in terms of some of the other Disney products available. For example, Indian students find the educational products, magazines and video games more appealing than any other group. Least popular is the Disney home page, with only 12 percent of students having visited it (although two-thirds of the visits have been made by male students).

In terms of merchandise, Indian students own the most Disney products, with toys (88 percent), Mickey watches (50 percent) and other collectibles (63 percent) being the most popular. African students are the least likely to own such products: for example, only half have owned a Disney toy. A significant proportion of all groups have owned Disney clothing (above 60 percent in all groups). All Disney merchandise is more popular with women than with men, clothing coming out on top for both sexes. As one White female student responded when asked about what Disney means: 'Cartoon characters, fantasy, fun. Everyone has heard of it. Everyone has a Disney product!'

Colored and White students are strongly in agreement with the idea that Disney is uniquely American (78 percent and 72 percent respectively), whereas only 35 percent of Africans and 38 percent of Indians agree. There were a large number of non-responses to this question, which is also significant: 30 percent of Africans, 25 percent of Indians, 11 percent of Coloreds, and 8 percent of Whites left the question unanswered. Interestingly, a significantly higher proportion of women agree that Disney is American (71 percent) as opposed to 51 percent of men. A high number of non-responses were again encountered in this question (22 percent of women, 10 percent of men).

Adjectives which at least 75 percent of all race groups believe are promoted by Disney are: family, fantasy, fun, good over evil, happiness and love/romance. There are no significant differences in the degree to which these groups subscribe to these adjectives, except in the case of love/romance, where African students (78 percent) are about ten percentage points behind their colleagues in other groups.

In the other adjectival categories where there is no overwhelming unanimity, such as bravery, imagination, magic and optimism, the tendency is for Indian and White students to score Disney high on promoting these attributes, while African students (and to a lesser extent, Colored students) are 10 to 15 percent more conservative in their willingness to identify Disney as promoting them.

The adjectives (statements) which are most uneven in terms of students' willingness to identify them with Disney are: physical beauty (where all groups were in two-thirds agreement, except Coloreds, of whom only half were prepared to acknowledge Disney's role in promoting this attribute); respect for difference (where less than half of African students, nearly 90 percent of Colored students, and just over 60 percent of White and Indian students felt that Disney

263

promoted this value); technological progress (where Whites were equally divided on promoting and discouraging, Coloreds and Indians nearly two-thirds in favor of Disney promoting, and African students overwhelmingly in support of Disney promoting this idea); work ethic (where less than half of African and White students, and nearly two-thirds of Indian and Colored students believed this value was promoted by Disney).

While there were no adjectives that all groups identified as being discouraged by Disney (except for racism, which I will comment on below), there are those which are viewed in markedly different ways. The value of individualism, for example, which Indians (75 percent), Coloreds (67 percent) and Whites (54 percent) believe is promoted by Disney, is seen as being discouraged by the majority of Africans who responded to the question. This would seem to resonate with Thomas Oosthuizen's comment, that, 'our own research reveals the importance of society for blacks [*sic*] as far exceeding that of the individual' (Oosthhuizen, 1995: 46). It is noteworthy that there were a high number of 'not applicable' responses to this question, but it is not clear why so many people did not answer this question.

Patriarchy, too, is seen as being promoted by just over half of the Indian and White students, whereas over 30 percent of all students see this as a descriptive which is not applicable to Disney. Patriotism, too, is not unequivocally a value recognized in Disney products, with nearly 40 percent of students feeling that it is a value that is not applicable. Racism is generally seen as being discouraged by Disney, but the scores for this descriptive are almost outweighed by those respondents who see it as not applicable.

Viewing these adjectives through the gender prism reveals that more women students see Disney as promoting bravery, family, fantasy, fun, good over evil, happiness, imagination, love/romance, and magic than do their male counterparts (although the rates for both sexes are high). More men students feel that Disney promotes optimism, individualism, respect for difference, and technological progress, although the scores in all of these except optimism are much lower generally than for the descriptives above. While both sexes agree that Disney promotes physical beauty and discourages racism, the response rates are interesting: in the former, more women (71 percent) than men (61 percent) support this characterization of Disney, and in the latter, the response rates for discouraging racism and finding the descriptive not applicable are virtually the same. The adjectives of patriotism and patriarchy are scored more highly by women, although in both cases there is not a clear majority of students who support the idea that Disney promotes them. Finally, while half the women students believe that the idea of a work ethic is not applicable to Disney, a good majority of men believe the notion to be promoted by the company.

On matters of Disney promoting individualism and technological progress, where there are significant differences across groups, it is only too easy to fall into cultural stereotypes, and further research would need to unpack the various milieu, particularly the domestic viewing milieu, in order to develop a coherent understanding of these differences.

The divided responses

So, what can be said about these responses to the questionnaire? It seems as though the severe divisions between White and African people are reproduced in their contact with, and interpretations of, Disney artifacts (film and video, in particular). When we consider the enormous disparities between these groups in terms of access to infrastructure assets, education levels, income and employment, it comes as no surprise that levels of contact, the likelihood of owning Disney merchandise and the consequences in terms of characterizations differ markedly. The stark reality of nearly half of all African households being without electricity (Hirschowitz and Orkin, 1997: 125) impacts directly on TV watching (and video rental); the fact that average monthly earnings of Africans (for those who are employees) is just 32 percent of that for Whites (Schlemmer and Moller, 1997: 28) impacts directly on the disposable cash available for the expensive outings to cinemas (which, while close to most campuses surveyed, are not close to the townships). However, when we consider that the students represent an elite, particularly the African group, we are drawn towards the conclusion that Disney does have a presence in an increasingly significant layer of African society.

However, there are responses which raise questions about the reference points for different groups in terms of certain crucial characterizations of Disney. The fact that there is a high non-response rate to the matter of Disney being uniquely American points to the ubiquity of American programs on television (our staple diet during the cultural boycott), and perhaps to a relatively unsophisticated audience. Guy Berger's comment, that 'while figures exist on the sizes of (some) audiences, very little research has been done on how they decode, negotiate, and make use of the contents of media' (Berger, 1999: 111) is apposite.

As for those who did respond to this question, there were some interesting contradictory statements. As noted above, many White students felt that Disney was uniquely American, and some ascribed more specific characteristics. For instance:

> Disney is a wholly American cultural phenomenon which seems to perpetuate the false consciousness of economic liberalism, gender-stereotypes, patriarchy and the land of the brave and the free as a model for the rest of the planet to aspire to! Yes, it's very American. All the characters with other accents (for example, British – Jeremy Irons as Scar) are EVIL, RACIST BASTARDS.

However, several White students were more ambivalent, as indicated in these responses:

> Yes, Disney is American to me and is unique to the U.S.A. No, all Western cultures strive to educate and make their kids be optimistic and ambitious.

> Yes, it is an ideology; the perception of a perfect world, a type of euphoria. It creates a fantasy yet tends to avoid the underlying issues of humanity and reality. Overall, it is an excellent tool of escape for young children. Therefore I believe that it does not represent or reflect an entirely American culture, but is definitely heavily influenced by the American culture.

> Disney's actually got a mixed bag for me, because on a political level I've got a lot to say against them, but at the same time I mean, there are highly creative individuals who do all the films and that, and I admire that ... I am a bit of an anti-American a lot of the time and Disney symbolizes a lot of America for me. It's just another sort of level of the mass propaganda. But anyway, I think that it's OK. You know, it's not that bad. You know, you can't really stress about everything in your life. I don't really stress about anything in life, so Disney's cool.

Two Colored students responded similiarly:

> No and yes. It shows you American culture. But it shows you another world. It promotes dreams.

> No. It is a part of growing up that cannot be spoiled. It shows that with differences we can always go back to something we all can relate to.

The theme of 'differences' was also picked up by a few of the Black students, who generally were less sure that Disney represented American culture, as noted above. Two Black, Zulu students provided the following commentaries:

> Disney is universal because it promotes the cultures across nations. Black/white enjoy Disney products.

Yes, [Disney is American], as Africans what appears [in] some videos is not applicable to us. So, as a result we tend to imitate what is done and think is the best 'cause it appears in movies.

Another Black student who agreed to be interviewed said the following:

I'm not too sure, but I think Disney is everything. It's South African, it's American, it's everything. If you are a South African, you enjoy Disney. If you are American, you enjoy Disney. It doesn't matter if you are South African, or what, you enjoy Disney.

An Indian student echoed these sentiments: 'No, [Disney is not uniquely American] as it is universal in terms of morals, values, etc.; it is a part of every culture, to be enjoyed by everyone.'

Conclusions: towards a common culture?

Disney products in South Africa still occupy a relatively small part of the field of cultural resources available to the country's people, a field that it must be recognized is changing fast, both from the perspective of who has access (and how appropriation takes place relative to other resources) and from the range and diversity of these resources. While 'there are no essential links between what matters to people and the "cultural" groups people belong to' (Van Staden, 1997: 48), the legacy of apartheid imposes the reality of a racially divided society like a grid over the field of cultural consumption. This grid may be wearing thin at the more affluent levels of the society, but this blurring of divisions will not necessarily result in a common set of values as new matrices of the popular take hold (for example, the notion of an African Renaissance, which is already a significant popular discourse). Oosthuizen's remark that ' not only is there a substantial convergence of values between black and white youth' (Oosthhuizen, 1995: 48) ignores the very real questions posed by the turbulent and unpredictable process of de-racialization of the society.

Nevertheless, Disney is not a sideshow for the rich and mobile only. As television viewing expands (which it is), in contexts where collective viewing gradually gives way to more individualized viewing (as is happening in township contexts), there is a strong probability that 'children's Disney' will increase in popularity. By this I mean a more general identification with animated characters as Disney characters, and a revised sense of the forms of storytelling (rather than novelty value) available in the society. The lack of rootedness of the original characters (like Mickey and Donald) in South Africa does require that we consider less the nostalgic aspects of Disney (which seem to be a feature of longer exposure), and more the question of Disney as an interface between young people coming from markedly different backgrounds.

Notes

1. For the purposes of this chapter, determined to some extent by the research method informing the global study, 'groups' in South Africa refer to ethnic groups, although ethnicity has for decades been little more than racial classifications established in the legislative program of apartheid. In political terms, this has meant a division between 'Black' and 'White,' while culturally (and spatially and economically) there are four major groups: African, Colored and Indian ('Black'), and people of European descent ('Whites'). With capitalism having taken a racial form in South Africa, and a central platform for the democratization of South African society being its 'de-racialization,' it is not a racist approach to engage the issue of cultural transformation from the perspective of these fraught categories.

References and other sources

AMPS (All Media Products Survey) (1999) Johannesburg, South African Advertising Research Foundation.

Berger, G. (1999) 'Towards an analysis of the South African media and transformation, 1994-99,' *Transformation*, 38.

'Disney sets South Africa subsid' (1997) *Daily Variety*, July 9, p. 19.

Hirschowitz, R. and Orkin, M. (1997) 'Inequality in South Africa: findings from the 1994 October Household Survey,' in V. Moller (ed.), *Quality of Life in South Africa*. London, Kluwer Academic Publishers. (Reprinted from *Social Indicators Research*, 41(1-3), 1997.)

Independent Newspapers (1999) Reality Check Supplement, April 28.

Leggett, T. (1997) ' "South Africa is beautiful as seen on television:" media, culture, consumerism and sport,' in T. Leggett, V. Moller, and R. Richards (eds), *My Life in the New South Africa: A Youth Perspective*. Pretoria, Human Sciences Research Council.

Oosthuizen, T. H. (1995) 'South African paradigm shifts and the communications revolution,' *Communicatio*, 21(1).

Pearson, B. (1997) 'Disney into South Africa,' *Daily Variety*, July 11, p. 26.

Schlemmer, L. and Moller, V. (1997) 'The shape of South African society and its challenges,' in V. Moller (ed.), *Quality of Life in South Africa*. London, Kluwer Academic Publishers.

Van Staden, C. (1997) 'Policing the field of the popular,' *Communicatio*, 23(2).

CHAPTER 13

United Kingdom: Disney Dialectics: Debating the Politics of Children's Media Culture

DAVID BUCKINGHAM

In December 1998, just as I began working on this chapter, the radical British magazine *The New Internationalist* published a special issue on Disney. The front cover image says it all: a little Asian child, no more than two or three years of age, is being embraced – almost crushed – by a gigantic Mickey Mouse. The headline reads: 'The Mousetrap: Inside Disney's Dream Machine.'

The New Internationalist is a socialist publication, with a particular interest in world development issues. Its position on Disney is thus perhaps predictable. The articles repeatedly condemn the Disney corporation's cultural imperialism, its exploitation of workers in developing countries and its shady business practices. Disney theme parks are seen to offer 'safe,' 'sanitized,' 'predictable' fantasies; while the movies are full of gender and racial stereotypes, and riddled with historical misrepresentations. Disney are the 'racketeers of illusion,' 'undermining people's faith in themselves,' 'seducing' them away from their true identities and cultural traditions, and leading them inexorably towards a uniform, mass-produced consumer culture. And above all, it is children who are the primary victims of this process: Disney, we are told, 'colonizes children's minds,' 'betrays' childhood and turns children into mere 'swallowers of fictions.'

The New Internationalist is not an academic journal; although in fact this kind of critique of Disney is one that can easily be found in more academic works.[1] Indeed, it could be said to represent a 'common-sense' position on Disney that is easily accessible to popular consciousness. Most adults in Britain, I would argue, would understand the pejorative implications of a term like 'Disneyfied.' They might condemn a historical site or a museum by comparing it to a Disney theme park; or a movie by comparing it to a Disney cartoon. As I shall indicate in this chapter, the very mention of Disney almost automatically invokes negative associations.

For the writers of *The New Internationalist*, of course, these associations are primarily and overtly *political*. Like McDonald's, Disney is a 'bad object' *par excellence* for the political left. Disney somehow stands for and encapsulates everything that is wrong with contemporary capitalism: the destruction of authentic culture, the privatization of public space, the victory of consumerism over citizenship, the denial of cultural differences and of history – not to mention exploitation, racism, (hetero-)sexism and the wholesale destruction of the natural environment.

Yet these negative associations are by no means always straightforwardly 'political,' as they might appear to be for *The New Internationalist*. As I shall indicate, they also invoke judgements of taste and cultural value, as well as assumptions about childhood and about children's vulnerability to the influence of the media. Indeed, such outwardly 'political' condemnations of Disney almost inevitably invoke and depend upon prior beliefs about what should *count* as 'true' or 'authentic' forms of cultural expression and cultural identity.

In her influential book *Watching Dallas*, Ien Ang (1985) identifies a similar tendency in some of her respondents' arguments about another such 'bad object.' One of her primary interests is in what we might now call the *discourses* that people use to account for their responses to popular culture – in this case, how Dutch viewers describe their responses to the U.S. soap opera *Dallas*. According to Ang, people who profess to hate *Dallas* routinely employ what she (somewhat confusingly) terms 'the ideology of mass culture.' Like the writers of *The New Internationalist*, they condemn this apparently typical product of mass culture as merely inauthentic, unrealistic, reactionary and worthless. Yet, as Ang indicates, their arguments are couched primarily in terms of what they take *Dallas* to *represent*. *Dallas*, in other words, is merely a *symbol* of something much broader.

Ang's book was written some years before the emergence of 'critical discourse analysis' in Cultural Studies. Nevertheless, her argument prefigures some of the later insights of this approach. She implies that, in adopting a 'critical' stance towards *Dallas*, these respondents are laying claim to a powerful subject position – a position that will differentiate them from *other* viewers, who (by implication) are seen to be incapable of seeing through the program's illusion of reality, and the values it is held to convey. In condemning 'mass culture,' they also disassociate themselves from the 'mass audience' – that undifferen-tiated agglomeration of individuals who (in the words of *The New Internationalist*) are merely 'swallowers of fictions.'

This approach to analyzing audiences' critical discourse about the media has been developed more explicitly in subsequent research.[2] From this perspective, discourse is not seen simply as a neutral reflection of what is going on inside people's heads. On the contrary, it is regarded as a form of *social action*, which serves particular social functions and purposes. As such, it cannot be taken at face value, as straightforward evidence of 'attitudes' or 'beliefs.'

Likewise, critical discourse about the media should not be seen merely as an indication of people's psychological 'skills' as readers, or indeed as a reflection of their pre-given social position.[3] In making judgements about the media, people are simultaneously attempting to define themselves in particular ways – to lay claim to, and to construct, particular social identities. In the context of a research interview, and in more general social encounters, critical discourse thus becomes a valuable means of enacting social power – of displaying *and claiming* what Pierre Bourdieu (1984) calls 'distinction.' This approach has troubling implications, both in terms of how we assess the *status* of audience data, and for education about the media – whose overall aims have precisely been to *cultivate* the 'critical reader.'[4]

In this chapter, I intend to apply this approach in analyzing discussions of Disney held among groups of adult students in the U.K. As I shall indicate, such discussions are typically dominated by the kind of critical discourse that permeates the special issue of *The New Internationalist*. Disney is routinely condemned in terms that are drawn directly from Ien Ang's 'ideology of mass culture.' And yet there is also a considerable degree of ambivalence here. 'American' (that is, U.S.) culture is not merely rejected, but also admired and valued. Disney's 'dream' of childhood is seen as illusory, and yet as simultaneously attractive and even necessary. The values of the movies are easily condemned, but they are also recognized to be quite ambivalent in themselves. And while there are concerns about the 'effects' of all this on children, there is also a feeling that such concerns can be overstated.

As I have implied, Disney poses fundamental questions about the *politics* of popular culture – and it does so in very stark (and indeed traditional) terms. It necessarily invokes questions about influences and effects, about the relations between ideology and pleasure, and about the space of identity and human agency. Yet in my view, an alternative politics cannot be based simply on rhetorical condemna-tion, on appeals to the authority of oppressed groups, or on rationalistic forms of 'demystification.' On the contrary, it needs to start by recognizing the fundamental *ambivalence* of audiences' relationships with popular culture.

Talking Disney

In autumn 1997, my colleagues and I convened a series of ten focus groups, each consisting of four or five adults. These groups were effectively commandeered from among our own students. Three groups were drawn from an MA class on Children's Media Culture, which I was teaching at the time; three from a class of teachers following an in-service training course in media education; and four from a class of undergraduates at a drama school.[5] These individuals had earlier completed the project questionnaires on Disney, which I also draw upon here.

The groups were self-directed: we gave the participants a handout with a list of prompt questions, suggested that they appoint a chair, and left them to get on with their discussion. The discussions lasted an average of 30 minutes, and all the tapes were subsequently transcribed.

The questions we used were only very slightly adapted from those developed by the Global Disney Project team.[6] They were as follows:

- What have been your experiences with Disney products, both as a child and as an adult?
- What values do Disney and Disney products represent to you? Do you think they reflect or reinforce particular ideologies?
- What influence does Disney have on children? What advice would you give to parents on exposing their children to Disney products, and why?
- Do you experience Disney as uniquely 'American,' and in what ways? Is the 'Americanness' of Disney positive or negative, in your view?
- Why do you think Disney has been so popular for so many years and in so many different cultures?

These were, in our view, distinctly leading questions. The notion that parents might *need* 'advice' on 'exposing' their children to Disney products, for example, clearly signaled that there might be a problem in them doing so; while the use of words like 'ideologies,' and the introduction of the issue of 'Americanness' may have elicited more 'critical' responses than might otherwise have occurred. The context of the interviews was also, of course, far from neutral in this respect. The MA and teachers' groups were following courses in Media Studies; while most of the undergraduates were also taking Media Studies components as part of their degree. Albeit in somewhat different ways, all of them would have approached the activity with certain expectations about what they were required to say.[7]

Particularly in an educational setting such as this, the act of asking people their views about the media is obviously far from neutral: participants are often very aware of the kinds of responses that are socially desirable – although whether or not they choose to play what they perceive to be the game is another matter.[8] Yet in a sense, this was precisely the intention. We wanted to gather instances of adults' *critical discourses* about Disney, in an attempt to understand how those discourses might operate, the social functions they might serve, and the contradictions which might be encountered in using them.

These groups were self-evidently unrepresentative of the general population; and they were also heterogeneous in themselves. The extent to which it is meaningful to generalize on the basis of this sample is therefore fairly limited. One of the key hypotheses of the Global Project, for example, was that people of different ages are likely to have different experiences of Disney, and hence to attach different associations to it. People who have grown up since the 1980s resurgence of the Disney corporation will be very differently positioned here compared with those who grew up in the 1960s or 1970s. Although our groups were somewhat mixed in terms of age (the MA and teachers' groups ranged between 23 and 45, and there were some mature students – and a couple of parents – in the under-graduate group), this hypothesis was to some extent confirmed here. The younger participants were simply more aware of Disney as a brand than the older ones; and while the older participants recalled *Fantasia* and *Bambi* from their early childhood, the younger ones looked back to *The Lion King* and *Aladdin* from their more recent teenage years.

However, there were also differences both *between* and *within* these groups in terms of which media products they associated with Disney in the first place. In most cases, the groups defined 'Disney' with reference to the animated feature films. Only eight participants claimed to have visited Disney theme parks, either in the U.S.A. or in France (not least because it is prohibitively expensive to do so, as some pointed out); and there was no mention of comic strips, which (to my knowledge) have barely been distributed in the U.K. Some of the older participants were aware that Disney produced live-action features (*Mary Poppins* was mentioned on a couple of occasions), and some also referred to the fact that Touchstone is a Disney company. Nevertheless, there was some confusion among some of the older participants about whether Tom and Jerry, for example, was a Disney creation.

It is even more difficult to generalize about the distribution of different perspectives on Disney among these groups. The dominant voices in all groups were consistently the most 'critical' ones – a phenomenon which itself reflects the authority carried by this discourse. While the teachers were more inclined towards ideological critique, the undergraduates were more likely to focus on aesthetics (which could perhaps be seen to reflect their position as drama students). Broadly speaking, older teachers and parents were the most vehemently critical, particularly in respect of Disney's influence on children, although again this can be seen as a socially desirable response: 'good parents,' like 'good teachers,' are largely expected to adopt a protectionist stance, and may have a great deal invested in doing so. Interestingly, the MA students – particularly those with the most previous experience of Media Studies – were the most overtly (and indeed self-consciously) ambivalent.

Ultimately, however, this is a qualitative analysis, not an opinion poll. My interest is not so much in the views that were expressed, or in how they were distributed, as in *how* they were expressed – that is, in *the processes by which people account for their relationships with popular culture*. From the perspective I have outlined above, the *rate of incidence* of a particular discourse does not necessarily indicate its significance to the individuals concerned. Performance does not necessarily indicate competence; and it may tell us much more about the social context of the discussion than it does about individuals' 'attitudes' or 'readings.'[9]

My initial aim in what follows, therefore, is to map out a kind of taxonomy of the discourses that emerged, based on my coding and comparative analysis of the transcripts. The examples I have selected for more detailed commentary are symptomatic, rather than necessarily representative – symptomatic, in particular, of the *tensions between* the discourses I am concerned with here.

The unacceptable face of capitalism

Throughout these discussions, Disney was consistently represented as a kind of symbol of capitalism itself. In the large majority of instances, the implications of this were distinctly pejorative. Some of the charges against Disney in this respect were quite specific, even if the information on which they were based was somewhat vague. Thus, several participants rehearsed accusations about the company's exploitation of its workers, particularly in developing countries. Disney was accused of paying workers 'in Mexico and South America' or 'in Taiwan' minimal wages to produce goods that were sold at vast profits; and of exerting an almost paranoid control over their

Figure 13. The Disney Store in Chester, England. Photo: Carlos R. Calderon

employees in theme parks, 'even down to making them shave their beards off.' For some, this was symptomatic of a more general process of increasing social control. One participant likened Disney's employment practices to Huxley's *Brave New World*, while another offered a kind of paranoid fantasy of Disneyland: 'Like, you can go and live in Disneyland and send your children to a Disney school … And people try to get out, and people can't get out. It's almost like a brainwashed city' (UG/F[10]).

Similarly, there were criticisms of what was implicitly seen as devious marketing practice. The strategy of releasing movies on a seven-year cycle, or videos for only a few months, was seen to create 'an artificial rush to buy'; while integrated marketing – the symbiosis between advertising, movies, theme parks and merchandising – was seen as similarly manipulative.

However, Disney was also perceived to be symptomatic or symbolic of a more general form of 'commercialization' – of what one teacher described as the 'extraordinarily commercial environment in which we live.' The very scale of its activities, and the fact that some of them were effectively 'hidden' under other brand names, itself provided grounds for suspicion in this regard: 'You don't realize what a power base it is –

it's like a Murdoch thing. There's loads more than you think. Is *that* Disney? You didn't realize that it is' (UG/F).

At the same time, many participants noted the expansion or greater visibility of the Disney corporation in recent years, in the form of shops and merchandising. This was particularly apparent among the older participants, although several of the younger ones also distinguished in this respect between 'old' and 'new' Disney:

> *The Jungle Book* was really good, but that was old-style Disney – and now it's gone out of – with all the Disney shops you get in Oxford Street like, for example, huge plastic Disney shops just selling Disney crap. ... The old style that we were brought up on, it was less commercial – obviously because it was appreciated. (UG/F)

> It was better packaged as well. The Walt Disney machine is far bigger now than it was. (UG/F)

Even for these younger participants, there is an element of nostalgia for a less commercial time – the time of their own childhoods – in which products were genuinely 'appreciated.' By contrast, contemporary Disney is seen (as it is in *The New Internationalist*) as a 'machine' that just produces 'plastic' – as a form of mass production that is fundamentally incompatible with quality or authenticity.

According to several participants, there had been a process of *commodification* here: something that had formerly existed in a purely cultural sphere had been steadily overtaken by the marketplace, and transformed in the process.[11] Some of the older participants could recall buying Disney products when they were younger – one man described the peer-group 'status' attached to a Mickey Mouse watch – but there was a general feeling that this emphasis on merchandising and commercial exploitation was something new. For some, this process was not especially sinister. One female undergraduate, for example, suggested that commercial success had been discovered almost inadvertently: 'Disney realizes that they are on to a good thing with these cartoons, and they commercialize it – and they're exploiting the fact that they have such a wide audience.' In general, however, the commodification of Disney was defined in much more explicitly pejorative terms, as a decline from a more innocent time – or even a betrayal of it.

Of course, there are questions that might be raised about the accuracy of these accounts. While the scale of the Disney operation – and particularly of the merchandising – has undoubtedly expanded, it was always part of the picture. Indeed, historians have suggested that the success of the Disney corporation has always been dependent upon these 'ancillary' activities, and could not have been sustained on the basis of the movies alone (Bryman, 1995; Gomery, 1994). Nevertheless, these arguments attest the powerful connection that is often drawn between ideas of 'culture' and 'childhood,' and the related opposition between 'culture' and 'commerce.' In this account, authentic culture is often identified with a form of innocent pleasure – and it is this that is so deviously exploited by the operations of the market.

A view from the 53rd state

This view of Disney as a symbol of contemporary capitalism was strongly reinforced by the perception of it as uniquely 'American.' Disney's success as a global corporation was partly accounted for in terms of the position of the U.S.A. as 'the super-power of the Western world' (T/M). To some extent, this was seen as simply an inevitable fact of life:

> It seems to me that America has been the global culture, and Disney is part of that. That doesn't strike me as being different to anything else – just Hollywood. It's there, and it's part of your life from way back. We've just come to accept it. (PG/M)

Nevertheless, the global dominance of the U.S.A. was also seen to reflect a kind of arrogance and insularity. 'Americans,' it was argued, 'like to think of themselves as universal' (UG/F); they are 'unaware of what the rest of the world is like' (PG/M); and they 'buy into this idea of the moral rightness of America – they don't question it' (PG/F). In one instance, this was directly linked to arguments about U.S. foreign policy:

> I'm not suggesting that Disney affects the way Americans treat other people. But when you think about the way they seem to feel they have the right to walk over everybody, you know, walk over the rest of the world. ... (UG/M)

> U.S. foreign policy – it's interventionism internationally. (UG/F)

Of course, what lies behind these arguments is the widespread concern that Britain is particularly at risk from U.S. economic and cultural imperialism. In the words of the man just quoted, 'the British *are* Americans – we're the 53rd state.' This resentment was fueled by Disney's representation of the British, and particularly by the use of British accents to identify the villains in the animated movies. Several groups were able to list such characters, from Scar in *The Lion King* through to the wicked witch in *Snow White* – although they also noted that this was something Disney shared with many Hollywood films. Meanwhile, others condemned the representation of British life in movies like *101 Dalmatians* – 'everyone lives in Knightsbridge' (PG/ F)[12] – as symptomatic of Disney's tendency to 'caricature every other culture in the world' (PG/M).

Meanwhile, 'Americanness' was overwhelmingly defined as a negative quality that could not be endorsed. On one level, this was a matter of cultural or aesthetic *style*. American culture was 'big and brash,' 'larger than life,' 'loud,' 'colorful' and 'extravagant'; but it was also 'crass,' 'saccharine,' 'corny,' 'trite,' 'sentimentalized' and 'anodyne.' This cultural style was thus partly defined as *extrovert*, but it was also seen as *inauthentic* and *simplistic*. The exploitation of emotional responses, 'formulaic' narratives, 'happy endings,' simple oppositions between good and evil, moralistic messages, and 'stereotypes' were all seen as characteristic of U.S. popular culture more broadly.

However, these criticisms also fed into a critique of the value system Disney was seen to promote – a system which was repeatedly described as 'the American Dream.' On one level, the American Dream was seen as a form of idealism, which valued achievement and generated a necessary self-confidence. Yet on the other hand, it was condemned as an 'illusion,' a 'misrepresentation of society' and an 'idealized world' – an image of 'how America would like to see itself' (T/F) that encouraged a form of 'false optimism.' The American Dream was associated by several participants with conservative notions of 'family values.' It was seen to embody a 'WASP' view of the world, which denied the continuing existence of inequalities in U.S. society:

> There's this uniquely American idea that racism doesn't exist any more [laughs], sexism doesn't exist any more. It started about fifteen years ago, where there was this great denial of all the problems … but underneath there, it's going up. And I think Disney's the same. It's got this great thing that there are no problems, but underneath it it's run by a fascist regime. (UG/M)

In the Disney version, the American Dream is one in which wealth is an unproblematic virtue, 'to be approved of, to be striven for' (PG/M), yet in which 'you only succeed if you already belong to the dominant group' (PG/F). Here again, this value system was not seen as unique to Disney: it was also believed to be present in Hollywood movies and in American sitcoms. Nevertheless, what one of the teachers called the 'transparency' of Disney made such values much easier to detect – and hence to condemn.

According to some, this value system was simply being imposed on other cultures. It represented a 'blind charging in on other cultures,' an 'invasion,' something that was simply 'ingested' (T/F):

It's part of the Hollywood project, which has been a clear national aim, you know, the industry has received support to export the American way of life. So you have the films, on the back of which you have the products. It's commercial imperialism of the highest order. And I think it's probably a bit paranoid to say that it's a concerted project, but it's certainly happened, you know. The kids watch Disney, the adults watch the Hollywood films, everybody wants a bit of Americana, so you go out and buy the products. You buy the Ford, the Pepsi and the Coke. (T/M)

Nevertheless, the consequences of this were not necessarily so predictable. For some, this response to being 'othered' seemed to lead to a sense of superiority:

I actually think that's a bonus of obvious American culture, because it makes our children and ourselves be very discriminating about how much better our values are than the Americans. It makes you very aware of the superficiality of Americans. (UG/F)

Likewise, it was argued that the problems of U.S. society – most notably racism – that Disney sought to deny were not so apparent in the U.K. On the other hand, some felt that this reinforcement of 'Britishness' was not necessarily positive, and that a celebration of British national identity might be equally artificial: 'Well, it does conflict with my sense of national, or cultural, identity. But, kind of, being British – would you go round and be happy and have people hugging you and smiling – hooray, I'm British!?' (PG/F). Yet however desirable or problematic a 'British' identity might be seen to be, an 'American' one was almost universally rejected here. There was only one instance in these interviews of a more positive response to 'Americanness.' Of course, as some of the above quotations suggest, the 'Americanness' of some American popular culture is very attractive to many British people – and the marketing of many products strongly accentuates this quality.[13] Yet for the reasons I have implied, the context of these interviews effectively prohibited such expressions. In this respect, it is very notable that even this solitary example of a generalized enthusiasm for American culture was firmly located in the speaker's childhood: 'As a kid I loved things American. I always thought that Americans do it better than the British. I don't know why. I always thought that if it was American, it was done properly [laughs]' (PG/M).

Spotting the stereotypes

Of course, not all the values identified with Disney were perceived as uniquely American. Indeed, in some cases, participants identified values – such as an apparent preoccupation with royalty and aristocracy – that were seen to be somewhat at odds with the 'rags-to-riches' ideology of the American Dream. Others argued that the values of Disney were effectively 'universal' or at least more broadly 'Western' – although there was some debate about whether this was a result of their general human relevance (their status as what one teacher called 'cultural archetypes') or simply a consequence of U.S. imperialism (as in the quotation at the beginning of the previous section).

Nevertheless, many participants had little hesitation or difficulty in defining Disney as an ideological 'bad object.' Again, some of the grounds for these charges derived from popular knowledge about the Disney corporation in particular. Uncle Walt himself was described (somewhat ironically) by one participant as a 'mad fascist' – a view that he had partly drawn from a television documentary about the man's life, which others had also seen.[14] (This was perhaps also implicit in the quotation above about the 'fascist regime.')

However, most of the argument here derived from the application of more general discourses of ideological critique – discourses that are an increasingly common dimension of what Ien Ang terms 'the ideology of mass culture.'[15] Few participants had problems in spotting the racism and sexism in Disney films, although some appeared to be rather bored by the somewhat 'obvious' nature of the activity. Much of this discussion was directed at 'stereotyping':

> It's stereotypes, isn't it? Look at Hercules, he's a tall strapping man. Snow White is this peaceful, feminine [woman]. (UG/M)

> You have to be white and attractive, and if you're a woman you have to have big tits, big eyes, long hair. And if you're a bloke, you've got to have a square jaw, all-American, with big pectorals and a six-pack. (PG/F)

Likewise, in the case of 'race,' it was argued that evil characters were often coded as black, and good ones as white; and that Disney minimizes differences by giving 'ethnic' characters Caucasian features. Ugly characters were inevitably evil, good ones inevitably beautiful; while disabled heroes like Quasimodo in *The Hunchback of Notre Dame* or the Beast in *Beauty and the Beast* had to be rendered 'cute' in order to be acceptable. Several participants argued that such stereo-typical representations derived in turn from a naïve moralism: 'There's a very direct kind of cause-and-effect Christian morality, isn't there? That virtue will be rewarded or else you'll be damned for ever in hell fire. It's very simplistic, isn't it?' (PG/M)

There were equally familiar criticisms of Disney's 'distortions' of history and mythology: *Pocahontas* was condemned as a misrepresentation of the experience of native Americans, and for sanitizing and ignoring historical fact; *Hercules* was dismissed as a 'bastardized' version of the Greek myth, with a 'youngish typical Disney-type figure' replacing the 'grizzled old hero' of the original; and there were several complaints about the American accents in versions of classic British texts such as *The Sword in the Stone* and *The Jungle Book*.

There was a general agreement throughout these discussions that Disney 'reaffirmed' or 'reinforced' existing stereotypes, and hence encouraged a kind of conformity:

> It certainly doesn't step outside the mainstream, does it? ... It reinforces ideas about what makes a stable society. Like, you know, if you don't agree with your parents, you're going to be in trouble. You've got to grow up and take your rightful place in society. (PG/M)

For this man, there was often 'something suspect about intellectualism' in Disney films: 'Those who use words and who use ideas are often portrayed as the villainous ones. And there's an approval of simplicity and harmony with nature, and not questioning too much. And facility with words is slightly suspect' (PG/M).

This shared position thus represents 'Disney' as a homogeneous, coherent ideological bloc, which successfully represses any potential contradiction or resistance. While there was some recognition of more 'liberal' representations in recent Disney films, this was seen to have significant limitations:

> Like the feminist things in things like *Aladdin*. You know, you have this woman who says 'I want to marry someone on my own, I want to, you know, make my own choice.' But actually it's all within a very specific box ... it's always within this very prescribed way. (UG/F)

If 'spotting the stereotypes' was implicitly seen by most of the participants as a mundane, easy exercise, this kind of critical discourse nevertheless serves to guarantee the speaker's superior authority. Condemning the tokenism and the liberal rhetoric of the more recent films positions the speaker as a more discerning viewer, whose criteria for judgement are much more rigorous and stringent than those of ordinary people. Likewise, condemning Disney's suspicion of 'intellectualism' and 'facility with words' implicitly vindicates the position of the intellectual adult critic. In this way, those who employ such critical discourses are able to distinguish themselves from what one of the teachers in our sample referred to as 'the undiscerning masses.'

David Buckingham

Save the children?

As I have implied, many of the critical discourses that are applied to Disney come to rest upon a particular notion of childhood. Throughout these discussions, children were repeatedly positioned as passive victims of Disney's 'exploitation,' 'manipulation,' and 'brainwashing.' For obvious reasons, these arguments were particularly strongly voiced by the parents and teachers in our sample.

Thus, the child audience was repeatedly described using terms like 'passive,' 'captive,' and 'impressionable.' Disney, it was asserted, had an 'enormous' influence on children. It was accused of 'taking over and monopolizing childhood' (T/F); of giving 'bad messages to little girls' (PG/F); of 'cheating children of their childhood imaginations' (T/F); and of 'brainwashing [children] into this very commercial world' (UG/ F). This power was seen to be exercised through a process of mass identification, which children were powerless to resist:

> Like in *The Lion King*, they all – the little kids really respect Simba when he gets older. And little girls really identify with Snow White and want to be like her....Children look up to the stereotypes. They identify themselves with the stereotypes. (UG/F)

Others argued that the 'fantasy world' of Disney somehow reflected children's view of the world: 'It's a fantasy land where everything is perfect, and that's how kids see the world. And that's why kids love it so much, because it is just so perfect, and there isn't all this shit that's going on outside, you know' (UG/M).

Three groups explicitly entertained the possibility of 'banning' Disney outright, although this was generally rejected as unworkable or as counter-productive. For parents, there seemed to be few choices here: either they could refuse to buy their children Disney merchandise, leaving them 'distraught,' or they could 'spoil' them by doing so (UG/F). Yet for teachers – at least those opposed to censorship – there was the possibility of a form of counter-pedagogy: 'I think it's up to us to educate ourselves and our children to be able to deal with this stuff. ... I can't see any other way than arming people with basic literacy skills to deal with it' (T/M).

However, there were some dissenting views on these issues in several groups. On one level, there were those who asserted that children simply did not notice – and hence were unaffected by – the things that so concerned them as adults. Some of the undergraduates, in particular, argued that children would not be 'harmed,' because they regarded Disney films just as 'entertainment' and did not 'analyze them at that age in that way' (UG/F). This reflected a more general sense among the undergraduates that popular culture should not be taken too seriously: 'it's not that deep' (UG/F).

Meanwhile, several of the postgraduates argued that children were not so easily duped: they refuted the idea that the influence of Disney was 'straightforward' or that children were likely to become 'stooges of the Disney corporation.' Children were more likely to be defined here as 'sophisticated' and 'discriminating' viewers, particularly as they grew older; and the influence of the media needed to be seen in relation to other influences such as the family. Such arguments reinforced a more general belief that children should be exposed to such material, and allowed to make up their own minds. Nevertheless, even among those who adopted this view of the child audience, the meretricious nature of Disney productions themselves was taken for granted:

> I think it's important for them to see it, and to see its flaws and its shallowness, than not let them see it. (PG/M)

> You have to show things that have got stereotypes, but you are encouraging them to wonder, and want to question things. (T/F)

What remained conspicuous by its rarity was the argument that Disney might actually have any positive influence upon children. A couple of parents argued that Disney films were likely to be both safer and of better quality than other films they might watch with their children:

> If I'm taking the children to a film and I have a choice of a Disney film or another film, I would know that the Disney film would be very pretty to look at, it would have a very good ending, and there would be a strong moral theme to it. I would know that it would be a safe film to take children [to]. (UG/F)

Even here, however, such positive assessments were often couched in the form of faint praise: another parent, for example, asserted that she would choose Disney on the grounds that it was likely to be 'bland entertainment' (T/F) – in a sense, on the grounds of what it was *not*, rather than for any more positive reasons.

Here again, I would assert that a more positive view of Disney must be more widespread among the population at large; but that the context of these interviews made it very difficult to assert. As we shall see in the following sections, there were in fact several positive assessments of Disney – particularly those associated with the participants' own childhood memories and fantasies – but there was a strong sense that such contributions went against the grain of the discussion. To claim in more general terms that Disney might actually be *good* for children seemed to be well-nigh impossible.

David Buckingham

The limits of critical discourse

To sum up, while there were some divergent views about the potential influence of Disney upon children – and about how adults might respond to this – there was a remarkable uniformity in the participants' critical assessments of Disney productions themselves. There was general agreement that Disney represented and embodied a certain set of values, and that those values were fundamentally negative. Disney was by turn identified with commercialism, cultural imperialism, fascism, deceptive marketing, exploitative employment practices, sexism, racism, class bias, the denial of history and the brainwashing of innocent children. Against the dominance of this position, it was much more difficult to argue that Disney was just innocent fun or entertainment, much less that it was any good for you.

My purpose here is not to judge the *validity* or *accuracy* of these criticisms, or indeed to take them as evidence of the 'attitudes' of particular audience groups. On the contrary, I have sought to raise questions about the *social functions* they might serve. As I have implied, this kind of critical discourse serves to position its users in particular ways. On one level, it positions them as *discriminating agents* in their dealings with the media – and thus distinguishes them from those who are implicitly seen to lack this discrimination, and hence to be easily deceived. It also positions them as *'politically correct'* – that is, as people who are free from bias, who reject inequality and injustice, who see the world without the distortions of stereotypes or false ideologies. In the case of Disney, this discourse also serves to position its users as *mature adults*, who are able to perceive things that children cannot, and are thus less impressionable or vulnerable to influence. And in these interviews, the discourse also positions its users as British – or at least as *not American* – and hence as immune from the negative values that are seen to be inherent both in American popular culture and in the U.S.A.'s dealings with the rest of the world.

In each case, therefore, the discourse operates by creating *distinctions between self and other*. In each case, what is disavowed is the position of the powerless other – the incompetent child, the ideological dupe, the undiscriminating masses. And in each case, the claim for a 'critical' position is thus implicitly a claim for greater rationality and competence – and hence for *social power*.

In this context, any positive judgements of Disney must necessarily bypass or escape *both* of these positions: that is, the positions that are claimed in critical discourse and the positions that are disavowed. To proclaim one's enjoyment of mindless pleasure, to profess an enthusiasm for all things American, or to celebrate one's infantile desires are simply untenable positions – at least if one wishes to avoid the ridicule or disdain of others. Particularly in a context such as that of our interviews, and in relation to a topic such as Disney, the presentation of self can therefore become a fraught and risky business.

Recovering childish things

Nevertheless, this is not to say that pleasure was wholly unspeakable. The first question on our handout, and one of the more open-ended questions on the Project questionnaire, invited the participants to recall their childhood memories of Disney. As we have seen, they often responded by distinguishing between old and new Disney, and between themselves in the present and themselves as children. This was most evident in some of the questionnaire responses:

> Q: As you look back at your experience of Disney's media, products and services, what descriptions instantly come to mind? What terms express your perceptions of 'Disney'? List as many words and phrases as you wish.

> Now: manipulative, money machine, ghastly Hercules, characterless Pocahontas. As a child: pleasure, romance, adventure, excitement, color, music. (T/F)

> Fun (as a child). Corrupting (as an adult): racist/fascist, anti-communist, unethical, consumerist, etc. (T/M)

> As a child, Disney was *magical*. I wanted to be the *princess* in the fairy-tale castle, and a trip to see the latest feature was always a *treat*. Nowadays, I'm much more skeptical [although] I still think there's something magical, particularly about the early films. (PG/F; her emphases)

On one level, this kind of response entails a form of disavowal – although, at least in the last extract, this is clearly equivocal. As I have implied, the responses of the child self are implicitly defined as a kind of illusion, and the 'critical' stance of the mature adult is thereby vindicated.

Nevertheless, the invitation to recall childhood memories also provoked a genuine nostalgia for the fantasies and pleasures of childhood. Of course, this *idea* of childhood is absolutely crucial to the continuing appeal of Disney, both for adults *and* for children. Disney self-consciously mobilizes a particular construction of childhood, which is intimately connected with ideas of our essential selfhood. For adults in contemporary Western societies, childhood is often seen to represent a more natural, less artificial form of subjectivity: our 'inner child' is frequently seen as something we have lost, and must strive to recover if we are to become whole once again.[16] As David Forgacs (1992) has noted, many of the key Disney films are not so much about childhood as about its loss: both for adults and for children, they mobilize anxieties about the pain of mutual separation, while simultaneously offering reassuring fantasies about how this can be overcome.

Some of the childhood memories recalled by our participants were of this kind – the pathos of *Bambi* (recalled by several older participants) being a particular case in point. Nevertheless, what was particularly striking here was the emphasis on the *context* of viewing. As in the last extract above, a trip to the movies to see a Disney film in the company of your parents was often described as a 'special occasion' or a 'treat' – although, of course, this impression was partly a result of the company's strategy of controlling their release in cinemas, as described above. For several participants, these were also their first memories of the cinema itself:

> I used to love going to the cinema. I remember queuing up – one showing of *Snow White* was completely full, so we had to queue for the entire length of the film, and there were other people getting in the queue, and it was so exciting. You could feel it was like a special treat to go to see this, a big deal. (PG/F)

Several also recalled being given the merchandise (particularly records, books, and posters) as presents. One participant described at great length how he had become a member of a Mickey Mouse Club:

> Every year till the age of 12 or something, I'd get a birthday card. And I'd go with my father to the cinema in London – I can't remember which one – they'd call my name and I'd walk down the stairs and all the audience would applaud and I'd get a birthday card.... It was always very memorable, and I remember it with nostalgia. It was a really good experience.... And the other thing I remember is that I had a [Disney] poster that I really cherished, and it got torn. On one of those birthdays, actually. I was very upset. (T/M)

While such expressions of emotion were often located in the safety of the past, many of the younger participants attested the continuing appeal of Disney films. Several praised the 'technical quality' and 'realism' of the animation, while others noted the use of well-known actors' voices and enthused about the songs. Such things were seen as 'powerful,' irrespective of one's critical views: 'you do relate to it, you can't help yourself – you do become engaged' (UG/F). Likewise, while it was recognized that the narratives might be formulaic, they were also acknowledged to be 'appealing': 'it's the ultimate fantasy world – you're made to feel excitement and danger in the same environment, which is incredibly appealing' (UG/M).

These more aesthetic responses were particularly prevalent among the undergraduates, and seemed to sit fairly easily alongside their vociferous condemnations of the ideological shortcomings of Disney. Several praised the 'beauty' or 'quality' of contemporary Disney animation: it was described as 'well done' and 'stylish.' By contrast, the teachers were more inclined to reject the aesthetics of Disney as 'slick' and 'glossy,' and to condemn it for 'not taking risks' (T/F). Among the teachers and the postgraduates, there was more suspicion about emotional responses, and a concern about what was defined as the 'gushiness of Disney style' (PG/F). Disney was defined as a 'feel-good' experience – uplifting while it lasts, perhaps, but essentially superficial. In this context, the use of aesthetic criteria had to be argued for:

> I really like the animation, to be honest. I would like to see – the new film *Hercules* – to see the actual drawings, because Gerald Scarfe designed them, didn't he? And that's another thing they seem to have done lately, to bring in other influences to broaden their style.... There's some fine things to look at in some of their cartoons. Putting aside some of the ideology, they're incredibly well constructed. And especially in the 1930s and 1940s, they were – things like *Snow White*, it was an extraordinary piece of artwork at the time. You know, absolutely light years in advance of anything else. You could go to *Fantasia* or whatever – you could go to the cinema as a spectacle. (T/M)

Working against the grain of criticism, the approval of Disney here requires a degree of apology ('to be honest,' 'putting aside some of the ideology') and an appeal to specialist knowledge ('Gerald Scarfe designed them') and an alternative discourse of 'art appreciation' ('bring in other influences to broaden their style,' 'well-constructed,' 'an extraordinary piece of artwork,' 'the cinema as a spectacle'). In this context, the appeal to 'old' Disney – and particularly to the 'art movie' *Fantasia* – seems quite inevitable (Luckett, 1994).

Yet the appeal of Disney identified here was not merely aesthetic. It can perhaps best be described as *utopian* – although it is a utopia of comfort and ease, rather than of energy and excess.[17] Thus, several participants referred to the image of the magic castle that features in the Disney logo, attesting its attraction for them as children: 'I wanted to live in that fairy-tale castle at the beginning' (PG/F). As we have seen, this sense of Disney as a self-contained 'world' could generate a degree of paranoia – as in the 'brainwashed city' – yet it could also prove to be an attractive fantasy:

> When I was a kid I thought that Disney was like a big escape. It was like a
> different world. And I always wanted the world to be real, as well. I
> always wished there was a place like Disney. And then when I heard
> about things like Disney World and Disneyland, I thought 'it's true,' you
> know, to some extent.... It's that amazing sense that there's a different
> world. (PG/M)

Here again, accounts of such utopianism were surrounded with
qualifications and distancing strategies of various kinds. Thus, the
world of Disney was frequently described as 'nice,' 'easy' and 'simple' –
words that almost inevitably seem to imply that real life is rather more
nasty, difficult, and complicated. While the 'magic' of the utopia was
recognized, it was simultaneously dismissed as 'escapism,' or as a form
of 'over-the-top happiness.' This sense of comfort and ease also
extended to the experience of viewing itself:

> It's just entertainment, you switch off. You know, it's easy to watch. When
> you're very young it's sort of comforting. When you become a teenager,
> you get, you know, you get into other things. (PG/M)

> It's a very good formula. It's this formula that they've developed. Easy
> viewing. (PG/M)

Here again, the pleasures of the utopia are seen as particularly
appropriate for children, and dismissed as formulaic by the adult critic.
Such escapist desires implicitly seem to be confined to *other* people:
'Lots of people want to buy into that idea of – simple ideas of what life
is and what culture is and what society is. Simple rights and wrongs,
and to see those ideas of rights and wrongs reflected back to them'
(PG/M).

While recognizing the appeal of the utopia, therefore, the
participants also sought to distance themselves from it. They did so
primarily by locating it in the past, in their own childhoods. Yet in
thereby claiming a degree of maturity – a recognition of harsh realities,
an unwillingness to settle for easy comforts – they also expressed a
passing regret that they were now 'too old' to surrender themselves to
it (PG/M, F). The desire for 'simplicity' and 'innocence' was somehow
more than just empty nostalgia: something, it seemed, had genuinely
been lost.

Ideological dilemmas

The analysis outlined thus far has depended upon short extracts from
group discussions and questionnaire responses. As such, it has tended
to underplay the considerable ambivalence – and indeed the contra-

dictions – that characterized these discussions as a whole. While the various 'critical' positions I have mapped out were certainly dominant, the repressed dimension of pleasure frequently returned to disruptive effect. Across the course of a discussion, participants could move between these positions at considerable speed; and in some instances, the contradictions were quite overt. The speakers whom we have just heard extolling the fantasy world of Disney, for example, were forcefully condemning Walt himself as a fascist not a minute later. One of the teachers complained bitterly about the 'rip off' of Disney theme parks, yet immediately confessed that she had attended no fewer than four of them.

These tensions create which Michael Billig and his colleagues (1988) call an 'ideological dilemma' – an awkward contradiction between conflicting discourses that has to be effaced or rationalized away. Ideological dilemmas are partly to do with *self-presentation* – that is, with the positions one is *seen* to adopt – and they can sometimes be resolved through a form of 'identity work.' Thus, one solution here was to construct an opposition between a rational and an emotional self, and to claim that you had been 'won over' by the pleasures of Disney 'despite yourself.' Thus, Disney was described as 'infectious,' 'appealing' or 'overpowering' – words that implicitly represent the consumer as passive and helpless. This seemed to be particularly the case with the theme parks:

> I didn't think I would, but in fact that magical world of happiness – and even if you're sort of cynical going in there, by the end of the day you're smiling….You know, I'm a very cynical person, but I was completely taken over by it. (T/F)

> I enjoyed Disneyland in Paris. Against all my better judgement, I really enjoyed it. I went with a party of school kids – ten kids – and I really expected to hate it…. I went with all those assumptions of 'Disney, bloody Disney' – Americanization of culture, modulization of culture, all that. But it was really fun. I had a lovely time. I had a really, really good time. (PG/F)

As we have seen, expressions of pleasure were also accompanied by a considerable amount of apology and rationalization. The man quoted above, extolling the aesthetic merits of Disney animation, was a particular case in point:

> I mean, I may be seen as a philistine here, but to be honest, I associate, I can see some positive aspects of Disney films. Especially the cartoons. I mean, I like the way that they actually – they can encourage children to think imaginatively…. I know there's the sinister side to Disney as a

whole, but, you know, the way it celebrates – a lot of the cartoons celebrate childhood and fun and … (T/M)

The hesitations and qualifications here point to the difficulty of sustaining this position. In fact, this speaker was quickly interrupted by another contributor condemning the lack of authentic French culture at Disneyland Paris – a response which implicitly sustained the charge that he was merely a 'philistine.'

By contrast, there was little indication of the potential for 'ironic viewing,' which proved so attractive to some of Ien Ang's (1985) respondents.[18] One of the postgraduates described how she was looking forward to going back to Disneyland in a few years' time without her children, 'just for a really clichéd good time;' while one of the undergraduates referred to the popular legend about sexual images being secreted in the backgrounds of *The Lion King*. Such ironic or subversive responses could be seen to provide a further resolution of the ideological dilemmas at stake; yet there seemed to be fewer opportunities for such an approach here.

Some participants commented explicitly on these contradictions and the dilemmas to which they gave rise. For example, one group of undergraduates had discussed at some length the relationships between Disney and U.S. foreign policy, and the accusations of fascism. Yet they were able to shift gear instantly at the mention of *The Lion King*. As one subsequently observed: 'These questions have been addressed to us, and now we've got to start thinking about it. But as soon as somebody said a minute ago "Have you seen *The Lion King?*" [Imitates enthusiasm] "Oh, oh, yes, it's brilliant"' (UG/M). As this participant implies, the dominance of the 'critical' stance was partly an artifact of the research context. As another speaker in the same group suggested, 'you only analyze something when you're asked to, like this – [normally] you don't think about it, people don't think about it.'

This led some to actively resist the critical stance, on the grounds that it was somehow pretentious or inappropriate – a matter of 'reading too much into it.' Thus, particularly among the undergraduates, criticism was seen as incompatible with pleasure: 'I think that Disney has to be taken at face value, because if you start reading all sorts of deep, meaningful things into it, then – it's just a story – the whole magic is missing' (UG/F).

Despite their criticisms, several of the undergraduates were keen to conclude by proclaiming that Disney was just 'fun' and 'entertainment,' albeit with a certain self-consciousness: 'what we've got to remember is that there's nothing wrong with fantasy' (UG/F). Yet, against the grain of adult criticism, this naïve, pleasure-seeking stance was also seen to require some effort: 'I don't try now to read into it – I just try and watch it and enjoy it' (UG/F).

Other groups explicitly acknowledged the hidden pressure towards adopting a critical stance. Rather like McDonald's (with which it was compared by a couple of participants), Disney was seen as an 'easy target' that symbolized and focused much broader concerns:

> I can appreciate why people dislike it. But I don't think it's any more saccharine than a lot of American organizations, or many world organizations. It's just that it's become – it's iconographic, it's symbolic, that's why it's so despised. Rather than for the fact of what it actually is. (T/M)

In a sense, the official air of harmlessness and innocence that Disney has sought to create appears to have *provoked* a search for its opposite. As one male undergraduate argued, 'if something is as innocent as Disney, people are looking for things [to criticize].' The need to identify the 'dark side' of Disney which dominated all these discussions could even be seen to reflect a distinctly 'adult' (or perhaps adolescent?) cynicism – an almost willful desire to shatter childhood illusions, and thereby to prove one's ability to see the world as it really is.

Yet this 'cynical' position remains insecure, and has to be constantly reasserted. As one female undergraduate put it: 'I wanted to believe that the world is like Disney – I want to believe that. But it's not.' Here the desire to believe is not just in the past tense of childhood but also in the present tense of adulthood. As one of the teachers acknowledged, it was *adults* who bought Disney videos: 'it's not for children, they're buying them for themselves' (T/F). As such, these dilemmas were particularly acute for the parents in our sample, who were having to negotiate, not only with their own desires but also with those of their children:

> I actually quite enjoy seeing the reruns of the things I saw when I was a child. It's like buying the first train set, isn't it, you know. Buying your six months old baby a train set! That's what I did. It's reliving it, isn't it? (PG/F)

As this speaker implies, the adult's desire to relive their childhood experience may override their understanding of what is actually appropriate for the child at that age. Likewise, another parent argued that part of the appeal of Disneyland Paris was the fact that it could accommodate both adults' and children's different needs. Far from being the 'cultural Chernobyl' described by the French Minister of Culture, this parent argued that it allowed 'the cultural snobs' to visit Paris and 'pull the kids around' (PG/M).

Nevertheless, the dilemma remained more acute for parents than it appeared to be for others. As I have noted, it was the parents (along with the teachers) who were most vociferous in their condemnations of Disney – and indeed most inclined to be censorious. One parent, who took a more liberal view of Disney, drew an interesting analogy with McDonald's here:

> I'm swearing blind that under our own power [my son] will never go to McDonald's. … But that's a kind of hypocrisy for me because, you know, Disney can be seen as a corporate illusion. And it can be just as destructive as bad food and chopping the rain forest down. And buying a McDonald's – we're talking about the effects on children, so it's a tricky one, this. Because if my child gets pleasure out of Disney, and enjoyment, that's on one level. But if he gets a duff couple of hamburgers and it actually makes him physically ill, that's another thing. Working at an ideological level, or a kind of – it's not physically good for you. There's a kind of struggle there. And Disney have these cross-promotional activities with McDonald's anyway, and that is another [thing] – if you're a parent who has strong views about McDonald's. Then what do you do about Disney? (PG/M)

As a parent myself, with similarly strong views about McDonald's, I share this dilemma. One may not believe that children are witless dupes of the media or of consumer culture. One may recognize that, alongside the objectionable stereotypes, Disney products do genuinely reflect the desires we have invested in childhood. And one may accept that the 'effects' of such material on children are neither predictable nor straightforward. But, ultimately, what *do* you do about Disney?

Beyond ambivalence

Discussions of the politics of popular culture have often been caught in a dialectical tension between ideology and pleasure. Traditionally, pleasure has been seen as the mechanism whereby audiences are deceived into an acceptance of ideology; while more recently, it has come to be celebrated as something that exceeds and thereby undermines ideology. Putting the debate in these crude terms draws attention to its limitations. Ultimately, it tends to come down to a series of either/or choices: between ideology and pleasure; between reason and emotion; between powerful media and powerful audiences. Both theoretically and pragmatically, such choices are much too simplistic. If it is to do more than issue rationalistic denunciations of popular pleasures, cultural politics will need to move beyond them.

In drawing attention to the limitations of ideological critique, therefore, it has not been my intention simply to vindicate pleasure. The critical arguments made by the participants in these discussions – about the economic, ideological and cultural biases of Disney – are, for the most part, hard to refute. At the same time, they do give cause for doubt about the *consequences* of those biases. Of course, these are educated people; but if they find it easy to see through and to challenge Disney, can we necessarily assume that 'uneducated' people are unable to do so as well? And, more to the point, are we right to assume that children are merely 'swallowers of fictions,' with lasting consequences for their beliefs and values?

I would assert that the ambivalence I have identified here is in fact characteristic of very many – perhaps most – adults' relationships with Disney. It is not some kind of deviation from an 'authentic,' 'popular' viewing position, or indeed a form of misplaced snobbery, as some critics seem to imply.[19] It is a consequence – perhaps an inevitable consequence – of the position of the adult in relation to the child, and hence of the adult critic in relation to the culture of childhood. This fundamental difference is accentuated here by cultural differences – British viewers, American media – and by more overtly political concerns. Taken together, it is hardly surprising that Disney should emerge as the 'bad object' *par excellence*; and yet that it should also evoke such unresolved desires and fantasies.

Ambivalence is perhaps an appropriate conclusion for such an academic investigation. Yet can it be a sufficient basis for cultural politics – or even for cultural pedagogy? In this respect, I am intrigued – and slightly troubled – by the fact that the *most* ambivalent discussions were those among my own postgraduate students. In general, their arguments – both about Disney, and about the broader issues that were at stake – were less trenchant and forthright, and more nuanced and even-handed, than those of the other groups. I do not assume that this is simply the result of my own teaching. However, I do wonder whether this is the subject position my teaching implicitly seeks to produce: equivocal, self-aware, sophisticated – but ultimately paralyzed.

Yet whatever position they may have adopted, all these individuals were able to speak at length about what Disney meant to them. For most of them, Disney was an integral part of their childhoods; and for the parents, it was now being 'relived' with their own children. As one of my students pointed out: 'Disney has come almost to embody childhood. And of course they position themselves to do that' (PG/M). It is certainly hard to imagine any similar company or brand enjoying a similar status (even though there are increasing numbers that try to do so). In Britain, as in many other countries around the world, children today are Disney children; and parents are Disney parents. We may all be consuming Disney in complex and ambivalent ways; but in the end, we are all still consuming the same things. The space for alternative childhoods, for alternative stories to be told, may be steadily reducing. So what *will* we do about Disney?

Notes

1. Recent examples would include Giroux (1997), Michel (1996), and Roth (1996).
2. It has particularly informed my own work about children's relationships with television: see Buckingham (1993a, 1996, 1999). Potter and Wetherell (1987) and Fairclough (1989) provide useful introductions to critical discourse analysis. Barker and Brooks (1998) offer a trenchant evaluation of its uses in media audience research.
3. This is very much the dominant approach to audience discourse in psychology and in Cultural Studies respectively. Liebes and Katz (1990), for example, develop a valuable analysis of critical viewing, yet it is one which largely neglects the social functions of discourse.
4. For further discussion, see Buckingham (1993b).
5. I would like to thank Hannah Davies and Julian Sefton-Green for their help in convening these groups; and Betty Mitchell for the transcribing.
6. The Project team's 'schedule' for these interviews is very detailed, although it is designed to be used by a group leader rather than in the context of a self-directed group, as was the case here.
7. Needless to say, this contextual effect is completely ignored by mainstream mass-communication researchers, who readily use their own students as subjects without ever appearing to doubt their representativeness.
8. For a fuller discussion of these issues in relation to interviewing children, see Buckingham (1993a), particularly Chapter Three.
9. I would not necessarily oppose those who have called for a return to quantification in audience studies (for example, Murdock, 1997); but there are self-evident problems in using *qualitative* data of this kind to support *quantitative* conclusions.
10. I identify participants by group (UG = undergraduate, PG = postgraduate, T = teachers) and gender. All quotations are taken from the interview or questionnaire data.
11. For a discussion of these arguments in relation to children's culture, see Buckingham (1995).
12. Knightsbridge is an extremely up-market area of London.
13. There is a long history of this somewhat schizophrenic relation with American popular culture, in which social class plays a prominent role: see Hebdige (1988) and Worpole (1983).
14. The program in question was a Channel Four documentary in the series *Secret Lives*, transmitted in 1997. Disney's connections with fascism, and its implications for the movies, are explored by Roth (1996).

15. By comparison, it is striking that very few of Ang's respondents condemn 'racism' or 'sexism' in *Dallas*.
16. See Steedman (1995) for a discussion of the cultural origins of these beliefs; and Ivy (1995) for an analysis of the tensions that surround this notion of the 'inner child.'
17. The obvious point of reference here is Richard Dyer's analysis of the 'utopian' dimension of popular entertainment (Dyer, 1985).
18. Some have implied that this stance is effectively invited by the soap opera form: see Geraghty (1991) and Buckingham (1993a), Chapter Four.
19. This seems to me to be the implication of Ang's argument, particularly her somewhat hostile account of the 'ironic viewing attitude' (Ang, 1985).

References and other sources

Ang, I. (1985) *Watching* Dallas: *Soap Opera and the Melodramatic Imagination*. London, Methuen.

Barker, M. and Brooks, K. (1998) *Knowing Audiences:* Judge Dredd, *Its Friends, Fans and Foes*. Luton, University of Luton Press.

Billig, M., Condor, S., Edwards, D., Gane, M., Middleton, D., and Radley, A. (1988) *Ideological Dilemmas: A Social Psychology of Everyday Life*. London, Sage.

Bourdieu, P. (1984) *Distinction: A Social Critique of the Judgment of Taste*. London, Routledge and Kegan Paul.

Bryman, A. (1995) *Disney and His Worlds*. London, Routledge.

Buckingham, D. (1993a) *Children Talking Television: The Making of Television Literacy*. London, Falmer.

Buckingham, D. (1993b) 'Going critical: the limits of media literacy,' *Australian Journal of Education*, 37(2): 142–52.

Buckingham, D. (1995) 'The commercialisation of childhood? The place of the market in children's media culture,' *Changing English*, 2(2): 17–40.

Buckingham, D. (1996) *Moving Images: Understanding Children's Emotional Responses to Television*. Manchester, Manchester University Press.

Buckingham, D. (1999) *The Making of Citizens: Young People, News and Politics*. London, University College London Press.

Dyer, R. (1985) 'Entertainment and utopia,' in B. Nichols (ed.), *Movies and Methods Volume II*. Berkeley, University of California, pp. 221–32.

Fairclough, N. (1989) *Language and Power*. London, Longman.

Forgacs, D. (1992) 'Disney animation and the business of childhood,' *Screen*, 33(4): 361–74.

Geraghty, C. (1991) *Women and Soap Opera*. Cambridge, Polity Press.

Giroux, H. (1997) 'Are Disney movies good for your kids?' in S. R. Steinberg and J. L. Kincheloe (eds), *Kinderculture: The Corporate Construction of Childhood*. Boulder, CO, Westview, pp. 53–67.

Gomery, D. (1994) 'Disney's business history: a reinterpretation,' in E. Smoodin (ed.), *Disney Discourse: Producing the Magic Kingdom*. London, British Film Institute, pp. 71–86.

Hebdige, D. (1988) *Hiding in the Light*. London, Routledge.

Ivy, M. (1995) 'Have you seen me? Recovering the inner child in late twentieth-century America,' in S. Stephens (ed.), *Children and the Politics of Culture*. Princeton, NJ, Princeton University Press, pp. 79–104.

Liebes, T. and Katz, E. (1990) *The Export of Meaning*. New York, Oxford University Press.

Luckett, M. (1994) '*Fantasia*: cultural constructions of Disney's "masterpiece," ' in E. Smoodin (ed.), *Disney Discourse: Producing the Magic Kingdom*. London, British Film Institute, pp. 214–36.

Michel, C. (1996) 'Re-reading Disney, not quite Snow White,' *Discourse*, 17(1): 5–14.

Murdock, G. (1997) 'Thin descriptions: questions of method in cultural analysis,' in J. McGuigan (ed.), *Cultural Methodologies*. London, Sage, pp. 178–92.

New Internationalist (1998) 308, December.

Potter, J. and Wetherell, M. (1987) *Discourse and Social Psychology*. London, Sage.

Roth, M. (1996) 'A short history of Disney fascism,' *Jump Cut*, 40: 15–20.

Steedman, C. (1995) *Strange Dislocations: Childhood and the Idea of Human Interiority, 1780–1930*. London, Virago.

Worpole, K. (1983) *Dockers and Detectives*. London, Verso.

CHAPTER 14

United States: A Disney Dialectic: A Tale of Two American Cities

NORMA PECORA AND EILEEN R. MEEHAN

'Disney' – for Americans, that word alone conjures up dozens of contrasting images: Minnie Mouse and Esmeralda; Disneyland and Disney Stores; Uncle Walt and Michael Eisner; Silly Symphonies and Tarzan; 'Who's Afraid of the Big, Bad Wolf?' and 'Circle of Life;' Mickey Mouse watches and Hercules underwear, dolls, games, books, sandals, jewelry, tapes, CDs, website, etc.

For the nostalgic among us, the 'old' Disney signals all that is good in this dialectic: an individual genius, the family-run company, artful animations. While the 'new' Disney builds on that legacy, it also commands a business empire that depends on aggressive programs of corporate acquisition, product marketing, and commercial exploitation. In living memory, there seem to be two distinct Disney companies, but the ubiquity of Disney's fantasy world appears constant.

Rather than reiterate Disney's transindustrial structure (presented in the Introduction), from which its symbolic ubiquity derives, we focus in this chapter on variations in Disney's physical presence and technological accessibility inside the U.S.A. To do this, we present a tale of two cities – Athens, Ohio, and Tucson, Arizona – comparing and contrasting Disney's operations at a local level with the national operations that ensure its symbolic ubiquity. We then trace that symbolic ubiquity through our respondents' replies. But first, let us explain our selection of these two, relatively minor markets.

We selected Athens and Tucson for three reasons, the most obvious being that, as residents, we could systematically monitor the local retail scene over a fairly long period of time. Both of us had moved to our respective cities to secure employment: Norma Pecora at Ohio University in Athens, Eileen Meehan at the University of Arizona in Tucson. This was our second reason for selecting Athens and Tucson: we would have access to university students. Our third – and perhaps most important reason – was that Athens and Tucson are neither major economic centers nor peripheral outposts. Each city has a relatively sound economy and access to the major media in the U.S.A. But each needs to be contextualized in terms of sharp contrasts rooted in regional politics and economics. By examining cities that reflect the uneven development of U.S. capitalism, we hope to draw a more nuanced picture of Disney's presence. To do this, we begin by describing each city's retail and media systems, and then Disney's penetration of those systems.

Athens, Ohio: a snapshot

According to the most recent data available,[1] Ohio is the seventh largest state in population, with over 11 million residents (1999); 81 percent of the population lives in urban areas (1996); and, the majority of Ohioans are of European descent, with approximately 13 percent of African/Asian/Native American descent (1990). When states are rated in terms of the market value of their goods and services, Ohio ranks seventh in the U.S.A. The unemployment rate overall in the state is about 3.6 percent, though in some counties the rate is over 10 percent. The median household income was $38,925 (1998), with 11.2 percent living below the poverty level (1998).

In the north of the state, cities like Cleveland and Toledo have been traditionally industrial areas supported by steel mills and manufacturing plants; southern Ohio is mainly rural, with rolling hills and small subsistence farms. The county of Athens, and hence the city and Ohio University, are situated in the southeast area of the state and within the larger area designated as Appalachia. Although unemployment in the county is low, primarily because of the university, the counties that border Athens County have among the highest unemployment figures in the nation, ranging from 5 percent to 12.1 percent (2000). And at $26,020, the median household income is almost $12,000 below the state figures (1995). In Athens County, 20.1 percent of the population lives in poverty and 26 percent of those under 18 live in homes with incomes below the poverty level (1996). Many of the families in the region are single-parent homes and a significant number of Appalachian children are raised in poverty. Severe economic conditions have persisted in Appalachia for decades. While there have been periodic attempts by the federal and state government to address this economic situation, the attempts are sporadic at best, leaving the residents suspicious of government intentions.

The city of Athens is the county seat and the home of Ohio University, where the disparities in income are often evident. Faculty and administrators live in designer homes costing well over $150,000, while their neighbors live in trailers on land handed down through the family. Most of these long-term residents also work at the university but hardly under the same conditions as university faculty and administrators. The 'locals' are more generally underemployed in less skilled, low-waged support jobs. While the surrounding hills are pictures of rural poverty, the campus closely resembles Hollywood's image of college life: stately trees surround the campus, and buildings replicate an earlier architecture. Each Fall, the town nearly doubles, as over 18,000 undergraduates return to the university from their homes in Ohio's more prosperous cities – in our sample over half were from the major metropolitan areas of Ohio such as Cincinnati, Cleveland, Columbus, Dayton, and Toledo. Athens' population over the summer reverts to about 21,000.

Given Athens' retail outlets, students tend to leave their shopping to their trips back home. Most residents drive to other cities such as Columbus and Parkersburg, West Virginia – both about a two-hour drive – to shop. Athens could not be mistaken for a retail hub. The major department stores are J. C. Penney, the only national chain in Athens, and Elder-Beerman, a regional department store. Two national discount stores hover on the fringes of town, Ames and KMart, each one anchoring a small local mall. Occasionally rumors surface that Wal-Mart will build a store, but the rumors seem more wishful than possible.

Tuning in: Disney media in Athens

Athens' only local television station is the university-owned public broadcasting station, WOUB. The town is considered a part of the Charleston–Huntington (West Virginia) market some 90 miles to the south and in another state. Within the city limits, residents have access to nationally distributed television through Time Warner Communications, but in the surrounding area people must rely on satellite-distribution systems for access to television programing. It is not unusual to see large satellite dishes in most yards, though more recently small, roof-mounted dishes have been sprouting up. In part, this is a function of the hilly terrain that makes reception difficult, but it also represents the limited access of much of rural U.S.A.

Nonetheless, we do have Disney media.

In Athens, the Disney Channel is offered by Time Warner Communications as a premium channel to its 6200 subscribers at an additional fee of $6.95; however, only slightly more than 200 people subscribe to Disney. This is perhaps a consequence of a high student population living around the university and hence in Athens. Most residents receive programing via satellite or, if they live in town, as a part of Time Warner Communications: consequently, some Disney is available to most people. However, the students living in school dormitories have limited access to cable and Disney is not one of the channels they receive.

Families in the surrounding area who rely on satellite distribution have a wider range of programing available, though at a cost. Depending on the system, Disney East, Disney West, and Toon Disney are either a part of the basic package or are charged as premium channels. In Pecora's home, the ABC network-affiliated stations come out of New York City at an add-on cost of $4.99 per month, but Disney East and West and Toon Disney come as part of the basic service of $28.99 per month. In this household, television costs over $400 a year. Because the area relies on either cable or satellite access, there are few problems with reception, except in a good rainstorm. However, in this area access is also determined by economics. At an extra $7.00 per month on top of a cable bill of $28.54 or a satellite bill of $29.95 a month, in an economically depressed area not everyone has 'access' to Disney. More recently, Athens residents have gained access to the latest in Disney television through ABC network television and ESPN. For an extra $10.00 a month, viewers can watch the Columbus, Ohio, local ABC affiliate WSYX from 90 miles to the north, or the Huntington, West Virginia, station WCHS from 90 miles to the south. Neither is truly local.

Mulan, the most recent Disney movie at the time of this writing, just closed at the local cinema. Disney videos are available at the three local rental stores and the major supermarket video rental section. Some are available for purchase at Blockbuster Music, and KMart has the most recently released Disney video prominently positioned at the entrance to the store. Disney videos, including *Hercules*, are also available at the local library.

Athens is not really a comic-book kind of town and those sold at the Mini Maul, the local comic-book store, or the two local bookstores are generally action-adventure or adult comics, with only a few copies of *Mickey Mouse* or *Donald Duck*. A range of storybooks are available at the bookstores and coloring books are on the shelf in the Kroger grocery store and two discount stores, though on most shelves Disney books compete with *Sesame Street*, Barney, and Barbie. Records and music are available in the discount stores, Blockbuster Music, and the public library. The music stores near campus tend not to carry show tunes, musicals, or Disney.

Local entrepreneurs also own the two local movie theaters, the Athena and Movies 10. Until recently there was only the Athena, and, although it has three screens, rarely does it show family-oriented films, but caters rather to the college audience. Although the Athena will usually have a brief one-week run of new Disney releases, located just off-campus, it generally runs only adult-oriented, first-run films briefly. About a year ago a ten-screen theater, Movies 10, was built 5 miles north of town, drawing in a more family-oriented audience, where first-run Disney movies play more frequently and for longer periods of time. For example, *Tarzan* recently had almost a month-long run. Consequently, video rentals are very popular. The major grocery store, Kroger, has a large section devoted to video rentals featuring children's videos, including any of the Disney releases, as do the two other grocery stores, Bob's and Big Bear. There are three video-rental agencies in town, Athens Video and Premiere Video, which offer a wide range of videos including all Disney video releases. Although Disney products are available at Magic Video, the campus video-rental store, their eclectic collection is targeted at the college taste, so Disney competes with the latest foreign release or Japanese anime. Like most businesses in Athens, the video-rental agencies are locally owned. There is a small, by most standards, Blockbuster located in the larger mall, but its primary stock is music not videos. In Athens, tuning in general means either a very local experience – watching videos at home – or someone else's local experience – watching the local New York City news.

The only truly local media are the university-based public television and radio station, which, because of their impoverished budgets, have limited programing. Programs like those featuring Garrison Keillor are simply too expensive for the station's small budget. Pledge drives are victorious when they bring in $50,000. The students, more accustomed to major city markets, describe the two locally owned radio stations, in addition to public radio, with disdain. There is no way that Radio Disney would be a part of our local media landscape. We have access to Disney videos, movies, and television, but at a price. These limitations in media distribution are reflected in the way Disney products, so important for synergy, are merchandised here in Athens.

The one arena where Disney is potentially available to all, again within limits of access, is through the Disney website. However, although the SchoolNet Program has wired all schools in the southeast region of Ohio, it does not mean there is access. Many of the schools are wired only on paper, as there is little money in their budget for maintenance and some have no computers hooked in to the Internet. Where schools do have access to the Web, some have restricted access, using software programs to control availability; others have a policy that requires an adult in the room; and in some cases parental permission is necessary to access the computers. Often surfing the net is seen as goofing off. On the other hand, one school in the state built a day around Disney and made it available on their web site. In this third-grade classroom, the students celebrated Disney Day and the 25th anniversary of Disney World. They dressed in Disney clothes, shared Disney toys, ate Mickey Mouse ice-cream treats, read Disney books, and saw a Disney movie: http://www.perryschools.lgca.ohio.gov (July 20, 1998).

No doubt children, particularly those of the academic faculty and administrators, have computers or access to computers in their home. But for many of the rest of Athens' children, access to Disney media is somewhat limited, reflecting both the disenfranchisement and the limitations of media in rural America.

Market analysis: Disney doesn't do Athens

The popularity of Disney products and media has been well established, both by others contributing to this book and by the students we talked with in Athens. Yet issues of availability pose an interesting problem. Because of its isolation and size, Athens has very few retail outlets. The students tend to shop in their home town, where they are familiar with the shops and parents pay the bills. Those in the university community shop in the nearby cities and during visits to academic conferences. Columbus, the nearest metropolitan area and Disney Store, is about a two-hour drive.

The three strip malls at the east end of town dominate the retail business; two are anchored by discount stores – KMart in University Mall and Ames in Athens Mall – the third contains a variety of service agencies, such as a check-cashing service and a barber shop, a bulk grocery store and an auto supply store. The small department stores, J.C. Penney and Elder-Beerman, are located in University Mall, while the Athens Mall contains a range of small stores that sell fabric, paint, guitars, leather goods, and ice-cream. Although the paint store features Disney wallpaper and the fabric store a few Mickey Mouse needle-point kits, most Disney products are found in the discount stores and grocery stores. There are no up-market shops in Athens.[2]

At some level, this market analysis reveals that almost every Disney category of licensed product can be purchased in Athens.[3] Clothes for adults and teens as well as products for toddlers, babies, and infants are available at both department and discount stores; diapers, bottles, and toys are for sale in the grocery stores, too. (These were particularly difficult for the new mother who conducted this market analysis to resist, even though she is a poor and jaded graduate student.) Housewares and party goods, toys, games, personal adornments, some decorative products, and carry-alls are available at KMart and Ames, Revco and the grocery store. Other products are less available: for instance, this author was unable to find Mickey Mouse ice-cream treats.

A visit to the major stores revealed that, though the area cannot compete with major metropolitan areas for shopping, one could put together a substantial collection of Disney memorabilia from the local suppliers. For example, one of the campus card shops has been regularly expanding its section of Disney's Winnie the Pooh products, and at the last visit it accounted for perhaps the largest display area, second only to Beanie Babies. The locally owned card shop also carried coffee cups, clocks, umbrellas, posters, figurines, stationery, and balloons, among other things. The grocery stores had items ranging from toothpaste to pacifiers, activity books to band-aids, but no food items. And even one campus bookstore offered calendars and mousepads.

The two McDonald's in town, where Disney movies and products are often heavily promoted, are off-campus and not easily accessible to the students on campus, so tend to be more community-oriented. As would be expected, the discount stores accounted for the majority of items. In all, we found over more than 100 different Disney-themed items available. Not bad for a town with so few shopping opportunities. What type of products are available is more interesting than the fact that there are Disney products available.

Although this is a small town with limited retail opportunities, one can find Disney, with Disney merchandising particularly ubiquitous among items aimed at babies (bibs, pacifiers, layettes, wallpaper, mobiles, toys, rattles, and bottles) and young children (toys, activity books, pencils, and clothing). What is perhaps most interesting is the Disney that is not available. Unlike other places where a 'new campaign takes center stage,' things come slower, if at all, to Athens. The characters available are the traditional Mickey, Minnie, and Winnie the Pooh. Mulan, Disney's latest media character, was barely in evidence, though it was the featured Disney media event in the movie theaters at the time. The only Mulan items were a few backpacks in the back-to-school display, one action-figure doll, and some coloring books in the grocery store. However, Disney's Winnie the Pooh is featured everywhere, and even Mickey and Minnie have taken a back seat to him. He is the character most featured on all of the items available here, both in the baby and toddler sections and in the card shop in the campus retail area.

So Disney does do Athens but only in a way that maintains a symbolic ubiquity for the Disney Empire. The characters that are a part of the tradition of Disney – Winnie the Pooh, Minnie and Mickey – are here, and available in a range of merchandise. However, those that have a shorter shelf-life, connected to and promoting a movie, then fading away, are less evident.

Responding to Disney at Ohio University

The 63 Ohio University students who participated in this study were all in their freshman year of college, many away from home for the first time. The respondents were identified by the numbers JO01–JO63. The survey was conducted early in the fall in a large-lecture introductory journalism class where Disney had not been discussed to date. Since all but a few had grown up in the U.S.A., home of the Disney Empire, one would expect them to be familiar with the characters and movies created by Disney – and they were. They were also white, middle-class, young people who were born in the U.S.A. and had grown up in Ohio, with an average age of 18.4. The age range of 18 to 22 reflected the fact that most were in their first year of college. That the group included proportionately more women (73 percent) than men (27 percent), was overwhelmingly white (89 percent), and was comprised of citizens of the U.S.A. (98.4 percent) is comparable to the make-up of Ohio University undergraduates, particularly in the Scripps School of Journalism where this survey was conducted. Given their age, they are of the new Disney generation and this is reflected in their memories of the company, as the majority (87.9 percent) said their first contact with Disney products occurred before they were 5 years of age.

Three of the students had been to EuroDisney, while 58 students (92 percent) had been either to Disneyland in California (22.2 percent) or Disney World in Florida (82.5 percent). Since Disney World is only a long day's drive away, while California and Disneyland involve much longer journeys, it is not surprising that most of the Ohio University students had visited the Florida theme park, where 46 percent had stayed at a Disney hotel and attended Epcot (71.4 percent) and Disney-MGM (54 percent).

Clearly, these students are Disney-media savvy as all had seen a Disney film, many had come into contact with the Disney Channel (87.3 percent), rented videos (88.9 percent), or bought videos (87.3 percent). Fewer students had much contact with Disney video games

(60.3 percent), perhaps because the games tend to be simplistic and not very exciting, as anyone who has played the *Beauty and the Beast* 'Game Girl' will attest. These students, however, have had contact with books (90.5 percent), records (87.3 percent), magazines (34.9 percent), and comics (20.6 percent), though clearly Disney print media is not as popular as the movies and television. Only seven students had contact with the Disney home page, which is perhaps a function of their age.

When it comes to Disney products, these are material girls – and boys. Over 90 percent (92.1 percent) have had contact with Disney merchandise, with 55 receiving gifts of Disney merchandise (87.3 percent) and 49 giving Disney gifts (77.8 percent). Almost all, 61 of the 63 students, had been in a Disney Store. Their material Disney world has consisted of toys (85.7 percent), clothing (76.2 percent), collectibles (65.1 percent), Mickey Mouse ears (54 percent), watches (49.2 percent) and jewelry (46 percent). A surprising 30.2 percent claimed to have artwork, but only one student admitted belonging to the Disney Club. The total number of products Ohio University students reported having contact with after prompting was fifteen, though without prompting they only averaged 4.6 items.

Recognizing the ubiquity of the material world known as Disney, we turn our attention to the symbolic world. When asked to describe their perception of 'Disney,' the respondents chose adjectives such as: happiness (6), fun (6), imagination (4), love/romance (2), and generous (1), as well as cute (6) or wholesome (2). But a few students saw the darker side of Disney and cited: cowardly (1), overpriced and expensive (4), and manipulative (1), with bad films (1) and long lines (1). When prompted with a list of values that Disney could be seen as either promoting or discouraging, the company was unanimously seen as promoting family (100 percent), happiness (100 percent), and magic (100 percent), and as promoting fantasy (98 percent), fun (98 percent), good over evil (98 percent), imagination (98 percent), and bravery (92.1 percent). The students here were less sure or disinclined to respond to terms like individualism, where 39 students (61.9 percent) said Disney promoted the idea, but only 2 (3.2 percent) said Disney discouraged it, while 22 gave no answer. This ambivalence was also seen in other more complex descriptors, as presented in Table 14.1.

It also should be noted that the students either avoided or claimed that some of the more complex descriptions did not apply. Out of the 63 students who participated, fewer responded to the question of whether or not Disney encouraged or discouraged optimism (50), individualism (41), work ethic (40), racism (32), technological progress (31), patriotism (27), patriarchy (18), and thriftiness (13). Were they consciously avoiding identifying Disney with these notions or simply

Table 14.1 Responses to Disney descriptors

	Promote		Discourage	
	Number	*%*	*Number*	*%*
Optimism	49	77.8	1	1.6
Patriarchy	17	27.0	1	1.6
Technological progress	33	52.4	1	1.6
Patriotism	25	39.7	2	3.2
Physical beauty	50	79.4	2	3.2
Thriftiness	10	15.9	3	4.8
Work ethic	37	58.7	3	4.8
Respect for difference	48	76.2	6	9.5
Racism	6	9.5	26	41.3

in a hurry to finish? The students were equally divided on whether Disney is uniquely American, with 25 saying yes and 25 saying no.

According to some students, Disney is uniquely American for practical reasons, as it was created in the U.S.A. (JO30, JO61) and is symbolic of the country (JO58, JO62, JO39). Others said it reflects and promotes uniquely American values (JO23) and ideals of strength, perseverance, courage, triumph, beauty, happiness, and contentment (JO27), and that it is representative of the 'parity and freedom' of American culture (JO50):

> [it is] people struggling and learning to be all they can be (excuse the Army lingo). Americans are always fighting for a better way, and Disney reminds us that eventually there will be a happy ending. (JO50)

> Disney, to me has created a world of wonder, happiness, and imagination. In American society, our free-spirit 'freedom-based' society is then, in a way reflected. (JO04)

Only one student was clearly what Wasko (2001) has identified as a resister and saw Disney as representing corporate America and its greediness (JO05). To others, Disney belongs to the world because of its global distribution (JO24, JO19, JO43) or representation of global or universal values, such as reaching people's hearts (JO21), imagination (JO67), diversity (JO40), and a common ground (JO71), or simply because the animated figures are the same everywhere (JO65).

'Disney – how could you not like it?'

Themes of happiness, fun, imagination, family, and good versus evil were repeated throughout the interviews that were also a part of this study. Five students who completed the questionnaire agreed to participate in more extensive interviews, which were conducted by a graduate student.[4] These three women and two men had all grown up in Ohio and with Disney. They offered very little in the way of ambiguity or confusion about the role of Disney. All of them appeared to be committed Disneyphiles or, as defined by Wasko, fanatics, who strongly supported the values inherent in Disney. Unfortunately, no resisters were willing to be interviewed and as a consequence the conversations give us a one-sided view of the students' perceptions of Disney. Nonetheless, the interviews do allow us some insight into the role of Disney in the lives of five students from Ohio.

Each of the students had a different favorite character – Cinderella, Goofy, Mickey Mouse, and Winnie the Pooh were favorites. One student's favorite changed with each new movie (Walt would be proud). Cinderella was favored for the fantasy she created, Goofy because of his 'happy aura,' Mickey and Minnie Mouse because they 'always put[s] a smile on your face,' and Pooh because he represented 'hugs and niceness.' Perhaps this accounts for his ubiquity in a university town.

In the context of defining these students as 'consumers,' all five had been to Disney World, most at least twice. One student reported having been to Disney World about twelve times and Disneyland twice during her 18 years. All had visited the parks with family on vacation and regarded the fact that it was a family trip as a special occasion. When asked to describe the experience, one male said:

> I was being in awe, it's always like this is the stuff I saw on TV and pictures and stuff like, wow, I'm looking at it right there. I'll never forget looking at the Epcot ball representation: just like wow, you know, I looked at it as a kid, even the castle, you just see it, yeah, OK, it's just something that doesn't really exist and then I'm there, so it's like wow, 'cause I was just, it was just a really, really fun, fun time. (JO12)

His experience seemed to reflect that of the others, who expressed the 'fun' of the adventure, though one student's memory was limited to a parent getting sick at Epcot and cool candy treats.

The films

These students are still apparently Disney fans, as three of the five had seen the then-current release *Hercules* and the other two had seen *The Lion King* and *Beauty and the Beast*, two other recent releases, and all were familiar with the movies, moving in and out of various films to illustrate their comments. Those who saw *Hercules* did so with friends.

One woman reported going as a 'girl's night out': she and her friends went because their boyfriends wouldn't go, claiming it was not a guy thing to do. But the women went, loved it, and cried.

When asked to describe their expectations of a Disney film, they often recounted an element of predictability and the narrative of good versus evil and magic as important to the experience. One student appreciated the fact that you knew nothing would be depressing and you would leave feeling good (JO12). In their words, they would expect

> a fantasy … like most of the time it's going to be a situation where there's something that would not normally be … like animals talking … geared toward kids … with a lesson … entertainment with a twist of magic. (JO23)

> good versus evil … the usual conflict … animals that talk, friendship, people learning things about each other and growing and experiencing new things … following their hearts. (JO50)

> there's a good guy and the bad guy … something goes wrong and the good guy always wins, but it is always so much more than that … You can probably sit there and say well that's the good guy, you know he's going to win in the end. You know they add the other stuff in it just to keep it interesting. (JO26)

Although the 'good guy' or hero is most often seen as 'handsome,' the exception was the Beast in *Beauty and the Beast*, whose attraction was perceived to be that he was very 'caring and loving.' But generally the heroes were described as 'studs,' who were independent with 'hoardes (*sic*) of followers or something.' As one female pointed out, they are usually 'some macho stud, who's out to save some fair dame, who's in distress … and then usually, he battles some evil monster, witch or something to win her over … they all kind of look alike' (JO03). For the most part, except for the obvious Beast, the heroes were described by their physical prowess and strength (JO03, JO23, JO26, JO50), and by their ability to overcome evil (JO12).

Heroines, on the other hand, are seen as beautiful, though as one female student said: 'I don't remember seeing any of them sitting back and saying "Well, that's probably not what I should do." They're all saying "I'm going to do [it], this is my dream and I'm going to do [it]," all of them' (JO50). In fact, the young women who were interviewed were inclined to describe the Disney heroines as bold and strong, while the two men saw things differently. When asked about the heroines, one of them questioned whether there was always such a character and described the movies almost entirely in the context of the battle between good and evil (JO23). The other described the heroine as 'Pretty ... always subject to almost like manipulation ... like eating the apple or whatever' (JO12). Other characters in the films were described as the evil villain and the sidekick, who acts the silly fool for comic relief.

When describing the typical story line, one student had an interesting observation about the conflict or problems in the films. She pointed out that the conflict is generally external, and characterized by simple conflicts, because that is what a child can understand. They understand at a surface level why he (the hero) had to fight the bad guy, whereas internal conflict is lost on young children.

Each student claimed that the obstacles were always presented as moral battles of good versus evil, with the stories ending happily ever after.

Values and child-rearing

For whatever reason, not unexpectedly, the students from Ohio who participated in these interviews believed that exposing children, their own or friends', to Disney was only a good thing. A few offered cautionary advice about too much exposure; but overall, Disney was seen as a way of transmitting good values. One young man's response was representative of the others:

> There's nothing wrong with Disney ... everything they have is geared towards children. It helps in forming a child's, you know, their right and wrong, their – not morals, I wouldn't say that – just stuff you need when you're a kid. Disney helps to bring out just little simple things that parents using Disney things could tell their children as an example, I suppose, of what needs to be taught to children, when they're at that age. Like movies are good to show them. The books that you read to them always have good stories, good messages ...

Moving to the material, he points out:

> Clothes, I suppose, are fun to wear, like the best would be when you're young – those little footy pajamas with things on the bottom, those are the coziest little things I ever [saw] – so you couldn't go wrong with those. (JO23)

To him, even the material Disney, the cozy footy pajamas, was recognized as a good thing, reinforcing, no doubt, the values of his years of growing up with Disney. His response points to how closely childhood memories and consumption are linked in the mind of Disney consumers.

Popularity and meanings

When asked what Disney meant to them personally, most responses centered on 'happiness.' One student characterized Disney as a 'big huge company of happy things ... a big, huge company that does good for society and children and everybody.' Others responded by defining Disney as 'companionship ... good family ties' or 'friendship' and 'sticking together'; another that it was a 'fantasy world that ... warms the heart.'

When asked what Disney meant to them as Americans, those who answered the question said that Disney represents the U.S.A. because

> it originated here and the free expression of ideas is always prevalent in their themes. But the characters hold a lot of American values but ... are very universal, everyone cries, everyone falls in love. (JO50)

> it's something you can be proud of ... the main goal of Disney was just to keep people happy ... everything that they promote, that they do, it seems to encourage like happiness and like fun, you know, all good things, so I guess I would be proud to have it represent us as American. (JO26)

> it's obviously a symbol ... I think everybody in the world likes Disney and I think they identify with the fact that it is American and people have a fascination with American things. (JO23)

> freedom is pretty synonymous with a Disney film. Disney is very American in its nature, it's something that all people can sort of strive for which is good, you know, all of what America is about, good, striving and achieving goals. (JO12).

As a representative of the U.S.A., one student stated that through Disney, 'America is expressed as multicultural and very united and strong.' Another sees it as representing 'the basis of what we believe, that if you work hard and you live your dream, then you're going to, you know, reap the benefit.'

A variety of reasons were offered for Disney's appeal, but those participating in the interviews centered primarily on its ubiquity and its 'happiness.' Some of the other reasons they cited were: 'it's fun and everyone likes to have fun'; 'it's everywhere'; 'it appeals to everyone'; 'it's a happy place'; 'it's a fantasy world.' For these students there was no 'resisting' Disney: for most of them it was a part of their life and culture since before they could really remember. Except for a few who participated in the survey and expressed their dissatisfaction with the 'overpriced' nature of Disney, these Ohio students were very much of the New Disney, their memories of the movies proving to be as strong as those of the material goods. In the interviews only one student described a vague uneasiness with what she described as 'sad as it may seem,' Disney is 'a really big part of American culture' (JO03).

As one student said, 'Disney – how could you not like it?'

Tucson, Arizona: another snapshot

Located in the southwest, Arizona shares borders with California, Nevada, Utah, Texas, and the Mexican state of Sonora. The terrain is rugged, with mountain forests in the north and sparse deserts punctuated by mountain ranges in the south. Approximately 4.5 million people live in Arizona, making it the 21st most populous state. In the last five years, a population boom has made Arizona one of the fastest-growing states in the nation. Arizona also boasts a highly diverse population: 68 percent non-Hispanic whites; 22 percent Hispanics (the fastest-growing identity group); 6 percent Native American (various nations); 3 percent non-Hispanic blacks; and 2 percent Asians. Most of Arizona's population (88 percent) lives in urban areas, with the largest concentrations in the southern section of the state, first in the Phoenix metropolitan region and then in Tucson.

In terms of the market value of its goods and services, Arizona ranks 26th, with a gross state product in excess of $74 billion; it is 35th in both per capita income ($20,489) and median household income ($30,863) (Morgan *et al.*, 1997). In other comparisons, however, Arizona does not do well. Overall, wages are lower in the state than in the U.S.A. generally. Household incomes (either per capita or median) generally reach 87 to 90 percent of national levels. Among the 50 states, Arizona ranks in the bottom ten in terms of funding for education and in the top fifteen for residents without health insurance (14 percent). While 16 percent of Arizona's total population and 24 percent of its school-age children live in poverty, only 7 percent of Arizonans receive public aid.[5] This reflects a combination of chronic economic underdevelopment (particularly on the many native reservations in the state) and power blocs dominated by conservative and reactionary elites, who harbor hostility towards organized labor, social safety nets, and public schools.

Arizona's economy from the first Spanish incursion in 1539 to the end of World War II in 1948 was largely based on the exportation of cattle, cotton, and copper. In the Cold War period, the federal government extended the number and size of its military bases in Arizona, providing employment for some civilians and incomes for local businesses. Other growth industries were found in tourism, renting winter residences, retail operations, and building housing estates for retirees moving to Arizona. In the 1990s, economic growth was centered in telemarketing, business services, light manufacturing, construction of up-market housing, and administrative and support services.

Arizona's political and economic center is Phoenix, which is also the seat of Maricopa County. The Phoenix metropolitan area has all the earmarks of a major American city: an international airport, sports arenas, museums with significant collections, a public university, cross-town freeways, poor public transportation, air pollution, etc. Historically, the state legislature has paid more attention to Maricopa County than any other county.

About 125 miles to the south lies the city of Tucson, the seat of Pima County. Tucson is located about 50 miles from the U.S.–Mexico border. The nearest urban center in Mexico is Hermisillo, approximately 150 miles from the border, in the State of Sonora. This makes Tucson an important retail center for southern Arizona and northern Sonora.

Although the residential demographics are similar, Phoenix and Tucson are opposites in terms of appearance, tenor, and economics. Tucson's City Council has a reputation (rightly or wrongly) for liberalism. The city's skyline has few skyscrapers. Although adjacent to a freeway, Tucson has no cross-town freeways. Despite redevelopment efforts, downtown and most of central Tucson remain relatively ungentrified – even 'funky.' As in Phoenix, housing developments for the well-to-do sprawl across the foothills of the four mountain ranges encircling Tucson. Unlike Phoenix, Tucson's public university is located in the city's central district.

The 'brickyard,' as locals call the University of Arizona, recalls universities built in the Midwest: multistoried, brick buildings with big windows line a long quadrangle planted with grass. At one end of the quad is the university's original wooden building (the only territorial-style edifice on campus); at the other end, a monumental abstract sculpture resembling clothespins. Over the years, new buildings have been added – usually brick, always multistoried, and typically with much glass and no shade. The campus' horticulture mixes non-native trees and grasses with cacti and mesquite trees. Numerous parking lots and structures dot the campus. The resulting look is distinctive, but hardly Hollywood's vision of university life or of southwestern architecture. The university enrolls about 35,000 students annually, with out-of-state students coming primarily from California.

Adjacent to the university is a small 'campus town' retail area; within walking distance is the Fourth Avenue shopping district. Both are dominated by local establishments, among them bars, eateries, travel agencies, barber shops, boutiques, and record shops. While the national chain, The Gap, has opened a clothing store in the campus town, neither shopping area has a grocery store or drugstore owned by a national chain.

Tuning in: Disney media in Tucson

Because of its distance from Phoenix and its rugged terrain, Tucson is relatively insulated from Phoenix-based broadcasting. Yet, like any other medium-sized market, Tucson's media are integrated into the national media system. To describe this, we briefly sketch Disney's media presence in exhibition venues, then in retail outlets.

In Tucson, television can mean broadcast, cable, or satellite operations. The city has nine broadcast stations: six affiliated with national, commercial networks (KGUN-9 with Disney's ABC); two with Spanish-language networks; and one with the non-profit public broadcasting system. Technical peculiarities in the U.S. television system give stations allocated channels 2 through 12 an advantage in signal strength and receivability, which accrues to the Disney/ABC, General Electric/NBC, and PBS affiliates.

As in most cities, the owner of Tucson's local cable operation has been a horizontally integrated, nationally oriented company. The current owner, Cox Cable, offers several subscription packages. The least expensive package (currently $13.69 per month) provides the nine local stations, seven public service/access channels, ten commercially programed channels (four of which share an allocation), a shopping channel, and a channel listing shows currently running. For $16.57 more, the second package adds 27 commercial channels, including six connected to Disney: A&E, ESPN, ESPN2, History, Lifetime, and the Disney Channel. This is the most typical level of subscription, which means a monthly bill of approximately $36 (when various minor charges are added), resulting in an annual cost of approximately $432. For an extra $10 monthly fee, subscribers can gain access to 22 digital channels, including Disney's ESPN News and ESPN Classic.[6]

Providing a semblance of competition for Cox is People's Choice satellite television, which carries the nine broadcast stations, 20 basic cable channels, 3 premium channels, and 3 pay-per-view channels. People's Choice offers Disney's local affiliate and five Disney owned or co-owned channels (A&E, Disney, ESPN 1, ESPN 2, Lifetime). Costs are similar.

Tucson has an unusual number of movie theaters: two art houses, one multi-screen drive-in, six first-run multiplexes, and four second-run multiplexes. First-run multiplexes are in or near the town's four malls and so follow the tendency to build new developments far from the downtown or central districts. Except for the smaller art house, all theaters show films owned by Disney, but only the national chains show films with the Walt Disney imprimatur. Films are released in Tucson only slightly later than in Phoenix. Typically, a single title will run on multiple screens and in all first-run multiplexes. This makes each new Disney animation available at each first-run multiplex.

In video rental, the Tucson market is dominated by two national chains: Blockbuster (eleven stores) and Hollywood Video (eight stores). But even in the locally owned store (Casa Video) that specializes in foreign, independent, and experimental films, videos with the Walt Disney signature are heavily featured. At Casa Video, renting Truffaut's *Jules et Jim* or Sayles' *Matewan* is as easy as renting *The Lion King*. Disney videos are sold in various national retail chains, including department stores like Target, specialty stores like Sun Coast Video, and grocery stores like Albertsons. Other Disney media – books, magazines, recorded music, and computer games – are similarly available in stores run by local merchants and national chains like Borders, Barnes and Noble, and The Wherehouse.

However, national chains have a significant advantage over local media retailers. Much of the media product that Disney ships to retailers is tied to the release of its animated films. Coordinating national release dates with the saturation of local markets becomes particularly important and a limited number of deals with national chains deliver that saturation efficiently. With a single deal, Disney can ensure the media products coordinated with the animation will saturate local markets across the nation and thereby promote the new animation while earning independent revenues. The same is true in terms of non-media merchandise. We turn to that in our next section.

Malling it: Disney does Tucson

In 1996, four shopping malls operated in Tucson, but only one, Tucson Mall, had the occupancy rates and look of a modern, urban mall. Both Time Warner and Disney opened stores in the Tucson Mall. Six department stores served to anchor the mall: three mid-market retailers (Sears, J. C. Penney, Mervyn's) and three upscale retailers (Dillard's, Robinsons-May, Macys), with numerous specialty shops filling the space between. Taking Tucson Mall as the site of our primary observations, Meehan's graduate students entered the stores and recorded the product type, price, and country of origin for merchandise connected to *The Hunchback of Notre Dame*.[7] Although these systematic observations occurred after the peak of *Hunchback* merchandising, 320 different products were identified and that list closely approximated lists compiled earlier in the summer.[8]

Our observations confirmed that *Hunchback* merchandise was everywhere. Up-market department stores, mid-market department stores, and many specialty stores offered *Hunchback* products as well as other Disney merchandise. The same Esmeralda dress could be bought in both the anchors and at the Disney Store; the same *Hunchback* T-shirt was offered in the anchors as well as in gift shops. Small stores specializing in greetings cards, paper goods, candy, books, recorded music, pre-recorded videos, toys, etc. offered numerous *Hunchback* items as well as other Disney items. The Disney Store expanded on these offerings, stocking *Hunchback* merchandise that was only available through Disney's own retail operations. Given Disney's promotional agreement with McDonald's, the McDonald's in the mall had been decorated with *Hunchback* streamers and promotional displays. It offered special *Hunchback* meals with *Hunchback* toys and served all meals with *Hunchback* place mats, napkins, paper cups, etc. In contrast, *Hunchback* or other Disney merchandise was noticeably absent in mid-sized, up-market clothiers – Eddie Bauer, The Gap, Miller's Outpost, etc. – and in the Disney Store's immediate rival, the Warner Bros. store. Still, to most shoppers walking through Tucson's main mall, Disney merchandise would be ubiquitous.

Some differences arose when we repeated these observations for *Hercules* merchandise.[9] Again, the same licensed clothing, leather goods, jewelry, toys, bed linens, decorative items, and trinkets were offered in Sears, J. C. Penney, and Mervyn's. Again, most of the small shops carried *Hercules* merchandise; McDonald's promoted the movie, and the Disney Store foregrounded Hercules as the newest hero in its galaxy of characters. However, the three up-market department stores joined the up-market clothiers in eschewing *Hercules* merchandise. When queried, clerks explained that you could buy Disney merchandise in Sears. We interpreted this as an attempt to preserve a distinction between up-market and mid-market stores, as well as a reaction to the Disney–Sears contract restricting the Winnie the Pooh product line to Sears for the August–September back-to-school retail season.

The general ubiquity of *Hunchback* and *Hercules* merchandise was confirmed in secondary observations of products in chain stores, whether general retailers like Target and KMart, or targeted retailers like Toys 'R' Us. Across these stores, the same merchandise was heavily featured in similar departments. Indeed, we noted the presence of Disney's non-media products in almost any national retail operation. Even grocery stores had displays of merchandise related to *The Hunchback* or *Hercules*: toys, cups, shampoo, key-rings, paper goods, ice-cream novelties, and similar objects promoted the films to grocery shoppers. The ubiquity of Disney merchandise extended to campus, including merchandise sold in the university bookstore. With a McDonald's restaurant in the Student Union, a second McDonald's within walking distance, and a third several blocks away, students could easily acquire the toys, figures, and cups that promoted *Hunchback* and *Hercules*. In the local swap meet, vendors offered a mix of licensed and unlicensed merchandise, ranging from piñatas to T-shirts, emblazoned with characters from *Hunchback*, *Hercules*, and 'classic' Disney animations.[10]

Overall, then, our observations confirm the impression that Disney merchandise saturates retail operations targeting the average shopper, especially that merchandise connected to specific theatrical animations. The absence of *Hercules* products in up-market department stores, given Disney's contract with Sears, suggests that retail saturation has both advantages and drawbacks. A constant presence may make a product line or brand name less special, more common – perhaps even slightly 'down-market.'

Responding to Disney: fantasy, fun, goodness, and happiness

That concern seems less pressing when we review the questionnaire and interview data for Tucson, as Disney has clearly been part of our 41 students' lives.[11] These were the students enrolled in Meehan's upper-division class on commercial intertextuality in spring 1997. No Disney characters, movies, or television programs were discussed in the class. In demographic terms, the class was fairly typical of the University of Arizona. More women than men were enrolled (60 percent versus 40 percent); the average age was 22 years old, although the age span ranged from 20 to 40. Despite some diversity in national origin and self-described identity (1 each born in Chile, Ireland, and Korea; 1 each self-identified as Asian, black, Jewish, or mixed; 3 self-identified as Hispanic), 40 students were U.S. citizens and 33 self-identified as white. All students were either majors or minors in Media Arts.

These students recalled their contacts with Disney products starting at the average age of 3.18 years. Reacting to a scale where 1 indicated 'no contact' and 7 'much contact,' students reported most contact as a child (average score 5.22), less as a teenager (4.24), and more as a young adult (4.85). These averages, however, suggest that students did not remember being inundated with Disney goods, given that a score of 4 is the neutral response on this scale. When asked to indicate their feelings about Disney on a similar scale (1 was 'strongly liked,' 7 'strongly disliked') students were more neutral than positive or negative. They remembered liking Disney most as children (2.1), less as teenagers (3.2), and least as adults (3.54). For these respondents, Disney products and services were part of their life cycle. Disney was and remains a constant, though not overwhelming, presence. Well liked in childhood, Disney is now regarded somewhat fondly and rather more often than in their teenage years.

While no student had visited EuroDisney or Tokyo Disneyland, 40 students (98 percent) had been to one of the U.S. theme parks: 88 percent to Disneyland in California; 54 percent to Disney World in Florida; 44 percent to Epcot Center; and 22 percent to Disney-MGM in Florida. Proximity to Arizona may account for the popularity of the original Disneyland. While at a theme park, 44 percent stayed at a Disney hotel.

As might be expected in a Media Arts class, 100 percent had seen Disney films; 100 percent reported watching television programs made and distributed by Disney in venues other than the Disney Channel; 95 percent watched the Disney Channel available over Tucson's cable system as a basic channel; 95 percent and 93 percent reported owning, respectively, Disney books and records. While 83 percent reported renting Disney videos, only 68 percent reported buying them. This may be indicative of the 'kid stuff' status accorded to many Disney products. For example, Disney educational materials were owned by 73 percent, magazines by 49 percent, video games played by 46 percent, comic books read by 42 percent, the Disney home page visited by 24 percent, and 2 percent (one student) joined a Disney Club.

In contrast, 95 percent had visited a Disney Store. While 98 percent reported having Disney merchandise, 85 percent had received such merchandise as gifts and 73 percent had given such goods as gifts. The most popular items were toys: 85 percent reported owning toys; 78 percent clothing; 76 percent Mickey Mouse ears; 42 percent Disney artwork; 39 percent owned household items as well as Mickey Mouse watches; and 34 percent owned Disney jewelry. Although students reported contact with an average of four items without prompting, that average number rose to sixteen after students completed the checklist of product types. Overall, then, these 41 students would seem well acquainted and still involved with Disney media, theme parks, and merchandise.

Students' responses to the unprompted request to describe Disney presented no clear trends. Forty-four terms were offered, with minimal agreement that Disney could be described as fun (8 or 19 percent) or happy (5 or 12 percent). When offered the list of descriptors, our 41 respondents agreed unanimously that Disney promoted fantasy, fun, happiness, and good over evil. They strongly endorsed Disney as promoting love and romance (98 percent), imagination and family (95 percent), and magic and bravery (93 percent). Weaker ties were registered between Disney and optimism (88 percent), physical beauty

(83 percent), and technological progress (81 percent). To these respondents, Disney barely encouraged a work ethic (68 percent), respect for differences (63 percent), individualism (61 percent), or patriotism (61 percent). While 56 percent found that Disney promoted patriarchy, 37 percent identified thriftiness and 34 percent racism as part of the Disney vision. Finally, 59 percent found Disney uniquely American. The interviews shed some light on these findings.[12]

A closer view: the interviews

Five undergraduates who completed the questionnaires volunteered to be interviewed. All were women; one was an Hispanic born in Chile who had returned to the university when her daughter was old enough to attend school. The others were traditional students – two in the honors program and one self-identified as Jewish. One had traveled in Europe, another in Israel. Because of Meehan's previous history with these students, a research assistant conducted the interviews. As we contemplated the interview data, we used Wasko's (2001) typology of Disney audiences, which identifies as extremes Disney fanatics and Disney rejecters.

In terms of Wasko's typology of Disney audiences, the group included three Disney resisters (R1, R2, R3) and two Disney consumers (C1, C2). Interviewees did not include anyone with a strong emotional connection (positive or negative) who might go out of their way to express their feelings about Disney. For the resisters, Disney animations and products were problematic as both cultural expressions and commodities. Disney's treatments of gender, ethnicity, and race were particularly troubling given the company's perceived ability to influence young children. For the consumers, such items were inescapable given the nature of American culture and familial traditions. Consumers sorted the films into two categories: artistic animations with positive role models and mere cartoons that were harmless even when negative role models appeared. In terms of merchandising, the resisters worried that peer pressure on children and children's pressures on parents would lead to arguments and also teach children to value hyper-consumerism and overcommercialism. In contrast, the consumers believed that children needed to own some Disney items and go to Disneyland as a natural part of growing up in the U.S.A. They believed that parents could deal with children's requests through reasoning – an interesting claim, because C1 is a parent – especially when merchandise was too expensive, poorly made, or stereotypical. With resister and consumer as our guiding structure, we now review the main topics pursued in the interviews.

Consumers: the interviews

The two consumers both found Disney to be part of growing up. As a child growing up in Chile, C1's favorite character had been Donald Duck. She had been shocked to discover that Mickey Mouse outshone Donald when her family moved to the United States. Similarly, C2 recounted the story of her parents decorating her room with Winnie the Pooh gear when she was a young girl. While her parents hadn't grown up with such Disney characters, they had given her that experience, which she intended to share when she had children of her own. Both C1 and C2 had visited Disneyland as children. C1 had had a wonderful and memorable time, while C2's trip had been ill-timed ('the second busiest day of the year'), leading to a nine-hour visit in which they took eight rides. Annual visits with her church's youth group changed C2's impressions of Disneyland: with only 2000 people in the park, the rides had a quick turnaround that satisfied everyone. When describing her daughter's trip to Disneyland, C1 clearly communicated the delight that the two had shared in the Magic Kingdom.

Both C1 and C2 demonstrated considerable familiarity with the titles and contents of Disney's recent animations. Perhaps more cautious because of her daughter, C1 found some of the recent animations too violent or otherwise inappropriate for a very young child. Stating that she would love to have the 'full collection' of Disney videotapes, C1 nevertheless purchased only those that she found acceptable. She was particularly outspoken about *Pocahontas*, which she saw as stereotyping Native Americans despite Pocahontas' portrayal as a relatively strong woman who refused to abandon her home and sail away with the English hero. C2 was less troubled by such representations, suggesting that Disney had made a poor decision in selecting the figure of Pocahontas, as the story itself provided too much opportunity to offend people. While C2 thought the company tried 'too hard' to integrate its films by adding people of color, overall she believed that Disney did a good job when it followed the logic of the original story:

> the more they try, the more they botch at it. I think they should just go with it … if a character, like for instance, in *Aladdin*, the characters were obviously from India … so obviously that was what their skin color was going to be and that was what their facial features were going to be, and what not. And I think they just had to run with it … I mean like it wasn't like 'oh, we gotta like try to please everyone – have this shade of darkness so that it pleases African Americans, this shade of lightness so that it pleases the whites' … I think the less they try with it, the better they'll do.

In terms of gender, both agreed that the new animations presented

319

heroines more positively than the old ones. Female characters were more independent, less passive; drawings were more realistic. However, C1 worried that Disney's buxom heroines like Esmeralda could encourage the same unrealistic expectations about female bodies as the Barbie doll. Overall, then, C1 tended to judge Disney's treatment of race, gender, and ethnicity on a film-by-film basis; C2 believed that, when Disney sought to entertain, it did a good job in providing positive role models, whether it meant to or not.

Merchandise was more problematic for C1 than C2, partly because C1 dealt with frequent requests for Disney merchandise, clearly ran her household on a budget, and wanted her daughter to be a somewhat critical consumer. For example, C1's concerns about the distorted body images meant that she did not buy Barbie dolls for her daughter. However, having explained this decision, C1 would allow her daughter to accept Barbie dolls as gifts and to play with them. Similarly, when refusing her daughter's request for Disney merchandise, C1 gave her reasons for denying the request (for example, expense, body image) so that her daughter would understand why she could not have a certain object. For C2, her acquisition of Disney merchandise was limited to gifts from family and friends, who occasionally bought her Winnie the Pooh merchandise. Such gifts were not systematic, so C2 had not become a *de facto* collector of Pooh products. She regarded them as essentially harmless and, for families, unavoidable. C2 found Disney products to be everywhere and regarded them as a natural part of childhood; she saw no reason for parents to be cautious in selecting products or exposing their children to Disney. C1 offered parents more guarded advice: pick what's best, leave the rest. After all, both agreed, Disney was part of being an American. C2 went further, describing Disney as

> very symbolic of how American culture is; it's a dominating type of thing. ...You have no choice, like I said before, but to do something Disney-ish. But ... it's the fun part of America. Everybody comes from other countries to go to Disneyland or Disney World....There's the Grand Canyon ... [and there's] ... Disneyland ... and it's all encompassed together as being America ... It's the American dream ... It's something to achieve. ...

Resisters: the interviews

Of the three resisters, R1 and R3 were honors students and R1 self-identified as Jewish. These students did not reject Disney automatically; nor did they avoid all contact with Disney products. Instead, they shared a sense of unease, particularly with Disney's representations of gender, race, and ethnicity given their perception of Disney's strong influence over children in their formative years. Both R1 and R2 had visited Disneyland as children and later as adults. Although acknowledging that it was fun, R1 stated that she had felt Disneyland 'really wasn't a place for people like me' and that the park didn't seem to admit 'Hispanics or black people' at that time. For R2, Disneyland was a place for her extended family to visit and then separate, so that 'kids could do kid things and adults, adult things.' In contrast, R3 had not, and actively intended never to, visit Disneyland despite her friends' offers to correct (what they perceived as) this sad state of affairs.

All three resisters expressed grave doubts about Disney's treatment of gender. R2 was the most emphatic, arguing that the Disney heroines taught girls to think of themselves only in terms of the men with whom they might fall in love. The students agreed that the average Disney plot boiled down to an innocent female caught in a bad situation that was not of her choosing, who needed to be rescued. A muscular white man would save her, disposing of the villain and introducing her to her rightful role: namely, as the hero's bride. Other characters only provided comic relief.

For these women, the major change that Disney had made to its heroines was in their body type and bra size: the too thin body with a tiny waist and large breasts *à la* Pocahontas and Esmeralda reminded these interviewees of Barbie dolls. Even if the heroines displayed some independence, they remained trapped inside a distorted, impossible Barbie body. For these students, the repetition and idealization of that body type provided an overwhelmingly negative message to young girls, many of whom would engage in self-destructive behavior in their attempt to emulate these heroines. The importance given to this message by these healthy, trim, young women cannot be overstated.

Similar doubts were voiced regarding Disney's treatment of race and ethnicity. All three commented on racism in the older animations, finding the newer animations to be more subtle in their presentation of ethnic and racial stereotypes. Disney's use of characters from non-European backgrounds was dismissed as 'one-dimensional ... window dressing – "we're PC now" – they put in a little window dressing so they can get money from those people, too' (R3).

Although all three students had received Disney merchandise as gifts, they expressed reservations about exposing children to Disney products. Two were adamant:

Don't do it! (R3)

Don't expose them to Disney when they are younger ... wait until they are old enough to understand, when you explain to them, that a lot of what goes on in Disney films is BS. (R2)

R2 went on to say that she would let her children have Disney toys that could be used in imaginative play (stuffed animals, dolls) but not Disney books, where the readers could 'get slammed with stereotypes and certain ideas.' All three expressed reservations rooted partly in the stereotyped content of the animations and partly in synergistic business practices that they see as typical of Disney. As R3 noted, the products

> seem so innocuous ... but all the commercial tie-ins, all the dealings ... the economic structures that we don't see are the problem ... that's a cute little movie they made there. Let's look at the cute little doll I have with interchangeable clothes. But you have to wonder: where was this made? Who made this? Were they paid a penny a day? What plant got shut down so they could move it to somewhere where they could have cheaper labor, where they could lock them up in rooms and make this cute little doll that you're holding in your hand.

All three suggested that Disney's popularity and current success was tied to the company's longevity and its corporate practices. Students decried Disney's 'commercialism ... that buy-buy-buy attitude ...' (R1), 'corporate greed' (R2), and 'products, merchandise, tie-ins up the wazoo' (R3).

They agreed that Disney was uniquely American, but for reasons far removed from those cited by the consumers. Noting Disney's longevity and mass marketing, R1 suggested that adults' nostalgia for their own childhood was manifested in the purchase of Disney products for children. But she also contextualized that nostalgia and consumption: 'This country is lacking so in culture that [Disney is] something people can hold onto and share and its tradition, and it's something to do with family – which is pretty disturbing.'

In a slightly different vein, R2 characterized both Disney and much of the U.S. population as immature and authoritarian – 'stuck in' simplistic ways of thinking, unable to deal with sexuality, or tolerate differences in lifestyles. R3 stated that Disney's commercialism linked it to the 'American dream of being a consumer, but with quotes around American dream.' When asked if Disney represented the U.S.A., R3 responded: 'God, I hope not ... It doesn't represent my life.'

Yet these students had some pleasant memories associated with Disney. For R1, a lunch-box with Mickey Mouse and some pirates – one of whom was 'bending over and his butt was showing'– afforded much amusement in grammar school. At home, a Mickey Mouse cheese plate provided a family tag line. For R2, visits to Disneyland provided a chance to 'escape into a fantasy world' without the stereotypes and ideology typical of Disney films. As a child, R3 had also found a Mickey Mouse lunch-box amusing and, in high school, had two friends – 'Disney fanatics' – whom she thought rather odd.

Conclusion: unequal peripheries; symbolic ubiquity

This contrast of Athens, Ohio, and Tucson, Arizona, demonstrates clearly that Disney enjoys a symbolic ubiquity in the U.S.A. Similarly, the contrast shows that Disney, like any other nationally oriented retailer or distributor, is present in a local marketplace only to the degree that the local marketplace is integrated into the national system.

While both Athens and Tucson are relatively peripheral in the U.S.A., the two cities are not equally so. This inequality means that Disney is differentially available. Tucson has more direct access, receiving movies and licensed products as a second-tier market while getting broadcast and cablecast simultaneously with the rest of the nation. Athens, however, has a more constricted access. As a market for television, Athens is subsumed by a market centered on a city in another state. Disney movies arrive late in Athens and play for short periods. Athens' residents must either travel in order to buy Disney merchandise or rely on mail order, Internet, and similar impersonal modes of purchase – no wandering the aisles of a Disney Store. Athens is clearly on the fringe despite being a county seat, university town, and an economic highlight of Appalachian Ohio. The deep-seated nature of Athens' peripheral status testifies to the unequal development that exists in the U.S.A. and to capitalism's willingness to simply write off certain places.

Tucson's status indicates the degree to which unequal development is itself an uneven process in the U.S.A. Although Arizona is economically inferior to Ohio overall, Tucson emerges from the comparison as significantly more integrated into the national systems of media and retail sales. Despite differential access to Disney products in physical and technological terms, Disney's symbolic universe extends deep into these peripheries, creating a 'magic kingdom' in which our students assume Disney's presence even when they resist Disney's ideals.

As we have seen, however, resistance is not an option for most students. Their current attitudes towards, and memories of, Disney naturalizes Disney's intellectual property as a central part of a person's life cycle and a family's existence. Parents, grandparents, and family friends naturally provide Disney goods to infants in order to get the child's life off to a good start. Family vacations, media use, and everyday objects naturally involve Disney theme parks, movies, and merchandise. Over time, as a child becomes independent of its family, contact with Disney lessens somewhat as the child gains adult status. The differences between freshmen at Ohio and seniors at Arizona suggest this shift. Those on the verge of graduating – and thereby completing the middle-class rite of passage to adulthood – see themselves as somewhat more sophisticated, though nonetheless enthusiastic about Disney. As they contemplate their future, most imagine that their lives will center on marriage and children, thus returning Disney to the nucleus of their home. For these students, the notion of a happy childhood is firmly imprinted with the Disney trademark.

To what degree can these findings be generalized across American college students and Americans in general? The market study in Athens indicates that, should there be a dearth of the latest merchandise in town, people will seek out Disney products. In Tucson, the market study suggests that secondary retail centers do provide the full complement of Disney product lines. Regardless of the range of media outlets available to a city, Disney media products saturate rental, first-run, broadcast, and cable venues. This contrast between Tucson and Athens is essentially a contrast, respectively, between ease of access and the willingness to seek out access. In either situation, Disney remains constant as an assumed part of American culture and Americans' lives. Disney's symbolic ubiquity remains generally unquestioned, even when the company's marketing raises questions. This creates a peculiar situation in which one can criticize Eisner's synergistic strategies and still perceive the Mickey Mouse watches, Esmeralda dolls, *Hercules* sandals, *Mulan* videos as magical – ad infinitum, ad nauseam. While Disney the company can be exploitative, Disney the merchandise remains innocent, familial, imaginative, and fun. What marketer could ask for anything more?

Notes

1. The economic profile of Ohio and Athens County came from several web-site databases including:

   - http://www.census.gov/ststab/www/states/oh.txt
   - http://www.census.gov/cpcd/www/92profiles/county/3909.TXT
   - http://web.lexis-nexis.com/universe.docu
   - http://www.obes.org/emp_stats/apr00corts.htm
   - http://www.odod.state.oh.us/osr/profiles/PDF/ATHENS.PDF

   The figures in parentheses represent the year of the data.
2. This analysis was carried out in the two major commercial districts in town. The first is a strip of highway on the east side of town about 5 miles from campus, where there are three strip malls with two large name-brand grocery stores, Kroger and Big Bear, and several bulk grocers, the discount stores Ames and KMart, J. C. Penney and the local department store chain, Elder-Beerman. Other stores in the malls are local businesses; Blockbuster Music, CVS (formerly Revco) pharmacy, Radio Shack, Foot Locker, and

Bath and Body are the only national retail chains stores in town. The only toy store was a locally owned business that was located in one of the malls but carried only 'educational' toys; it went out of business within a year.

The second area lies on the fringes of campus and has three bookstores that stock textbooks and supplies for the students, a used bookstore (which closed after the analysis and by the time of this writing), and a small, locally owned Little Professor Bookstore; two card shops (oops, one of those closed too), several record stores that carry mostly used items, two dress shops that feature size 4 (one of which has recently closed), several hairdressers and T-shirt shops, copy shops, bars, and restaurants.

There are other grocery stores, hardware stores, gun shops and the like scattered throughout the town but most people, including students, shop at one of the two major areas.

3. Norma Pecora would like to thank Monica Pombo for her trips to the mall.
4. Norma Pecora would like to thank Mike Newberg for his enthusiasm and interview skills.
5. In contrast, nationally 14 percent of the total population and 19 percent of school-age children live in poverty, while 8 percent of the national population receive public aid. In Ohio, 16 percent of the total population and 17 percent of school-age children live in poverty, but 8 percent receive public aid. For further comparisons, see Morgan *et al.* (1997) and Slater and Davis (1999).
6. Cox has five premium channels for $10.95 each. None of the premium channels are owned by Disney, although theatrical films released under Disney's other imprimaturs play on these channels. Four 'bundles' of digital and premium channels can be added on to the second package, for a total monthly cost ranging from an $43.20 to $66.42.
7. For an analysis of the *Hunchback* merchandise, subcontracting, and sweatshops see James Tracy (1999).
8. Eileen Meehan would like to acknowledge and thank Denise Chaytor, Rick Emrich, Jasmin Proisos, James Tracy, Katheryn Vlesmos, Brian Yecies for the August observations, and Brian Yecies for his assistance in observations over summer.
9. Eileen Meehan would like to acknowledge and thank Anthony Defazio, Joann DiFilippo, Nate Fisher, Derek Frank, Roxanne Green, Maris Hayashi, Chris Kirschenpfadt, Mike Malcomb, Brian McCall, Cristel Russell, and Judy Schultz for their observations.
10. Swap meets are more commonly called flea markets in the U.S.A. The terms refer to places where individuals can rent stalls or spaces and offer their wares for sale. Some of the goods are used (and some stolen); some are made by the seller; some are bought wholesale and sold for prices lower than those charged by retail stores. Much of the merchandise emblazoned with trademarks, logos, or copyrighted characters are unlicensed.
11. Given the odd number of students responding, percentages are rounded off. For example, when one student responded 'yes,' the precise percentage would be 2.4 percent, but is reported here as 2 percent. When

33 responded 'yes,' the precise percentage would be 80.5 percent, but is reported here as 81 percent.

12. Eileen Meehan would like to acknowledge and thank Denise Chaytor for conducting these interviews as part of her research assistantship.

References and other sources

Morgan, K. O., Morgan, S., and Quitno, N. (1997) *State Ranking 1997: A Statistical View of the 50 United States*, 8th edn. Lawrence, KS, Morgan Quitno.

Slater, C. M. and Davis, M. G. (1999) *State Profiles: The Population and Economy of Each US State*. Lanham, MD, Beman Association.

Tracy, J. (1999) 'Whistle while you work,' *Journal of Communication Inquiry*, 23(4) (October): 374–89.

Wasko, J. (2001) *Understanding Disney: The Manufacture of Fantasy*. Cambridge, Polity Press.

PART IV

Conclusions and Directions for Future Research

CHAPTER 15

Dazzled by Disney?
Ambiguity in Ubiquity

JANET WASKO AND EILEEN R. MEEHAN

The Global Disney Audiences Project has only scratched the surface in our attempt to understand the significance of the Disney phenomenon. While it is dangerous and foolish to draw generalized conclusions across cultures, especially based on such limited and narrow samples, the Project's results do tell us quite a lot about Disney's pervasiveness and symbolic ubiquity, as well as the ambiguities and contradictions that exist among Disney audiences.

Disney's pervasiveness: it's (almost) everywhere

It was obvious before we started this research that the Disney company had expanded its global marketing in recent decades. While Disney characters and products have been distributed and recognized in many countries since the early 1930s, the company's more recent corporate expansion has further reinforced the global recognition of the Disney brand. The research not only bolstered these initial suspicions but also provided some convincing evidence of Disney's global pervasiveness.

Perhaps the most telling evidence is the study itself, in which over 1250 respondents in eighteen different countries not only recognized and discussed the Disney brand but also reported a relatively high degree of interaction with the company's products. Access to and use of Disney products by college-educated populations is clearly extensive, to the point of being virtually universal among our respondents. If these groups are indicative of the rest of their nations, and if the range of Disney products and prices are replicated, then we expect that the great majority of populations recognize, have access at least to inexpensive products, and use such materials.

From this perspective, the recognition of Disney seems to be a global phenomenon. Of course, marketing wizards and industry pundits might well respond, 'We could have told you so!' However, this study provides information regarding Disney's presence that is not tainted by the usual distortions associated with commodifying and commercializing the production of information.

From the respondents, we confirmed that Disney is typically first experienced at a young age (first contact was generally between 4 and 5 years of age), and the experience is usually positive. More specifically, the questionnaires indicated that nearly 98 percent of the respondents had seen a Disney film, nearly 82 percent were familiar with Disney books, and around 79 percent had experienced Disney television programs and merchandise. In addition, we found that people generally tend to underestimate their exposure to Disney products, selectively reporting only a few examples until confronted with a specific list of the many Disney products and services that are available.

While the respondents generally felt most positive (or 'liked') Disney products at a younger age, by and large they still like Disney products as young adults and continue to come into contact (or consume) these products. Further, they generally imagine a future in which they will introduce their own children to Disney products. In this way, most of our respondents incorporate Disney into their life cycles, treating the products as naturally attractive to children, enjoyable enough for adults, and important parts of the happy childhood that all parents want for their children.

Of course, there are certainly variations in the familiarity with and popularity of Disney in different countries. The most common experiences are with films and television programing, and various kinds of merchandise. However, some countries and geographic regions have incorporated Disney into cultural rituals, such as the ritualized reading of Disney comics in Scandinavia, or visits to theme parks for Brazilians marking their passage into adulthood. But even where Disney products are not as pervasive or ubiquitous, respondents report a sense that 'Disney products are everywhere.'

This general sense of Disney's ubiquity is undiminished even when Disney products are less available: whether due to undeveloped markets within a country (as in Appalachia in the U.S.A.), national underdevelopment of markets (as in Greece and South Africa), or continental underdevelopment (as in Africa generally), respondents in such areas not only recognized the Disney brand but also demonstrated familiarity with the products. As one of Simon Burton's South African respondents explained, 'Everyone has heard of it. Everyone has a Disney product.'

This theme surfaced routinely in the national profiles indicating, as Ingunn Hagen notes, 'children's everyday lives are saturated with Disney products.' In this sense, Disney's drive for corporate synergy has succeeded in creating a commercial intertext that connects Disney characters, stories, and merchandise across all media, saturating not only markets but lives. This constitutes Disney's symbolic ubiquity and raises questions about the relationship between this ubiquity, individual consciousness, and culture.

Some respondents and researchers are troubled by those questions. Respondents generally used two tactics to resolve such concerns. Some divided Disney into the good provider of fun and the bad overcommercializer. While enjoying the good Disney, they criticize the bad Disney's high prices and merchandising. Others sought comfort in the possibility of a general backlash against Disney, vowing to exercise selectivity in purchasing Disney products, or displaying uncertainty about introducing children to Disney. Such reflections formed the basis for the ambiguous or even negative positions taken by some respondents to Disney. Overall, however, the multitude think positively about Disney, as well as quite a few ardent fans who were definitely dazzled.

Love it or hate it? Attitudes about Disney

The multitude not only favors Disney but also often considers as taboo any serious examination – never mind any criticism – of Disney's meaning and impact. Resistance to study or criticism of Disney was especially marked in the U.S.A. and Japan. This strong affirmation may well lie in the connection between Disney and childhood – a connection that confers a special status to Disney products. Overall, Disney was linked to strong and positive memories of childhood, family, and ritualized activities – even by those who criticized the company. For Americans, of course, Disney's role in childhood is legendary. However, this also is true for children in other countries. In both Norway and Denmark, where printed material is especially popular, Disney is part of the ritual of reading, as well as being associated with the Christmas holidays, when a special Disney program was broadcast each year. Thus, Hagen describes how, for Norwegian adults, Disney is associated with 'an annual ritual embroidered with nostalgic feelings,' as well as being integrated into children's everyday life in various ways. In Brazil, visiting Walt Disney World represents another kind of ritual – a rite of passage – for some Brazilian teenagers. While in Mexico, birthday parties are often celebrated with a plethora of piñatas, decorations and presents with Disney themes. Along the same lines, in Greece, some respondents thought there was something wrong with those not 'touched by Disney films,' and view Disney products as necessary for children.

Whether it was the link between the *Donald* books and grand-parents in Denmark, birthday parties with Disney themes and presents in Mexico, or the family fun experienced at one of the theme parks for Brazilians, the association with childhood and memories seems to place Disney in a special, almost sacred, category.[1] This connection with childhood may seem obvious given Disney's product line. But this association also played into the contradictions and ambiguities that were evident in many cases, as will be discussed further below.

There are other reasons why people think positively about Disney. The products often are viewed as high-quality and well-made entertainment. Many respondents told us that Disney products were especially appropriate and positive for children, and even explained how they were harmless and often educational. These students essentially argued the case for using Disney products based on rational appeals of quality, innocence, and educational value, thus separating themselves from those who embraced Disney because of its significance in familial rituals.

Others taking the approach of the rational consumer found Disney's intense marketing problematic. They were troubled by the commerci-alism that transformed a Disney film into a product line and that touted the product line over every available medium. Often they described Disney products and the Disney parks as overpriced and too expensive for the average family. Some ascribed the success and popularity of Disney to the company's marketing, which was described as pervasive and effective. They connected such marketing power with concerns about overcommercialization, aggressive mer-chandising, and expense.

While some of these respondents separated the good Disney that provides us with imaginative fun from the bad Disney that saturates markets with merchandise, others rejected Disney, critiquing both the company and its products. Researchers offer various explanations for this, attributing it to 'adult reflections on childhood' (Hagen), or respondents 'constructing their own identities' (Buckingham). Never-theless, the negative responses or forms of resistance to the Disney 'magic' are worth further explanation.[2]

For some Disney resisters, the company epitomized all that is negative about the U.S.A.: commercialism, materialism, mass produc-tion. The groups interviewed by Buckingham were especially cynical, as they discussed Disney as a 'bad object,' consistent with American culture and consumerism. Indeed, many respondents agreed that Disney teaches consumerism, which encourages conflicts between parent and child. Some interviewees recalled how they themselves had pressured their parents for Disney products. In other groups, respondents discussed the difficulty of dealing with the demands of their children (or, in the Tucson interviews, the demands of children under their care) for expensive Disney merchandise. These generally negative discussions were balanced by some of the Greek respondents, for instance, who observed that other forces are more responsible for a consumerist society, and that Disney should not be blamed.

Besides criticizing Disney's corporate synergy and pricing, many resisters found fault with both Disney's narratives and its depiction of women. The moral content of Disney's tales was often described as heavy-handed and the treatment of romance stereotypical. This was especially important in the depiction of female protagonists, whose primary tasks were usually centered on romantic relationships. Adding in the tendency for recent Disney heroines to resemble Mattel's Barbie dolls, some of those interviewed found a negative subtext to Disney heroines. They noted that, although Esmeralda or Pocahontas were supposed to be more independent than classic heroines like Cinderella or Snow White, the Barbie-body type and emphasis on romance undercut any independence the new heroines might aspire to and relegated them to the status of sexual object. This suggests that some respondents recognized that Disney's new heroines were supposed to be read in a certain way – as independent women – but resisted that reading. Instead, they deconstructed the apparently progressive message of Esmeralda's or Pocahontas' independence to discover the same old sexism lurking underneath as a latent message. These resisters read against the grain, not to produce an oppositional reading, but rather to uncover an oppressive subtext. In this process, we may see some clues regarding the degrees of freedom and the constraints of cultural expectation that shape the work of resistant audiences as they negotiate a text.

Balancing this resistance, however, were respondents who also recognized problems with Disney's moralistic tales and stereotyped heroines, but who avoided criticizing Disney by arguing that the company was simply reflecting human nature or social institutions. While strong resisters easily critiqued the company's current operations, they became more ambiguous when recalling their own childhood experiences with Disney, assessing its ultimate value through that lens of personal memory and shared experience, as we shall see in the next section.

Disney's meanings: symbolic ubiquity and ambiguity

One of the strongest findings of the study was the commonly shared understanding of what Disney means. Whether or not respondents liked Disney, they generally agreed on the core values represented in the company's products. As reported in Chapter 2, over 93 percent of the respondents agreed that Disney promoted fun and fantasy, while over 88 percent agreed on happiness, magic and good over evil. Other terms that ranked very high (in the 80 percent range) were family, imagination, and love/romance. In other words, as Pecora and Meehan observe in their chapter, Disney represents a kind of symbolic ubiquity – the core values and ideas that it promotes are understood similarly everywhere.

Unsurprisingly, these are the same values that the Disney company itself reinforces in its marketing campaigns. As Jacques Guyot observed in his chapter on France, the consistency of the respondents' identification of Disney values 'confirms that Disney's marketing policy is well adjusted to its target.' Another example of specific targeting is represented in Raul Reis' description of the 'Temporada Mágica' campaign that encourages Brazilians to visit the Florida theme parks.

Alternatively, one might argue that submersion in Disney's symbolic universe as a child, and incorporation of that symbolic universe into many people's life cycle, effectively teaches people what Disney ought to mean, regardless of people's acceptance of or resistance to Disney's message. The contrast here is between interpretations that emphasize Disney's targeting of consumers and interpretations that emphasize enculturation via submersion and constant reinforcement.

A similarly high level of agreement was found in respondents' ability to articulate the classic Disney formula. Respondents agreed not only on the abstract core values but also on the details of narrative structure and character types – that is, on the semiotic structures and functions undergirding multiple Disney animations over the generations. They also recognized Disney's attempts to tweak its formulae. Overall, expectations about Disney films were quite consistent – beautiful heroines seeking romance, brave heroes, evil villains, and happy endings with good triumphing over evil and the chaste couple united. Our respondents are strongly disposed to read Disney texts in these terms, regardless of an individual's particular feelings about the company.

These results raise questions about claims that audiences freely negotiate meanings or engage the texts regardless of the semiotics of the text. Our respondents suggest that they are constrained by the text and by their expectations of the Disney brand. To follow Stuart Hall's model, our respondents clearly decode the overt messages encoded in Disney's products. In fact, our respondents expect to find those messages – an expectation that, when met, reinforces either their affirmation of or their resistance to Disney.

These seemingly universal expectations and predispositions, how-ever, are not entirely determinative of respondents' readings. The individual national profiles show some variations across different cultures, as illustrated by the numerous examples of contradictions and ambiguities discussed by the project's researchers.

For instance, Reis identified a major contradiction between Brazilians' love of the Disney theme parks and the rather negative attitudes about Disney in general. Similarly in Norway, Hagen reports a number of critical comments about the company, as represented in many respondents' ambivalent postures: 'they love the entertainment, the fantastic characters, the imagination, the fun – the innocent dreamworld of Disney. While most of them continue to take part in "the wonderful world of Disney," they also condemn the business of Disney.'

As noted previously, some respondents pointed to differences between the traditional Disney and the 'new Disney.' The classic Disney was often associated with the image of Walt Disney and a company that was more interested in providing entertainment and pleasure. In contrast, the 'new Disney' represented commercialism and the ugly side of American capitalism. For the French, the contrast represents a fundamental opposition between 'the world of creation and the logic of business.' Thus, the 'new Disney' – with its emphasis on synergy across media and heavy merchandising – is seen as the 'merchandisation of culture,' and is rejected.

In some countries, Disney's appropriations of classic folk and fairy tales elicited negative reactions. But even though some respondents were insulted by representations of their own culture, as in France and Greece, they were forgiving and even amused by other Disneyfied stories and characters from other cultures.

In another variation, some of the respondents from Korea reported that they wanted to like their own country's cultural products, but they could not 'resist the familiarity and pleasure of Disney.' As Kim and Lee report, even though they may suffer from 'guilty consciences from consuming Disney products,' they still thought positively about them.

While the responses of Mexican students were overwhelmingly positive towards Disney, Molina detected a form of distancing due to the traditional Mexican nationalism in relation to American culture. It was as though they wanted to think about Disney as separate from American culture or the U.S.A.

The question of whether or not Disney is viewed as uniquely

American or universal provides another example of these contradictory attitudes. Overall, nearly 50 percent of the respondents across
cultures thought Disney 'promotes and represents a vision of
American culture that is distinct from other cultures,' with close to 28
percent disagreeing. Interestingly, a good number of participants in
the survey did not respond to this question. While many were adamant
that Disney is universal, in other situations, those interviewed
explained that Disney products and characters seemed to represent
their own culture, as in Drotner's discussion of 'Donald as Danish.'[3]

Clearly, then, respondents are engaging and negotiating Disney
texts, but within the contexts of national cultures, ritualized use of
media, expectations and predispositions learned from Disney about
Disney texts, and the relative degree of critical consciousness achieved
by individuals. This suggests that although some negotiation occurs, it
takes place within the intersection of the political economy of the
mediated text, the national context within which that text plays
economic as well as cultural roles, the cultural practices of a society
and its social units (like families), and finally individual consciousness.
This indicates that negotiation is quite diverse and often complex,
requiring an interdisciplinary approach that integrates political
economy, cultural studies, sociology, and anthropology. While each
approach is crucial, no one approach is enough.

Disney's influence: cultural identity/imperialism revisited

Beyond the points that emerged directly from the questionnaires and
interviews, the project researchers pursued inquiries in six related
areas: cultural industries, consumer culture, Americanization, global
culture, cultural identity and cultural imperialism.

Cultural industries

Disney's dominance of children's entertainment in many parts of the
world has affected indigenous media and cultural production by
setting Disney products as the standard by which local and regional
productions are judged. Virginia Nightingale in her chapter on
Australia, and Sophia Kaitatzi-Whitlock in the chapter on Greece, detail
how the popularity of the Disney model of entertainment has
influenced the definition of entertainment in their countries in many
ways, leading to significant economic and cultural consequences.
Other authors point to the dominance of Disney products in their
country, where there is little choice other than Disney for children's

entertainment. In Korea, for instance, Disney was preferred over other similar entertainment, such as Japanese products that were considered 'morally debased,' and local Korean animation that is regarded as 'uninteresting and inferior.' Of course, this has had economic implications for national and local cultural industries, as Disney and other transnational companies drain local economies of resources (as noted, especially, in the chapters on Greece and Korea).

Consumer culture

Disney's relationship to consumer culture involves not only its own promotional activities and synergistic practices but also respondents' ritualized cultural practices and children's lobbying of parents and family for Disney goods. On the one hand, the company aggressively promotes its core values through its image advertising. Disney is similarly aggressive in promoting each of its animation-based product lines over long periods of time. Merchandise precedes the release of films, continues through the film's run in theaters, and reappears with each repackaging of the animation or recycling of its elements. These corporate activities promote consumption by defining happiness, fun, romance, magic, etc. as the outcome of purchasing a Mickey Mouse watch or a Tarzan action figure. The image and product advertising ultimately teaches that buying a brand name results in the satisfaction of a human being's most basic emotional and social needs.

On the other hand, ritual and interpersonal practices associated with Disney products also promote consumerism. This is seen most clearly through the ritualized consumption of Disney products during national or religious holidays, at family events celebrating the life cycle (birthdays, for example), or during peer-based events celebrating inclusion in the group. It is notable that even resisters who complained about the abundance of Disney merchandise and the negative aspects of overconsumption often were Disney consumers. The processes of being human and moving through the socially defined life cycle from child to adolescent to parent becomes intimately linked with Disney products. Buying the Disney brand in order to complete the ritual transforms rites of passage into rites of purchase.

Thus, consumerism is again linked to the national definition of being Danish, Mexican, American, Korean, etc. The impact of familial and cultural rituals plus aggressive advertising and merchandising is evident in our respondents' memories of themselves as children lobbying parents and family for Disney goods. Immersed in cultures that have been or are becoming wholly commercialized – and that are being fully integrated into a world economy dominated by the capitalist First World – children learn that being human means owning

337

name brands. Disney's historical and current business strategies have positioned it to exploit the opportunities presented by a globalized economy dependent on a commercialized media system for the promotion of consumption. These dynamics militate for global consumerism and for the dominant definition of one's humanity to be one's purchases.

Americanization

Undoubtedly, Disney contributes to consumerism, but does it contribute to Americanization? Some countries and individuals have historically been attracted to various aspects of American culture, including such core values as rugged individualism, movie icons like James Dean or Jerry Lewis, products like Levi Strauss jeans, and entertainment bearing the Disney brand. Yet, that attraction does not predict national or individual responses to Americanization or American policy. One can embrace Disney while still resisting Americanization or critiquing American policies. This inconsistency is manifested differently in different cultures and is influenced by historical, cultural, economic, and political factors. The fact that, historically, Walt Disney and the Disney company have participated in U.S. efforts to Americanize other nations must also be taken into account.

Unsurprisingly, the Disney brand is associated with Americanization in many countries. While this has been more recent in some countries (such as South Africa), in many countries, it has a much longer history and quite complex roots. For instance, Yoshimi has discussed cultural Americanization in Japan, which dates back to the 1920s: 'During this process, the world of Disney was introduced and gradually became accepted as the core of what people in Japan perceive as American-ism.' With the success of Tokyo Disneyland and the expansion of cultural Americanization in Japan since the 1970s, Yoshimi has detailed how Disney has contributed to the transformation of 'America' as symbol to 'America' as system.

In contrast, Kim and Lee have reported that the attitudes of Koreans are 'intermingled with their feelings about the U.S.A. ... the ambivalent feelings towards, as well as the trust of, Disney products, is associated with the historical context of modernization in Korea.' This interweaving of a corporate brand, Americanization, and modernization takes on greater significance in the context of globalization, as we shall see below.

Global culture

As some of the discussions reveal, Disney is not always associated exclusively with Americanization, but with a growing global culture, often strongly influenced by American products and values. Guyot observed that many of the French respondents were well aware of Disney's contribution to a 'globalization of culture.' This analysis was echoed in many other settings, as respondents found 'Disney culture' to be either universal or at least consistent with the Western values of many other cultures. As one of the Australians interviewed noted, 'The Disney movies do not promote American culture as such, but promote the standards of any wealthy Western culture.' In other words, Disney contributes to a cultural standardization or cultural hybridity, as discussed by Morley and Robins.[4]

This raises the issue of cultural hegemony and media imperialism: in the so-called 'American Century' or 'Pax Americana,' which stretches from the end of World War II to the downfall of the Soviet Union to the current day, to what degree are the 'standards of any wealthy Western culture' determined by the standards of the nation that dominates the world's political economy? And, to what extent can local audiences 'denature, redefine, and appropriate' – as Molina observes in Mexico – the media products bearing these implicit values? Both processes are clearly at work and further research is necessary to map the extent of each and the interactions between each dynamic.

One approach to these issues was undertaken by Nightingale (Australia), Yoshimi (Japan), and others, who examined Disney texts within the national economic and cultural environment. In the Australian context, for example, Nightingale found not only that the Disney formula became the national standard in media productions but also that respondents had a 'broad acceptance of the stereotyping conventions of mass culture' and that few missed anything distinctly 'Australian' in these globally oriented cultural products. If the future holds a global system of distribution where production remains oligopolized and formulae remain rooted in the model of U.S. commercial culture, then one has to wonder if and how localities, regions, and nations will maintain identities adjacent to the identities provided in global commercial media.

Cultural identity

Indeed, many authors addressed the issue of identity. Molina (Mexico) observed that local audiences might use Disney products in ways that foster cultural diversity. Buckingham (U.K.) discussed how Disney and other cultural objects serve as a means by which audience members construct identities and define themselves. He argued that respondents' ambiguity over Disney was a form of social action – or, a process of forming their own identities in relation to cultural products like Disney – and needs to be evaluated accordingly.

On the other hand, Yoshimi describes how many Japanese have accepted American culture, and Disney. He suggests that Disney is used as a form of self-identification: 'they can see no distance between themselves and the world of Disney.' For example, this phenomenon has contributed to a cutesification trend (*'kawaii* culture') that is well known in contemporary Japanese society. Furthermore, cultural identity is a significant theme in Nightingale's chapter, in which the issue of a national cultural identity is raised in the context of cultural production for global markets and Disney's specific influence on cultural expression.

Cultural imperialism

For some respondents and researchers, these concerns regarding globalization, identity, and Americanization were interrogated through the lens of cultural imperialism. Some respondents made the connection specifically and voluntarily. Others used language that evokes the work of dependency theorists as well as researchers tracing the extent of media imperialism. For example, French respondents linked Disney with words such as 'propaganda, manipulation, domination, and influence.'

Across nations, and regardless of whether respondents affirmed or resisted Disney, many related Disney's business practices and cultural products to the imperialist and expansive logics of capitalism. Yet, frequently respondents and researchers reminded us of the need to balance the local with the global. In their reflections on past discussions of cultural imperialism, Kim and Lee argued for the creation of research concepts that would more accurately describe and analyze global and local processes.

While Disney is not directly imposing its products and values on the rest of the world, its business practices make those products ubiquitous. This ubiquity, the incorporation of Disney products in family rituals, and the early contact with Disney products in childhood combine in complex and often contradictory ways to communicate Disney's core values and to set the terms within which audiences evaluate Disney. Clearly, this process is what Gramsci meant by the term 'hegemony.' Molina describes it as the 'soft, friendly side of globalization, whose penetration is so intense and persistent that it resounds in all local ambits and generates specific forms of appropriation ...' Disney is accepted because its products and values appear innocent and compatible with local culture.' As Molina suggests, Disney and other brands of commercial culture 'don't appear as an imposition from outside the local system, but rather as a prolongation or continuation, as something that naturally adheres to fit within local culture. The perception of global culture thus remains partially veiled by its soft interaction with local culture.'

Thus, through its domination of children and family entertainment, through its insinuation into family rituals, Disney promotes consumer culture, as well as specific tastes and values. Because of its special links to childhood and family, Disney and its products take on a nearly sacred status. That status makes criticism difficult, although, as we have seen, not impossible.

Significantly, criticism seems to be easier when directed at the company's market saturation and commercialism. The contradictions between Disney's core values and its aggressive merchandising provide the ground upon which individuals can achieve a more critical consciousness about Disney, and perhaps more generally about cultural industries operating in a global, capitalist system. Could the contradictions of capitalism ultimately unravel on a matter as simple as Disney's exploitation of children?

Further research? Of course

First, we encourage scholars to extend this collective project by taking our materials and using them to map Disney's meaning wherever they can. We also hope that scholars will examine Disney's significance for groups that are less accessible than college students. For example, given the significance of Disney for our respondents and their understanding of their life cycles, studies of extended families and their ritual celebrations would seem especially promising. Certainly, more research on Disney's role in childhood and parenting is needed. By contextualizing such research in terms of the local culture as well as the global culture industry, scholars should be able to trace the interpenetration of local and global meanings and thereby to track people's resistant, ambiguous, and celebratory understandings. While such research can be carried out as individual projects, we hope that more scholars will undertake collective ventures like this one.

Second, we encourage scholars to coordinate efforts in order to deepen our understanding of Disney's core values and audiences' reactions to them. For instance, if several scholars agreed to work on a specific Disney film, they could combine audience/reception studies with textual analyses to tap into contextual differences as related to awareness of the research process. Working in various cultures and using the same techniques and instruments, each scholar might first study audiences' reception of the film to gauge the 'common sense' readings produced by casual decoders in 'naturalistic' settings. Then, using textual analysis, each scholar might produce a reading to determine how they, as culture members and media scholars, see Disney's core values deployed within the particular film. The reception study and the researchers' decodings could then be contextualized in terms of local and global cultures. This might lead to another round of audience research in which respondents decoded the film for researchers. Differences and similarities between casual decoding, scholarly decoding, and self-conscious decoding could tell us much about the process of reception and the relationship between global products and local cultures.

While we realize that collaborative research across cultures is fraught with difficulties, and often not encouraged in some university settings, we suggest that even the informal coordination of individual projects on an aspect of the ubiquitous Disney would enrich the field's understanding of media audiences, their work as decoders of media products, and the roles actually played by transindustrial media conglomerates in shaping human consciousness by controlling the world's commercial media.

Notes

1. Contemporary with Disney is Warner Bros., now Time Warner, soon to become AOL Time Warner. Warner Bros. also produced cartoons in the 1930s and merchandised its cartoon characters (Bugs Bunny, Daffy Duck, etc.). However, when Disney was only a small independent animation studio, Warner Bros. was a horizontally integrated film studio and played an important role in the oligopoly termed 'Hollywood.' To this day, Warner's Looney Tune characters remain staples of American commercial culture and target children (and adults) through merchandise, cartoons, animated films, television shows, etc. Bugs and Daffy also are featured at Six Flags amusement parks; however, they do not seem to enjoy the same status as Mickey Mouse and Disneyland.

2. Note that samples often included media students, who may have been introduced to the critical analysis of media before the questionnaire was administered. It is interesting to note that some participants found the questionnaire 'offensive' (Greece), while others found it 'leading' (U.K.).

3. Also, in Norway, some interviewees said that when they were children, they thought that the characters were Norwegian. Drotner notes that Disney texts in Denmark are 'unmarked,' or translated into Danish. In other settings, where printed material is less popular, and Disney movies

include subtitles, the American trademark may be stronger. However, in most markets, Disney films are dubbed. It is also unclear if aspects of Disney's marketing in different countries encourages audiences to think of Disney as American.

4. D. Morley and K. Robins (1995) *Spaces of Identity: Global Media, Electronic Landscapes and Cultural Boundaries*. London, Routledge.

APPENDIX 1

Questionnaire

———————

Scholars are very interested in how people react to mass media and related products. We believe that we can better understand the role that mass media play in our lives if we ask people about their impressions, contact, and feelings about the media. We hope that you will help us in this research by filling out this questionnaire.

Although we will ask about your contact with media and merchandise made by the Disney company, you should know that the Disney company has no connection with this project.

Please go through the questionnaire, answering the questions in order. There are no right or wrong answers; there are no 'trick' questions. Don't spend too much time on any particular question. Your first reaction is what we are looking for. Once you have completed a page, move on to the next page. Don't look back to previous pages or look ahead to subsequent pages while you are completing the question-naire.

We are interested in how people as a group respond to these questions. We will report the data for the entire group with no reference to individual persons. Your anonymity is guaranteed.

Thank you for your participation and cooperation. Your input is very valuable.

For statistical purposes please fill in the following:

1. Your age: _____

2. Your sex: Female _____   Male _____

3. Country of origin: _____

4. Current nationality: _____

5. Ethnic group: _____

Do not write anything on this page that would identify you as an individual. When you are ready, turn the page and continue with the questionnaire.

Each person has their own understanding of the Disney company and their own history of contact with Disney's products and services. We would like to understand your contact with Disney. Answer each question by circling the number on the scale that best reflects your contact. A '1' indicates no contact, a '7' indicates much contact.

6. How much contact have you had with Disney materials in general?

    no contact   much contact
       1   2   3   4   5   6   7

7. As a child (1 to 12 years old), how much contact would you say you had with Disney materials?

    no contact   much contact
       1   2   3   4   5   6   7

8. What contact did you have as a teenager (13 to 17 years old)?

    no contact   much contact
       1   2   3   4   5   6   7

9. As an adult (18 and older)?

    no contact   much contact
       1   2   3   4   5   6   7

10. How old were you when you first came into contact with Disney products?

    Age: _____

Different people like different things at different points in their life. The following items ask you to express your like or dislike using a scale on which '1' means that you strongly liked Disney products and '7' means that you strongly disliked Disney products.

11. When you were a child (1 to 12), how did you feel about Disney products?

    strongly liked   strongly disliked
       1   2   3   4   5   6   7

12. When you were a teenager (13 to 17), how did you feel about Disney products?

strongly liked   strongly disliked

    1   2   3   4   5   6   7

13. As an adult (18+), how do you feel about Disney products?

strongly like   strongly dislike

    1   2   3   4   5   6   7

14. As you think about your contact with Disney products, you have probably remembered some specific items that you had contact with. In the space below, please list all of those Disney products, services, and presentations that you remember having contact with. If you need more room, use the back of this page.

We have made a list of some Disney theme parks and park services. Check YES if you have personally visited the park; check NO if you have never visited the park.

	YES	NO
15. Disneyland/California	____	____
16. Disney World/Florida	____	____
17. Disneyland/Japan	____	____
18. Disneyland/France	____	____
19. Epcot Center/Florida	____	____
20. Disney-MGM Studios/Florida	____	____
21. Have you ever stayed in a Disney Hotel?	____	____

Below is a list of some media produced by Disney. Check YES if you have come into contact with that type of media during your lifetime; check NO if you have not.

	YES	NO
22. Films	____	____
23. The Disney Channel	____	____
24. Television shows not airing on the Disney Channel	____	____
25. Video cassette or video disc	____	____
26. Video games	____	____

	YES	NO
27. Books	____	____
28. Records, audiotapes, or CDs	____	____
29. Comic books	____	____
30. Magazines	____	____
31. Educational products	____	____
32. Disney home page on the World Wide Web	____	____

The Disney company also sells many products in stores, at the Disney Stores, and through catalogs. For the following questions, please check the answer that describes your experience.

	YES	NO
33. Have you ever rented a Disney video?	____	____
34. Have you ever bought a Disney video?	____	____
35. Have you owned any Disney merchandise at all?	____	____
36. Have you ever received any as a gift?	____	____
37. Have you ever given any as a gift?	____	____
38. Have you ever been in a Disney Store?	____	____

Below is a list of some types of Disney merchandise. Please check off the products that you have owned, received as a gift, or given as a gift. Again the Disney company has no connection with this project and no information about you as an individual will be given to anyone.

39. Clothing _____

40. Jewelry _____

41. Mickey Mouse watch _____

42. Mickey Mouse ears _____

43. Toys _____

44. Household items _____

45. Artwork _____

46. Do you now or did you ever belong to a Disney Club? Yes _____ No _____

47. As you look back at your experience of Disney media, products, and

services, what descriptions instantly come to mind? What terms express your perception of 'Disney'? List as many words or phrases as you wish.

48. Which of the following does Disney, in any of its activities, promote or discourage. For each item please indicate whether Disney, on balance, tends to promote OR discourage, OR, in your opinion, the item does not apply (NA) to Disney.

	Promote	Discourage	NA
Bravery	――――	――――	――――
Family	――――	――――	――――
Fantasy	――――	――――	――――
Fun	――――	――――	――――
Good over evil	――――	――――	――――
Happiness	――――	――――	――――
Imagination	――――	――――	――――
Individualism	――――	――――	――――
Love/romance	――――	――――	――――
Magic	――――	――――	――――
Optimism	――――	――――	――――
Patriarchy	――――	――――	――――
Patriotism	――――	――――	――――
Physical beauty	――――	――――	――――
Racism	――――	――――	――――
Respect for difference	――――	――――	――――
Technological progress	――――	――――	――――
Thriftiness	――――	――――	――――
Work ethic	――――	――――	――――

49. Do you feel Disney is uniquely 'American'? Does it promote and represent a vision of American culture that is distinct from other cultures? Please explain.

Thank you for helping us with this research. We value your information.

Of course, this questionnaire cannot fully reflect your experience with the media, products, and services provided by the Disney company. We would appreciate the opportunity to explore your opinions and attitudes toward Disney in greater detail. If you would be willing to participate in an interview lasting approximately 30 minutes (the length is really at your discretion) conducted at a time of your choosing (we will accommodate your schedule), please provide the information below so that we may contact you.

NAME _____

ADDRESS_____

                _____

                _____

PHONE #_____

As with the questionnaire, any interviews will be totally confidential and all respondents will remain completely anonymous. Thank you again for your help.

APPENDIX 2

Interview

The follow-up interview is designed with two goals in mind:

- to delve more deeply into questions of influence and meaning;
- to explore more fully the ideology represented by Disney.

At the end of the questionnaire is a request for volunteers to participate in a brief interview. The interview should produce further data for cross-cultural comparison but also allow the researcher to pursue matters of particular, individual interest as well as delve into matters perhaps idiosyncratic to a given culture and/or geographic area. We would like at least five (5) interviews from each researcher, although you can administer more than that number to help in preparing your National Profile, or for your own research.

In order to ensure that data are comparable, we ask that each interviewer pursue some basic issues/questions listed below with each respondent. After covering these issues, interviewers are free to pursue their own research interests.

We are especially interested in following up on some of the issues/questions covered in the questionnaire, so please focus on the following areas during the interviews:

a. **What EXPERIENCES did you associate with Disney products, as a child and as an adult?**
b. **What VALUES do Disney products and Disney represent to you?**
c. **What MEANINGS do you attribute to Disney products and Disney?**
d. **How, from your perspective, can we explain Disney's POPULARITY?**
e. **Do you experience Disney as uniquely 'AMERICAN'?**

(A more extensive version of this interview template that was used by some researchers is not included here.)

APPENDIX 3

Market Analysis

We are interested in grounding our audience study with a description of the Disney products and media available in the different countries in the study. The market analysis of products, distribution systems and media outlets is designed with two goals in mind:

- to determine the availability of Disney's trademarked products in specific countries;
- to determine the availability of Disney media products and to trace the systems of distribution by which Disney products are made available.

Some researchers may have a good deal of experience assessing product markets and media systems; others may need more guidelines on how to proceed. (Still others may want to work with another researcher for this part of the study.)

What we are interested in is a description of the Disney products and media generally available in your country, as well as their relative popularity. For instance, in some countries, a number of Disney comic books are published weekly and read by adults as well as children. In other countries, comic books are not as popular (or available), yet Disney feature films are extremely well attended. Certainly, the presence of Disney theme parks and the number of Disney Stores must be accounted for in these analyses, as well as the ratings or audience numbers for Disney television programing.

Attached is a list of the wide array of Disney trademarked products, media outlets, etc. that may be available in your country. You may want to make a visit (or assign one of your students to visit) a local shopping mall or major retail outlets to get a sense of the range of Disney products for sale (make sure that a toy store or a store selling toys is included). Other sources can be used to assess Disney's media presence in your country.

You may also want to note any specific promotions for Disney films, products, services, or theme parks being conducted in the media generally or any special promotions for Disney products being conducted in stores, etc.

Trademarked products/merchandise

Clothes for adults and teenagers
T-shirts, underpants, pajamas or nightgowns, ties.

Products for toddlers, babies, infants
T-shirts, underpants, pajamas, shirts, pants, dresses, diaper covers or diapers, layettes or blankets, cribs or bedroom furniture, bed linens, curtains, wallpaper or similar decorator items, posters, pictures, mobiles, lamps, toys (stuffed, soft, or plastic), cups, bottles, cutlery, plates, and similar items.

Housewares
Kitchen items: coffee cups, cutlery, plates, cookie jars, etc., kitchen appliances, curtains, bed linens, clocks, etc.

Toys, games, children's furniture
Soft toys, stuffed animals, cloth dolls, etc., hard plastic toys, dolls, action figures, settings or accessories for play with dolls or figures, games based on films or characters, small items like playing cards, jump ropes, balls, etc., chairs, tables for children, swing sets, slides, wading pools.

Personal adornment
Jewelry, Mickey Mouse watches, other Disney watches, key chains, hair barrettes, etc.

Decorative products
Figurines, holiday decorations, posters, framed artwork (animation cels, drawings, lithographs, etc.), commemorative plates for display in the home, lamps, pillows, furniture.

Food products
Candy, breakfast cereals, ice-cream novelties, frozen foods.

Personal hygiene products
Soap, shampoo, perfume or cologne, band-aids, antiseptic products, first-aid kits, hairbrushes, combs, toothbrushes, toothpaste, cups or glasses, bubble bath, ceramic covers for tissues, razors, shaving brushes, shaving mugs, shaving cream or soap.

Paper and stationery goods
Pencils, pencil boxes, pens, school supplies generally, stationery, cards, postcards, wrapping paper, party goods: paper plates, cups, table covers, party favors.

Carry-alls
Book bags or backpacks, purses, cloth or plastic bags meant to be kept and reused, luggage.

Recreational equipment
Sleeping bags, tents, lanterns, bicycles, skates.

Distribution systems and media products

Media outlets
- Disney movies shown in movie theaters
- the Disney Channel
- Disney television programs appearing on a regularly scheduled basis (daily, weekly) but not on the Disney Channel
  - describe the channel's ownership and main source of income
  - include audience ratings/data
- Disney television programs appearing for special events like holidays, but not on the Disney Channel
- Disney Stores
  - how many Disney Stores are there in your country?
- video rental stores that offer Disney videotapes
- live performances of Disney musicals, plays, ice shows, etc.

Disney media products available for purchase or rental (include availability at public libraries)
- picture books
- story books
- comic books
- comic strips (in newspapers or magazines)
- books that compile Disney strips
- magazines
- activity books (coloring books, sticker books, etc.)
- home videos (theatrically released films, Disney television shows, or materials originated for the home video market)
- records, audiotapes, CDs
- trading cards
- CD-ROM 'books'
- educational materials for use on computers
- games for use on computers
- screen savers for computers

Worldwide Response to Disney Questionnaire

———————

N = 1252

Question number

1. Age		Avg. 21.12 years	Range	13–52 years

2. Gender	F	730	58.3
	M	514	41.1

Response on scale of 1–7

6. Contact in general	Avg.	4.56
7. Contact 1–12	Avg.	4.65
8. Contact 13–17	Avg.	4.03
9. Contact 18+	Avg.	3.74
10. First contact	Avg.	4.61
11. Like 1–12	Avg.	2.48
12. Like 13–17	Avg.	3.25
13. Like 18+	Avg.	3.52

		Number	%
14. Products (unprompted)	Avg.	4.24	
15. Disneyland/California	Yes	333	26.6
16. Disney World/Florida	Yes	310	24.8
17. Disneyland/Japan	Yes	149	11.9
18. Disneyland/France	Yes	72	5.8
19. Epcot Center/Florida	Yes	255	20.4
20. Disney-MGM/Florida	Yes	199	15.9
21. Disney Hotel	Yes	187	14.9

Number of respondents visiting any one of the theme parks:	675	53.9

For questions 22 to 46 numbers reported are 'Yes' responses:

	Number	%
22. Films	1221	97.5
23. Disney Channel	620	49.5
24. TV not Disney	987	78.8
25. Rent video	906	72.4
26. Buy video	551	44.0
27. Video games	515	41.1
28. Books	1026	81.9
29. Records	815	65.1
30. Comics	668	53.4
31. Magazines	577	46.1
32. Educational	518	41.4
33. Disney Home Page	173	13.8
34. Any Disney merchandise	994	79.4
35. Received gift	902	72.0
36. Give gift	745	59.5
37. Disney Store	796	63.6
38. Clothing	764	61.0
39. Jewelry	258	20.6
40. MM watch	374	29.9
41. MM ears	325	26.0
42. Toys	912	72.8
43. Collectibles	273	40.6
44. Household	368	29.4
45. Artwork	350	28.0
46. Disney Club	64	5.1

Total number of products respondents report having had contact with after prompting via questions 15 to 46: prompted average 11.36; unprompted average 4.24 (Question 14 above).

48. Terms to describe Disney (prompted):

	Promote		Discourage	
	Number	%	Number	%
Bravery	961	76.8	33	2.6
Family	1055	84.3	45	3.6
Fantasy	1176	93.9	20	1.6
Fun	1193	95.3	13	1.0
Good over evil	1110	88.7	41	3.3
Happiness	1112	88.8	27	2.2
Imagination	1078	86.2	76	6.1
Individualism	507	40.5	308	24.6
Love/romance	1066	85.1	38	3.0

Worldwide Response to Disney Questionnaire

	Promote		Discourage	
	Number	*%*	*Number*	*%*
Magic	1111	88.7	37	3.0
Optimism	962	76.8	64	5.1
Patriarchy	486	38.8	163	13.0
Patriotism	512	40.9	134	10.7
Physical beauty	857	68.5	121	9.7
Racism	235	18.8	483	38.6
Respect for difference	596	47.6	248	19.8
Technological progress	625	49.9	126	10.1
Thriftiness	308	24.6	306	24.4
Work ethic	491	39.2	179	14.3

49. Is Disney uniquely American?

	Number	*%*
Yes	620	49.5
No	346	27.6

APPENDIX 5

Nationalities Represented in the Sample
(Country of Origin, Self-Reported)

Australia
Austria
Brazil
Bulgaria
Canada
Chile
China
Columbia
Costa Rica
Cyprus
Denmark
France
Germany
Greece
Guam
Hong Kong
India
Indonesia
Iran
Ireland
Israel
Japan
Korea
Malaysia
Malta
Mexico
Namibia

The Netherlands
New Zealand
Norway
Philippines
Poland
Rhodesia
Romania
Russia
Saudi Arabia
Scotland
Singapore
Slovenia
South Africa
Sweden
Syria
Tahiti
Taiwan
Thailand
Trinidad
Ukraine
United Kingdom
United States
Wales
West Indies
Vietnam
Zimbabwe

Index